VEII

CITIES OF THE ETRUSCANS

Nancy Thomson de Grummond and
Lisa C. Pieraccini, series editors

What defines an Etruscan city? How did Etruscan cities arise, and what can they tell us about urbanism in ancient Italy? How did each Etruscan city create its own identity, and how did they differ from each other? This innovative new series aspires to facilitate discussion of such issues among scholars and students of the ancient Mediterranean at large and thereby contribute to the vigorous dialogue currently under way regarding Etruscan culture and urbanism, state formation, trade and craft connectivity, and the socioeconomic characteristics of settlements in Etruria. The series uses an interdisciplinary approach grounded in the latest research in order to reveal the social, religious, economic, architectural, artistic, and civic fabric of each Etruscan city. This perspective highlights the unique Etruscan contribution to ancient Italy without relying heavily on previous methodologies that looked to Greece or Rome to explain Etruscan customs, culture, and traditions.

VEII

EDITED BY JACOPO TABOLLI
WITH ORLANDO CERASUOLO

University of Texas Press
AUSTIN

This book has been supported by an endowment dedicated
to classics and the ancient world and funded by the Aretē
Foundation; the Gladys Krieble Delmas Foundation;
the Dougherty Foundation; the James R. Dougherty, Jr.
Foundation; the Rachael and Ben Vaughan Foundation;
and the National Endowment for the Humanities.

LIBRARY OF CONGRESS
CATALOGING-IN-PUBLICATION DATA

Names: Tabolli, Jacopo, editor. | Cerasuolo, Orlando,
1977– editor.
Title: Veii / edited by Jacopo Tabolli with Orlando Cerasuolo.
Other titles: Cities of the Etruscans.
Description: First edition. | Austin : University of Texas
Press, 2019. | Series: Cities of the Etruscans | Includes
bibliographical references and index.
Identifiers: LCCN 2018012484 | ISBN 978-1-4773-1725-9
(cloth : alk. paper) | ISBN 978-1-4773-1726-6 (library
e-book) | ISBN 978-1-4773-1727-3 (nonlibrary e-book)
Subjects: LCSH: Veii (Extinct city) | Excavations
(Archaeology)—Italy—Veii (Extinct city) | Material culture—
Italy—Veii (Extinct city)
Classification: LCC DG70.V3 V44 2019 | DDC 937/.595—dc23
LC record available at https://lccn.loc.gov/2018012484

doi:10.7560/317259

CONTENTS

LIST OF ILLUSTRATIONS

PLATES

PREFACE

JACOPO TABOLLI

"Of all the cities of Etruria, none takes so prominent a place in history as Veii," wrote George Dennis at the beginning of his *Cities and Cemeteries of Etruria*. Almost 170 years after the beautiful and mysterious description was published, Veii continues to reveal the characteristics of its historical importance. I have accepted with enthusiasm the challenge of editing this volume—which is the first entirely written in English on the Etruscan city of Veii since the publication of *Veii: The Historical Topography of the Ancient City*, by J. B. Ward-Perkins—and I am grateful for this opportunity to present to an international public the historical importance of Veii as revealed in the new results of research focused on the town, its necropoleis, and its territory.

Over the past twenty years, none of the other cities of Etruria has had the privilege of being so intensively and continuously excavated as Veii. The archaeological record together with our understanding of Veii has tremendously increased and changed in this short time. Since 1996, each year between May and November, under the summer sun or the autumn rain, dozens of students have received their training in field archaeology in different sectors of the town as part of the "Veii Project" of the Sapienza University of Rome. Fieldwork took place in a landscape that still preserves the beautiful bucolic appearance described by Propertius (4.10.27–30; see the introduction). Inspired by that poet, I have imagined the different chapters of this volume as parts of a unique narrative that unifies the different studies of the settlement *nunc intra muros*

("now within your walls") and of the cemeteries, *in vostris ossibus* ("over your bones").

Another goal in creating this volume has been to bring together scholars who belong to different schools. From protohistorians to Etruscologists and historians, the different voices of researchers on Veii have indeed found their place in this volume. The result is a polyphonic narrative, with a number of important different views on relevant issues appearing in the chapters, illustrating the vibrant current debate on Veii among scholars. The appendix to this book, "A Chronology of Veii," provides a useful timeline as a backdrop and unifying element for these dialogues.

In the introduction, Gilda Bartoloni, Jacopo Tabolli, and Orlando Cerasuolo and describe the work of the "Veii Project" as the logical outcome of the history of research at Veii. A new periodization for Veii is now possible in light of the past twenty years of excavation. This introduction also presents the general topography of Veii and the characteristics of the town.

Part I then presents an overview of the most significant methods used by the different projects in recent years at Veii. Valeria Acconcia synthesizes in her chapter the results of the several recent excavations on the plateau and focuses especially on a case study of Piazza d'Armi (the small area south of the main plateau of Veii), where a lengthy sequence has been revealed that encompasses all the phases of the Etruscan town. The stunning discovery there of a male inhumation burial set within a protective hut leads to the hypothesis that an early leader or even founder of Veii was revered in this area. Roberta Cascino next addresses the importance of the survey conducted by the British School at Rome in the 1950s and 1960s at Veii, together with some of the most important discoveries achieved in those years. Finally, Stefano Campana presents the preliminary results of the "Emptyscapes," a Marie Skłodowska-Curie EU-funded project, which involved the use of noninvasive magnetometry covering the entire town of Veii and has resulted in the creation of exciting new maps of the road system of the plateau that are without parallel in the study of Etruscan cities. The combination of the different projects, approaches, and methods has created the potential for a holistic understanding of the archaeology of Veii. In addition, this part of the volume constitutes the foundation for part II of the volume, which is focused on the diachronic history of the Etruscan town.

In part II we thus present our narrative of Etruscan Veii. Data from the settlement, from the necropoleis, and from the territory are combined in the description of the history of Early, Orientalizing, Archaic and Late Archaic Veii. Too often the description of Veii—and many other Etruscan towns—lacks a systematic discussion of the formative periods between protohistory and history, which, especially for Veii, is crucial to fully illuminating the archaeology of the town. First, the long journey from small Middle Bronze Age villages widespread in the territory to proto-urban Veii is described by Francesco di Gennaro. Folco Biagi then discusses the evidence from the time of the passage from the Final Bronze Age to the Early Iron Age, which corresponds to the birth of Veii. Alessandra Piergrossi next addresses the complex theme of the eighth century BCE at Veii, a moment of great richness for this early city, when the local aristocracy revealed all its power. The vivid network of interactions between Veii and "the others" is described as a journey, moving first outside the territory and reaching the closest neighbors, narrated by Jacopo Tabolli. A quite significant find is a drinking cup from the cemetery on via d'Avack decorated with a scene of vessels and cargo that is highly suggestive as to the shipping prowess of Veii.

Orlando Cerasuolo introduces the group of chapters focused on the Orientalizing period (seventh century BCE), presenting the various kinds of evidence,

especially for the years of continuous interactions between Rome and Veii. Gilda Bartoloni and Anna De Santis offer a synthesis of the characteristics of the political structure and organization of the territory during the Orientalizing period, suggesting a possible original model for the exploitation and control of the land operated by Veii. Next are chapters on interactions with faraway lands, with the Greeks discussed by Francesca Boitani, and the Near East by Annette Rathje.

A general introduction to Archaic Veii is presented by Gilda Bartoloni and Laura Michetti, with an overview of the settlement, the sanctuaries, the necropoleis, and the territory of Veii. They include the recently discovered terracotta sculptures from Piazza d'Armi that allow for the reconstruction of the charming image of a large dog and his owner (a leader or lord?). The central role of the sacred areas in the definition of the Archaic culture of Veii is addressed in two chapters, by Giovanni Colonna and Ingrid Edlund-Berry. Colonna discusses the fascinating history of the most important sub-urban sanctuary of Veii, Portonaccio—and the famous Veientine terracotta masterpiece statues of Aplu and Hercle (Apollo and Herakles). Edlund-Berry presents in detail the cult evidence from the urban sanctuaries. At the end of this part of the volume, Daniele Federico Maras addresses the complex topic of the epigraphic evidence from Veii, where a local school of scribes in the sanctuary of Portonaccio was one of the most important in all Etruria. Finally, Luca Pulcinelli describes the history of the defensive fortifications of Veii, from the Final Bronze Age ditch to the Iron Age ramparts, to the monumental Archaic tufa city walls.

Part III summarizes the different aspects of material culture at Veii. In the first chapters the authors describe the pottery production typical of Veii during the Iron Age (Sara Neri), during the Orientalizing period (Silvia ten Kortenaar), and during the Archaic, Late Archaic, and Classical periods (Maria Teresa Di Sarcina and Federica Pitzalis). Luciana Drago and Matteo Milletti next describe the different metal products. Francesca Boitani focuses on the wall paintings, providing new data from the Tomb of the Roaring Lions and the Tomb of the Ducks, which constitute the earliest evidence of wall painting in the western Mediterranean. Iefke van Kampen presents an overview of extant stone sculpture at Veii. Barbara Belelli Marchesini describes the evidence for pottery production, presenting also the first workshop where bucchero was certainly produced, in the area called Comunità. An analysis of the evolution of architectural terracottas at Veii, by Nancy A. Winter and Claudia Carlucci, marks the end of this part.

The final part (IV) of this volume, "Legacy of the City," focuses on the end of the Etruscan town of Veii. In this part Christopher Smith discusses the well-known historical event of the Roman conquest of Veii (396 BCE), especially in relation to the complex figure of the Roman consul M. Furius Camillus and his role between Veii and Rome. The survival of Veii and its re-foundation by Augustus in 12 BCE as the Municipium Augustum Veiens, together with the medieval history, are parts of another fascinating story, echoing the legacy of Etruscan Veii.

I am particularly grateful to Nancy de Grummond and Lisa C. Pieraccini, the editors of the Cities of the Etruscans series, and to the University of Texas Press for giving me the privilege to edit this, the first to follow the series's inaugural volume, *Caere*. My greatest thanks to the Irish Research Council and the Trinity College Dublin for allowing me to work on the editing on this volume as part of my Postdoctoral Fellowship at TCD between 2016 and 2018. I would like to thank Orlando Cerasuolo for sharing with me the initial plan of this work and for his continuous contributions and valuable work on the images of the volume. I would also like to thank the anonymous referees for their suggestions, which guided the final editing of the volume. I hope this book will allow the archaeology of Veii to prove again its historical importance worldwide. To all the authors, who are colleagues and friends, my most sincere thanks for having shared this amazing journey through the archaeology and the history of Etruscan Veii.

ABBREVIATIONS

In this volume the abbreviations of journals and series as well as of basic reference works in classical studies are those used by the *American Journal of Archaeology* and listed in *AJA* 104 (2000): 10–24. An updated version is maintained on the website of the *AJA*, currently under http://www.ajaonline.org/submissions /abbreviations.

The following abbreviations are especially relevant for Etruscan studies and for this volume.

AION = *Annali dell'Università degli Studi di Napoli «L'Orientale» Dipartimento di Studi del Mondo classico e del mediterraneo antico*

ArchCl = *Archeologia Classica*

Artigiani = M. Cristina Biella, R. Cascino, A. F. Ferrandes, and M. Revello Lami, eds., *Gli artigiani e la città: Officine e aree produttive tra VIII e III sec. a.C. nell'Italia centrale tirrenica. Atti della giornata di studio, British School at Rome, 11 January 2016, ScAnt* 23.1 (Rome, 2017)

BaM = *Baghdader Mitteilungen*

BPI = *Bullettino di Paletnologia Italiana*

Bridging the Tiber = H. Patterson, *Bridging the Tiber: Approaches to Regional Archaeology in the Middle Tiber Valley*, Archaeological Monographs of the British School at Rome 13 (London, 2004)

BullCom = *Bullettino della Commissione Archeologica Comunale di Roma*

CIE = *Corpus Inscriptionum Etruscarum* (Berlin-Rome-Pisa)

Città murata = *La città murata in Etruria. Atti del Convegno di Studi Etruschi e Italici, Chianciano Terme–Sarteano–Chiusi 2005* (Pisa, 2008)

Culto degli Antenati = G. Bartoloni, ed., *Il culto degli Antenati a Veio: Nuove testimonianze da scavi e ricerche recenti* (Rome, 2011)

DialArch = *Dialoghi di Archeologia*

Dinamiche = *Dinamiche di sviluppo delle città nell'Etruria meridionale: Veio, Caere, Tarquinia, Vulci. Atti del XXIII Convegno di Studi Etruschi e Italici (Roma, Veio, Cerveteri/Pyrgi, Tarquinia, Tuscania, Vulci, Viterbo, 2001)* (Pisa, 2005)

Formello = I. van Kampen, ed. *Dalla capanna alla casa: I primi abitanti di Veio*, exh. cat. (Formello, 2003)

MAV = I. van Kampen, ed. *Il nuovo Museo dell'Agro Veientano a Palazzo Chigi di Formello* (Rome, 2012)

MÉFRA = *Mélanges de l'École française de Rome*

Mercator Placidissimus = F. Coarelli and H. Patterson, eds., *Mercator Placidissimus: The Tiber Valley in Antiquity. New Research in the Upper and Middle River Valley. Atti del seminario di Roma, 2004* (Rome, 2008)

MonAnt = *Monumenti Antichi dei Lincei*

Necropoli arcaiche = G. Bartoloni, ed., *Le necropoli arcaiche di Veio: Giornata di studio in memoria di Massimo Pallottino* (Rome, 1997)

Novità = R. Cascino, U. Fusco, and C. Smith, eds., *Novità nella ricerca archeologica a Veio: Dagli studi di John Ward-Perkins alle ultime scoperte. Atti della Giornata di Studi su Veio — British School at Rome, 13 gennaio 2013* (Rome, 2015)

NSc = *Notizie degli Scavi di Antichità*

PBSR = *Papers of the British School at Rome*

Portonaccio I = G. Colonna, ed., *Il santuario di Portonaccio a Veio* I: *Gli scavi di Massimo Pallottino nella zona dell'altare (1939–1940), MonAnt 58, ser. misc. 6.3* (Rome, 2002)

ProcDanInstAth = *Proceedings of the Danish Institite at Athens*

QF = *Quattro Fontanili*

QF 1963 = "Veio (Isola Farnese) — Scavi in una necropoli villanoviana in località 'Quattro Fontanili,'" *NSc* 1963:77–272

QF 1965 = "Veio (Isola Farnese) — Continuazione degli scavi nella necropoli villanoviana in località 'Quattro Fontanili,'" *NSc* 1965:49–236

QF 1967 = "Veio (Isola Farnese) — Continuazione degli scavi nella necropoli villanoviana in località 'Quattro Fontanili,'" *NSc* 1967:87–286

QF 1970 = "Veio (Isola Farnese) — Continuazione degli scavi nella necropoli villanoviana in località 'Quattro Fontanili,'" *NSc* 1970:178–329

QF 1972 = "Veio (Isola Farnese) — Continuazione degli scavi nella necropoli villanoviana in località 'Quattro Fontanili,'" *NSc* 1972:195–384

QF 1975 = "Veio (Isola Farnese) — Continuazione degli scavi nella necropoli villanoviana in località 'Quattro Fontanili,'" *NSc* 1975:63–184

QF 1976 = "Veio (Isola Farnese) — Continuazione degli scavi nella necropoli villanoviana in località 'Quattro Fontanili,'" *NSc* 1976:149–220

QuadAEI = *Quaderni di Archeologia Etrusco-Italica*

RendPontAcc = *Atti dell'Accademia Pontificia dei Lincei. Rendiconti*

Repertorio = C. Belardelli, M. Angle, F. di Gennaro, and F. Trucco, eds., *Repertorio dei siti protostorici del Lazio: Province di Roma, Viterbo e Frosinone* (Florence, 2007)

ScAnt = *Scienze dell'Antichità*

Sepolti tra i vivi = G. Bartoloni and M. G. Benedettini, eds., *Evidenze ed interpretazione di contesti funerari di abitato. Atti del Convegno Internazionale, Roma, 2006, ScAnt 14* (Rome, 2007–2008)

StEtr = *Studi Etruschi*

Survey = R. Cascino, H. Di Giuseppe, and H. L. Patterson, eds., *Veii: The Historical Topography of the Ancient City. A Restudy of John Ward-Perkins's Survey, Archaeological Monographs of the British School at Rome 19* (London, 2012)

Tetti di terracotta = A. Conti, ed., *Tetti di terracotta: La decorazione architettonica fittile tra Etruria e Lazio in età arcaica. Atti delle giornate di studio, Roma, 2010, Officina Etruscologia 5* (Rome, 2011)

Veio I = G. Bartoloni, ed., *L'abitato etrusco di Veio: Ricerche dell'Università di Roma "La Sapienza,"* I: *Cisterne pozzi e fosse* (Rome, 2009)

Veio II = G. Bartoloni and V. Acconcia, eds., *L'abitato etrusco di Veio: Ricerche dell'Università di Roma "La Sapienza,"* II: *Un edificio tardo-arcaico e la sequenza stratigrafica* (Rome, 2012)

Veio III.2 = G. Bartoloni, S. Neri, and F. Pitzalis, eds., *L'abitato etrusco di Veio: Ricerche dell'Università di Roma "La Sapienza,"* III.2: *Il complesso residenziale: I materiali* (Rome, 2016)

Veio, Cerveteri, Vulci = A. M. Moretti Sgubini, ed., *Veio, Cerveteri, Vulci: Città d'Etruria a confronto*, exh. cat. (Rome, 2001)

ALBUM OF MAPS

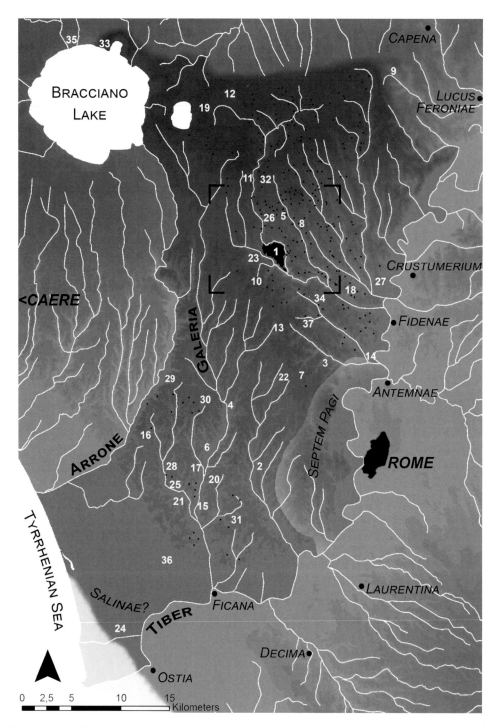

MAP 1. The territory of Veii with the major centers mentioned in the volume. (Copyright: O. Cerasuolo and J. Tabolli)

Unlabeled dots represent secondary sites discovered during surveys. The area in brackets is detailed in map 2. 1. Veii; 2. Acquafredda; 3. Acquatraversa; 4. Boccea-Casalotti; 5. Casale Pian Roseto; 6. Cava ESI; 7. Colle S. Agata; 8. Domusculta Capracorum; 9. Fontanile Nuovo (Morlupo); 10. La Storta; 11. Le Rughe; 12. Mansio ad Baccanas; 13. Marmo Nuovo; 14. Monte delle Grotte; 15. Monte Ficone; 16. Monte La Vignola; 17. Monte Roncione; 18. Monte S. Michele; 19. Monte Sant'Angelo; 20. Muracci di Malagrotta; 21. Pantano di Grano; 22. Pian del Marmo; 23. Poggio Verde; 24. Portus; 25. Prati Madonna; 26. Prato La Corte; 27. Torre di Prima Porta; 28. Quarto della Vipera; 29. Riserva della Casa; 30. S. Rufina; 31. S. Cecilia–Casale Basini; 32. Terre di Bettona; 33. Trevignano; 34. Via d'Avack; 35. Vicarello; 36. Vignole–Maccarese–Piana del Sole; 37. Volusia.

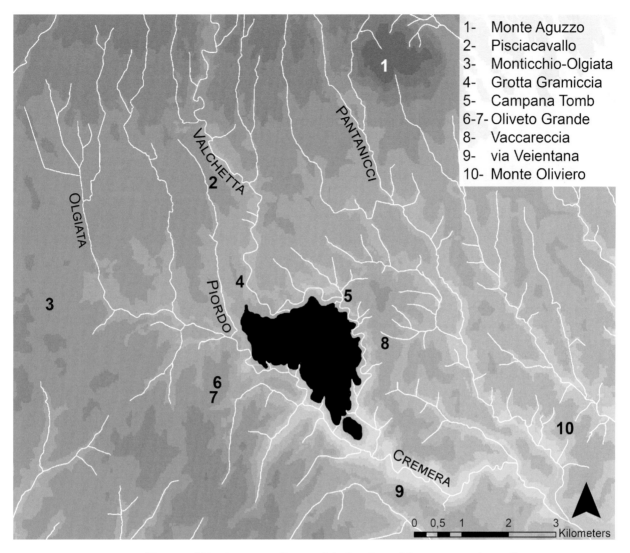

MAP 2. The area of Veii, its surroundings, and the locations of the monumental tumuli.
(Copyright: O. Cerasuolo and J. Tabolli)

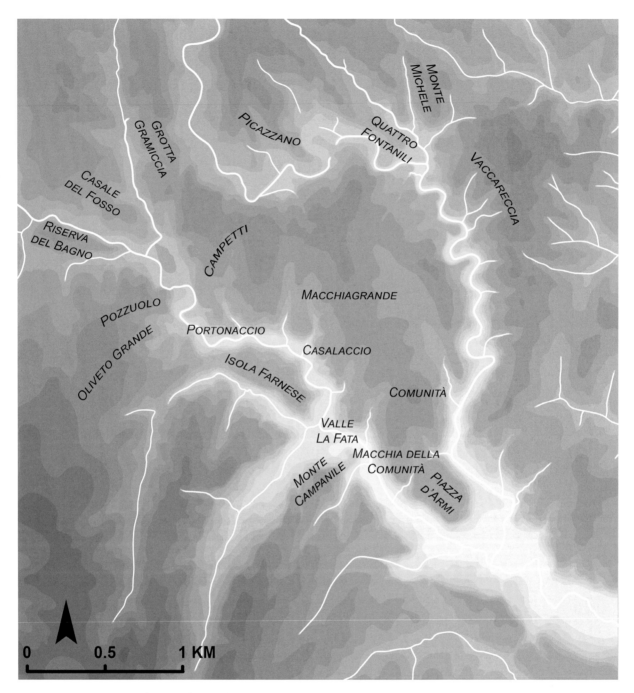

MAP 3. The area of Veii and its surroundings, with the toponyms mentioned in this volume.
(Copyright: O. Cerasuolo and J. Tabolli)

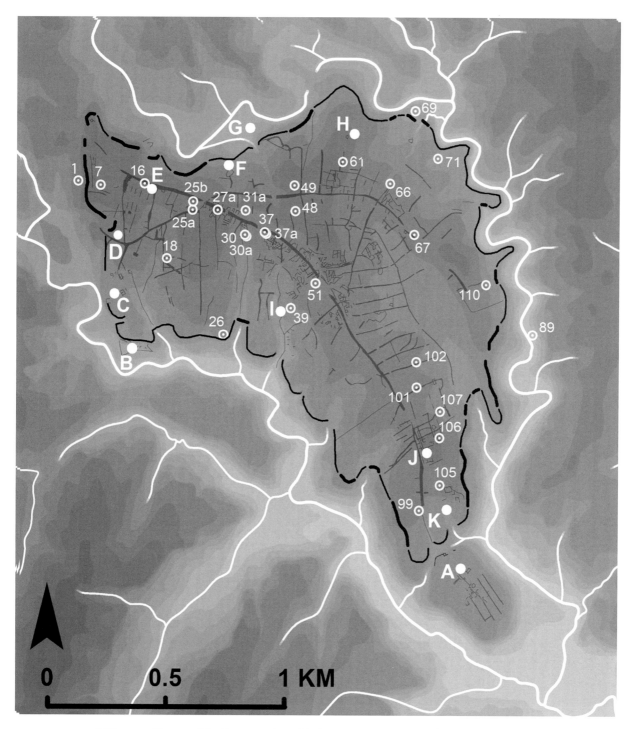

MAP 4. Veii: general layout of the Etruscan city, with the major sites, remains of the defensive walls and their tentative reconstruction, names of the gates, and features detected through geophysics and aerial photography. (Copyright: O. Cerasuolo and J. Tabolli)

A. Tomb of the Roaring Lions; B. Monte Michele, tomb 5; C. Tomba Campana; D. Ponte Sodo; E. Grotta Gramiccia; F. British excavation at the North-West Gate; G. Excavation at Campetti Bastion; H. Campetti, North Area; I. Campetti, Central Area; J. Tomb of the Ducks; K. Campetti-Caere Gate; L. Casale Caprioli; M. Macchiagrande-Forum; N. Vaccareccia tumulus; O. Campetti South-West; P. Macchiagrande-Vignacce; Q. Valloncello; R. Oliveto Grande Tumulus 1; S. Portonaccio; T. Cannetaccio; U. Oliveto Grande Tumulus 2 and tomb; V. Isola Farnese (excavation of the Bronze Age settlement); W. Excavation at Comunità; X. So-called Stipe Lanciani; Y. Piazza d'Armi.

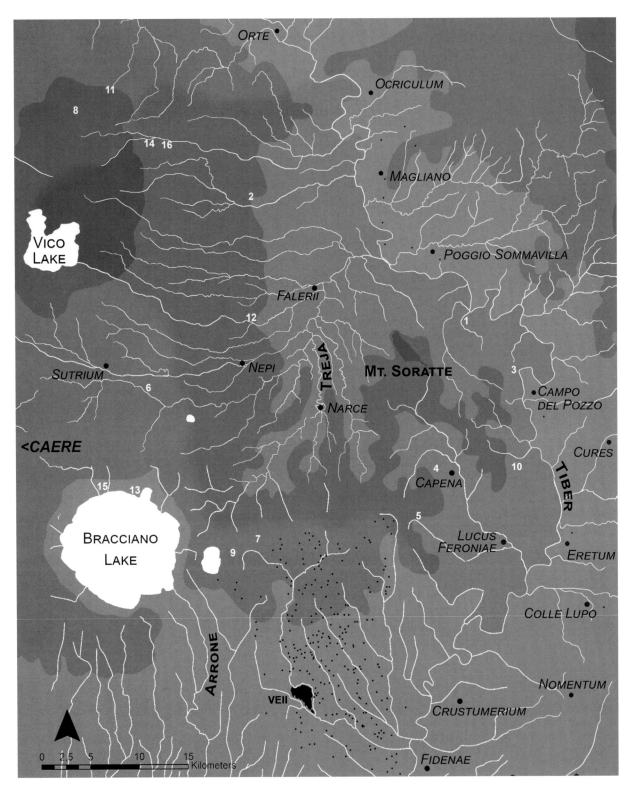

MAP 5. The territory of the Faliscans with the major centers mentioned in this volume. Dots represent secondary sites discovered through surveys. (Copyright: O. Cerasuolo and J. Tabolli)

1. Badia; 2. Castellaccio di Corchiano; 3. Colle S. Antimo a Nazzano; 4. Fontanile Nuovo (Morlupo); 5. Monte Pelliccia;
6. La Ferriera di Sutri; 7. Mansio ad Baccanas; 8. Monte Cimino; 9. Monte Sant'Angelo; 10. Rocchetta di Fiano;
11. Soriano nel Cimino; 12. Torre Stroppa; 13. Trevignano; 14. Vallerano; 15. Vicarello; 16. Vignanello.

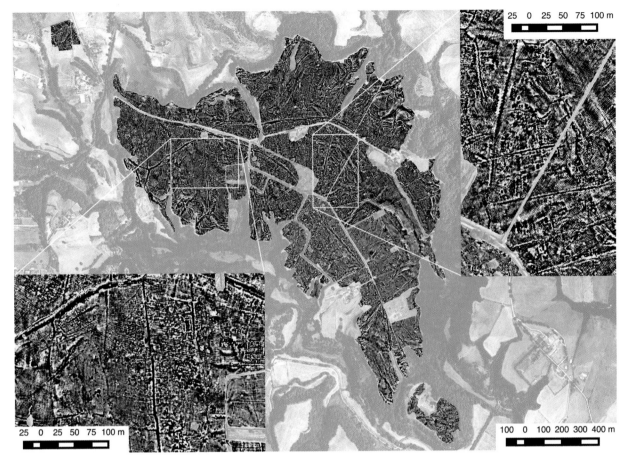

PLATE 1. Layout of the surveyed area on the plateau of Veii, with close-up showing the detail and density of the archaeological features. (Copyright: S. Campana)

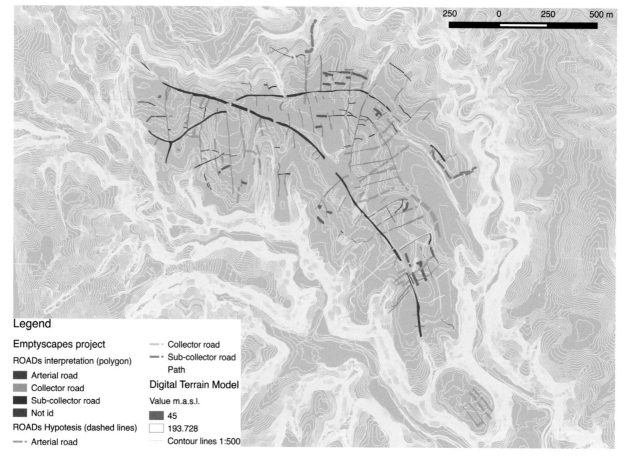

PLATE 2. Interpretative mapping of the magnetic data showing only the road system, classified as arterial road (high-capacity urban road), collector road (low-to-moderate-capacity road which serves to move traffic from local streets to arterial roads) and sub-collector roads (connecting collector road and providing access to residential properties). Dashed lines are magnetic features particularly difficult to be interpreted that could be only hypothetically associated with the road system. (Copyright: S. Campana)

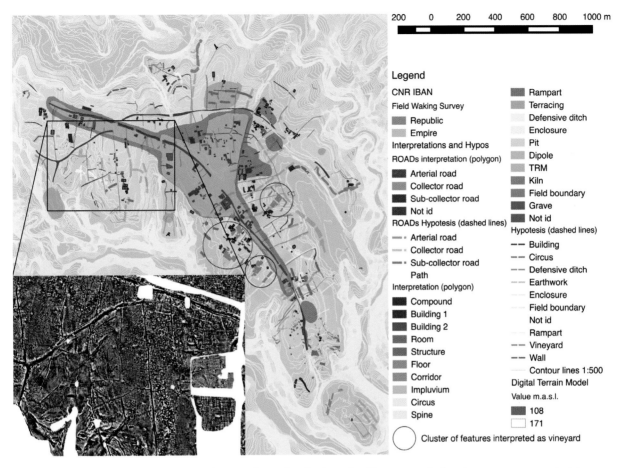

200 0 200 400 600 800 1000 m

Legend

CNR IBAN

Field Waking Survey
- Republic
- Empire

Interpretations and Hypos

ROADs interpretation (polygon)
- Arterial road
- Collector road
- Sub-collector road
- Not id

ROADs Hypotesis (dashed lines)
- – · Arterial road
- – · Collector road
- – · Sub-collector road
- Path

Interpretation (polygon)
- Compound
- Building 1
- Building 2
- Room
- Structure
- Floor
- Corridor
- Impluvium
- Circus
- Spine

- Rampart
- Terracing
- Defensive ditch
- Enclosure
- Pit
- Dipole
- TRM
- Kiln
- Field boundary
- Grave
- Not id

Hypotesis (dashed lines)
- – – Building
- – – Circus
- – – Defensive ditch
- – – Earthwork
- Enclosure
- Field boundary
- Not id
- Rampart
- – – Vineyard
- – – Wall
- Contour lines 1:500

Digital Terrain Model

Value m.a.s.l.
- 108
- 171

◯ Cluster of features interpreted as vineyard

PLATE 3. The Late Republican and Imperial Age distribution of artifact scatters (red and green areas respectively) is clearly less extensive compared with the Etruscan period, when artifacts covered the whole of the plateau, including the parts of the magnetic map showing clear evidence of structures that can be interpreted as dwellings, roads, workshops, temples. (Copyright: S. Campana)

PLATE 4. Jar with a "monster-lion" from the Tomb of the Roaring Lions. (Copyright: F. Boitani)

PLATE 5. Chigi Vase (*olpe*). (Copyright: F. Boitani)

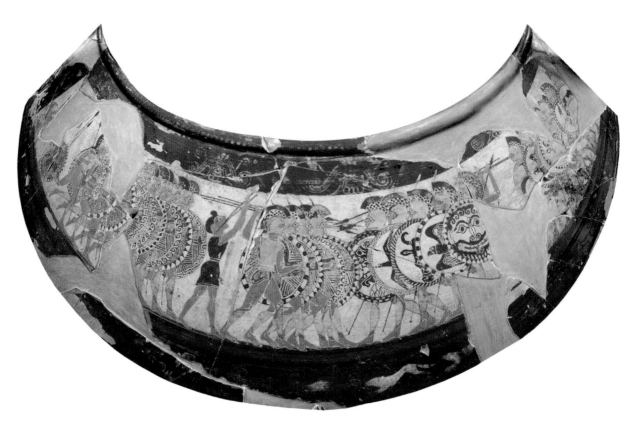

PLATE 6. Detail of the Chigi Vase. (Copyright: F. Boitani)

PLATE 7. Tomb of the Roaring Lions, back wall. (Copyright: F. Boitani)

PLATE 8. Tomb of the Roaring Lions, waterfowl (detail). (Copyright: F. Boitani)

PLATE 9. Tomb of the Ducks, back wall. (Copyright: P. Brocato)

PLATE 10. Tomba Campana, the back wall of the entrance room. (Copyright: F. Boitani)

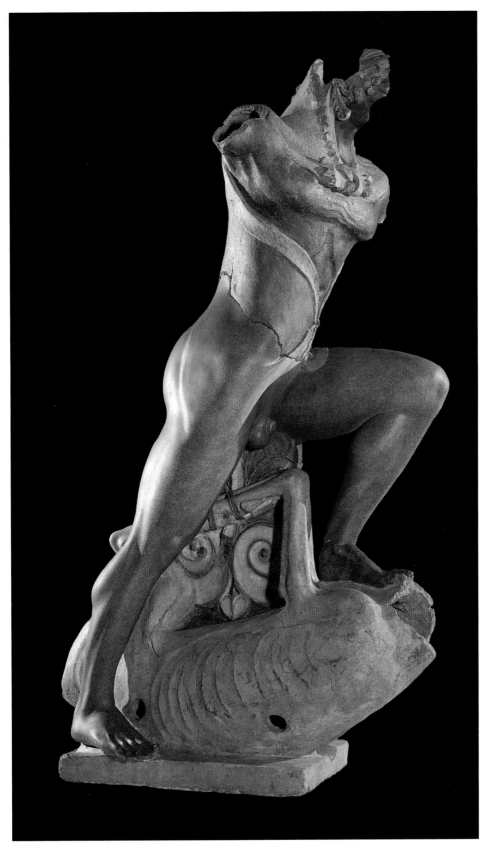

PLATE 11. Statue of Hercle (Herakles) and the deer from Portonaccio, 500 BCE.
(© MiBACT, Museo Nazionale Etrusco di Villa Giulia)

PLATE 12. Statue of Aplu (Apollo) from Portonaccio, 500 BCE. (© MiBACT, Museo Nazionale Etrusco di Villa Giulia)

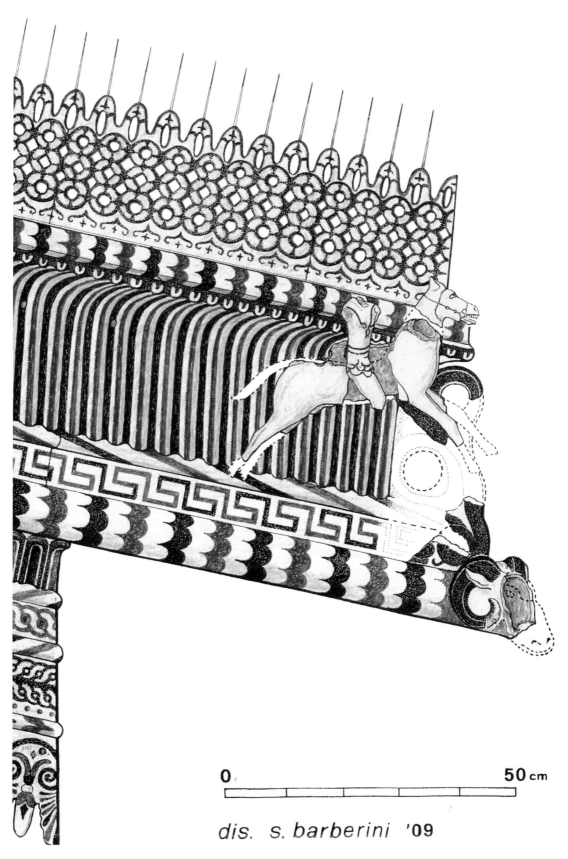

dis. s. barberini '09

PLATE 13. Portonaccio temple, graphic reconstruction of the architectural decoration, 500 BCE.
(Drawing by S. Barberini; copyright: C. Carlucci)

PLATE 14. *Top*: Antefix with *gorgoneion*, from Portonaccio, 500 BCE. *Bottom*: Antefix with head of a maenad, from Portonaccio, 500 BCE. (© MiBACT, Museo Nazionale Etrusco di Villa Giulia)

PLATE 15. Full-figure antefix with a maenad, from Campetti North, 485–480 BCE. (Copyright: C. Carlucci)

PLATE 16. Full-figure antefix with a woman, from Macchiagrande, 470–460 BCE. (Copyright: C. Carlucci)

INTRODUCTION

Exploring Veii

GILDA BARTOLONI, JACOPO TABOLLI, AND ORLANDO CERASUOLO

Since the Early Iron Age Veii has played a fundamental role as the principal link between the Etruscans and the Latins, thanks both to its peculiar geographical location and to its status as an affluent community with powerful leaders. Therefore, even if the Etruscan town had an early rivalry with Rome, as they fought to control the Lower Tiber Valley, a mutual cultural exchange and stimulus occurred between the two cities from the time of their foundation until the destruction of Veii.[1]

THE LANDSCAPE OF VEII

The city of Veii developed on a wide plateau of about 185 hectares (*maps 2 and 4*). The limits of the urban plateau correspond to the high natural cliffs that were formed over millennia by the two major rivers of the area, the Piordo (also known as Olpeta) and the Cremera, joining together as the Valchetta River, one of the tributaries of the Tiber. The roughly triangular shape of the city is characterized by a hilly morphology and reaches the highest elevation (ca. 125 masl) in the southern part, called Comunità (*maps 3 and 4:W*) or Piano di Comunità. The central area of the town, where Augustus in 12 BCE established the Roman "Municipium Augustum Veiens," goes by the name of Macchiagrande (*maps 3 and 4:M*), while the northern and western parts together are called Campetti (*maps 3 and 4:F, G, K, I, and O*).

Even in antiquity, the margins of the settlement were reinforced by strong defensive structures in the areas where the natural cliffs of the plateau are more gradual in their ascent. At different points, the cliffs were naturally interrupted by small rock-cut passages that led to the river valleys. The main gates of the city (*map 4*) were located in coincidence with these passages. Scholars have named these gates after the ancient cities around Veii (e.g., Caere Gate), or the modern villages (e.g., Formello Gate), or after their geographical position (e.g., North-West Gate).

Several different funerary areas have been discovered around the city, especially along the major roads departing from the settlement (*map 3*). A few monumental burial mounds (or tumuli) were set amid the higher hills surrounding the city and are among the most characteristic landmarks of the region (*map 2*).

In Etruscan times, the territory controlled by the city of Veii would have measured approximately 960 square kilometers (*map 1*), extending from the Tiber on the east to the Arrone River to the west, and from the Tyrrhenian Sea on the south up to Lake Bracciano in the north. Hills and valleys still characterize this beautiful landscape. Extensive, though not homogeneous, territorial surveys undertaken in the last two centuries have provided a large body of archaeological evidence for the ancient occupation and use of the land.

THE REDISCOVERY OF VEII

After the Roman period, the city of Veii suffered from massive depopulation and the archaeological remains disappeared rapidly. Propertius (4.10.27–30), in the first century BCE, gives a mournful description of the site during his time:

Oh ancient Veii, once you were a kingdom
And in your forum was placed a golden throne:
now the horn of the shepherd resounds within your
    walls
and over your bones they reap the harvest.[2]

The location of the site was later forgotten, and it was only after 1641 that historians such as L. Holstenius and F. Nardini began to search for evidence of the Etruscan city of Veii. Greater interest in Veii arose in the 1820s, when some prestigious international scholars (A. Nibby, W. Gell, E. Gerhard, G. Dennis) joined the Roman cultural scene and undertook the earliest explorations, providing the first documentation of the ruins of Veii. Systematic excavations began in 1838 and were conducted by "antiquarian archaeologists" such as S. Campanari, followed by L. Canina, G. P. Campana, F. Vespignani, R. Lanciani, and others. These scholars promptly published their research and began to disseminate information about the most important discoveries, such as the paintings from the so-called Tomba Campana.[3]

At the beginning of the 1900s, the newborn Archaeological Superintendence of Italy (Soprintendenza Archeologica) began to coordinate archaeological research at Veii within a broad plan of activities. Several necropoleis were investigated (Grotta Gramiccia, Casale del Fosso, Pozzuolo, Monte Campanile, Valle La Fata, and Macchia della Comunità; *see map 3*), and other excavations were carried out inside the city (Piazza d'Armi, Macchiagrande, and Portonaccio; *see map 3*). Since then, all archaeological activities at Veii have been directed and controlled by the Archaeological Superintendence based at the National Etruscan Museum in the Villa Giulia in Rome.

A new period of research began in the 1950s thanks to the British School at Rome, under the enlightened and tireless direction of John Bryan Ward-Perkins.[4] His dedication and the work of a group of English and Italian colleagues rescued an enormous amount of archaeological data that had been brought to light all over the territory north of Rome because of the introduction of mechanical cultivation. The British School initiated excavation, using modern techniques,

of the Etruscan necropolis of Veii at Quattro Fontanili (*map 3*), in a joint collaboration with the Sapienza University of Rome, and in particular with Massimo Pallottino and his students,[5] and promoted the quick publication of raw data for scholars.

In more recent times, the continuous effort to protect and investigate the site of Veii through the collaboration of different institutions resulted in the creation of the ongoing "Veii Project," a research initiative promoted by La Sapienza and the Archaeological Superintendence of Southern Etruria.[6] Since 1996, professors, scholars, and students (both graduate and undergraduate) from La Sapienza have joined the Veii Project, bringing with them a dynamism that the archaeological site had never seen before in the two hundred years of research undertaken there. Along with this project, a great effort has been made to answer all the major archaeological and historical questions concerning both the settlement and the necropoleis of Veii.

A NEW CHRONOLOGICAL SEQUENCE FOR VEII

Combining past and new data, the urban evolution of Veii can be divided now into seven main periods (see the appendix), as follows.

1. Final Bronze Age (FBA; twelfth through tenth centuries BCE): Villages widely distributed in the territory. In the area of Veii, the earliest evidence of a continuous occupation dates back to the Final Bronze Age.[7] In the most recent excavations, a small settlement dating to the Final Bronze Age was discovered in the area of Isola Farnese (*map 4:V*), a small, naturally defended hill close to the urban plateau, together with a corresponding necropolis at Pozzuolo.[8] At the end of this period the territory, which until that moment was characterized by a widespread occupation, was gradually abandoned in favor of the new plateau of what would become the historical town. It is possible to suggest that, similarly to Tarquinia and Vulci, the plateau of Veii was occupied before the beginning of the Early Iron Age.[9]

2. Early Iron Age I (EIA I; tenth or ninth century BCE to ca. 800 BCE): From the small villages to the town

on the main plateau. The wide plateau where the entire population was resettled was preferred to the previous series of small highland Bronze Age villages, where the defensive character prevailed over the agricultural needs. During the Early Iron Age the occupation of the plateau of Veii appears to be in small groups of huts. The recent excavations at Campetti revealed rampart fortifications (*map 4:G*) built in the tenth century BCE, in an area that was not well defended naturally.[10] On the small plateau of Piazza d'Armi (*map 4:Y*), identified as the acropolis of the early Etruscan town, the burial of a thirty-year-old man was discovered and dated to the beginning of the ninth century BCE.[11] The man was respected and evidently worshiped as a "founder" in a structure that seems to be a *heroon*, for the following four centuries (*see fig. 5.1*). The tomb-groups at Quattro Fontanili, Grotta Gramiccia, and Valle La Fata shed light on the social and cultural development of Veii. During the tenth and ninth centuries BCE, cremation is the only mortuary custom so far attested. The earliest tomb-groups revealed no apparent status differentiation. The necropoleis seem to represent an egalitarian society.[12]

3. Early Iron Age 2 (EIA 2; ca. 800–720 BCE): the monarchy. Between the ninth and the eighth century BCE (Veii IIA), during the so-called precolonial phase, Veii functioned as the preferred "arrival gate" in Italy for Greek and Levantine merchants.[13] We must imagine that local kings (or chiefs) led the trade. Latin and Greek literary sources stressed the presence of powerful kings at Veii, more than anywhere else in Etruria, for example the legendary Vel Vibe mentioned by Naevius (Festus 334 L).[14] Veii is indeed the acknowledged source of famous Roman insignia such as fans, stools, scepters, and other status items, testimony to Veii's historical significance and meaning to the Romans.

In the mid-eighth century BCE social changes transformed both urban settlement planning and territorial control, while the city ramparts were also strengthened. In the second half of the century, economic differentiation resulted in a more complex articulation of the society, as evidenced by the numerous rich burials.[15] A subdivision into separated groups consisting of rather numerous graves connected by family links appears in the different necropoleis. The existence of "families" can be perceived in the spatial distribution of tombs, and the occurrence of similar common grave goods or rituals.

4. Orientalizing period (ca. 720–575 BCE): the age of the princes. A main necropolis (like the Esquiline cemetery in Rome) did not exist at Veii in the Early Orientalizing period; on the contrary, a series of different cemeteries was distributed all around the plateau; some of these, sometimes very small, were newly established, along the roads toward the nearer settlements and cities, mostly near the gates of the town.[16] Chamber tombs appear to have belonged to members of the same family, and some of those hold the earliest wall paintings in Etruria.[17] These new necropoleis and the few monumental tumulus burials (*map 2*) marked the beginning of a resettlement of the territory, with the rise of groups of aristocrats who based their power and prestige on the ownership of the land.[18] The urban settlement was reorganized and divided into rectangular blocks featuring the so-called wooden houses, which constituted an architectural development from the previous elliptical huts. At Piazza d'Armi, the *heroon* was renewed in the shape of a small temple *in antis*, now surrounded by a structure interpreted as a gentilicial building.[19]

5. Early Archaic period (575–540 BCE): the residences. At the beginning of the sixth century the town was surrounded by a massive town wall made of squared tufa blocks (*opus quadratum*) with several town gates.[20] The foundation of a sanctuary at Portonaccio occurred during this period (*map 4:S*).[21] In the earliest phase an open-air cult probably surrounded the altar of Menerva. This sanctuary corresponded to one of the most important sacred places in all of Etruria, as the rich architecture, the statues, the votives, and the inscriptions reveal. At Piazza d'Armi the major wooden structures were replaced by structures with stone foundations, L-shaped porches, and roofs decorated with terracotta slabs.[22] An acroterion group of a man accompanied by his crouching dog probably represented the ancestor worshiped in the nearby funerary chapel (*figs. 12.2–12.3*).

6. Mid-Archaic period (ca. 540–480 BCE): the apo-

gee. The most recent excavations have revealed the building fervor that characterized Veii from the mid-sixth century BCE onward, especially at Piazza d'Armi, Campetti, Macchiagrande, Vignacce, and Comunità. New roads were built and gave access to rectangular houses with an internal division into three rooms and a front porch. It would seem logical to attribute this renewed building fervor at Veii at the height of its artistic flowering to the years of relative peace and stability in their political relations with Rome. This was the period, in the last part of the sixth century BCE, when Rome was governed by magistrates of Etruscan origin, after the events linked with Porsenna and before the conflict against the noble family of the Fabii (477 BCE).[23]

This cultural and artistic zeal of the final decades of the sixth century BCE led to the radical restructuring of the suburban sanctuary of Portonaccio, with the creation of a temple with three cellas on a square podium with a portico *in antis*. An examination of the recovered material highlights the rich decoration of the roof, which consisted of at least twenty acroteria statues. The most famous of these, such as the group of Aplu (Apollo) and Hercle (Herakles) (*plates 11–12*), recall the "Veientine expert in coroplastics" chosen by Tarquinius Superbus to create the chariot of Jupiter for the Capitoline temple in Rome.[24]

The necropoleis along the major roads were still used in this period, but from 575 BCE through the entire fifth century BCE, mortuary customs changed dramatically both at Veii and in its territory.[25] A return to the funerary ritual of cremation in chamber tombs (and in the new type of "vestibule tombs") was accompanied by the almost complete absence of grave goods. This phenomenon can be linked with the political decision to invest most of the city's economic resources in its sanctuaries and public buildings (such as palaces, public squares, and water tanks), revealing a significant shift from private to public, in contrast to the previous Orientalizing aristocratic society.

7. Late Archaic period (480–396 BCE): Toward the fall. At the beginning of the fifth century BCE the hill of Piazza d'Armi was abandoned,[26] and we have to search elsewhere for the temple of Uni/Juno Regina

mentioned in the ancient sources as present during the capture of Veii by M. Furius Camillus in 396 BCE. Recent investigations have allowed us to locate the temple on the southern hill of Comunità. Impressive finds appeared in this area: antefixes, votives, *louteria*, *thymiateria*, a helmeted head (probably from a life-size acroterion) dating to 520–510 BCE, and a fragment of a high-relief with a female forearm in high tension gripped by a male hand pointing in an excited way (possibly representing a scene of the rape of the Amazons).

An obvious reduction of building activity, though gradual, seems to affect the rest of the urban plateau during the fifth century BCE. In fact, little archaeological evidence is known for the decades just prior to the conquest by Furius Camillus and the fall of Veii.[27] We anticipate that future research will shed light on the years immediately surrounding this event and contribute to a greater understanding of the social and cultural legacy of the Etruscan city of Veii.[28]

NOTES

1. See especially chapters 6, 7, 8, 9, and 12.

2. "O Veii veteres, et vos tum regna fuistis / et vestro posita est aurea sella foro: / nunc intra muros pastoris bucina lenti / cantat et in vestris ossibus arva metunt" (trans. J. Tabolli).

3. The long and fascinating history of the early research at Veii has been described in detail by Delpino (1985, 1999). For the most important published works see Gell and Nibby 1827; Gell 1832; Gerhard 1832; Nibby 1837; Gell 1838; Canina 1847; and Dennis 1848.

4. See chapter 2.

5. See in particular *Necropoli arcaiche*.

6. On the history of the Veii Project, see *Veio* I, *Veio* II, and *Veio* III.

7. See chapters 4 and 5.

8. See chapter 4.

9. See chapters 4 and 5.

10. See chapter 5.

11. See chapters 1, 5, and 6.

12. See chapters 5 and 6.

13. See chapters 8, 10, and 11.

14. See chapter 6.

15. See chapter 6.

16. See chapter 8.

17. See chapters 8 and 21.

18. See chapters 8 and 9.
19. See chapters 1 and 6.
20. See chapters 12 and 16.
21. See chapter 13.
22. See chapters 1 and 12.
23. See chapters 12 and 25.
24. See chapters 13 and 24.
25. See chapters 12, 19, and 20.
26. See chapter 1.
27. See chapter 25.
28. See chapter 26.

BIBLIOGRAPHY

Canina, L. 1847. *Descrizione dell'antica città di Veii*. Rome.

Delpino, F. 1985. *Cronache veientane: Storia delle ricerche archeologiche a Veio*, 1: *Dal XIV alla metà del XIX secolo*. Contributi alla storia degli studi etruschi e italici 3. Rome.

———. 1999. "La 'scoperta' di Veio etrusca." In *Ricerche archeologiche in Etruria meridionale nel XIX secolo. Atti dell'incontro di studio (Tarquinia 1996)*, ed. A. Mandolesi and A. Naso, 73. Florence.

Dennis, G. 1848. *The Cities and Cemeteries of Etruria*. London.

Gell, W. 1832. "Gli avanzi di Veji." *Memoirie dell'Institutio di Corrispondenza Archeologica* 1:3–23.

———. 1838. *The Topography of Rome and Its Vicinity*. London.

Gell, W., and A. Nibby. 1827. *Carta dei dintorni di Roma secondo le osservazioni di Sir William Gell e del Prof. A. Nibby*. Rome.

Gerhard, Od. 1832. "Aggiunta d'osservazioni dell'Editore." *Memoirie dell'Institutio di Corrispondenza Archeologica* 1:23–29.

Nibby, A. 1837. *Analisi storico-topografico-antiquaria della carta de' dintorni di Roma*. Rome.

PART I

ARCHAEOLOGY OF THE CITY

The first part of this volume presents a general overview of the history of archaeology at Veii. The authors discuss the different approaches and methodologies that characterized archaeological research at Veii in the past and in more recent times. From the important South Etruria Survey of the British School at Rome in the sixties and seventies, to the excavations conducted as part of the Veii Project, and to the recent geophysical analyses of the Emptyscapes, the complexity of the investigation and elucidation of Veii is revealed in its entirety.

CHAPTER 1

VEII, THE STRATIGRAPHY
OF AN ANCIENT TOWN
A Case Study of Piazza d'Armi

VALERIA ACCONCIA

The small plateau known as Piazza d'Armi, located directly to the south of the main plateau of Veii, to which it is physically connected, serves as an important case study for an understanding of the urban development of Veii (*map 4:Y*). The site has an internal extension of 6.5 hectares, and it was used continuously from the ninth century until the first half of the fifth century BCE. After an intermission corresponding to the period of the conflicts against Rome (477–396 BCE), Piazza d'Armi was sporadically inhabited in the Middle Republican and Imperial periods. During early medieval times (ninth through eleventh century CE), it was settled again, in direct association with the development of the nearby Domusculta Capracorum, as suggested by some scattered funerary areas and by the defensive tufa walls around the small plateau, which had been previously ascribed by scholars to the sixth century BCE.[1]

Archeological research has been conducted on the site since the beginning of the twentieth century, by E. Gabrici, E. Stefani, and the Soprintendenza per i Beni Archeologici dell'Etruria Meridionale.[2] Since 1996, the area has been included in the Veii Project.[3] The intensity and extension of the research, recently supplemented by the application of noninvasive methods,[4] have shed light on the development of Piazza d'Armi and its internal organization during the Etruscan period but have also brought up new questions concerning such crucial problems as the origin and pattern of urban formation, its chronological framework, and the relationship of the site to the major plateau of Veii.[5]

Before the Veii Project began, the large majority of

scholars believed that Piazza d'Armi had been inhabited during the Early Iron Age in a nucleated settlement pattern consisting of sparse groups of huts, similarly to other areas of the settlement where huts have been discovered: the well-known hut at the North-West Gate (fig. 1.1:A); the hut underneath the sanctuary of Portonaccio (fig. 1.1:B; *map 4:S*); and the hut recently brought to light at Campetti (fig. 1.1:C). In addition, surface and residual finds appear in every excavated area and are scattered throughout the surface of the entire plateau.[6] At the end of the seventh century BCE, the area was organized according to a regular urban plan and divided by orthogonal roads, which were sometimes fronted by public buildings, such as the so-called *oikos* (fig. 1.2: no. 12; *see also fig. 24.1*). A wide octagonal "cistern," built of squared tufa blocks, occupied the center of a public square surrounded by different residential buildings (fig. 1.2: no. 13). The period of greatest prosperity at the site seems to have occurred during the sixth century BCE. A fixed chronology for the abandonment of Piazza d'Armi has not been yet established, and the different hypotheses that have been proposed are based on the apparent lack of archaeological evidence dating from the fifth century BCE through Republican times.[7]

The Veii Project allowed for a new definition of the development of the site. In 1996 the Sapienza University of Rome, under the direction of G. Bartoloni, commenced excavations in Piazza d'Armi, with the aim of understanding the chronological span of the use of the regular road system. Excavation work has been combined with a study of early orthogonal plan-

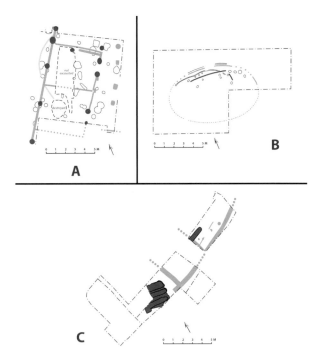

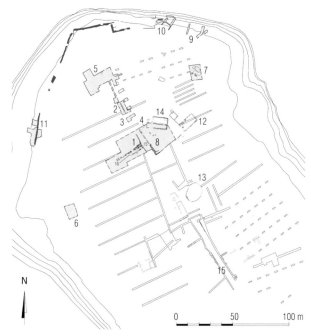

FIGURE I.I. Remains of early huts at Veii. A. Excavations at the North-West Gate; B. The hut at Portonaccio; C. The hut at Campetti. (Copyright: O. Cerasuolo)

FIGURE I.2. The finds on the plateau of Piazza d'Armi and the areas excavated by Sapienza University (Bartoloni et al. 2012). 1. The intersection between the *cardo* and a secondary route; 2–4. Areas II–IV; 5. Area V; 6. Area VI; 7. Area VII; 8. Area of Iron Age burials; 9–11. Excavations of the defensive walls; 12. The *oikos*; 13. The cistern; 14. Late Roman/early medieval building; 15. The *cardo*. (Copyright: V. Acconcia)

ning in ancient Italy, before its development in classical Greece and its diffusion in the Mediterranean.[8] The excavation area opened in 1996 corresponded to a road intersection opposite the *oikos*. A main road, oriented northwest–southeast (the so-called *cardo*) was connected to a secondary one, which had been detected through remote sensing (figs. 1.2: no. 15; 1.3). At the same time, a number of new excavation areas were opened at promising points around the entire plateau of Piazza d'Armi (fig. 1.2: nos. 2–7, 9–11).

One of the main achievements of the work to date is a new chronological framework, subdivided into periods connected to the internal development of the site itself. This outline has proved to be extremely useful in efforts to contextualize changes in the settlement.[9] This division reflects significant changes in urban and social organization over the life of the settlement. The Etruscan phases of Piazza d'Armi have been divided into four periods:

Veii I fits into Early Iron Age 1 and 2 (ninth century to third quarter of the eighth century BCE);

Veii II corresponds to the end of the Early Iron Age until the Early Orientalizing period and part of the Middle Orientalizing (last quarter of the eighth to mid-seventh century BCE);

Veii III and *Veii IV* correspond to the end of the Middle Orientalizing period until the Late Archaic period (mid-seventh to first half of the fifth century BCE); after the end of Etruscan times,

Veii V coincides with the abandonment of the site during the war against Rome; and

Veii VI corresponds to Middle Republican activity on the site.

The earliest traces of a permanent settlement, combined with evidence from the main plateau, suggest that Piazza d'Armi was essentially a small enclave within the larger community of Veii during the Early Iron Age.[10] New excavation in the area in front of the *oikos*

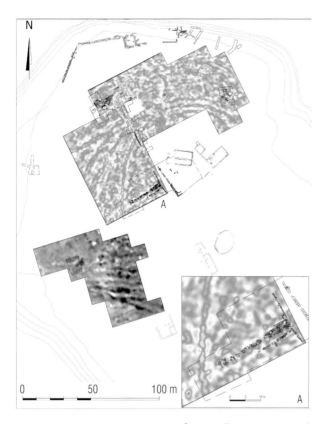

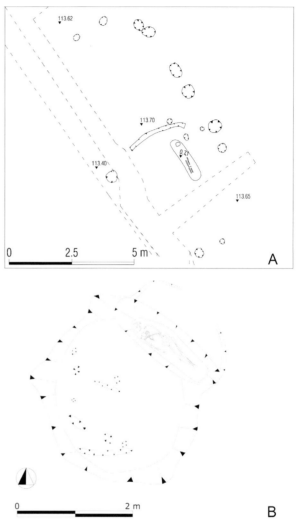

FIGURE I.3. Magnetometry map of Piazza d'Armi as surveyed by CNR-ITABC. A. Detail of the intersection between the *cardo* and the secondary route opposite to the *oikos*. (Copyright: V. Acconcia)

FIGURE I.4. Piazza d'Armi. A. The earliest burial in the plateau; B. The later burial. (Copyright: V. Acconcia)

allowed a reconsideration of the above-mentioned hypothesis regarding a nucleated settlement pattern; this earlier theory was based on the sparse remains of huts discovered there by E. Stefani, which were interpreted as evidence of a settlement still not unified.

We now know that during the first half of the ninth century BCE, an adult male aged between twenty-five and thirty years was buried in a simple trench in this area. The trench was surrounded by a series of small postholes, while larger postholes—at a distance of 2–4 meters and forming an oval around the trench—marked off the entire area. From this evidence it appears that the burial was fenced off and covered by an oval hut (figs. I.2: no. 8 and I.4:A; *see also fig. 5.1*). This discovery, made in 2003, is truly remarkable and raises numerous questions, especially concerning the identity of the interred individual and that person's standing in the contemporary community. This inhumation

represents a significant departure from the practice of cremation in use in the necropoleis of this period in Etruria. In addition, the location of the grave—inside the inhabited area and separate from the extra-urban funerary areas—reveals its strong symbolic value.[11]

This find has been hotly debated among scholars and variously interpreted. On the one hand, it has been considered to be the proof of a pre-urban phase of the settlement, when no clear division existed between inhabited and funerary areas. On the other hand, the burial has been connected to the tradition of the so-called *bidental*, the ritual burial of a victim of lightning.[12] Furthermore, it is most probable that the burial was the focus of the settlement system of Piazza d'Armi at its beginning, functioning as the center of its entire urban organization. The deceased has thus been identified as a powerful male member of the early community, maybe its leader, who was probably also perceived as a "founder" by his social group. This status was emphasized by the extraordinary burial.

This hypothesis seems to be confirmed by a first restoration of the funerary hut during the second half of the eighth century BCE. At this time, the structure was rebuilt according to a rectangular plan. Around this earliest burial, an impressive concentration of other evidence of ritual practices has been identified. For instance, another burial, of a young male, dating to the mid-eighth century BCE, was discovered in a wide bilobed pit associated with an area used for fires and rituals, thus functioning as an open-air altar (fig. 1.4:B).[13] Of importance among the various archaeological remains of Veii I and Veii II is the presence of another circular hut that was in use from the end of the eighth through the first half of the seventh century BCE (and which appears to have been similar to huts found by E. Stefani).[14]

New research also sheds light on the actual chronology of the initial regularized urban system that characterized Veii III and Veii IV. Around the mid-seventh century BCE, some years before the introduction of roof tiles for buildings, this part of the settlement was completely reorganized along a regular plan.[15] The surface of this small plateau was divided into square or rectangular units bordered by roads. Private residences or public buildings progressively occupied these units. Nevertheless, some of these units were never occupied at all, up to and including the time of the abandonment of the site during the first half of the fifth century BCE.

In addition, an intersection between the main road and a secondary pathway was uncovered during the excavations. In the mid-seventh century BCE a complex ritual of foundation for the street consisted of two lateral ditches dug into the natural bedrock (fig. 1.5). Immediately connected to the two ditches, the offering of a red impasto jar (*olla*), containing a broken chalice, probably underlined the transformation of the urban structure of the plateau. This event corresponded with

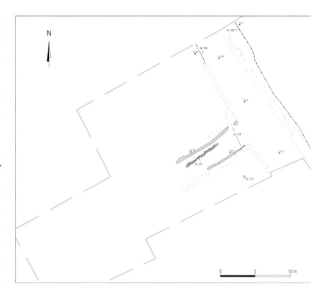

FIGURE 1.5. Piazza d'Armi, the area around the intersection of the two major routes, showing the grooves along the secondary route. (Copyright: V. Acconcia)

the complete removal or transformation of the previous huts, as evidenced by the quantity of residual pottery fragments discovered in later stratigraphy (Veii I to III).[16]

The area occupied by the EIA burials continued to mark the center of the settlement, emphasizing the continuity in the administration of power within this community. During the second half of the seventh century BCE, a rectangular wooden building, probably still covered by thatched roofing, bordered the area of the previous burials. At the end of the same century, it was transformed into another structure, with a portico, made of stone foundation blocks and covered by terracotta roofing (fig. 1.6). This building was bordered along its southeastern side by a road heading to the *oikos*.

THE *OIKOS*

The *oikos* was probably built at this time and covered by terracotta slabs decorated with processions of warriors and chariots.[17] The function of the *oikos* is still uncertain. It has been interpreted as one of the first expressions of sacred architecture (as also the temple of Juno Regina on the citadel of the town, mentioned by historical sources), although it lacks the typical

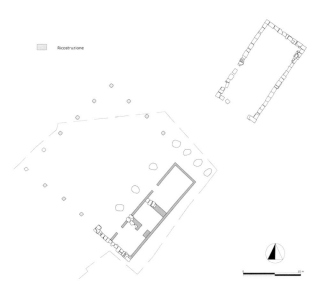

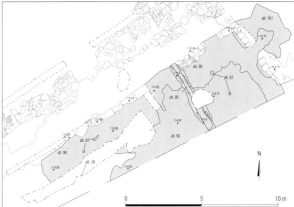

FIGURE I.7. Piazza d'Armi, the house of Veii IV, southeast of the secondary route. (Copyright: V. Acconcia)

FIGURE I.6. Piazza d'Armi, hypothetical reconstruction of the residential building in front of the *oikos*. (Copyright: V. Acconcia)

OTHER PUBLIC BUILDINGS

votive offerings that characterized the Late Orientalizing temples at Satricum, Rome, and Portonaccio in Veii itself.

The *oikos* at Piazza d'Armi is one of few examples of a peculiar building category seen in central Italy in the Late Orientalizing and Early Archaic periods. The term *oikos* derives from the Greek word for "house, home" and invokes its structural similarity to simple domestic buildings, widespread around the Mediterranean during the Archaic period. As already noted, the *oikos* had a simple rectangular plan. It was built with squared blocks of tufa, and its walls were probably made of wattle and daub. Terracotta roof tiles covered this public building. The presence of decorated architectural terracottas at several sites highlights the diversity of this building type and underlines the public relevance of the *oikoi* and their functions. It is uncertain whether they were used as sacred buildings before the introduction of the Greek concept of "temple" or were aristocratic residences. This feature is also highlighted by the position of the *oikoi* in the spatial organization of the settlement of Veii. An *oikos* was located in a central residential area at Piazza d'Armi but also in the nearby sanctuary of Portonaccio[18] and in Satricum, where traces of seventh-century BCE *oikoi* were found covered by later monumental temples.

It is likely that the *oikos* at Piazza d'Armi must be interpreted, together with the other buildings previously described, as part of a complex connected to the socially elite groups who controlled the site and held political and religious powers. Recently G. Bartoloni suggested that this complex should be compared with the well-known one in zone F at Acquarossa,[19] which was decorated by various terracotta ensembles, including plaques, acroteria, and antefixes.[20]

The monumental cistern found by E. Gabrici and another semi-subterranean one covered by tufa blocks at the northern edge of the area were built approximately at the same time.[21] The orthogonal urban plan was frequently restored, adding new buildings to the already planned units. In addition, the area southwest of the road intersection discussed above was never occupied by a building, but the unit on the other side of the secondary road was first used as an open productive area and then, during Veii IV, was occupied by a house (fig. 1.7).[22]

A group of fragments of architectural decoration indicates that around the mid-sixth century BCE the residential complex connected to the *oikos*, as well as other buildings, was completely dismantled. A square hollow carved in the bedrock was filled with a collection of pottery vessels, terracotta decorations, tiles, and bones (fig. 1.8).[23] Before its closure, the area functioned probably as the base of a residential building near the

FIGURE 1.8. Piazza d'Armi, the square cavity near the northwestern edge of the plateau. (Copyright: V. Acconcia)

FIGURE 1.9. Piazza d'Armi, the late sixth-century BCE (Veii IV) phase of reconstruction of the intersection between the *cardo* and the secondary route. (Copyright: V. Acconcia)

northwestern margin of the plateau. At the same time, northwest of the *oikos*, a natural crack in the bedrock was used for the same purpose. Fragments of acroteria were discovered in 2009 in the later filling of this crevice. These fragments have been identified as part of a statuary group: a standing man places his hand on a seated dog (*see figs. 12.2–12.3*).[24] Analysis of the group reveals its exceptional technical quality. The head of the dog (broken into thirty-two fragments) appears to be that of a hound. Despite the limited number of fragments, it has been possible to recognize traces of white painting (*ingobbio*) on the long dress of the man. This group, dating to the second half of the sixth century BCE, was probably part of the decoration of a gentilicial residence. The standing man may represent a member of the local elite together with his dog, which would have accompanied him in war or hunting.

POLITICAL TRANSFORMATIONS BEFORE AND AFTER THE ROMANS

The transition from Veii III and Veii IV was marked by a dismantling process reflecting either a radical change in the social and political structure of the community[25] or, as was recently proposed, a natural event such as an earthquake. This event corresponds in time to a break recognized by Swedish scholars at San Giovenale.[26]

During Veii IV (fig. 1.9), the buildings and the roads were continuously restored and partially monumental-

ized, until the first half of the fifth century BCE, when the site was apparently abandoned.[27] It is probable that the abandonment reflected contemporary historical events. The ancient sources mention conflicts between Veii and Rome, which took place around 480–477 BCE, when the *gens* of the Fabii tried to conquer Veii and set up an outpost in Etruscan territory.[28] The private army of the Fabii was heavily defeated in 477 BCE at the Battle of the Cremera, but it is likely that the fear caused by this war inspired calls for stronger control over the peripheral areas of Veii. From this perspective, the small plateau of Piazza d'Armi would have appeared inadequately defensible, and its community was probably absorbed inside the main plateau. The contraction of the settlement likely corresponded to a general decrease in the occupation of the rural sites in the territory of Veii occurring during the same period. This trend does not necessarily correspond to historical events.[29]

After the Roman conquest, Piazza d'Armi was again sparsely occupied. During the Middle Republican period, small productive farms corresponded probably to the assignment of land units to Roman plebeian citizens or to those Etruscans who had been faithful to Rome during its conflicts with Veii.[30]

NOTES

1. For the medieval period at Piazza d'Armi, see O. Cerasuolo and L. Pulcinelli in Bartoloni et al. 2013:147–150; Cerasuolo and Pulcinelli 2013. See also chapter 16.

2. E. Gabrici and E. Stefani worked at Piazza d'Armi at the beginning of the twentieth century: Gabrici discovered the "octagonal" cistern in the middle of the plateau (fig. 1.2: no. 13); Stefani excavated the *oikos* and the nearby Late Roman/early medieval building (Stefani 1944: see his figs. 2, 12, and 14), as well as some Iron Age huts, and uncovered the regularized urban layout of the Orientalizing/Archaic period: Gabrici 1913; Stefani 1922, 1944. The Soprintendenza per i Beni Archeologici dell'Etruria Meridionale carried on research at the site in 1968–1970: Nardi 1972; Bartoloni 2006. For an overview of the history of research at Piazza d'Armi, see Pitzalis 2011.

3. For the Veii Project, see the introduction to this volume; see also Bartoloni et al. 2013, 2014:1–3.

4. For the application of remote-sensing methods to archaeological research at Piazza d'Armi, as undertaken by the CNR-ITABC team managed by S. Piro (see his fig. 3): Piro 2005; Bartoloni et al. 2008.

5. The results of the Veii Project at Piazza d'Armi are published in *Veio* I, *Veio* II, and *Veio* III; and in a relevant number of preliminary reports (cited in the endnotes of those volumes).

6. For the North-West Gate: Murray Threipland 1963; *Survey*. For Portonaccio: 58, *Portonaccio* I, 146–147. For Campetti: Boitani, Biagi, and Neri 2009; more generally, *Formello*. Surveys and their interpretation: *Survey*; Guidi 1989. Residual finds at Macchiagrande and Campetti: D'Alessio 2001:17; Fusco and Cerasuolo 2001:9.

7. A synthesis of the data collected before the Veii Project appears in Colonna 1986:426; Torelli 1982.

8. See also Guaitoli 1981; G. Bartoloni compared the case of Piazza d'Armi to the development of regularized urban plans during the eighth century BCE at Megara Hyblaea and also at Oderzo (Bartoloni et al. 2006:51).

9. *Veio* II, 38, fig. 4; Bartoloni et al. 2014: table 1.

10. Bartoloni et al. 2006; Guidi 2008:177–178.

11. Bartoloni 2002–2003, 2007–2008, 2012; V. Acconcia in *Veio* I, 19; *Veio* II, 11.

12. Torelli 2007–2008.

13. S. Neri and F. Pitzalis in Bartoloni et al. 2013:139.

14. V. Acconcia in *Veio* I, 23–25.

15. V. Acconcia in *Veio* I, 15.

16. Bartoloni et al. 2012: 55.

17. S. Neri and F. Pitzalis in Bartoloni et al. 2013:139–140. For the *oikos*, see recently Bartoloni et al. 2011.

18. See chapter 13.

19. *Veio* II, 16–21.

20. G. Bartoloni in Bartoloni et al. 2011:140–142 and Bartoloni et al. 2012:118–120; S. Neri and F. Pitzalis in Bartoloni et al. 2013:140.

21. See no. 13 on figure 1.2. See also O. Cerasuolo and L. Pulcinelli in Bartoloni et al. 2013:148.

22. *Veio* II, 18, 22.

23. V. Acconcia in *Veio* I, 25–28.

24. See Bartoloni et al. 2011, 2012, 2014:21–23. In addition, see the introduction to this volume.

25. It is possible that a new leading group gained power and began to rule the community in this period.

26. Bartoloni et al. 2014:21n33.

27. V. Acconcia in *Veio* II, 32.

28. See chapter 12. V. Acconcia in *Veio* II, 25–32.

29. For the Battle of the Cremera: Livy 2.48–51; Dionysios of Halikarnassos 9.15.19–22; Diodorus Siculus 11.53; V. Acconcia in Bartoloni et al. 2012. For the Ager Veientanus in this period, Di Giuseppe 2008:438–440; H. Di Giuseppe in *Survey*, 359. See also chapter 12.

30. Livy 5.24.5–11, 30.8, 51–54, 6.4.4; Diodorus Siculus 14.102.4. V. Acconcia in Bartoloni et al. 2013:145–147.

BIBLIOGRAPHY

Bartoloni, G. 2001. "Le necropoli." In *Veio, Cerveteri, Vulci*, 89.

———. 2002–2003. "Una cappella funeraria al centro del pianoro di Piazza d'Armi-Veio." *AION* n.s. 9–10:63–78.

———. 2003a. "Veio e Roma: Considerazioni alla luce di recenti indagini." In *MAV*, 13–21.

———. 2003b. "Veio–Piazza d'Armi: Dallo scavo degli Ispettori alle ricerche attuali." In *Archeologia in Etruria meridionale. Atti delle giornate di studio in ricordo di M. Moretti, Civita Castellana*, ed. M. Pandolfini, 33–47. Rome.

———. 2006. "L'inizio del processo di formazione urbana in Etruria: Analogie e differenze venute alla luce nei recenti scavi." In *Tarquinia e le civiltà del Mediterraneo. Atti del Convegno Internazionale, Milano, 2004*, ed. M. Bonghi Jovino, 49–82. Milan.

———. 2007–2008. "La sepoltura al centro del pianoro di Piazza d'Armi a Veio." In *Sepolti tra i vivi*, 821–832.

———. 2012. "Una visita di Maria Bonghi agli scavi di Veio." In *Interpretando l'antico. Scritti archeologici offerti a Maria Bonghi Jovino*, ed. C. Chiaromonte Trere, G. Bagnasco Gianni, and F. Chiesa, 55–66. Milan.

Bartoloni, G., V. Acconcia, B. Belelli Marchesini, F. Biagi, O. Cerasuolo, S. Neri, F. Pitzalis, L. Pulcinelli, and D. Sarracino. 2013. "Progetto Veio: Novità dalle ultime campagne di scavo." *ScAnt* 19:131–154.

Bartoloni G., V. Acconcia, F. Biagi, B. Boitani, U. Fusco, and S. Neri. 2014. "Le ricerche dell'Università di Roma 'La Sapienza' a Veio." *RendPontAcc* 86:1–82.

Bartoloni, G., V. Acconcia, E. Biancifiori, C. Mottolese, D. Sar-
    racino, and V. Basilissi. 2012. "Lo scavo dell'Area VII e il
    contesto di rinvenimento del nuovo gruppo acroteriale con
    cane." *ArchCl* 63:55–126.

Bartoloni, G., V. Acconcia, F. Boitani, and S. Piro. 2008. "Inda-
    gini integrate nell'area dell'acropoli di Veio, Piazza d'Armi."
    In *Geofisica per l'archeologia: Possibilità e limiti. Atti del Con-
    vegno Internazionale, Roma, 2008*, 85–92. Rome.

Bartoloni, G., V. Acconcia, A. Piergrossi, S. ten Kortenaar, and
    I. van Kampen. 2006. "Veio: L'abitato di Piazza d'Armi. Le
    terrecotte architettoniche." In *Deliciae Fictiles* III: *Architec-
    tural Terracottas in Ancient Italy: New Discoveries and Inter-
    pretations. Proceedings of the International Conference, Rome
    2002*, ed. I. Edlund-Berry and G. Greco, 50–76. Rome.

————. 2011. "Veio, Piazza d'Armi: Riconsiderazioni e novità."
    In *Tetti di terracotta*, 116–174.

Bellelli Marchesini, B. 2001. "Comunità." In *Veio, Cerveteri,
    Vulci*, 23–28.

Belelli Marchesini, B., and R. Cascino. 2011–2012. "Veio.
    Comunità." In *Atlante dei siti di produzione ceramica*, ed.
    G. Olcese, 215–217. Rome.

Boitani, F. 2012. "La tomba tardo-orientalizzante '6' di Veio–
    Monte Michele." In *MAV*, 91–96.

Boitani, F., F. Biagi, and S. Neri. 2009. "Novità dall'impianto
    produttivo della prima età del Ferro di Veio–Campetti." In
    *I mestieri del fuoco: Officine e impianti artigianali nell'Italia
    preromana*, 23–42. Officina Etruscologia 1. Rome.

Cerasuolo, O., and L. Pulcinelli. 2013. "Nuovi dati sulle mura
    di Piazza d'Armi." In *Mura di legno, mura di terra, mura di
    pietra: Fortificazioni nel Mediterraneo antico. Atti del Con-
    vegno, Roma 2012*, ed. G. Bartoloni and L. M. Michetti,
    176–183. *ScAnt* 19.2–3. http://www.edizioniquasar.it/ScAnt
    /ScAnt19_poster.

Colonna, G. 1986. "Urbanistica e architettura." In *Rasenna: Sto-
    ria e civiltà degli Etruschi*, ed. G. Pugliese Carratelli, 369–
    530. Milan.

————. 2001. "Introduzione." In *Veio, Cerveteri, Vulci*, 3–4.

D'Alessio, M. T. 2001. "Macchiagrande-Vignacce." In *Veio, Cer-
    veteri, Vulci*, 17–18.

Delpino, F. 1985. *Cronache veientane: Storie delle ricerche archeo-
    logiche a Veio dal XIV secolo alla metà del XIX secolo*. Rome.

————. 1999. "La scoperta di Veio etrusca." In *Ricerche archeo-
    logiche in Etruria meridionale nel XIX secolo. Atti dell'incon-
    tro di studio, Tarquinia 1996*, ed. A. Mandolesi and A. Naso,
    73–85. Florence.

De Santis, A. 2012. "I 're' di Veio." In *MAV*, 77–80.

Di Giuseppe, H. 2008. "Assetti territoriali nella media valle del
    Tevere dall'epoca orientalizzante a quella repubblicana." In
    Mercator Placidissimus, 431–465.

Fusco, U. and O. Cerasuolo. 2001. "Campetti." In *Veio, Cerve-
    teri, Vulci*, 9–11.

Gabrici, E. 1913. "Veio: Brevi cenni intorno agli andamenti
    degli scavi che si fanno a Veio nella necropoli e nell'arce."
    NSc 1913:164–169.

Galante, G., A. Piergrossi, and S. ten Kortenaar. 2012. "Le ne-
    cropoli veienti della prima età del Ferro (IX–VIII sec. a.C.):
    Alcuni contesti da Grotta Gramiccia e Quattro Fontanili."
    In *MAV*, 65–76.

Guaitoli, M. 1981. "Notizie preliminari su recenti ricognizioni
    svolte in seminari dell'istituto." In *Ricognizioni archeolo-
    giche: Nuove ricerche nel Lazio*, 79–87. Quaderni di topogra-
    fia antica 9. Rome.

Guidi, A. 1989. "Alcune osservazioni sull'origine delle città
    etrusche." In *Atti del II Congresso Internazionale Etrusco,
    Florence 1985*, 285–292. Rome.

————. 2008. "Archeologia dell'Early State: Il caso di studio
    italiano." *Ocnus* 16:175–192.

Michetti, L. M., and I. van Kampen 2015. *Il tumulo di Monte
    Aguzzo a Veio e la collezione Chigi: Ricostruzione del contesto
    dell'Olpe Chigi e note sulla formazione della Collezione Archeo-
    logica della famiglia Chigi a Formello. MonAnt* 16. Rome.

Murray Threipland, L. 1963. "Excavations beside the North-
    West Gate at Veii, 1957–1958. Part II: The Pottery." *PBSR* 31:
    33–73.

Nardi, G. 1972. *Repertorio degli scavi e delle scoperte archeologiche
    nell'Etruria (1966–1970)*. Rome.

Patterson, H., H. Di Giuseppe, and R. Witcher. 2004. "Three
    South Etrurian 'Crises': First Results of the Tiber Valley
    Project." *PBSR* 52:1–36.

Piro, S. 2005. "Integrazione di metodi geofisici ad alta risolu-
    zione per l'indagine nei siti archeologici: Il caso di Piazza
    d'Armi–Veio." In *Dinamiche*, 125–134.

Pitzalis, F. 2011. "Le indagini a Veio Piazza d'Armi." In *Culto
    degli Antenati*, 7.

Stefani, E. 1922. "Esplorazioni dentro l'area dell'antica città di
    Veio." *NSc* 1922:379–404.

————. 1944. "Scavi archeologici in contrada Piazza d'Armi."
    MonAnt 40:177–290.

Torelli, M. 1982. "Veio, la città, l'*arx* e il culto di Giunone
    Regina." In *Miscellanea Archaeologica Tobias Dohrn Dedicata*,
    ed. H. Blanck and S. Steingräber, 117–128. Rome.

————. 2007–2008. "Exterminatio." In *Sepolti tra i vivi*,
    805–819.

Ward-Perkins, J. B. 1959. "Excavations beside the North-West
    Gate at Veii, 1957–58." *PBSR* 27:56–79.

————. 1961. "Veii, the Historical Topography of the Ancient
    City." *PBSR* 39:1–123.

CHAPTER 2

CITY AND LANDSCAPE
The Survey

ROBERTA CASCINO

During the 1950s, after the first mechanized plowing of the land, small teams of archaeologists walked across the fields of Veii and collected archaeological finds that had, until then, been buried in the ground for centuries. John Ward-Perkins, at that time director of the British School at Rome, led those "field-walks" (fig. 2.1). So began the South Etruria Survey, which constituted the first systematic archaeological survey conducted in the Mediterranean region. Within approximately twenty years, twenty-five hundred sites, dating to different periods, were identified over an area of more than one thousand square kilometers between the Tiber and the Tyrrhenian Sea, in the so-called Campagna Romana.

The survey followed a well-defined methodology and sought to answer questions concerning the historical development of the landscape.[1] Despite its differences from modern methodologies,[2] the scientific rigor applied during the survey still allows its findings to constitute today the basis for the protection and enhancement of the archaeological site of Veii, and indeed its results generated the paradigm for the subsequent sixty years of investigation of the area.[3] The relative rapidity of the field activities together with the resulting immediate preliminary publication[4] demonstrates the exceptional contribution of the survey of J. B. Ward-Perkins to the birth of modern landscape archaeology as an "archaeological study of the relation between people and the environment in antiquity and between people and the context in which they were living."[5] This methodology entailed an innovative approach, especially compared to the previous

nineteenth-century excavations,[6] which were limited in extent. For the first time, Veii and its plateau were investigated by means of a holistic approach.

THE SURVEY OF WARD-PERKINS

The methodology of the South Etruria Survey at Veii was essentially "site-oriented,"[7] with a focus on identifying concentrations of finds on the ground, which were only partially sampled.[8] The main features of the areas identified were listed on specific forms (fig. 2.2). The location of the areas was correlated with the 1:25,000 maps of the Istituto Geografico Militare.[9] Every site received a label consisting of six numbers that corresponded to an area of one hectare. This number was recorded both on the paperwork used during the survey and on the single artifacts discovered in the area.[10] Each form would have contained a description of the topography of the area, the types of finds, the current use of the area (fields for agriculture, vines, and pasture), and the visibility conditions at the time the area was surveyed. Unfortunately, only 50 percent of the original forms from the survey of Veii have been preserved. The loss of Ward-Perkins's notebooks might otherwise make it impossible to reference most of the data, but through a consultation of both published and unpublished material, 25 percent of the finds collected can be assigned to specific areas of the plateau, within an approximate area of one hundred square meters, only thanks to the six-number identification associated with individual objects.

The almost-complete survey of the area within the

FIGURE 2.1. John Bryan Ward-Perkins at Santa Cornelia, Domusculta Capracorum.
Remains of the church brought to light by a plow during the South Etruria Survey, 1954–1968.
(By permission of the BSR Photographic Archive, Ward-Perkins Collection, South Etruria Survey Series)

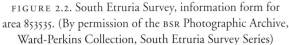

FIGURE 2.2. South Etruria Survey, information form for area 853535. (By permission of the BSR Photographic Archive, Ward-Perkins Collection, South Etruria Survey Series)

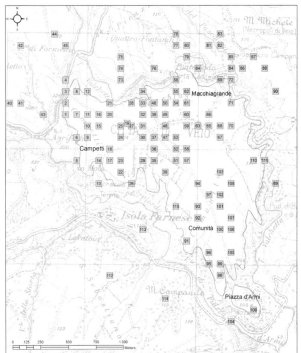

FIGURE 2.3. Archaeological sites around Veii documented by the South Etruria Survey. (Copyright: R. Cascino, after *Survey*, 32)

walls and in the surrounding necropoleis was achieved via continuous visits between the months of October and January, when deep plowing of the land and rain increased the visibility of exposed objects.[11] The large quantity of recorded finds demonstrates the speed of the collection, which took place immediately after plowing and before dispersal of the material. Remains of parts of structures were also noted (fig. 2.3).

During the survey, excavations at the North-West Gate were carried out within the urban area of Veii (*map 4:F*).[12] After the preliminary publication of 1961, the focus of the research moved to the so-called *ager*—the area of the territory of the town—and to the necropolis of Quattro Fontanili (*map 3*),[13] with only a few new explorations undertaken on the plateau. In 1964, a small but systematic survey was carried out in the area of Campetti, along the street that reaches the North-West Gate, to the south, and was organized into a grid system (34 squares of 27.6 meters on a side).[14]

THE RESULTS

The recent restudy of the data from the survey has confirmed the main assumptions of Ward-Perkins. At the same time, it has helped us to better understand the strategies used and to clarify various aspects of the ancient occupation of the plateau in some periods. The restudy has produced new data regarding areas where production activities took place,[15] and previously unknown sanctuaries have been identified.[16]

Regarding the early phase of the occupation of the plateau,[17] the protohistoric finds retrieved date exclusively to the Early Iron Age (approximately 1000–750 BCE). The distribution appears homogeneous, except for the cases of Comunità, Campetti, and near the North-West Gate (*map 3*), where a concentration of evidence has been identified. For the outer areas of the plateau, the distribution of finds essentially reflects the organization of the necropoleis around the settlement, with a great amount of evidence between the hill of Quattro Fontanili and the necropolis of Vaccareccia (*map 3*). During the proto-urban period—as at Tarquinia and more so than at Caere and Vulci—Veii shows a scattered but at the same time intensive occupation over the entire plateau. The settlement at Veii consisted of groups of huts linked by pathways and interspersed with animal enclosures, with open spaces for agriculture and pasture, within an environment that preserved patches of woodland.

During the Early Orientalizing period (720–675 BCE) there is an increase in the number of pottery finds together with a greater variety of types, as compared with the final phase of the Early Iron Age.[18] Continuity in the residential areas is accompanied by an increase in features along the main access roads and close to the city gates. Regarding the topography of the plateau, the areas occupied from the earliest phase and with greater continuity seem to coincide with the flatter spaces, which were particularly suitable for the construction of dwellings.

In terms of development of the settlement, data emerging from the restudy of the South Etruria Survey material confirms the theories that Ward-Perkins put forth. The pottery types characteristic of the transitional phase between the Iron Age and the Early Orientalizing period, in brown impasto, red impasto, and Italo-geometric wares, are most common in the area of Campetti. Ward-Perkins considered the northwestern area of the city to be of major significance in the development of the settlement, as it was crossed by the road corresponding to one of the main routes between the protohistoric centers of Vulci and Tarquinia and the centers of Latium in the Tiber area, with Veii functioning as a go-between.[19]

In the Middle Orientalizing period (675–630 BCE) both the number of fragments and the pottery types continue to increase, in parallel to the urban areas. Most of the Italo-geometric and bucchero pottery types belonging to this period come from the area of Comunità (*map 4:W*). Given the evidence of pottery production in some clusters, it appears that this sector underwent a substantial urban development at this time. The results of the survey have been confirmed in this instance by the recent excavations.[20]

For the Late Orientalizing period (630–575 BCE) the survey data document a strong increase in the number of sites and in the amount of material found, to such

an extent that the finds of this phase may reveal the apogee of the city (fig. 2.4). Settlements now occupied the entire plateau together with significant urban development in the area of Macchiagrande. Fragments of richly decorated vases and artifacts, in a number of areas corresponding to the highest points of the plateau, mark the presence of prestigious buildings in this phase. At Comunità, the activity of the pottery workshops increased, as attested by numerous fragments of Etrusco-Corinthian pottery wasters. The vitality of the urban center in this phase is reflected across the territory, where the survey data have revealed extraordinary growth in rural centers populating the countryside.

Analysis of the pottery from the Archaic period (575–480 BCE) has shown that important changes occurred at Veii between the end of the seventh century and the early years of the sixth century BCE.[21] The vessels used for banqueting in the Orientalizing period, made of fine polished and decorated impasto, were completely supplanted by the later production of bucchero tableware and fine-ware imitation or painted wares (cream wares). From this moment onward the production of impasto ware continued exclusively for domestic use, for the preparation, cooking, and preservation of food.

On the basis of the evidence from the survey, in some areas of Macchiagrande (*map 4:M*) the presence of religious structures (attested also for the Roman period) and monumental buildings has been surmised. In the area of Comunità a large quantity of overfired and wasted fragments has been connected to the production of painted cream ware. In addition, two fragments of architectural terracottas from monumental buildings recall the finds at Macchiagrande. In all these cases, the survey attests the common phenomenon of monumentalization during the Archaic period onward, with the construction of imposing religious buildings and the codification of cult practices and decorative schemes.[22]

The survey material provides useful elements for the reconstruction of the urban panorama of the Late Archaic and Classical periods (480–350 BCE). Especially noteworthy are the scarcity of Attic pottery, in comparison to other cities in southern Etruria,[23] and a certain vitality in the production of bucchero. On the

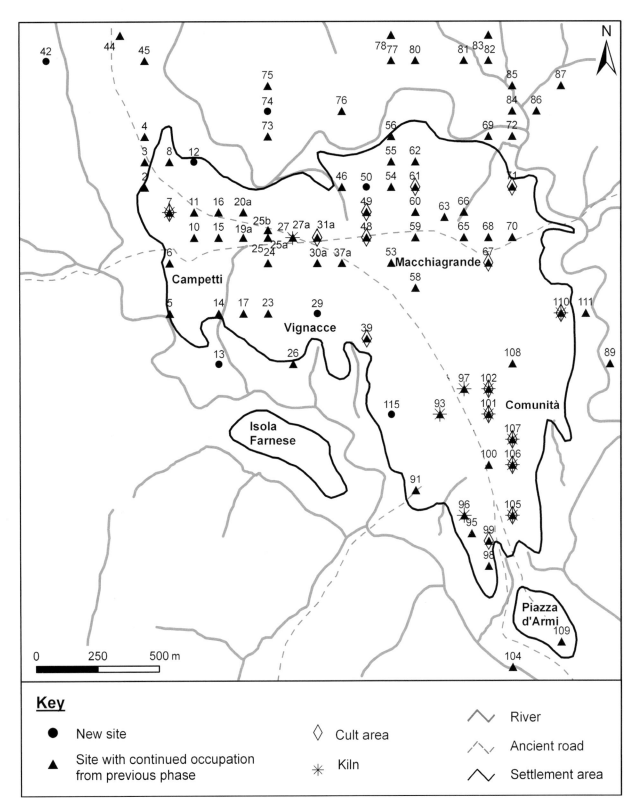

FIGURE 2.4. Distribution map of surface scatters around Veii dating to 630–580 BCE.
(Copyright: R. Cascino, after *Survey*, 350)

whole, the different areas of the plateau seem to preserve in this period the characteristics of previous periods. At Comunità the fine wares reach 60 percent of
the total of the material collected, with bucchero representing 27 percent of pottery sherds. This evidence,
together with the presence of impasto fragments of
vessels that appear to have been used in cult practices,
hints at the important sacred role that the area of Comunità played between the ends of the sixth and fifth
centuries BCE.

It has been suggested that, from the Orientalizing
period onward, the distribution of the areas with evidence for continuous occupation clusters close to the
gates of the city, where small sanctuaries were built,
and structures related to defense and guard posts were
located.[24] The survey material indicates the birth of
a potters' quarter in the area of Comunità, probably
sited there because of the proximity of the main sanctuaries and important public places. A comparison of
the vases found in the tombs of the Veientine cemeteries with those from tombs in the Ager Veientanus
shows that Veii can be considered to have been one of
the driving forces behind the distribution of imitation
wares such as Italo-geometric, Etrusco-Corinthian,
and painted cream ware pottery. The character of the
distribution of the material found during the South
Etruria Survey makes it possible to talk of a real urban
apogee, with the circulation and production of large
quantities of fine-ware pottery, comparable in quality
to that attested at Caere, Vulci, Tarquinia, and Rome.

Restudy of the periods of Roman occupation has
also yielded significant new insights: Archaic and Classical phases are better represented in areas of the city
that would later see major Republican development,
mainly situated along the roads and near the points
of access to the plateau. The areas yielding diagnostic
fragments, such as figured Attic pottery and architectural terracottas, on the one hand confirm the location
of previously known or hypothesized sanctuary sites;
on the other hand, several terracottas found during the
survey come from areas for which there had been no
previous evidence for monumental buildings or from
areas that have only recently been shown to have been
occupied by temples. The restudy of the Republican
material is revealing the "recent" history of Veii, the

period between the Roman conquest and the foundation of the Augustan Municipium Augustum Veiens,[25]
which is still fully to be reinterpreted.

During this period of transformation from an
Etruscan to a fully developed Roman town, the revival of cult and production activities by the Roman
colonists who settled in Veii is followed by a decline,
with the final revival only during the times of Augustus, when veterans reoccupied the plateau. In most
cases such areas, which had been occupied during the
Etruscan period, were reused after the Roman conquest. Most of these areas are situated in the central
part of the plateau, where the urban nucleus of the
Roman *municipium* was to grow up in the Augustan
period (*map 4:M*). Sanctuaries and artisan workshops
continued to be located along the main roads, close
to the town gates and on the highest points. Important indicators — especially the anatomical votives — of
Roman sanctuaries prove that in many cases these sites
continued to hold the same function until the third
or second century BCE. Fragments indicative of pottery production were found at the same sites, suggesting the presence of infrastructure able to satisfy production and cult requirements. Ceramic production is
attested by kiln spacers bearing traces of black-gloss
ware and by the evidence of overfired and therefore
wasted vases (black-gloss, red-gloss, and plain wares
and kitchen wares such as internal-slip ware) found in
large quantities and dating between the ends of the
fourth and third centuries BCE. Most likely these kilns
also produced the small Genucilia plates that are characteristic of Veii, following a style that has no parallels
elsewhere.[26]

By the early Imperial period large areas outside the
urban center were abandoned, and a continuous process of disintegration of the urban structures occurred
together with the gradual ruralization of the plateau
of Veii.[27] From the period of Julius Caesar and Augustus onward, the distribution of luxury items, and in
particular architectural fragments such as marbles and
mosaics, is concentrated in the central area, indicating
the remains of public buildings. In addition, there are
other sites outside the urban area from which a similar range of material was recovered and which, in the
majority of cases, can be interpreted as villas with *pars*

urbana. These structures, from the Late Republican period, favored the concentration of settlement and the depopulation of the surrounding area, with the disappearance of smaller settlements.

In late antiquity, the urban nucleus of Veii appears to have disintegrated totally, and some villas (on the edges of, or outside, the Roman *municipium*) remained the only places in the area of the former Etruscan town that continued to be occupied, resulting in the definitive transformation of the landscape. The majority of the material of the first and second centuries comes from the area of the *municipium*, but by the late second century CE there is a strong reduction in the quantity of material recovered from the center, and the beginning of an increasing decline in the surface finds, which become very scarce for the late Imperial period. Many areas produced material, including marble and mosaic fragments, that suggests the existence of structures with residential or official functions. In most cases these are situated along the principal road, and it is likely that they were either private *domus* that were monumentalized in the early Imperial period or possibly public buildings.

The distribution of finds in the period between 250 and 450 CE seems to indicate the definitive collapse of the urban structure and the total abandonment of the civic life. This decline does not seem to have influenced the richness of the villas on the plateau. Very few areas of the plateau have revealed consistent evidence of occupation into the period 450–650 CE. The South Etruria Survey did not reveal any evidence for activity on the plateau of Veii after the mid-seventh century.

AFTER THE SOUTH ETRURIA SURVEY

Despite Ward-Perkins's definition of a "systematic observation," the modern methodology for archaeological survey developed mainly during the forty years after the South Etruria Survey, perhaps thanks to the survey itself. Therefore, applying current standards to this pioneering work appears anachronistic.[28]

Between 1977 and 1980 the Istituto di Topografia Antica[29] of the Sapienza University of Rome again surveyed the entire plateau. The main result of this new study was the recognition of an overall occupation of the area during the Villanovan period, in contrast to previous theories on the existence of separated villages there.[30] In addition, the necropoleis appear to have formed a unified belt around the town. At Macchiagrande, near the Casale Caprioli (*map 4:M*), two new cult structures were identified. At Piazza d'Armi (*map 4:Y*), which was only partially investigated by Ward-Perkins, the regular pattern of the spatial distribution of the houses appeared to overlie the remains of numerous earlier huts.

In the same years, the Soprintendenza di Roma also started new surveys in the area of the *ager*, which resulted in the discovery of the necropolis of Pantano di Grano (*map 1: no. 21*).[31]

Between 1983 and 1984, Theodore Peña surveyed the plateau and the *ager* of Veii in order to confirm the presence of areas used for production activities, which Ward-Perkins had previously identified as workshops.[32] Peña studied poorly fired fragments and remains of kilns. Data were once again collected after plowing. He was able to define the types of production, to date the different activities, and to take samples from the various clay beds.[33]

Immediately afterward, Nicola King compared the data from his survey of the area of Campagnano di Roma (north of Veii, between via Cassia and via Amerina) with the results of the South Etruria Survey. After only thirty years, despite the fact that most of the sites were still visible, the identification of the finds collected on the ground appeared to have become more difficult.[34] The same conclusion was reached by T. W. Potter in his survey work in the Ager Faliscus during the late sixties (*map 5*).[35]

Rapid urbanization of the countryside resulted in a decrease in visibility of archaeological deposits, also accelerating erosion and re-deposition phenomena. Many areas now support arboriculture, two new *casali* (modern farms) were built, and the ancient street system has been modified.[36] A set of recent aerial photos of the plateau of Veii, when compared to the 1961 results published by Ward-Perkins, illustrate these dramatic changes in uses of the land. These new aerial photos were taken as part of a larger project that started in the 1980s and continues today.[37] These photos constitute the first comprehensive analysis of the entire archaeological site of Veii since the survey of the British School at Rome.[38] The tri-dimensional positioning data for all known archaeological evidence were integrated with the traces visible in existing aerial photos (dating from 1929 to 2010). The plotting of the finds within their urban context has allowed us to gain a clearer picture of activity on the site and has helped to refine the chronology.

Most recently, a systematic magnetometry survey encompassed the entire area of the plateau.[39] This new approach allowed a detailed mapping of the street system as well as certain features of the buildings. Chamber tombs and trench tombs (*tombe a fossa*) have been located in the hills surrounding the town, made visible in the aerial photos thanks to the humidity preserved by the tufa slabs comprising them, making them detectable in the aerial photos. Well-tombs (*tombe a pozzo*) for cremation, by contrast, are less visible because the soil used to fill in the wells was mostly the same soil surrounding the tombs.[40] Finally, in the *ager*, recent surveys have contributed to the discovery of the complex network of roads leading to Rome, Fidenae, Caere, and Capena (*map 1*), as well as numerous rural settlements. All of this evidence demonstrates the intensive use of the land.

SURVEY AND EXCAVATION IN COMPARISON

J. B. Ward-Perkins always sought a full integration between survey and excavation. Recent efforts using this methodology have helped us to correct and to confirm different interpretations.[41] For example, the locations of the forum and the villas in Comunità[42] and Campetti[43] were ascertained by combining data from survey and excavation, and two cult areas were able to be identified.

By combining the information from aerial photos[44] and archaeological excavation in the area of Campetti, researchers have been able to lay out a continuous sequence of occupation from the Early Iron Age to the Renaissance, pointing to the presence of huts, streets, structures for cult, and production areas.[45] This continuity was already attested on the basis of the finds of the survey,[46] where abundant material was discovered

in the area of the grid. The excavation added important data on the chronology of the site and the plans of the different structures.[47]

Also in the area of Comunità, the Veii Project excavation confirmed the presence of workshops for pottery production, which had only been hypothesized after the survey.[48]

As we have shown, among the most important outcomes of the survey was a greater general understanding of the site and its ancient occupation. A similar overview cannot be achieved through excavation, due to time and budgetary limits. The South Etruria Survey also had a specific historical value, because it provided a unique diachronic documentation of the transformation of the landscape in central Italy between the 1950s and the 1960s. The newly unearthed finds collected in those years could only illuminate the chronology, function, and spatial distribution of the ancient occupation of the site. Nevertheless, we need to be extremely careful in using these data for definitive interpretations and especially to hypothesize about areas with no data, as they were in reality characterized by an absence of archaeological sites.[49] Ward-Perkins himself was extremely careful to stress how the differences in depth of the plowings or the vegetation growth could affect the visibility of the structures and finds and, consequently, their interpretation. For this reason, he used to emphasize the importance of excavation in order to provide a correct interpretation of the areas where survey revealed the presence of superficial finds.[50] The excavations at the North-West Gate (1957–1958) and at Quattro Fontanili (1961–1972) confirmed this approach.

What we currently perceive to be the principal limit of the South Etruria Survey is the absence of a consistent strategy of sampling, in terms of both the selection of the areas to survey and the collection of the finds on the ground.

CONCLUSIONS

As I have shown, the South Etruria Survey at Veii constituted the first complete and systematic field survey of the town and surrounding territory; the preliminary reports on the survey, published in the 1960s and following, provided our initial knowledge of the historical development of the site.[51] The prompt publication program guaranteed scholars rapid initial access to most of the data, and the survey findings are still considered to underlie our current understanding of Veii.

Ward-Perkins's survey was particularly important because several different excavations originated from it, but at the same time the entire area has been protected and no urban development has been permitted in the area of the ancient town. The survey has constituted a framework for collaboration between different Italian universities, the Soprintendenza, and foreign institutions and scholars that continues into the present. Its future legacy will consist especially in the recognition of the value of intensive survey in gaining a general overview of archaeological sites. In this way, within a "tested and contextualized analysis,"[52] targeted excavation could prove the best possible form of objective confirmation.

Notwithstanding the different methodological problems and the limitations surrounding the South Etruria Survey, the quality and quantity of the data generated are still extraordinary. Integration of this data with modern surveys and excavation, together with the restudy of material culture from Veii based on a new chronology, will constitute the natural basis for future studies, enhancing such widely varying topics as changes in demography, ancient mobility, exploitation of natural sources, dynamics of communication, and the production and movement of goods over a long period of time.[53] Such research can only increase our understanding of one of the most important of all Etruscan towns, and one that was particularly closely associated with Rome.

NOTES

1. Ward-Perkins 1955:44.
2. On modern methodologies see, for example, the surveys in Mattingly 2000. Concerning the current debate on survey see Johnson and Millett 2013.
3. Cambi and Terrenato 1994:33–38.
4. Ward-Perkins 1961; Kahane, Murray Threipland, and Ward-Perkins 1968; Potter 1979. In particular, see *Survey*, where all the South Etruria Survey data from Veii were published after the Tiber Valley Project (see also Patterson et al. 2000).

5. Barker 1986:12.
6. Mostly consisting of "antiquarian" excavation, but often also of clandestine excavation and looting activities.
7. The methodology has been recently described by Witcher and Craven (2012).
8. The criteria for the collection of the samples followed different patterns. Common ware was not entirely collected, while fine ware was almost always collected. Containers such as amphoras and building materials were rarely collected.
9. The *tavola* for the area of Veii corresponds to IGM Formello *Foglio* 143 II SE.
10. The location of the areas with significant fragments was identified on the RAF aerial photos, taken during the Second World War for military purposes and left to the British School at Rome, which used them for the scientific investigation of the area (Ward-Perkins 1955:44).
11. Witcher and Craven 2012:16.
12. Ward-Perkins 1959; Murray Threipland 1963; Cascino 2012c, 2015.
13. Preliminary reports of a series of excavations were published in *Notizie degli Scavi di Antichità* between 1963 and 1976.
14. Witcher and Craven (2012: fig. 2.1, 11) describe the location of the grid.
15. See Cascino 2017 for a general picture of workshops evidence at Veii.
16. The most significant example is represented by the workshops for pottery production in the area of Comunità (*map 3*): see Cascino 2008. See Cascino 2012a:115–116 for Etrusco-geometric pottery; 127–128, for Etrusco-Corinthian; 134, for fine cream ware with bands; 139, for fine cream ware; and 152–153, for the bucchero.
17. Schiappelli 2012:334–336.
18. Cascino 2012b.
19. Ward-Perkins 1961:20.
20. Cascino 2008; Belelli Marchesini and Cascino 2012; Belelli Marchesini 2017.
21. Di Sarcina 2012b.
22. Di Sarcina 2012b:356.
23. Probably to be connected to the "fifth-century crisis." See Harris 1971:14; Colonna 1990.
24. Rendeli 2012:358.
25. Di Giuseppe 2012b:359.
26. In general on Genucilia plates see most recently Torelli 2014.
27. Fontana and Patterson 2012.
28. Cambi and Terrenato 1994; Francovich and Patterson 2000; Alcock and Cherry 2004.
29. Guaitoli 1981; Fenelli 1998.
30. As suggested by Ward-Perkins (1961:22) and Müller-Karpe (1962:48). See also chapter 5.
31. Bietti Sestieri 1984.

32. This project focused on regional trade during the Roman period, through the study of pottery (Peña 1987:4).

33. Veii corresponds to sites no. 16 (plateau), no. 17, and no. 18 (*ager*): Peña 1987: map 10, 561.

34. King 1993:119.

35. Witcher and Craven 2012:10.

36. Guaitoli 2003:167–177.

37. Guaitoli 2015, 2016.

38. This project involved the collaboration of the Sapienza University of Rome, the Università del Salento, the National Council of Research, and the Ministero per i Beni e le Attività Culturali. The results can be summarized as follows: a new survey of the entire area; a numeric cartography linked with GIS; photogrammetry and photorestitution; dataset and database; new masterplan for the protection and enhancement of the site.

39. See chapter 3. These methods demonstrate the potentials of a noninvasive approach at Veii (as in Piro 2015 and Campana 2017), similarly to Falerii Novi (Hay et al. 2010).

40. Guaitoli 2015:89.

41. See the introduction to this volume.

42. Torelli 1982; Colonna 2004.

43. Fusco 2015.

44. Guaitoli 2003:167–177.

45. This has been already suggested on the basis of the South Etruria Survey: Di Giuseppe 2012a:254 for the black-gloss ware; Cascino and Di Sarcina 2008, Di Sarcina 2012a:233, concerning the internal-slip ware; Di Sarcina 2012a:223, concerning the coarse cream ware.

46. *Survey*, 40–51, areas 19a, 20a, 25a, 25b, 27a, 30a, 31a, 37a.

47. Jaia and Cella 2015.

48. Belelli Marchesini and Cascino 2012; Belelli Marchesini 2015, 2017.

49. Witcher and Craven 2012:21.

50. For example, Ward-Perkins 1961:28, 41, 57, 77.

51. The drainage canals, tunnels, wells, and tanks scattered on the plateau and in the Ager Veientanus, which were created to control the flow of water and to protect the soft volcanic tufa from erosion, represented one of the main lines of research arising from the survey (Judson and Kahane 1963; Wilson 2000). Some of these structures, which continue to operate to this day, changed forever the natural landscape (Ward-Perkins 1962: 1642–1643).

52. Given 2004:20.

53. 1000 BCE to 1000 CE, from the Early Iron Age to the medieval period.

BIBLIOGRAPHY

Alcock, S. E., and J. F. Cherry, eds. 2004. *Side-by-Side Survey: Comparative Regional Studies in the Mediterranean World*. Oxford.

Barker, G. 1986. "L'archeologia del paesaggio italiano: Nuovi orientamenti e recenti esperienze." *ArchMed* 13:7–29.

Barker, G., and T. Rasmussen. 1998. *The Etruscans*. Oxford.

Bartoloni, G. 2015. "Introduzione." In *Novità*, 1–2.

Belelli Marchesini, B. 2015. "Comunità. La funzione del distretto: Strutture e infrastrutture produttive." In *Novità*, 21–27.

———. 2017. "Evidenze di attività produttive nel distretto meridionale di Veio: Indagini in corso." In *Artigiani*, 111–128.

Belelli Marchesini, B., and R. Cascino. 2012. "Veio. Comunità." In *Atlante dei siti di produzione ceramica (Toscana, Lazio, Campania e Sicilia): Con le tabelle dei principali relitti del Mediterraneo occidentale con carichi dall'Italia centro meridionale, IV secolo a.C.–I secolo d.C.*, ed. G. Olcese, 215–217. Rome.

Bietti Sestieri, A. M., ed. 1984. *Preistoria e protostoria nel territorio di Roma*. Rome.

Cambi, F., and N. Terrenato, eds. 1994. *Introduzione all'archeologia dei paesaggi*. Rome.

Campana, S., ed. 2017. *Mapping the Archaeological Continuum Filling "Empty" Mediterranean Landscapes*. New York.

Cascino, R. 2008. "Attività produttive ceramiche a Veio." *MÉFRA* 120.1:5–19.

———. 2012a. "Ceramica di epoca orientalizzante, arcaica e classica." In *Survey*, 103–162.

———. 2012b. "New Data for the Orientalizing Period from the South Etruria Survey." In *Survey*, 343–349.

———. 2012c. "La North West-Gate di Veio negli scavi della British School at Rome." In *MAV*, 51–56.

———. 2015. "Gli scavi Ward-Perkins a Porta Nord-Ovest." In *Novità*, 103–110.

———. 2017. "Il pianoro di Veio: Il quadro topografico della produzione." In *Artigiani*, 93–110.

Cascino, R., and M. T. Di Sarcina. 2008. "L'Internal slip ware nella media valle del Tevere." In *Mercator Placidissimus*, 559–585.

Colonna, G. 1990. "Città e territorio nell'Etruria meridionale del V secolo." In *Crise et transformations des sociétés archaïques de l'Italie antique au Ve siècle av. J.-C. Actes de la table-ronde organisée par l'École Française de Rome et l'Unité de Recherches Étrusco-italiques associée au CNRS (UA 1132), Rome, 19–21 novembre 1987*, 7–21. Rome.

———. 2004. "I santuari di Veio: Ricerche e scavi su Piano di Comunità." In *Bridging the Tiber*, 205–214.

Di Giuseppe, H. 2012a. "La ceramica a vernice nera." In *Survey*, 253–265.

———. 2012b. "Veii in the Republican Period." In *Survey*, 359–366.

Di Sarcina, M. T. 2012a. "Ceramica di epoca orientalizzante, arcaica e classica." In *Survey*, 162–235.

———. 2012b. "New Data from the South Etruria Survey for the Archaic and Classical Periods." In *Survey*, 354–358.

Fenelli, M. 1998. "Veio: Topografia generale e cartografia." In

Scavi e ricerche archeologiche dell'Università di Roma "La Sapienza," ed. L. Drago Troccoli, 137–138. Rome.

Fontana, S., and H. Patterson. 2012. "Veii in the Imperial, Late Antique, and Early Medieval Periods." In *Survey*, 366–376.

Francovich, R., and H. Patterson, eds. 2000. *Extracting Meaning from Ploughsoil Assemblages.* Archaeology of Mediterranean Landscapes 5. Oxford.

Fusco, U. 2015. "Veio: Osservazioni sulla topografia della città." In *Novità*, 40–45.

Given, M. 2004. "Mapping and Manuring: Can We Compare Sherd Density Figures?" In Alcock and Cherry 2004:13–21.

Guaitoli, M. 1981. "Notizie preliminari su recenti ricognizioni svolte in seminari dell'Istituto." *QITA* 9:79–87.

———, ed. 2003. *Lo sguardo di Icaro: Le collezioni dell'Aerofototeca Nazionale per la conoscenza del territorio.* Rome.

———. 2015. "Veio: Osservazioni sulla topografia della città." In *Novità*, 83–90.

———. 2016. "Veio: Osservazioni preliminari sulla topografia della cità." *Atlante Tematico di Topografia Antica* (ATTA) 26:177–214.

Harris, W. V. 1971. *Rome in Etruria and Umbria.* Oxford.

Hay, S., P. Johnson, S. Keay, and M. Millett. 2010. "*Falerii Novi*: Further Survey of the Northern Extramural Area." *PBSR* 78:1–38.

Jaia, A. M., and E. Cella. 2015. "Paesaggi urbani a Veio: Saggi di scavo della Sezione Topografia Antica della Sapienza." In *Novità*, 34–40.

Johnson, P., and M. Millett, eds. 2013. *Archaeological Survey and the City.* University of Cambridge Museum of Classical Archaeology Monograph 2. Oxford.

Judson, S., and A. Kahane. 1963. "Underground Drainageways in Southern Etruria and Northern Latium." *PBSR* 31:74–99.

Kahane, A., L. Murray Threipland, and J. B. Ward-Perkins. 1968. "The Ager Veientanus, North and East of Veii." *PBSR* 36:1–218.

King, N. 1993. "An Archaeological Field Survey near Campagnano di Roma, Southern Etruria." *PBSR* 61:115–124.

Mattingly, D. 2000. "Methods of Collection, Recording, and Quantification." In *Extracting Meaning from Ploughsoil Assemblages*, ed. R. Francovich and H. Patterson, 5–15. Archaeology of Mediterranean Landscapes 5. Oxford.

Müller-Karpe, H. 1962. *Zur Stadtwerdung Roms.* Heidelberg.

Murray Threipland, L. 1963. "Excavations beside the North-West Gate at Veii, 1957–1958. Part II: The Pottery." *PBSR* 31: 33–73.

Patterson, H., F. di Gennaro, H. Di Giuseppe, S. Fontana, V. Gaffney, A. Harrison, S. J. Keay, M. Millett, M. Rendeli, P. Roberts, S. Stoddart, and R. Witcher. 2000. "The Tiber Valley Project: The Tiber and Rome through Two Millennia." *Antiquity* 74 (no. 284): 395–403.

Peña, J. T. 1987. "Roman-Period Ceramic Production in Etruria Tiberina: A Geographical and Compositional Study." PhD diss., University of Michigan.

Piro, S. 2015. "Integrazione di metodi geofisici ad alta risoluzione per le indagini nel Parco Archeologico di Veio." In *Novità*, 90–97.

Potter, T. W., ed. 1979. *The Changing Landscape of South Etruria.* London.

Rendeli, M. 2012. "Conclusion: Veii in the Orientalizing, Archaic, and Classical Periods." In *Survey*, 358–359.

Schiappelli, A. 2012. "Veii in the Protohistoric Period: A Topographical and Territorial Analysis." In *Survey*, 327–336.

Terrenato, N. 2004. "Sample Size Matters! The Paradox of Global Trends and Local Surveys." In Alcock and Cherry 2004:36–48.

Torelli, M. 1982. "Veio, la città, l'*arx* e il culto di Giunone Regina." In *Miscellanea Archaeologica Tobias Dohrn Dedicata*, ed. H. Blanck and S. Steingräber, 117–128. Rome.

———. 2014. "Genucilia: Épigraphie et fonction, quelques considérations." In *Les potiers d'Étrurie et leur monde: Contacts, échanges, transferts*, ed. L. Ambrosini and V. Jolivet, 415–428. Paris.

Vermeulen, F., G.-J. Burgers, S. Keay, and C. Corsi, eds. 2012. *Urban Landscape Survey in Italy and the Mediterranean.* Oxford.

Ward-Perkins, J. B. 1955. "Notes on Southern Etruria and the Ager Veientanus (with an Appendix by Martin Frederiksen)." *PBSR* 23:44–72.

———. 1959. "Excavations beside the North-West Gate at Veii, 1957–58." *PBSR* 27:38–79.

———. 1961. "Veii: The Historical Topography of the Ancient City." *PBSR* 29:1–124.

———. 1962. "Etruscan Engineering: Road Building, Water Supply, and Drainage." In *Hommages à Albert Grenier*, ed. M. Renard, 1636–1643. Brussels.

Wilson, A. 2000. "Land Drainage." In *Handbook of Ancient Water Technology*, ed. O. Wikander, 303–320. Leiden.

Witcher, R., and M. Craven. 2012. "'Much that has long been hidden': Reconstructing the Survey Methodology." In *Survey*, 9–24.

CHAPTER 3

THE EMPTYSCAPES PROJECT

Filling Gaps in Space and Time at Veii

STEFANO CAMPANA

The purpose of the work described in the current chapter is best expressed by this quotation from C. Smith:

> To understand Veii is in part to understand both what Rome might have been, had history not favored her rise to power, and to understand better what made Rome the success she was, for in many respects Veii is Rome through a sort of looking glass. In their early history there were more similarities than differences between the two settlements, and Veii was more like Rome than she was like other Etruscan cities.[1]

Smith made this statement in his introduction to the volume dedicated by scholars of the British School at Rome to a reconsideration of the survey work conducted by John Ward-Perkins in the 1950s. That comparison presents us with a great challenge in undertaking further work at Veii.

RESEARCH QUESTIONS

In the spring of 2009 I was invited by Marcello Guaitoli and the Italian National Council of Research to undertake trials in the application of magnetic survey within the area once occupied by the city. In the years immediately before, as part of the Veii Project, Guaitoli in particular had closely examined a collection of photographs taken between 1929 and 2010. This work involved the accurate mapping of all features identified via detailed inspection of the aerial photos.[2] The initial results substantially improved our understanding of the city and its surroundings, demonstrating the high potential of this technique at Veii. It was then decided to extend the survey to cover the whole of the plateau; between spring 2011 and winter 2016, the project amassed magnetic readings for almost 170 hectares of land.

At the beginning of that work the aims and underpinning archaeological questions were set out as follows:

1. Although a very substantial amount of information has been collected in the last two centuries and a wide range of methodologies have been employed, there are still large areas on the plateau of Veii for which apparently no information is available. Filling in these gaps may provide a better understanding of the transformation of the city across time and a clearer picture of postdepositional processes.

2. Magnetic survey—preferably combined in specific areas with electrical resistivity tomography (ETR) and/or ground-penetrating radar (GPR)—could provide a detailed layout, or layouts, of Veii across the Iron Age and the Etruscan and Roman periods. This new information could be combined with that collected in the past, improving our understanding of the topography of the city and enabling us to better define its boundaries, its fortifications, the location of its gateways, the length and orientation of its streets, and the divisions between built-up and open areas.

3. In some cases, we would expect to have the

opportunity to go beyond the concept of "wall-following" by beginning to analyze economic and social patterns revealed by transformations of the urban layout and the expansion and contraction in the topography of economic activity in workshop areas, the religious center, public areas, agricultural activity and stock areas, and so on.

4. The implementation of this array of survey methods might allow us to identify unexpected features that will shed new light on chronological phases that on the current evidence appear to be "empty"; for instance, there is at present no consistent proof of Bronze Age or earlier cultural material having been found at Veii.

5. The influence of the environmental background (the geo- and bio-archaeological context) should be further investigated, as should the relationships between the city and the broader landscape over time.

NEW DATA FROM THE EMPTYSCAPES PROJECT

These research questions guided the Emptyscapes project as it began, with funding from the European Union as a Marie Skłodowska-Curie Actions grant.[3] The aim of the project is to stimulate changes in the traditional ways in which scholars, in Italy in particular but also more generally in the Mediterranean world, study the archaeology of landscapes—that is, to move from an essentially site-based approach to a more comprehensive landscape-scale perspective. The central purpose of this paper is to offer a preliminary overview of the first results achieved so far in the Veii case study.[4]

THE VEII LANDSCAPE

Although magnetic survey of Veii is almost completed, with just two fields yet to be surveyed at the time of this writing, the search for a fuller understanding of the environmental context is ongoing. However, it is possible at this stage to present a first interpretation of the magnetic data within the framework of the current view of the site provided by the long-standing research work described above.

As of February 2016 magnetic measurements had been collected for a total of 169.7 hectares within the city of Veii. Prior explorations had identified 1,886 archaeological and other features. As an indication of the potential of this method for identifying buried archaeological features, we note that in our investigation we classified 564 data points as buildings or part of them. *Plate 1* shows quite clearly the complexity of the information provided by the magnetic data, and the extraordinary density of the information makes it at first glance somewhat daunting.

Achieving a clear understanding of such a highly stratified context requires a strictly systematic approach and above all a well-defined starting point. The first step has therefore been the identification of the features that were relatively stable across the long time span of settlement activity.

THE URBAN ROAD SYSTEM

To build on previous experience, we decided to start by identifying the urban road system and in particular the two main axes of communication, one running from northwest to southeast and the other from west to east. Previous studies indicated that both initially developed during the Iron Age.[5]

As can be seen on the magnetic map, and on the graphic representation of the features in plates 1 and 2, the main axes present clear evidence of being what we have termed "arterial roads," high-capacity urban roads. One crosses the plateau from a gate at the north to another at the south, and the other from an access point at the west to another at the east. Likewise, it is easy to recognize a fairly regular pattern of linear features that start from the arterial roads and run for the most part in straight lines to cover most of the plateau; these have been designated "collector roads," moderate-capacity roads that served to connect arterial roads to different urban areas and provide access to public buildings and residential properties. In addition it has been possible to identify features connecting two or more collector roads, hence their classification as "subcollector roads," which provide access to public buildings and residential properties.

ISSUES OF VISIBILITY

Overall, the Veii road system conforms fairly closely to the physiography of the landscape. It also reveals a high level of sophistication in the layout of the city; this can be seen as the result of a long-term process of gradual development that nonetheless preserved a strong consistency across the long history of the urban center.

From a visual analysis of the features it is possible to recognize a single basic pattern that, in terms of its finer detail, probably developed gradually over a considerable length of time. Only a limited number of discontinuities within the general pattern have been detected.

A reasonable hypothesis is that the main axes took shape during a first occupation sometime between the end of the Late Bronze Age and the beginning of the Iron Age, the period for which the first artifactual evidence is available.[6] An overlay of the field-walking data and the magnetic maps indicates that by the end of the Archaic period the road system, including collector and even subcollector roads, had already been fully developed. Indeed, we know from the early survey by the British School at Rome and from the more recent work on behalf of CNR that it was during the Archaic period that the greatest development of the city took place and the built-up area of the city reached its greatest extent; artifact scatters from that time are present across the whole of the plateau. By contrast, for the Late Republican period and the Imperial age, after the conquest by Rome, the extent of the artifact scatters reduces substantially, confirming the historical sources and the excavation data.

MAGNETIC DATA

The magnetic data provide quite strong support for the view, developed from more traditional sources, of the city's expansion and subsequent contraction over time. Indeed, there are vast parts of the plateau where no Roman material has been recovered; on the magnetic maps these correspond to areas that display a pattern of collector roads and a dense distribution of buildings or other features (*see plate 3*). The consistency between the urban pattern revealed by geophysical prospection and the pottery distribution derived from the field-walking survey leaves no room for doubt about this. Moreover, within seemingly built-up parts of the city it is possible to recognize in the magnetic data patterns of parallel ditches that can readily be attributed to the cultivation of vines. The distance between the rows varies, from one allotment to another, between five and eight meters, closely matching excavation evidence from around Rome that has been dated to the mid- and late Republic (*see plate 3*).[7]

THE *LONGUE DURÉE* AT VEII

Another interesting point is the extraordinarily lengthy existence of the road system. To better clarify this point we might focus on what is known so far about the principal public buildings of the Roman period: the forum, theater, and thermal baths. None of these reveals any consistent effort to orient the structures with one another to form an orthogonal or regular pattern. In fact all of these structures clearly adopted orientations based on the system of roads laid out during the Etruscan period. We must note too that while on the one hand this continuity represents an important archaeological fixed data point for survey work, on the other it creates a sitewide chronological problem, making it different to distinguish different periods.

Among the first results of this present phase of research, therefore, is the conclusion that almost the entire road layout of the largest and most important Etruscan city in Italy has been detected through this application of geophysical prospection, in a way and with a clarity having few if any parallels elsewhere in Italy. The closest comparable case is that of Vulci, where there is a fairly similar pattern: main axes curving across the plateau and supplemented by a system of radial collector roads.[8] Another interesting parallel is found in a slightly different geographical and cultural context, in southern Latium, at Gabii.[9] In both cases remote sensing data played a major role in enabling archaeologists to determine the overall pattern of the urban layout; in Vulci this was accomplished through aerial photography, and in Gabii through large-scale magnetic prospection.

CONCLUSIONS

The Emptyscapes project is very much a work in progress. Further investigations, particularly test excavations and archaeometric analyses, are needed to extend the quantity and quality of the archaeological data gathered so far. In particular, further examination of the magnetic data already gathered—combined with the results of previous and current research by more traditional means—promises to shed light on many issues, such as the pattern of settlement distribution across time, the types of dwellings, the fortification system, previously unknown public buildings, and the ruralization and exploitation of the plateau during the Roman period.

It is worth emphasizing the extreme complexity of the overall situation at Veii, involving as it does an Etruscan layout that finds few parallels elsewhere, exhibiting a long-lasting development from the Iron Age onward—and with the added difficulty of determining the chronology of most of the detected features. Together with the interpretation and mapping of the magnetic data, it may be necessary in future endeavors to employ high-resolution electrical resistivity tomography (ERT) and ground-penetrating radar (GPR) survey on carefully chosen areas of the site so as to achieve 3D data for subsoil deposits that will resolve a number of crucial issues. A parallel series of targeted but minimalist test excavations will be also be needed to provide critical stratigraphical, artifactual, and chronological evidence at critical points throughout the site.

NOTES

The research for this paper would not have been possible without the financial support of Marie Skłodowska-Curie Action through its Emptyscapes project (FP7-PEOPLE-2013-IEF n. 628338) and the European Union's Culture 2007 ArchaeoLandscapes Europe Project (Grant Agreement nr. 2010/1486/001-001). I am particularly grateful to Prof. Martin Millett, Ken Saito, Dr. Simon Stoddart, Prof. Gilda Barto-loni, Prof. Maria Teresa d'Alessio, Prof. Marcello Guaitoli, Dr. Roberta Cascino, Prof. Christopher Smith, Dr. Salvatore Piro, Dr. Jacopo Tabolli, Michel Dabas, and Gianfranco Morelli. The University of Siena spinoff company ATS srl played a crucial role by sharing use of the Foerster magnetometer system used in the survey work.

1. Smith 2012:6.
2. Guaitoli 2015.
3. Campana and Forte 2001; Campana and Francovich 2003; Musson, Palmer, and Campana 2005; Campana 2009.
4. Within our context the research strategy falls into four interlinked categories: (1) so-called traditional approaches essentially based on archaeological literature, documentary sources, epigraphic sources, place names, iconography, technical, historical, and thematic maps, geomorphology, fieldwalking survey, and aerial photography; (2) environmental studies based on geoarchaeological and bioarchaeology analyses; (3) new technologies in the form of high-precision, high-speed, large-scale geophysical survey and the collection and analysis of high-resolution LiDAR data; and (4) minimalist test-excavations. The current situation in Italy and most of the Mediterranean area needs to be radically changed by developing and applying new and holistic research strategies, which can explore the whole landscape as a continuum; on this point see Bintliff 2000.
5. Guaitoli 2015.
6. See *Survey*. See in particular chapter 4.
7. Volpe 2009. It is important to mention that Republican vine trenches have been found in recent excavations at Piazza d'Armi (Cerasuolo and Pulcinelli 2015).
8. Pocobelli 2004, 2011.
9. Mogetta and Becker 2014.

BIBLIOGRAPHY

Bintliff, J. 2000. "Beyond Dots on the Map: Future Directions for Surface Artefact Survey in Greece." In *The Future of Surface Artefact Survey in Europe*, ed. J. Bintliff, M. Kuna, and N. Venclova, 3–20. Sheffield.

Campana, S. 2009. "Archaeological Site Detection and Mapping: Some Thoughts on Differing Scales of Detail and Archaeological 'Non-visibility.'" In *Seeing the Unseen: Geophysics and Landscape Archaeology*, ed. S. Campana and S. Piro, 5–21. Boca Raton.

Campana, S., and M. Forte. 2001. *Remote Sensing in Archaeology. Proceedings of the XI International School in Archaeology (Certosa di Pontignano, 6–11 dicembre 1999)*. Florence.

Campana, S., and R. Francovich. 2003. "Landscape Archaeology in Tuscany: Cultural Resource Management, Remotely Sensed Techniques, GIS Based Data Integration and Interpretation." In *The Reconstruction of Archaeological Landscapes through Digital Technologies (Boston, Massachusetts 1–3 November 2001)*, 15–28. Archaeopress BAR International Series 1151. Oxford.

Cerasuolo, O., and L. Pulcinelli. 2015. "Le mura occidentali e il quartiere presso le mura settentrionali." In *Survey*, 15–20.

Guaitoli, M., ed. 2003. *Lo sguardo di Icaro*. Rome.

———. 2015. "La città tra nuove metodologie e tradizione." In *Novità*, 83–97.

Mogetta M., and J. A. Becker. 2014. "Archaeological Research at Gabii, Italy: The Gabii Project Excavations, 2009–2011." *AJA* 118:177–188.

Musson C., R. Palmer, and S. Campana. 2005. *In volo nel passato: Aerofotografia e cartografia archeologica*. Florence.

Pocobelli, G. F. 2004. "Vulci: Il contributo della fotografia aerea alla conoscenza dell'area urbana." *Archeologia Aerea* 1:127–142.

———. 2011. "Vulci ed il suo territorio: Area urbana, necropolis e viabilità. Applicazioni di cartografia archeologica e fotogrammetria finalizzata." *Archeologia Aerea* 4–5:117–126.

Potter, T. W. 1979. *The Changing Landscape of South Etruria*. London.

Smith, C. J. 2012. "Historical Introduction." In *Survey*, 1–8.

Volpe, R. 2009. "Vino, vigneti ed anfore in Roma repubblicana." In *Suburbium* II: *Il suburbio di Roma dalla fine dell'età monarchica alla nascita del sistema delle ville (V–II secolo a.C.)*, ed. V. Jolivet, C. Pavolini, M. A. Tomei, and R. Volpe, 369–381. Rome.

Ward-Perkins, J. 1961. "Veii: The Historical Topography of the Ancient City." *PBSR* 39:1–123.

PART II

HISTORY OF THE CITY

The second part of this volume presents our narrative of the history of Etruscan Veii. Newly gathered data from the settlement, from the necropoleis, and from the territory are combined in the descriptions of the history of early Veii, of Orientalizing Veii, and of Archaic, Late Archaic, and Classical Veii. The lively network of interactions between Veii and "the others" is detailed in the different chapters as a journey, moving outside the territory and reaching first the city's closest neighbors and then its farthest ones, the Greeks and the Near East.

CHAPTER 4

TOWARD VEII
The Bronze Age

FRANCESCO DI GENNARO

The territory of Veii had already been frequented by humans for a long time before the birth of the city, especially from the Paleolithic onward. Paleolithic remains have been identified all over Latium, which appears to have been significantly different at that time from the situation in the Holocene and Historical periods. Human groups lived in this area before the events of the Late Quaternary, when the final transformation of the landscape took place. Humans, winds, and rain have only slightly modified the region since then.

AT THE BEGINNING OF THE BRONZE AGE

During the Neolithic period, the earliest aggregation of families into single permanent settlements occurred. The location of the settlements on top of hills was a result of the widespread occupation of the territory in all its feasible locations, and in some cases was meant to provide a defensible position.

Nevertheless, it is only during the Bronze Age that we are able to recognize a unique and definitive process within the large amount of archaeological data available. In fact, in less than half a millennium, the territorial dynamics changed. Before the beginning of this process of transformation, settlements probably moved from one location to another, since the limited agricultural exploitation techniques did not permit long-term use of the land. During the Bronze Age, settlements became progressively more stable, probably due to the development and circulation of the use of bronze im-

plements and the availability of tools. During the Early Bronze Age axes began to be numerous. Their presence suggests the diffusion of the particular type of cultivation practice called "slash-and-burn." Their progressive typological transformation permitted refinement of the first wooden tools, such as plows, before the advent of sickles and other metallic tools.[1]

In any case, the development of agricultural production activities permitted a significant population growth, which in turn allowed for a better organization of the networks of settlements. We can imagine that, as soon as the opportunity to make settlements permanent became possible and evident, a rapid escalation occurred in conflicts between groups, and also at a more local scale among subsets of larger tribes. It is likely that some groups became aware of the fact that the skills and knowledge gained in agricultural practices would finally allow them to establish themselves stably in one agricultural area and to ensure their final possession of that land. This possession had nonetheless to be defended from competitors, and especially from those groups that were not yet settled, and later from the expansionism of the neighboring villages.

The decision to use and possess a specific portion of the territory, especially if shared by many communities, generated a run in the same direction by all groups. Some groups did not succeed, and for them the solutions were either permanence in a condition of instability or movement toward the less productive areas.

THE EARLIEST
FREQUENTING OF VEII

The earliest evidence that can be connected to events leading toward the historical development of the plateau of Veii dates to the Middle Bronze Age (around the mid-second millennium BCE; MBA). This frequenting of the future territory of Veii took place much earlier than the later and decisive process of urban formation of Veii, in parallel with the other major towns. Nevertheless, it is significant to stress that the MBA events were parts of long-lasting trends toward both the stabilization of individual settlements and the consolidation of the network of interactions between different settlements. The stability between the villages had been achieved, perhaps more than once, in previous centuries.

In the territory of Veii, and the immediate surroundings, Middle Bronze Age (MBA) and Recent Bronze Age (RBA) settlements are attested: Il Pino (MBA 1/2 and MBA 3); Terre di Bettona (MBA 3; *map 1: no. 32*); Cannetaccio, immediately under Veii-Portonaccio (MBA 3; *map 4:T*); Prato La Corte (MBA 3 and RBA; *map 1: no. 26*); Le Rughe (RBA; *map 1: no. 11*); Isola Farnese (RBA; *map 4:V*).[2]

At the beginning of the Middle Bronze Age (MBA 1–2), the main settlements were no longer seasonal but had already become stable. The following and final period of the Middle Bronze Age, the MBA 3, shows the easily recognizable presence of decorations engraved on the ceramic surface with a very strict style and technique. However, the patterns of the engraved designs are widely variable and therefore not completely repetitive. This style is known as "Apennine" (fig. 4.1:A). According to the data available, we can say that at the time when the Apennine style was widespread in central and southern Italy, many of the villages were already permanently settled[3] on naturally defensible hills. At the same time in northern Italy, the so-called *terramare* settlements were artificially defended. Many of these settlements in central and southern Italy would survive for more than five centuries.

The Apennine finds discovered at Veii seem to pertain mainly to secondary settlements or sporadic frequentation, although we need to take into account a

likely reduction in the number of fragments due to the passage of time. Study of the pottery suggests the direction and intensity of exchanges and mobility between the villages, which controlled movements in the territory. For example, a type of decorative filling within incised bands (consisting of small and coaxial lines) appeared along an "itinerary" from Veii–Il Pino to settlements on the Roman bank of the Tiber, such as Radicicoli Maffei,[4] but also in Faliscan territory, on the Apennine Mountains in the Marche, and in Abruzzo.

THE RECENT BRONZE AGE

The archaeological evidence from the Recent Bronze Age[5] in the territory surrounding Veii is notable for the continuation of many aspects of the previous archaeological phase, although it is not richly documented; the earliest evidence of occupation of the settlement of Isola Farnese dates to this period.

In order to understand the processes that took place at that time it is necessary to take a broader perspective and to look at southern Etruria in its entirety. In this region in this period a complete transformation in the decoration of pottery is attested. The RBA pottery style, referred to as "sub-Apennine," is typical of central Tyrrhenian Italy.[6] It was characterized by the complete absence of any decoration, of any drawing on the ceramic surface, while some continuity occurred in the form of the vases. The plastic attachments of handles projecting upwards occur now very frequently and are often zoomorphic (representing heads, especially of birds), a feature (fig. 4.1:B) only rarely documented for the Middle Bronze Age.

At this time, the occupation of the so-called *castelline*—naturally defended hills with sides consisting of vertical cliffs—involved a contraction in the number of secondary centers, mainly those in open positions. Taking into account this evidence (especially coming from surveys), it is possible to suggest that during the Recent Bronze Age the number of settlements located on top of defended hills surpassed the number of open sites as well as that of the minor settlements. This transformation marked a significant step in the progressive concentration of the settlements.[7] During the Recent Bronze Age, the hilltops of San Giovenale (fig.

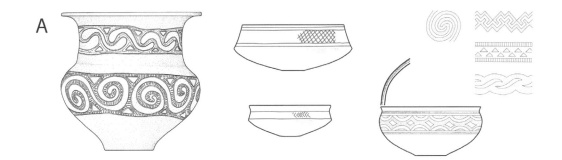

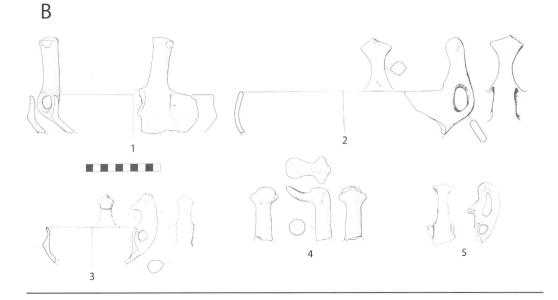

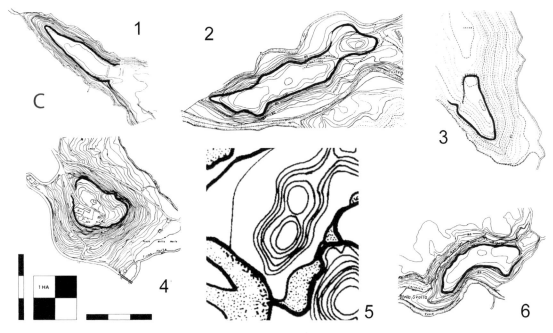

FIGURE 4.1. MBA and RBA remains around Veii. A. Selection of MBA 3 pottery and "Apennine" decorative patterns. B. Plastic attachments projecting upward, some zoomorphic, typical of the Middle Bronze Age. C. Topographical maps of typical RBA settlements: 1. Pontone di Barbarano; 2. Luni sul Mignone; 3. Ferleta; 4. Poggio San Pietro at Tuscania; 5. Campidoglio, Rome; 6. San Giovenale. (Copyright: F. di Gennaro)

4.1:C.6), Luni sul Mignone (fig. 4.1:C.2), Castellina del Marangone, and the Campidoglio in Rome (fig. 4.1:C.5) were occupied by settlements, while some open sites still survived (e.g., Sposetta, on the banks of Lake Bracciano).

In the area of the future town of Veii, Isola Farnese was occupied during the Recent Bronze Age and constitutes the most important site in the territory both for archaeological evidence and for its physical features. Looking at all the evidence of the surrounding regional area, we can imagine that this site was already inhabited during the Middle Bronze Age. At just 3.3 kilometers north of Isola Farnese (2 kilometers from the edge of the plateau of Veii), in the area of Prato La Corte (*map 1: no. 26*), MBA 3 and RBA fragments were found among other important Etruscan material. This evidence suggests a Bronze Age occupation followed by an Archaic settlement on this site.

In addition, at 5.7 kilometers from Isola Farnese (4.5 kilometers from Veii), at Le Rughe (*map 1: no. 11*), fragments dating to the Recent Bronze Age were found, unfortunately in a location not precisely recorded, along the main river of the area, the Cremera/ Valchetta.[8] A. M. Radmilli gave a brief description of the most significant finds, for example, the fragment of a carinated bowl (*capeduncola*) with a strap handle set on its wall midway between the carination and the rim, and fragments of a large vase with a cordon applied inside to create a supporting surface. Radmilli did not, however, mention any decorated pottery in his report. After the excavation, R. Peroni published the drawings of fifteen fragments from this context (fig. 4.2:A): several carinated bowls (nos. 1–8); one bowl with inverted rim (no. 10); one small cup with a light carination decorated by notches (no. 11); two cups with raised handles, one with a light carination (no. 12) and the other one more hemispherical, with a large horizontal groove (no. 13); and two "neck vases" with everted rims (nos. 14–15). The small fragment no. 9 may correspond to a spool even though it is represented as a handle in the form of a vertical cylinder. Another fragment of carinated bowl[9] is similar to nos. 3 and 6.[10] All these finds can be dated to the Recent Bronze Age, while no evidence from the site suggests its persistence during the

Final Bronze Age (as pointed out by Peroni when he referred to the "protovillanoviano" [Protovillanovan]).

THE FINAL BRONZE AGE

During the Final Bronze Age the decoration of vases recommenced. Unlike during the Middle Bronze Age, FBA decoration consisted of grooves (*solcature*; slightly larger than incisions) organized into repetitive motifs of groups of lines or single lines. At the same time, from a stylistic point of view, these decorations with grooves changed the tradition dramatically; in the later period, the practice of decorating vases with parallel grooves implies the use of a small comb tool with up to six prongs.

During the passage from the Recent Bronze Age to the Final Bronze Age most of the settlements survived, although the material culture shows a strong discontinuity, especially in regard to style. While the settlement of Isola Farnese (on a small plateau, ca. 5 hectares) survived during the Final Bronze Age, the contemporary evidence for the territory is very limited.

FBA SHERDS FROM EARLIER
INVESTIGATIONS

In the area near the North-West Gate of Veii, a fragment decorated with two bands of parallel grooves meeting at an angle was collected during field surveys (fig. 4.2:B). It would have been part of a large vase, and its decorative scheme and technique were characteristic of the Final Bronze Age.[11] Until recently, this discovery was isolated, since the restudy of the excavation at the North-West Gate and of the other finds collected during the British School at Rome survey, as well as all the previous excavations on the plateau, did not reveal any FBA evidence.[12] This situation contrasts with that of Vulci and Tarquinia, where intensive survey during the 1990s produced numerous FBA fragments, allowing dating of the earliest occupation of the urban plateaus in their entireties to this period and not to the Early Iron Age.[13] M. Pacciarelli has suggested that the proto-urban transformation at Veii, like that at Tarquinia and Vulci, be dated to the Final Bronze Age.[14]

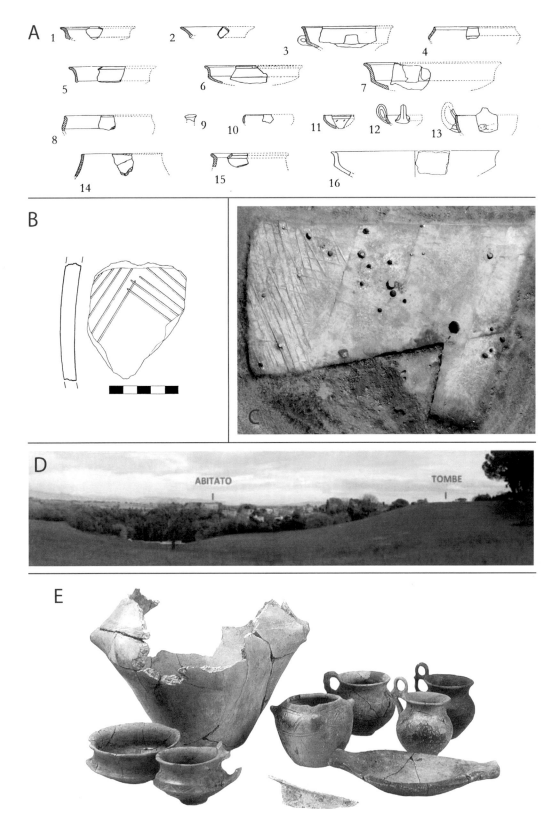

FIGURE 4.2. Bronze Age remains at Veii. A. RBA fragments discovered near the Cremera/Valchetta River (listed by A. Radmilli and first published by R. Peroni). B. FBA fragments from North-West Gate area. C. The area of the Pozzuolo necropolis. D. Pozzuolo with the urban plateau in the background. E. Casale del Fosso necropolis, assemblage from tomb 838. (A, B, and D, copyright: F. di Gennaro; C, copyright: Sabap-rm-met; E, copyright: L. D'Erme)

FBA SHERDS FROM LATER INVESTIGATIONS

Recent excavations have permitted F. Biagi to recognize similar FBA fragments (especially a cup with a trunco-conical or cylindrical neck) in association with the earliest fortifications at Veii.[15] These fragments point to the same date for the so-called proto-urban revolution in all the different parts of southern Etruria. Therefore, it is not possible anymore to suggest a "late" development at Veii, where "the proto-urban stage occurred only during the Early Iron Age, years before the same development at Rome."[16] At the same time, "the absence of an intermediate phase of occupation between Isola Farnese (and the North-West Gate FBA fragment) and the intensive EIA occupation of the plateau" needs to be reconsidered.

FROM SHERDS TO "PROTO-URBAN" TOWN

The significant new discoveries at Veii, although limited in number, have permitted a review of the issue of different chronologies for the foundation dates of the large towns. The Villanovan character appears to be the result of the new organization system, and especially of the urban system during its development. If the development of early Veii was delayed, the Villanovan style would have been imported from elsewhere and therefore would have presented the same distinctive aspects of one or two external towns.

On the contrary, as Peroni stressed, the Villanovan phenomenon corresponded to a unique cultural language, which followed different patterns at each proto-urban locale, as in the case of the Villanovan of Veii. Moreover, if the Villanovan trends were the result of a new organization of the community, the artifacts and materials the settlers brought with them onto the plateau would still have revealed earlier characteristics.[17]

FUNERARY EVIDENCE

The FBA funerary evidence on the hills near the plateau appears to have been more consistent. The razor (type *Croson di Bovolone*) that was discovered out of context in the necropolis of Quattro Fontanili (*map 3*) suggests the presence of disturbed FBA tombs in the area (more likely than the circumstance of its preservation in an Iron Age burial).[18]

A tomb dating to the Final Bronze Age has been identified inside the later necropolis of Casale del Fosso (fig. 4.2:E; *map 3*). The hill of Casale del Fosso lies approximately one kilometer from Isola Farnese (similarly to other FBA sites and their tombs),[19] and the distance between these two localities does not allow any direct connection (especially in terms of visibility). In addition, the two sites were located on opposite banks of the Piordo River, while at most of the FBA sites, settlements and cemeteries—with some relevant exceptions[20]—were located on the same bank. Finally, no evidence of the latest phase of the Final Bronze Age (FBA 3B) has been found at Isola Farnese. The tomb discovered at Casale del Fosso dates to this period, and it was at this time that the earliest occupation of the plateau of Veii occurred.

THE SIGNIFICANT ROLE OF ISOLA FARNESE

The recently discovered FBA urn-field of Pozzuolo (fig. 4.2:C, D; *map 3*), consisting entirely of cremations, has been connected to the settlement of Isola Farnese and confirms the importance of this FBA site within the entire region. In order to understand the process of urban formation at Veii, it is therefore extremely important to look at the evidence from Isola Farnese, which appears to have been the main "actor" for the foundation of Veii.

In fact, at many sites in Etruria, a pre-urban settlement was located on a small and naturally defended part of the future plateau of the town: (1) an FBA site occupying the so-called acropolis of Vulci (the hypothesis in favor of the presence of this settlement is justified by the orographic autonomy of the site, which would have permitted its occupation before the rest of the plateau); (2) Monte Bisenzo, in the large and homonymous EIA center; (3) the Castellina della Civita of Tarquinia; (4) the southern part of Caere; and now (5) the *castellina* of Isola Farnese.

The *castellina* of Isola Farnese appears to have been

physically divided from the plateau of Veii by the Piordo gorge. Comparison with Tarquinia indicates that the FBA settlement of the Castellina della Civita was not separated from the main plateau and therefore was later included inside the EIA proto-urban center of Tarquinia, while Isola Farnese was entirely detached from the Veii plateau, and thus the settlement did not survive into the Early Iron Age.

In the Final Bronze Age the Veii plateau was an open area entirely under the control of the village of Isola Farnese. Isola Farnese was also connected geographically with the slopes and hills ranging from La Storta up to Riserva del Bagno (with similar geological, morphological, and pedological characteristics).[21] While the FBA community of Castellina della Civita certainly made greater and greater use of the large plateau of Tarquinia as its main agricultural productive land, considering the deep separation between Isola Farnese and Veii, we must assume that the Veii plateau offered no particular attraction before its conscious and systematic occupation. It was only one of the nearby flat and well-drained land areas suitable for agricultural exploitation. In addition, despite the absence of FBA tombs, it is impossible to rule out the possibility that the plateau of Veii was once used also as a necropolis, since other Bronze Age tombs have been found further north, on the slopes of the plateau opposite Isola Farnese.

THE FINAL BRONZE AGE IN THE TERRITORY

Based on current evidence, the FBA settlements, which were abandoned as their population moved to Veii— apart from Isola Farnese—can be listed as follows: to the immediate north, Monte Sant'Angelo (*map 1: no. 19*), Trevignano (*map 1: no. 33*), Rocchetta di Fiano (*map 5: no. 10*), Pizzo di Nepi, and Narce; further north, Torre Stroppa (*map 5: no. 12*), Vignale di Civita Castellana (*map 5: Falerii*), and Vallerano (*map 5: no. 14*). Considering the significant distances involved, it is hard to determine whether the villages of Monte Cimino (*map 5: no. 8*), Soriano nel Cimino (*map 5: no. 11*), Vitorchiano, and Orte also participated in the process of foundation of Veii. It is possible that new dis-

coveries, especially in the areas of the modern villages near Veii, will reveal other sites.[22]

Monte Sant'Angelo is the only small settlement that shows a continuity of occupation between the Final Bronze Age and the Early Iron Age. The same continuity could be suggested, based on a few fragments, for La Ferriera di Sutri (*map 5: no. 6*). At Narce and at Il Pizzo di Nepi, single fragments could possibly attest an EIA presence.[23]

During a later moment of the Early Iron Age, it is possible that La Ferriera and especially Narce, together with the reoccupation of Vignale-Falerii and new sites such as Capena and Monte Lombrica,[24] were examples of the control and exploitation by Veii of a very large territory over the course of a gradual return of the population to the villages in the countryside, newly reorganized into an ascending hierarchy of power.[25] These new centers might also have absorbed groups coming from outside to compensate for a wave of immigration, as has been already proposed.[26]

In conclusion, the material from the region of Veii in these early periods, although fragmentary, emphasizes the strategic location of this area and the long frequenting and occupation of this land prior to the foundation of Veii. This material anticipates the early development of the settlement of Veii between the Final Bronze Age and the beginning of the Early Iron Age.

NOTES

1. Carancini 1984.
2. *Repertorio*, 43–44; D'Erme 2014. Other MBA fragments were recently discovered by the Veii Project in the area of Piazza d'Armi and Campetti.
3. The theory of a pastoral nomadism of Bronze Age human groups is still accepted in literature. Nevertheless, scholars expert in this period have stressed that the movements of herds (and particularly the seasonal transhumance) should be linked with permanent settlements, from which shepherds moved back and forth depending on the season.
4. di Gennaro and Barbaro (2008) identified this evidence (frag. 518160), before the discovery of the finds at Veii–Il Pino.
5. In Italian scholarship—unlike studies on protohistory in English—the Late Bronze Age is divided into the "Recent" (thirteenth and twelfth centuries BCE) and the "Final" Bronze

Age (twelfth and eleventh centuries BCE). Therefore the designation "Recent Bronze Age" should not be simplistically translated to "Late Bronze Age."

6. Because it is possible to further refine the dates for the evolution and transformation of the types of artifacts characteristic of this phase, the Recent Bronze Age has been divided into two different periods; see Damiani 2010.

7. The progressive concentration of settlements is discussed in Peroni and di Gennaro 1986.

8. Peroni 1959:248: "series of Subapennine and Protovillanovan with a complete absence of Apennine fragments." In the British School at Rome survey, the geographical location of this site corresponds to UTM 33TTG834609 with the description: "Bronze Age site on platform on the west bank of the Cremera, excavated by Peroni and published. Bronze Age material, bucchero, BIG": Hemphill 1975:146.

9. di Gennaro and Stoddart 1982: fig. 6, n. 9.

10. Peroni 1959.

11. The shape of the vase is not identifiable. It was decorated with sets of oblique lines consisting of no less than five grooves well drawn freehand, forming 90-degree angles. This decoration occurred in FBA sites and never in the Villanovan decoration style. Nevertheless, it characterizes EIA cups and bowls from Latium Vetus, with a zigzag of line segments: Bietti Sestieri 1992: tazza 22a var. 1; Gierow 1964: "calefattoio" (discovered at Castel Gandolfo 1816–1817).

12. di Gennaro and Schiappelli 2012.

13. Peroni 1969; Rittatore Vonwiller, Falchetti, and Negroni Catacchio 1977; di Gennaro 1982.

14. Pacciarelli 1994, 2001.

15. See chapter 5.

16. di Gennaro et al. 2002:41; 2004:150.

17. di Gennaro 1988: n. 26; 2015:126.

18. The same has been suggested for the fibula with serpentine bow discovered in the trench tomb 51α in the same necropolis (fig. 11b), belonging to a type which survived into the EIA.

19. Barbaro 2010.

20. For example, the settlement of Torre di Tragliatella–Monte Cucco (Fiumicino, RM), which was separated from the burials at Casale Campanella by the Fosso delle Pertucce. Similarly, the settlement on top of Vignale at Civita Castellana (VT) was connected to the necropolis of Celle–Montarano Sud on the other bank of the Fosso Sant'Anselmo.

21. di Gennaro and Guidi 2009.

22. Worth emphasizing is the reference (reported by Tim Potter) to some FBA pottery discovered near the Fontanile Nuovo in the territory of Morlupo (di Gennaro and Stoddart 1982:21 n. 40). All the other contexts are mentioned in *Repertorio*.

23. See chapter 6.

24. Iaia and Mandolesi 1993.

25. See chapter 6 for a different understanding of the phenomenon of reoccupation of the territory in the eighth century BCE.

26. Colonna 1991:38.

BIBLIOGRAPHY

Barbaro, B. 2010. *Insediamenti, aree funerarie ed entità territoriali in Etruria meridionale nel Bronzo Finale*. Grandi contesti e problemi della protostoria italiana 14. Florence.

Bietti Sestieri, A. M., ed. 1992. *La necropoli laziale di Osteria dell'Osa*. Rome.

Carancini, G. L. 1984. *Le asce nell'Italia continentale* II. Prähistorische Bronzefunde 9:12. Munich.

Colonna, G. 1991. "Le civiltà panelleniche." In *Storia e civiltà della Campania: L'evo antico*, ed. G. Pugliese Carratelli, 25–64. Naples.

Damiani, I. 2010. *L'età del Bronzo recente nell'Italia centro-meridionale*. Grandi contesti e problemi della protostoria italiana 12. Florence.

D'Erme, L. 2014. "Un ritrovamento dell'età del Bronzo nell'agro veientano." In *Etruria in progress: La ricerca archeologica in Etruria meridionale*, ed. L. Mercuri and R. Zaccagnini, 22–23. Rome.

di Gennaro, F. 1982. "Organizzazione del territorio nell'Etruria meridionale protostorica: Applicazione di un modello grafico." *DialArch* 2:102–112.

———. 1988. "Il popolamento dell'Etruria meridionale e le caratteristiche degli insediamenti tra l'età del Bronzo e l'età del Ferro." In *Etruria Meridionale: Conoscenza, conservazione, fruizione*, ed. C. Bettini, G. Colonna, and R. A. Staccioli, 59–82. Rome.

———. 2015. "Intervento di discussione su relazione T. Marino." In *Le città visibili*, 126–127. Officina Etruscologia 11. Rome.

di Gennaro, F., and B. Barbaro. 2008. "L'abitato del Bronzo Antico e Medio di Radicicoli Maffei: 1. L'indagine sul campo e prima analisi della ceramica." *BullCom* 109:9–56.

di Gennaro, F., O. Cerasuolo, C. Colonna, U. Rajala, S. Stoddart, and N. Whitehead. 2002. "Recent Research on the City and Territory of Nepi (VT)." *PBSR* 70:29–77.

di Gennaro, F., and A. Guidi. 2009. "Ragioni e regioni di un cambiamento culturale: Modi e tempi della formazione dei centri protourbani nella valle del Tevere e nel Lazio meridionale." *ScAnt* 15:429–445.

di Gennaro, F., and A. Schiappelli. 2012. "I reperti—Ceramica della prima età del Ferro." In *Survey*, 85–101.

di Gennaro, F., A. Schiappelli, and A. Amoroso. 2004. "Un confronto tra gli organismi protostatali delle due sponde del Tevere: Le prime fasi di Veio e di Crustumerio." In *Bridging the Tiber*, 147–177.

di Gennaro, F., and S. Stoddart. 1982. "A Review of the Evidence for Prehistoric Activity in Part of South Etruria." *PBSR* 50:1–21.

Gierow, P. G. 1964. *The Iron Age Culture of Latium* II: *Excavations and Finds*. ActaAth 24.2. Lund.

Hemphill, P. 1975. "The Cassia-Clodia Survey." *PBSR* 43:118–172.

Iaia, C., and A. Mandolesi. 1993. "Topografia dell'insediamento dell'VIII secolo a.C. in Etruria meridionale." *Journal of Ancient Topography* 3:17–48.

Pacciarelli, M. 1994. "Sviluppi verso l'urbanizzazione nell'Italia tirrenica protostorica." In *La presenza etrusca nella Campania meridionale. Atti delle giornate di studio, Salerno-Pontecagnano 1990*, 227–253. Biblioteca di Studi Etruschi 28. Florence.

———. 2001. *Dal villaggio alla città: La svolta protourbana del 1000 a.C. nell'Italia tirrenica*. Grandi contesti e problemi della protostoria italiana 4. Florence.

Peroni, R. 1959. *Per una definizione dell'aspetto culturale "Subappenninico" come fase cronologica a se stante. MemLinc*, ser. 8, vol. 9, fasc. 1. Rome.

———. 1969. "Per uno studio dell'economia di scambio in Italia nel quadro dell'ambiente culturale dei secoli intorno al mille a.C." *PP* 125:134–160.

Peroni, R., and F. di Gennaro. 1986. "Aspetti regionali dello sviluppo dell'insediamento protostorico nell'Italia centro-meridionale alla luce dei dati archeologici e ambientali." *DialArch* 2:193–200.

Rittatore Vonwiller, F., F. Falchetti, and N. Negroni Catacchio. 1977. "Preistoria e protostoria della Valle del Fiume Fiora." In *La civiltà arcaica di Vulci e la sua espansione. Atti Decimo Convegno di Studi etruschi e italici*, 99–165. Florence.

CHAPTER 5

VEII AND ITS TERRITORY FROM THE FINAL BRONZE AGE TO THE EARLY IRON AGE

FOLCO BIAGI

At the end of the Bronze Age, a revolutionary restructuring of the landscape occurred all over Etruria. This phenomenon marks the conclusion of a long-term political and ideological process, which began during the Middle Bronze Age and ended with the birth of the great Etruscan town-states. All the settlements, which until that moment were widely distributed in the territory, were abandoned.

As early as the tenth century BCE (Final Bronze Age [FBA] 3A), a contraction in the number of sites marks the beginning of this restructuring of the landscape, which was finally achieved at the beginning of the Early Iron Age, with the movement of communities toward the large tufa plateaus.[1] The selection of the plateaus occurred especially thanks to the large space available; the morphology of the area, with deep rivers that naturally defined and defended their borders; and their advantageous locations as compared to individual villages. The strategic importance of the new sites guaranteed their occupants the territorial control of vast sectors of land that now appeared almost completely free of settlements.

THE EARLY IRON AGE SETTLEMENT OF VEII

During the second half of the twentieth century CE, the different surveys in the area of the town of Veii recorded the presence of numerous finds, widely distributed on the entire plateau, dating to the Early Iron Age (EIA).[2] Remains of huts were identified in different excavations, and some of those can be certainly dated

to the first phase of occupation of the town. This evidence has been recognized at Piazza d'Armi,[3] Macchiagrande,[4] Pian di Comunità,[5] and Campetti.[6]

EIA HUTS AT PORTONACCIO

Small channels and post-holes have been discovered in the area of Portonaccio (*map 4:S*), which is located immediately outside the settlement on a small plateau, essentially a natural terrace at an elevation lower than that of the town. In this area was founded, in the first half of the seventh century BCE, the most important extra-urban sanctuary of Veii.[7] Traces of huts in this area could possibly testify to earlier evidence of the cult area rather than being part of the settlement.[8]

THE HUTS OF PIAZZA D'ARMI

Within the Veii Project, the most consistent EIA evidence discovered comes from Piazza d'Armi (*map 4:Y*). Piazza d'Armi constitutes a small tufa platform that is protected on all sides by tall, vertical cliffs. It is located to the southeast of the main plateau and connected to it by a narrow saddle.

Excavations carried out in the area surrounding the so-called *oikos* (which dates to the Late Orientalizing period) revealed a complex of sacred buildings. The most important among these buildings was created on top of the burial of an adult male,[9] whose grave was marked and protected by a series of wooden posts (fig. 5.1). Apart from this burial, little stratigraphical evidence can be dated to this early phase of occupation of

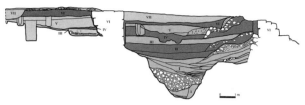

FIGURE 5.2. Campetti, excavation SBAEM 2003–2011, reconstruction of the stratigraphy. East–west section showing the sequence of Iron Age and Archaic defensive systems. I–V: Iron Age and Orientalizing contexts; VI–VII: Archaic and later contexts. (Copyright: F. Biagi and S. Neri)

FIGURE 5.1. Piazza d'Armi, hypothetical reconstruction of the heroic burial of the "founder" of Veii. (Copyright: G. Bartoloni)

the plateau of Piazza d'Armi.[10] Despite the later process of transformation and erosion of the site, the finds discovered in this area testify to the process of creation of the settlement, which should be considered to have begun already in the phase between the Final Bronze Age and the Early Iron Age.

CULT ACTIVITIES AT CAMPETTI SOUTH-WEST

Probable traces of cult activities are visible in the series of huts dating to the ninth century BCE that were identified in the area of Campetti (*map 4:O*). In the same location, in later periods, a sacred area was probably connected to a spring.[11] The earliest monumental evidence of this cult can be dated to the end of the seventh century BCE.

CAMPETTI NORTH-WEST WALLS

Excavation of the site of Campetti—referred to as the West Walls (map 4:G),[12] situated 80 meters to the south of the 1957 British excavations[13]—brought to light complex stratigraphy dating back to the Early Iron Age. This liminal area of the settlement was characterized by an articulated defensive system, necessitated by the fact that this northern side of the plateau was less naturally defended and more accessible to ene-

mies. Between the end of the tenth century BCE and the early ninth century BCE (at the passage from FBA 3 to EIA I), a great defensive rampart was built (figs. 5.2–5.4). It was formed by fillings of soil alternating with beds of stones used for anchoring or retaining the soil, and along its internal face a pavement, functioning as a service path, ran between two small mounds.

Excavation near the ramparts has revealed a series of domestic huts and areas for production. In the mid-ninth century BCE (Veii IA–IB), the area near the path was a polyfunctional artisans' district, housing ceramic production and other industry.[14] In addition to several hearths, numerous kilns for pottery production have been identified. These kilns, which conform to fully developed types known from elsewhere, were probably used for the firing of food-related pottery as well as for the production of prestigious vessels decorated with impressions and incisions made using combs.[15] Together with the evidence for manufacture of glass and the working of horn, metal production is indicated by the presence of dross with oxides of copper, tin lamina, and small tools with chisel tip used for finishing work.[16] Numerous spools and spindle-whorls, showing abundant signs of use, suggest the activities of spinning and weaving textiles in this area.[17]

At the end of the ninth century BCE, a great restructuring occurred in the entire area. On top of the earliest site of production a large hut was built, more than 13 meters long, featuring a small portico on the short side (figs. 5.5–5.6). In front of this portico was built a big pottery kiln with dual combustion chambers and a vertical draw, with an adjoining structure for the decantation of clay.

FIGURE 5.3. Campetti, excavation SBAEM 2003–2011, protohistoric defensive systems. (Copyright: F. Biagi)

FIGURE 5.4. Campetti, excavation SBAEM 2003–2011, excavation trench in the protohistoric ditch. (Copyright: F. Biagi)

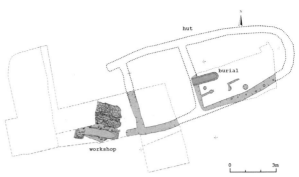

FIGURE 5.5. Campetti, excavation SBAEM 2003–2011, plan of the hut, the burial of the Lady of the Furnaces, and the workshop area. (Copyright: F. Biagi)

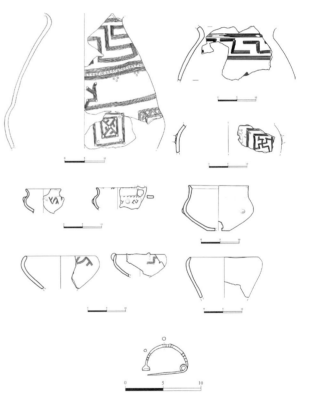

FIGURE 5.6. Campetti, excavation SBAEM 2003–2011, selection of pottery from the workshop area. (Copyright: F. Biagi)

Between the end of the ninth and the beginning of the eighth century BCE (Veii IC), the kiln and the hut were destroyed. This dismantling occurred together with the burial of an adult female, in the middle of the previous hut, now dubbed the "Lady of the Furnaces."[18] The whole area was then obliterated and leveled, and it was next used as the base for the reconstruction of a new rampart, while the earlier one at a lower elevation continued in use.

THE NECROPOLEIS

During the Early Iron Age the necropoleis, outside the area of the settlement, were located around the plateau, mainly on top of the closest hills, where the earliest burials have been found. Based on the available evidence from the necropoleis of Grotta Gramiccia, Casale del Fosso, and Quattro Fontanili (*map 3*), the main funerary areas appear to have been located to the north of the plateau. To the southwest were located the smaller necropoleis of Monte Campanile and Valle La Fata (*map 3*). Valle La Fata was situated on the bottom of the valley in a peculiar position.

FUNERARY RITUAL

At the beginning of the Early Iron Age, in the first half of the ninth century BCE, the funerary practice for the entire community was cremation. Ashes were deposited inside biconical urns, which were often ceremonially damaged by the breaking off of one handle.[19] Simple well-tombs (*tombe a pozzo*), having no lining of the sides with stones, represented the most common funerary architecture. The cinerary urns were often deposited on top of a tufa slab. Tomb-groups were always formed by a limited number of objects, and these stressed only the role and the gender of the deceased.[20]

Just at the end of the ninth century BCE, new types of tombs appeared, corresponding to a more stratified social articulation. The form of the well-tombs is now more complex, with a recess on the bottom and a niche on the side, which functioned as a place for the funerary vessels. At the same time, *custodiae* (stone containers) for cremation are attested.[21] Finally, the rite of inhumation in simple trenches (*tombe a fossa*) be-

came widespread.[22] Tomb-groups for males are generally characterized by a limited number of artifacts and especially personal ornaments, consisting in some cases only of fibulae with serpentine bow and a single bracelet. In the first half of the ninth century BCE, the very few references to the status of "warrior" corresponded to a terracotta helmet used as a lid to cover the cinerary urns.[23] In the second half of the century, this type of helmet changed into a type with a crest.[24] It is interesting to note that during the course of the entire ninth century BCE no weapons were ever buried inside the tombs.[25]

Tomb-groups for females appear to be more distinctive, especially at the end of the ninth century BCE.[26] At this time, the presence of ornaments (fibulae, bracelets, pendants, etc.) was widespread. The shapes of vessels were different, and in some cases artifacts connected with the activities of spinning and weaving were placed inside the tomb (spindles, spools, spindle-whorls, and distaffs).

Analysis of the horizontal stratigraphy of the necropoleis has demonstrated that, beginning with the different groups already formed in the mid-ninth century BCE, the development of the cemeteries followed a radial pattern during the entire eighth century BCE, one that emphasized family links and continuity between different generations.

THE EIA LANDSCAPE OF VEII

Between the Final Bronze Age and the Early Iron Age, the territory of Veii was an area of approximately 1,000–1,500 square kilometers (*maps 1 and 5*). The northeast border coincided with the Vezza River, while to the east and south the Tiber River marked the natural limits of the territory. To the west, the territory of Veii reached the sea, along a brief stretch of the Tyrrhenian coast between the Tiber and the Arrone River. The latter river marked the northwestern border, toward the territory of Caere. The eastern bank of Lake Bracciano, between Anguillara and Trevignano, was also controlled by Veii.

There is a likely frontier site at Vicarello, connected to the local hot springs, where evidence of protohistoric occupation has been found (*map 1: no. 35 and map 5: no. 15*). Hot springs and a place of worship were located there in historical times. From the Trevignano/Vicarello area, borders then passed by Sutri and Nepi and reached the foothills of the Cimini Mountains, following the left bank of the Vezza, from Centignano and Corchiano, and finally reaching the Tiber just below Orte (*see map 5*).

In ancient times, the Tyrrhenian coast consisted of extensive lagoons and marshes. Large sand dunes separated these internal waters and the open sea. The area of the delta of the Tiber, a landscape characterized by large ponds, was certainly subject to constant change and required continuous maintenance work.[27]

The hinterland, between the Arrone and the Tiber, rises gently toward Veii, without pronounced heights, creating a sequence of rolling hills and flat areas suitable to agricultural and pastoral exploitation. By contrast, the countryside just behind Veii was characterized by hills alternating with deep canyons formed by small streams, reaching the Tiber Valley and the foothills of the Cimini to the northeast.

EIA TERRITORIAL SETTLEMENTS AND COMMUNITIES

At the end of the Bronze Age, as in the rest of Etruria, all the settlements distributed throughout the territory of Veii slowly disappeared.[28] Only a few sites survived into the Early Iron Age, and their presence can be linked to Veii's new political control over the large territory.[29] At the beginning of the Early Iron Age, the long process of development of a territorial consciousness, which probably started in the Middle Bronze Age (seventeenth–fifteenth centuries BCE), reached its conclusion.[30]

The available data about the location of many of these settlements are still scarce and unfortunately not sufficient to enable us to draw up a profile of the political territory of Veii during the ninth century BCE. For instance, the apparent absence of a chain of coastal sites is striking. Satellite sites on the coast would have allowed the exploitation of maritime resources and control of the salt-pans, as such entities functioned for the other great cities of southern maritime Etruria.[31]

The few sites dating to the Early Iron Age are the following: (a) the small settlement of Monte Sant'Angelo (*map 1: no. 19*),[32] defended by a rampart wall and located on a hill at the center of a system of lakes (Martignano, Baccano, Stracciacappa, and Bracciano), which probably functioned as the control point of the frontier with Caere (*see fig. 7.1*); (b) the settlement of Torre di Prima Porta (*map 1: no. 27*),[33] located on a small hill near the bank of the Tiber and its confluence with the stream near Monte Oliviero; and (c) the settlement of the Ferriera di Sutri (*map 5: no. 6*).[34]

Very little evidence from the Ager Faliscus and the Ager Capenas can be dated to the Early Iron Age. During this period these areas, despite the fact that they had a well-defined ethnic and cultural autonomy and a specific historical and political identity, were certainly part of Veii, which controlled trade along the Tiber.[35] Several EIA sites have been identified: (1) Narce (*map 5*), along the banks of the Treja River, which controlled an important internal route;[36] (2) the settlement of Maleranca/Rosetoli, near Capena (*map 5*),[37] located near the Tiber, not far from the ford of Lucus Feroniae; (3) Pizzo di Nepi (*map 5*);[38] (4) Castellaccio di Corchiano (*map 5: no. 2*);[39] (5) Colle S. Antimo a Nazzano (*map 5: no. 3*); and (6) Monte Pelliccia a Ponzano (*map 5: no. 1*)[40] (on the basis of a few fragments discovered in the area).

CONCLUSIONS

As we have seen, recent discoveries are illuminating the complex sociopolitical profile of the early community of Veii between the Final Bronze Age and the Early Iron Age. The theory suggested by Ward-Perkins—of an occupation of the plateau consisting of different and separated villages[41]—is now refuted by the evidence of a unified community consisting of groups of huts and family plots, all spread along the plateau.[42]

Significantly, the data from Campetti push back the date of the earliest proto-urban settlement, to the end of the tenth century BCE (FBA 3B). The different communities that abandoned small settlements within the territory to move into the new area of the town at the end of the Bronze Age made this same conscious decision. This movement appears to be the result of a sociopolitical integration among all the villages, which during the Final Bronze Age gradually reached an acceptable level of prosperity, and allowed the constitution of a unified larger settlement. Only a high level of coordination among the groups, which does not exclude the preeminence of one of the communities over the others, could justify the impressive defensive complex that fortified one slope of the plateau in order to protect the entire new community.[43]

The earliest tomb-groups (ca. 900–825 BCE, Veii IA–IB) project the image of a society based on an egalitarian ideology but characterized also by charismatic leaders. This balance does not survive after the end of the ninth century BCE (Veii IC), when new types of burials with complex tomb-groups[44] testify to an ideological change and to a more stratified society, where the concentration of economic and social power anticipates the emergence of the aristocracies during the eighth century BCE.

NOTES

1. See chapter 4.

2. Ward-Perkins 1961; Delpino and Fugazzola Delpino 1980; Guaitoli 1981.

3. Stefani 1922, 1945; *Veio* II; and *Veio* III.

4. D'Alessio 2015:28.

5. Belelli Marchesini 2001:24.

6. The central area of the sanctuary of Campetti has been published in preliminary form by Fusco and Cerasuolo (2001:9). For the excavations at the walls of Campetti, see Boitani 2008; Boitani, Neri, and Biagi 2007–2008, 2009; and chapter 16.

7. See chapter 13.

8. Colonna (in *Portonaccio* I, 147) first suggested these were sacred huts.

9. In Etruria the presence of burials among the living inside the settlement is always connected with exceptional contexts. The burial in Piazza d'Armi has been interpreted as belonging to a man who might have played the role of leader at the beginning of the proto-urban development of the settlement (*Sepolti tra i vivi*). See also chapter 1.

10. Worthy of notice is the recent discovery of a circular structure—probably a hut—with numerous fragments of pottery dating to the beginning of the Early Iron Age (Veii IA), which was precisely aligned in relation to the later plan of the *oikos*.

11. Fusco 2015; Maggi and Latini 2015.

12. The excavation is located along the line of part of the Archaic defensive system.

13. Ward-Perkins 1959.

14. See also chapter 23.

15. The different forms attested are as follows: biconical jars (*ollae*), bowls, cups, small plates, and ship-shaped vessels.

16. These tools, probably chisel profilers similar to combs, were used to incise or impress the decoration on finished parts; see for example the technique used in an experimental reproduction of a fibula with decoration in "herringbone" in Formigli, Pacini, and Petti 2003:44–46, and fig. 18.

17. The presence of at least two bronze needles also confirms the hypothesis that this was an area for the production of textiles.

18. See chapter 23.

19. Generally, this type of jar, which was originally used as a container for water, had two horizontal handles located at the point of its greatest width. In the burials, the biconical urns—probably made for the funerary ritual—often have only a single handle.

20. Bartoloni et al. 1997:96.

21. The burial practice using the *custodiae* is attested especially in the necropolis of Grotta Gramiccia.

22. Quattro Fontanili tomb 307; Casale del Fosso tomb 439; Grotta Gramiccia tomb 254; Bartoloni et al. 1997:92.

23. Generally the upper part of the helmets is shaped like the roof of a small hut.

24. Starting from the phase Veii IC (ca. 825–790 BCE) and in the following Veii IIA (ca. 790–775 BCE), bronze helmets were used to cover the urns. The hemispherical type occurs, for example, in a tomb at Grotta Gramiccia (Berardinetti and Drago 1997:48, fig. 17); the crest type occurs in tomb 272 at Grotta Gramiccia (Berardinetti and Drago 1997:48 and fig. 15).

25. The earliest weapons attested, both as miniatures and life sized, date to Veii IIA (ca. 790–775 BCE).

26. Berardinetti and Drago 1997:40 n. 11.

27. It is important to mention here the FBA site Vignole-Maccarese (tenth century BCE), which was originally located near the lagoon at the Tiber delta. The settlement was similar to many lakeside sites, set atop artificial hills supported by posts and twisted branches (Ruggeri et al. 2010).

28. The Final Bronze Age occupation of large plateaus occurred in Tarquinia (Mandolesi 1999) and Vulci (Pacciarelli 2000). At Caere no data refer certainly to a Final Bronze Age occupation of the site, apart from a fragment of bowl from Vigna Parrocchiale that is dated to the end of the tenth century BCE (FBA 3B); see Moscati 1993:227 and fig. 439.H 17.1. Nevertheless, the presence of two Final Bronze Age cremations in the area of the Sorbo suggests, also for Caere, an early proto-urban evolution, as suggested by Arancio and D'Erme 1990–1991.

29. It is possible to suggest that all the settlements at the

end of the tenth century BCE (FBA 3B) were abandoned so that their inhabitants could join the creation of the new proto-urban town. Only after this political and formal act would the settlements later be reoccupied as satellite sites of Veii. See also chapter 7.

30. See chapter 4.

31. Recently, as a result of rescue excavations near Fiumicino (Maccarese–Le Vignole–Piana del Sole), traces have appeared of a settlement dating to the Bronze Age, which seems to survive into the Early Iron Age. Data on these discoveries are unfortunately almost entirely unpublished (Ruggeri et al. 2010). Among the very few finds dating to this period, of great importance is the presence of a Sardinian bronze *navicella* (small ship) discovered in the area of Portus, in the 1863 excavations of the tombs of the Principi Torlonia, and preserved at the Hermitage Museum (Colonna 1981:171–172 and pl. 9b; and recently Milletti 2012:144.9 and pl. 87.2). The importance of this area also relates to salt production, attested here until the Middle Ages, which was especially important for medieval and Renaissance Rome (Pannunzi 2013:18–19).

32. Among the different sites within the territory of Veii that belong to this period, the best known is Monte Sant'Angelo, although it is not yet fully published (Cozza and Pasqui 1894; Tabolli 2015). Concerning this site see also chapter 7.

33. The only published EIA fragment (Carbonara, Messineo, and Pellegrino 1996:135, and fig. 267) can be dated to Latial period II, and finds comparanda from the necropolis of Osteria dell'Osa in tomb 352 (first quarter of the ninth century BCE, Latial period IIA1) and tomb 374 (ca. 900–830 BCE, Latial period IIA?) (Bietti Sestieri 1992:595 and fig. 3a.87; 597–598 and fig. 3a.93).

34. See di Gennaro 1995.

35. During the ninth century BCE the Faliscan and Capenate territories were probably entirely under the political and cultural control of Veii, while during the eighth century BCE the northern borders of the territory of Veii moved south of the springs of the Treja River. See chapter 7.

36. Of the several finds discovered and published in the small test trench excavated by Fugazzola and Peroni Fugazzola, different fragments can be dated to the Early Iron Age. The comb-shaped incisions suggest a cultural influence by Veii at this time (Peroni and Fugazzola 1969).

37. The surveys revealed the presence of numerous fragments with comb-shaped incisions, probably still dating to the ninth century BCE; see Turchetti 1995:94–95.

38. The Faliscan nature of Nepi—always considered between Etruria and the Ager Faliscus—has been recently stressed, due to the study of finds discovered in different surveys and excavations (recently, di Gennaro et al. 2002, 2008).

39. See di Gennaro et al. 2002.

40. *Repertorio*.

41. Ward-Perkins 1959.

42. Bartoloni (2009:100) summarizes the evidence for the earliest occupation of the plateau of Veii.

43. The excavations in progress in the area of Campetti Bastion revealed a stretch of the protohistoric defensive system of Veii more than 200 meters long.

44. In this period, trench tombs and complex tomb-groups appeared and cremations were placed in larger *custodiae* (Bartoloni et al. 1997:92–93). At the same time were found two peculiar objects now identified as scepters: one was discovered in tomb 542 of Grotta Gramiccia and had undergone a ceremonial destruction (published by A. Piergrossi, G. Galante, J. Tabolli, and S. ten Kortenaar in Arancio and Massimi 2012:79, II.27); the second one comes from Quattro Fontanili (Berardinetti Insam 1990:9). The scepter from Grotta Gramiccia was placed inside the urn together with a fibula, in accordance with the very modest funerary ritual of the ninth century BCE (Veii IA and IB). These objects probably do not represent the politic and social power of the contemporary elite but instead stress the power of the earliest leaders in relation to the ancient communities. In the Early Iron Age, new leaders, more distinctive in social and economic status, arose amid a more structured society after a process of formation that lasted almost one hundred years.

BIBLIOGRAPHY

Arancio, M. L., and L. D'Erme. 1990–1991. "Una tomba del Bronzo Finale da Cerveteri: Nuovi dati per la conoscenza del territorio." *Origini* 15:375–398.

Arancio, M. L., and S. Massimi, eds. 2012. *Ambra dalle rive del Baltico all'Etruria* (exh. cat.). Rome.

Bartoloni, G. 2007–2008. "La sepoltura al centro del pianoro di Piazza d'Armi a Veio." In *Sepolti fra i vivi*, 821–832.

———. 2009. "I primi abitanti di Roma e Veio." In *Gli Etruschi e Roma: Fasi monarchica e alto-repubblicana. Atti del XVI Convegno Internazionale di Studi sulla Storia e l'Archeologia dell'Etruria*, ed. G. M. Della Fina, 93–117. Annali della Fondazione per il Museo "Claudio Faina" 16. Orvieto.

Bartoloni, G., A. Berardinetti, A. De Santis, and L. Drago. 1997. "Le necropoli villanoviane di Veio: Parallelismi e differenze." In *Necropoli arcaiche*, 89–100.

Belelli Marchesini, B. 2001. "Comunità." In *Veio, Cerveteri, Vulci*, 23–28.

Berardinetti, A., and L. Drago. 1997. "La necropoli di Grotta Gramiccia." In *Necropoli arcaiche*, 39–61.

Berardinetti Insam, A. 1990. "La fase iniziale della necropoli villanoviana di Quattro Fontanile: Rapporti con le comunità limitrofe." *DialArch* 1:5–28.

Bietti Sestieri, A. M., ed. 1992. *La necropoli laziale di Osteria dell'Osa*. Rome.

Boitani, F. 2008. "Nuove indagini sulle mura di Veio nei pressi di Porta Nord-Ovest," with an appendix by S. Neri and F. Biagi. In *Città murata*, 135–154.

Boitani, F., S. Neri, and F. Biagi. 2007–2008. "La donna delle fornaci di Veio-Campetti." In *Sepolti tra i vivi*, 833–868.

———. 2009. "Novità dall'impianto produttivo della prima età del Ferro di Veio-Campetti." In *I mestieri del fuoco: Officine e impianti artigianali nell'Italia preromana*, 23–42. Officina Etruscologia 1. Rome.

Carbonara, A., G. Messineo, and A. Pellegrino, eds. 1996. *La necropoli etrusca di Volusia*. Rome.

Colonna, G. 1981. "La barchetta nuragica di Porto ritrovata." In *Gli Etruschi e Roma. Atti dell'incontro di studio in onore di Massimo Pallottino (Rome 1979)*, ed. M. Cristofani, 171–172. Rome.

Cozza, A., and A. Pasqui. 1894. "Monte Sant'Angelo e la sua necropoli." *MonAnt* 4:33–94.

D'Alessio, M. T. 2015. "Macchiagrande: Il paesaggio urbano tra l'età del Ferro e la tarda età imperiale." In *Novità*, 27–33.

Delpino, F., and M. A. Fugazzola Delpino. 1980. "Qualche nuovo dato sulla topografia storica di Veio." *ArchCl* 32: 174–181.

D'Erme, L. 2001. "Necropoli di Casal del Fosso, tomba 838." In *Veio, Cerveteri, Vulci*, 90–91.

———. 2003. "Necropoli di Casal del Fosso, tomba 838." In *Formello*, 54–56.

di Gennaro, F. 1986. *Forme di insediamento tra Tevere e Fiora dal Bronzo Finale al principio dell'età del Ferro*. Florence.

———. 1995. "Le Ferriere di Sutri." In *Preistoria e Protostoria in Etruria: Tipologia delle necropoli e rituali di deposizione: Ricerche e scavi. Atti del II Incontro di studi, Farnese 1993*, ed. N. Negroni Catacchio, 277–279. Milan.

———. 2012. "I ritrovamenti protostorici del territorio di Formello e le fasi formative di Veio." In *MAV*, 33–46.

di Gennaro, F., O. Cerasuolo, C. Colonna, U. Rajala, S. F. K. Stoddart, and N. Whitehead. 2002. "Recent Research on the City and Territory of Nepi." *PBSR* 70:29–77.

di Gennaro, F., U. Rajala, D. Rizzo, S. F. K. Stoddart, and N. Whitehead. 2008. "Nepi and Territory: 1200 BC–400 AD." In *Mercator Placidissimus*, 879–888.

Formigli, E., A. Pacini, and M. Petti. 2003. "Studio tecnico e riproduzione sperimentale di una fibula con arco semplice a gomito del bronzo finale." In *Fibulae dall'età del Bronzo all'alto Medioevo: Tecnica e tipologia*, ed. E. Formigli, 40–48. Florence.

Fusco, U. 2015. "I santuari presso Campetti, area SO." In *Novità*, 40–45.

Fusco, U., and O. Cerasuolo. 2001. "Campetti." In *Veio, Cerveteri, Vulci*, 9–11.

Guaitoli, M. 1981. "Gabii: Osservazioni sulle fasi di sviluppo dell'abitato." In *Ricognizione archeologicae nuove ricerche nel Lazio*. *QITA* 9:23–57.

Maggi, M., and T. Latini. 2015. "Prime evidenze di paleocircolazione di acque idrotermali." In *Novità*, 34–39.

Mandolesi, A. 1999. *La "prima" Tarquinia: L'insediamento protostorico sulla Civita e nel territorio circostante*. Florence.

Milletti, M. 2012. *Cimeli d'identità: Tra Etruria e Sardegna nella prima età del ferro*. Officina Etruscologia 6. Rome.

Moscati, P. 1993. "Impasti dell'età del Ferro." In *Lo scarico arcaico della Vigna Parrocchiale*, ed. M. Cristofani, 217–235. *Caere* 3.2. Rome.

Pacciarelli, M. 2000. *Dal villaggio alla città: La svolta protourbana del 1000 a.C. nell'Italia tirrenica*. Florence.

Pannunzi, S. 2013. "La laguna di Ostia: Produzione del sale e trasformazione del paesaggio dall'età antica all'età moderna." *MÉFRM* 125.2. http://mefrm.revues.org/1507.

Peroni, R., and M. A. Fugazzola. 1969. "Ricerche preistoriche a Narce." *BPI* 78:79–145.

Ruggeri, D., M. Gala, A. Facciolo, M. C. Grossi, C. Morelli, M. L. Rinaldi, S. Sivilli, E. Carrisi, D. Citro, and F. R. De Casto. 2010. "Località Le Vignole, Maccarese (Fiumicino, Roma): Risultati preliminari dello scavo protostorico." In *Preistoria e Protostoria in Etruria: L'alba dell'Etruria: Fenomeni di continuità e trasformazione nei secoli XII–VIII a.C.: Ricerche e scavi. Atti del IX Incontro di Studi, Valentano, Pitigliano 2008*, ed. N. Negroni Catacchio, 327–338. Milan.

Stefani, E. 1922. "Veio: Esplorazioni dentro l'area della città." *NSc* 1922:379–404.

———. 1945. "Scavi archeologici a Veio in contrada Piazza d'Armi." *MonAnt* 40:177–290.

Tabolli, J. 2015. "Nuovi dati sulla necropoli di Monte Sant'Angelo." In *Novità*, 141–146, 157–160.

Turchetti, R. 1995. "Osservazioni sulle fasi di sviluppo del territorio in epoca antica." In *Capena e il suo territorio*, ed. M. C. Mazzi, 91–110. Rome.

Vianello Cordova, A. P. 1967. "Una tomba 'protovillanoviana' a Veio." *StEtr* 35:295–306.

Ward-Perkins, J. B. 1959. "Excavations beside the North-West Gate at Veii, 1957–58." *PBSR* 27:38–79.

———. 1961. "Veii: The Historical Topography of the Ancient City." *PBSR* 29:1–23.

CHAPTER 6

VEII IN THE EIGHTH CENTURY BCE

ALESSANDRA PIERGROSSI

At the beginning of the Early Iron Age, the organization of the territory in southern Etruria was based mainly on agricultural and pastoral exploitation of the land.[1] Villanovan villages evolved into proto-urban settlements through a swift process of aggregation. Soon afterward, however, a growing interest in seafaring activities can be detected in the evidence of frequent contacts with other populations of the Tyrrhenian Sea, prior to the earliest encounters with the Greeks and Phoenicians, following the foundation of Euboean settlements around the Gulf of Naples: Pithekoussai in 770–760 BCE and Cumae in 740–730 BCE.

Funerary evidence dating to the ninth century BCE reveals an apparently egalitarian society: the community followed a strict ritual, as evidenced in the consistent adoption of generic markers of gender and role by most of the members of the group. Almost no reference to the status of the dead appeared in the burials. However, two or three generations after the foundation of the Etruscan cities in the early eighth century BCE, a progressive increase in wealth together with the display of symbols of political and religious power is evident. Tomb-groups reveal a hierarchical social structure, which can be considered the natural outcome of the processes that had already begun in the previous phase.

LEADERS AND "KINGS"

With the emergence of leading groups, power seems to have converged in the hands of family heads who were warlords and priests (in this phase no recognizable distinction between military and religious powers is visible in the archaeological record) and acted as mediators between the divine and human spheres. These leaders probably organized this power via a form of monarchy, where the king represented the entire community and ensured prosperity and continuity. The family—meaning an extended group—marked the core of this community. The leader, of high rank, coordinated the interactions between the different families living in the same area and sharing land and resources. This "king" held great powers, which were recognized and respected by the entire community. It is possible to imagine the existence of a form of primitive and religious monarchy, based on economic differentiation, that was transferred by birthright and gained by attaining honor in war.

Among the different kings of Veii, several legendary names have survived, despite the impossibility of providing a contextual and historical date to any of those names. For at least three of them, the ancient sources suggest that they belonged to the early phases of the city: (a) Vel Vibe (Naevius in Festus 334 L), who was connected to Amulius, the usurper king of Alba Longa overthrown by his grandsons Romulus and Remus; (b) Morrius, who appears to be similar to Numa, according to Servius (*ad Aen.* 8.285), for the religious introduction of the cult of Salii;[2] and (c) Propertius, the founder of Lucus Feroniae (Cato in Servius, *ad Aen.* 7.697).[3]

THE TERRITORY IN THE EIGHTH CENTURY BCE

This rising aristocracy needed to control its rural territories. This necessity explains the desire to create a dependent and productive *ager* surrounding the urban area, which also appears in the different narratives of the wars between Rome and Veii. The earliest conflicts between the two cities date back to the reign of Romulus and were followed, according to the sources, by a hundred years of peace.[4]

In comparison to other Villanovan sites, such as Tarquinia and Vulci, the archaeological record of Veii is significantly different. From this phase, and up to the beginning of the seventh century BCE, there is a clear absence of archaeological evidence in the territory between Rome and Veii and toward the coast.[5] This absence might be explained in the light of the conflicts against the rising Latin center and the conditions established during the truce.

However, it is also possible that Veii did not need to control the territory by means of a permanent occupation, because its population was essentially in a demographic balance between the ninth and the eighth centuries BCE, as the funerary evidence so far has shown (see below). Even if the rivalry with Rome consisted mainly of a continuous series of conflicts, quarrels, truces, and betrayals, right up to 396 BCE, among all the Etruscan cities, Rome had its closest cultural and artistic ties with Veii.

The location of Veii may also have been determined by the control of the area along the Middle Tiber Valley by the Faliscans and the Capenates (*map 5*).[6] Different scholars have suggested that this area was bolstered at the beginning of the eighth century by the establishment of Narce, considered by some to be a "Veientine outpost"[7] in the Treja Valley, when the great Etruscan center began encouraging the repopulation of the area.[8]

The importance of the Tiber Valley and the inland roads had grown markedly following the establishment of Greek colonies in Campania. Veii, from this moment on and throughout the entire eighth century BCE, held a primary role in the trade between Etruria, Rome, and Latium, serving as a communication hub between the north and south regions of Apennine Italy.[9] With its location close to the Tiber River, Veii became an essential transit point for travel to the Bolognese area and consequently the Transalpine area, as well as the Campania region and southern Magna Graecia.

After the second half of the seventh century BCE, the prominent position of Veii was diminished, as shown by the account of the Roman king Ancus Marcius, who reconquered the Veientine salt-pans and Silva Maesia, the largest of the coastal forests in Latium along the Latin shores of the Tiber, both of which were previously controlled by Veii.[10] The loss of these valuable assets, which were permanently absorbed into Roman territory at the expense of the Veientine land, compromised the influence of Veii, while the future via Cornelia, which led from Caere and the coast toward Praeneste and Campania, prevailed as the preferred route.

THE CHARACTER OF THE SETTLEMENT

The growing displays of wealth in the tombs around Veii did not correspond to any real change in its housing structures. The same type of dwelling was used as in the previous century: circular huts with conical roofs supported by a central post, clustered in groups all over the plateau, spaced out across open areas intended for domestic production (hearths, ovens for ceramic production, etc.), and with orchards and enclosures for livestock.

For the most part, areas used for worship and ritual practices are not identifiable in the archaeological record. They may have been nondurable structures resembling those used for residential purposes or altars in the open air. It is probable that they were located in places that would someday be built over and thus were completely eradicated by later buildings.

The only sacred material evidence identified thus far is on the small southern plain of Piazza d'Armi (*maps 3 and 4:Y*). It was uncovered during the excavations directed by G. Bartoloni: a trench tomb protected by an oval hut inside an enclosure, which was preserved from the ninth to the seventh century BCE (*see fig. 5.1*).[11] The man who was buried in this tomb (the inhumation was an exceptional practice, cremation being the prevalent ritual at that time) may have been the community's unifying element, somehow connected with the origins of the settlement. This man was probably an acknowledged ancestor and object of veneration, and/or a king of mythical and legendary character. If other discoveries do not bring to light similar early burials in other areas of the ancient city, we might suggest that the presence of this noble burial would have justified the royal status of the family (or, to use a modern word, "lineage") that lived at Piazza d'Armi, a place that already manifested a distinctive character, as confirmed in later phases by the construction of the *oikos*. During the second half of the eighth century BCE, this hut underwent significant change, and was transformed into a wooden building with a double-arched hearth to the north. In addition, a second burial has been found, which belongs to a boy aged between twelve and eighteen years, probably a descendant of the person buried earlier.[12]

All over the settlement, there is archaeological evidence for ditches, canals, and post-holes that mark the perimeter of the structures, but in most cases the earliest occupation is indicated by the high incidence of early residual ceramic fragments within the later contexts.

During the Veii Project—aside from the discoveries at Piazza d'Armi—inhabited areas have been found as in earlier excavations:[13] in the southern part of the plateau at Comunità (*map 4:W*);[14] in the middle of the plateau at Macchiagrande (*map 4:M*)[15] in the vicinity of the Augustan forum; in the area of Campetti (*map 4:O*),[16] a northwestern offshoot near the sanctuary at Portonaccio and in the same area of the great polyadic sanctuary dedicated to the deities that protected the city (*map 4:S*).[17]

During the survey by the British School at Rome in the mid-1950s, the excavation of a residential quarter near the North-West Gate, in front of the necropolis of Grotta Gramiccia, revealed an elliptical structure that appears to have survived until the end of the eighth century BCE, as indicated by the deposits of Villanovan materials (*map 4:F*).[18]

The distribution of the structures allows us to believe that during the Early Iron Age, without any distinction between the ninth and the eighth centuries BCE, the entire plateau was extensively occupied, although it is not possible to determine what relationships and arrangements linked the different groups.

Some changes in the internal organization of the site began during the second half of the eighth century BCE, as highlighted by the excavation of the fortification discovered at Campetti (*map 4:G*), where the easiest access to the plateau required an early defense structure. A renovation of the defensive system, which had been installed in the Final Bronze Age, was carried out, with the construction of wall embankments.

THE FUNERARY EVIDENCE

The best glimpse of the social and political processes of the second phase of the Early Iron Age at Veii, as in the rest of Etruria, comes from the funerary evidence. Taking into account the ideological filters that may have altered the historical reality, the "city of the dead" existed in parallel with the living society, even if through an idealized representation. The analysis of the subjective system of signs represented by a single tomb and by an entire necropolis—though the language is complex, symbolic, mediated, and selective—shows the variations within the funerary ritual, and portrays an image both of the identity of individual persons and of the various relationships within the social group.

We can observe some general trends, such as the following:

an increased complexity and variety in the funerary structures;

the diffusion of the use of inhumation together with progressive growth in the number of grave goods;

the presence of artifacts explicitly related to the high social status of the deceased: banqueting sets and metal vases, high-value goods such as ornaments made from precious materials, symbolic objects, signs of prestige, and imported goods; and

an increase in weapons in the case of male tombs and in jewelry and instruments for spinning and textiles in female tombs.

Within some of the necropoleis, however, it is possible to distinguish separate funerary groups by their own particular structures and rites, as well as by the arrangement of the funerary goods. These variations probably reflect the constitution and differentiation of various bloodlines within the community, whose traditions and privileges were inherited.

The main burial grounds of the Villanovan age continued to be in use from the ninth through the eighth centuries BCE.[19] At Quattro Fontanili (*map 3*)[20] the most elevated part of the cemetery has been destroyed by deep plowing. The earliest burials of this cemetery were probably located in this area and therefore have been lost. Most of the tombs (approximately six hundred) belong to the later phase of the Early Iron Age, as do the three hundred tombs at Casale del Fosso (*map 3*),[21] located respectively in the northeast and northwest areas just outside the city. The best example of the EIA community of Veii, dating to the ninth and eighth centuries BCE, comes from the necropolis of Grotta Gramiccia (eight hundred tombs, of which only half were undisturbed),[22] located close to the plateau and especially the northern side of Campetti (*map 3*).

Other isolated tombs of the eighth century BCE have been identified at Valle La Fata–Monte Campanile,[23] at Vaccareccia near the slopes of Piazza d'Armi, and at Isola Farnese (*see map 3*).[24] Among the four Late Villanovan burials at Valle La Fata, tomb 23 stands out. Following a custom that was typical of the mid-eighth century BCE and onward, this cremation in a well-tomb inside a tufa container (*custodia*) uses as the ossuary a jar covered by a laminated bronze bowl with cross-shaped attachments (fig. 6.1). This bowl has an unusual decoration, showing a series of human figures in relief alternating with bird-shaped protomes. It is similar to products from central Europe and especially from Hallstatt and was possibly imported from the Danube area. However, it is more likely that the vase was produced locally by traveling artisans or by local artisans who learned new skills from traveling artisans.[25]

Taken as a whole, the data provided by the northern necropoleis of Grotta Gramiccia, Casale del Fosso, and Quattro Fontanili (approximately two thousand tombs) constitute one of the largest bodies of knowl-

FIGURE 6.1. Ossuary from Valle La Fata tomb 23.
(Copyright: A. Berardinetti)

edge for EIA Italy. Approximately half of the tombs belong to the eighth century BCE. Given our current state of knowledge, different scholars have suggested there was significant demographic stability between the first and second phases.[26] During the first half of the eighth century BCE—and in line with the last twenty years of the ninth century BCE—besides the simple cremations in well-tombs, more complex structures such as tufa containers or *dolios* (large vases) are used. According to a practice attested in a privileged group of men and women, the ashes were placed in the usual biconical vase (generally without decoration) or in a jar (*olla*), inside a niche.

At the same time, inhumation became increasingly widespread: the body, fully dressed and accompanied by a large suite of grave goods in bronze and ceramic, was laid supine in a rectangular trench (*fossa*). The architecture of these trenches varies from simple to more complex, with some characterized by a deeper area on the bottom for the body. After the second half of the eighth century, the lateral burial recess or a wooden coffin appears in the trenches.

Children are often placed inside a tufa sarcophagus with a semi-cylindrical lid, and they are provided with a limited number of grave goods or miniaturistic vases. The cremated men—who probably were of a high rank—were accompanied by a crest helmet (fig. 6.2:A) and occasionally by a miniature spear and sword, which is a rather rare phenomenon in Veii (fig. 6.2:B). The inhumated men had full-size weapons, generally spears and, more rarely, swords and/or axes.

The female tomb-groups were enriched by a con-

A

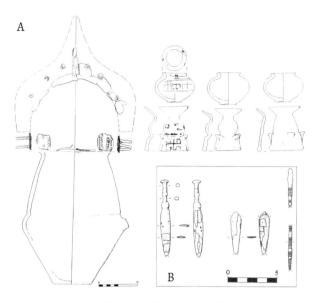

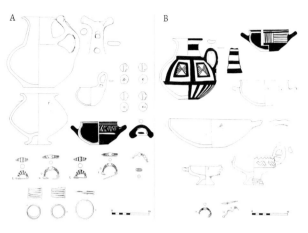

FIGURE 6.4. Grave goods from Grotta Gramiccia female tombs with Greek imports: A. Tomb 779; B. Tomb 581. (Copyright: L. Drago)

FIGURE 6.2. Grave goods accompanying males at Grotta Grammicia: A. Tomb 272; B. Tomb 312. (Copyright: L. Drago)

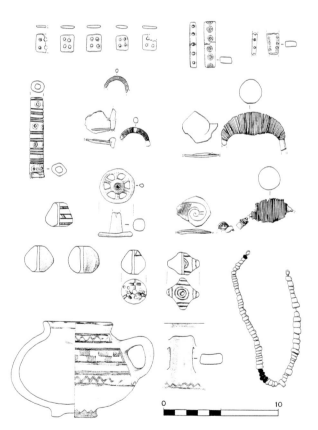

FIGURE 6.3. Grave goods from Grotta Gramiccia female tomb 377. (Copyright: L. Drago)

siderable amount of clothing and personal ornaments, as well as earthenware crockery and *instrumentum* linked to spinning and weaving, among which a set of burials with bronze utensils particularly stands out (fig. 6.3). Throughout antiquity, no matter what their social position was, women appear to have been primarily assigned to spinning and weaving, even if they were the wives or daughters of kings.[27]

The necropolis of Grotta Gramiccia is where most of the *skyphoi* (two-handled deep wine cups) in refined painted clay, of Greek import or inspiration, have been found, in a limited number of female tombs[28] (fig. 6.4), especially those of the first half of the eighth century BCE. This discovery may indicate that these women came from outside the community, in accordance with the role of women in ancient times: often in antiquity marriages were arranged to establish trade relations and strengthen alliances.[29]

Regarding the topographical distribution of tombs at Grotta Gramiccia, we observe a progressive enlargement radiating from the two original nuclei of the eighth century BCE (fig. 6.5:A, B). Some groups of tombs were organized around one or more cremations of high status. At Casale del Fosso and Quattro Fontanili, some tombs were located at the edges of the cemetery, while others occupied areas used previously. From the third quarter of the eighth century BCE onward at Grotta Gramiccia, the number of finds diminishes in comparison with the other necropoleis, and although

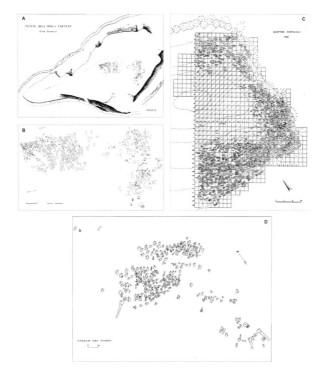

FIGURE 6.5. Plans of necropoleis at Veii: A–B. Grotta Gramiccia; C. Quattro Fontanili; D. Casale del Fosso. (Maps A, B, D, copyright: L. Drago; map C, copyright: A. Guidi)

the home, the married couple should be in close proximity, and the members of the *gens* (descendants of a common ancestor) who inherited the family land and homes also acquired property rights over their burial plots.

The composition of the funerary goods assembled, ranging from complex to simple, displayed a horizontal subdivision according to the role and gender of the deceased, and at the same time a deep vertical subdivision according to wealth and social rank, without any reference to age and gender.[32] The society was arranged around warrior values, and people who were equipped with a rich and full array of arms probably constituted its center. Apart from these important warriors, other dead were accompanied by a limited number of goods. Finally, a third rank was represented by poorer funerary goods.

High-ranking men and women lived a lifestyle characterized by participation in banquets and ownership of horses and chariots. At Casale del Fosso,[33] in some of the tombs, skewers and andirons were found alongside chisels and other metal instruments, suggesting that the interred had been skilled in artisanal activities—duties worthy of aristocratic people—which recalls the example of Odysseus.[34] These were warriors who were leaders in both the military and the sociopolitical spheres. They led sacrifice and banquet rituals, including the consumption of meat and wine.

The economic basis on which the aristocratic conditions of the dead would have been created can be outlined as follows: the production of wine, a valuable and sought-after agricultural product in this age, evidently made possible by the permanent possession of extensive and privileged portions of rural territory; and the raising of horses, an aristocratic activity par excellence and the most characteristic indicator of rank in funerary self-representation. To these we should add (as testified by the arrival of Near Eastern and Hellenic handmade goods) sea travel and commerce, which were a source of social prestige focused on interweaving relations with other nobles on an international level.

The necropolis at Casale del Fosso is the only one in which nearly all the tombs date from within the Late Villanovan and the Orientalizing periods. The complex topographical distribution of the graves has

it is possible to identify high-rank tombs, these never reached the level of wealth of the warriors' tombs that we know of from other necropoleis.

The burial evidence from the Quattro Fontanili necropolis begins in the advanced phase of the Early Villanovan period, and becomes more and more consistent in the later phase. The extensive nature of the excavation, the complete publication of the tomb-groups, and the numerous analyses undertaken on this body of material permit a more in-depth analysis of funerary custom and the social structure at Veii in the later phase of the Early Iron Age.[30] Here too, even though the topographical organization of the burials developed radially, more recent tombs overlap or lie next to the older ones (fig. 6.5:C).

A group of burials from the first half of the eighth century BCE was placed around more ancient tombs and is organized into family groupings that aim to emphasize their relationship and identity.[31] Often, a deceased pair—probably a married couple—are buried together or closely connected: in the cemetery, as in groupings of tombs, sometimes positioned chaotically on top of each other, separated by strips of land without graves. From the last thirty years of the eighth century BCE, it is possible to distinguish a pair of tombs—one male and one female—separated from the others (fig. 6.5:D),[35] including the princely tomb 871. This particular practice of isolating a married couple not only confirms the significance given to noble birth but also shows that the woman shared the same wealth and distinctive emblems as her partner, and thus had equal status.

In the central sector is located the earliest nucleus of the necropolis, with cremations in well-tombs inside a tufa container holding the biconical ossuary or the jar-ossuary, covered by a crested earthenware helmet. From the middle of the century, in addition to a few cremations, numerous trench tombs with the characteristic funerary goods already described are attested. The conclusion and culmination of the hierarchical processes and of the construction of the noble-aristocratic identity is visible in some princely tombs of the highest rank, dating from 750 to 720 BCE, uncovered in the excavations at Quattro Fontanili and at Casale del Fosso.[36]

These people of the highest class (genuine *principes*) were probably endowed with actual royal power, and were buried following a "heroic" style of funeral. Clearly, the mechanisms of inheritance among these elites are still invisible, making it difficult to understand the coexistence of such prominent figures within such a limited time frame. Still, we find ourselves undeniably confronted by historical figures whose own graves were above the standard of other contemporary tombs, and who represented the central authority of their society. We should mention for instance tombs AA1 (fig. 6.6:A) and Z15A (fig. 6.6:B) in the necropolis at Quattro Fontanili, and later tomb 1036 (fig. 6.6:C) and tomb 871 at Casale del Fosso (fig. 6.7). The first two followed the more traditional ritual of cremation, while tombs 1036 and 871, dating to the Orientalizing period, were inhumations.

The choice of the ritual of cremation, which harks back to the tradition of the ancestors, lent a heroic character to these burials. The cremation ritual required a greater expenditure of energy and time, and took on

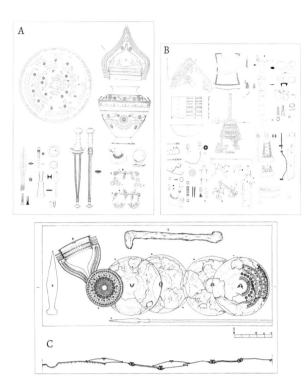

FIGURE 6.6. Grave goods from princely tombs in Veii's necropoleis: A. Quattro Fontanili tomb AA1 (copyright: M. Pacciarelli); B. Quattro Fontanili tomb Z15A (copyright: M. Pacciarelli); C. Casale del Fosso tomb 1036 (copyright: G. Colonna)

a strongly symbolic character when we consider that death was seen as part of a rite of passage. Total dissolution by fire is the fastest way for the body to reach its new state, assuring separation from the soul. This separation guarantees the reestablishment of the social order, and the brevity of the passage allows a quicker cancellation of the *miasma* (pollution) evoked by the death itself, which would have upset the entire community, especially when a prominent person was concerned. It also would spare the soul its period of transition before being received into the afterlife.[37]

In tombs AA1 and Z15A (fig. 6.6:A, B), which represent two consecutive generations, the ashes of the dead were laid in a precious bronze receptacle covered by parade helmets; every type of weapon is attested, along with a lavish collection of ceramic vases, a scepter, horses' bits, and parts of a horse cart. In tomb Z15A, there were also a *flabellum* (fan), bronze vases, and fireplace tools.

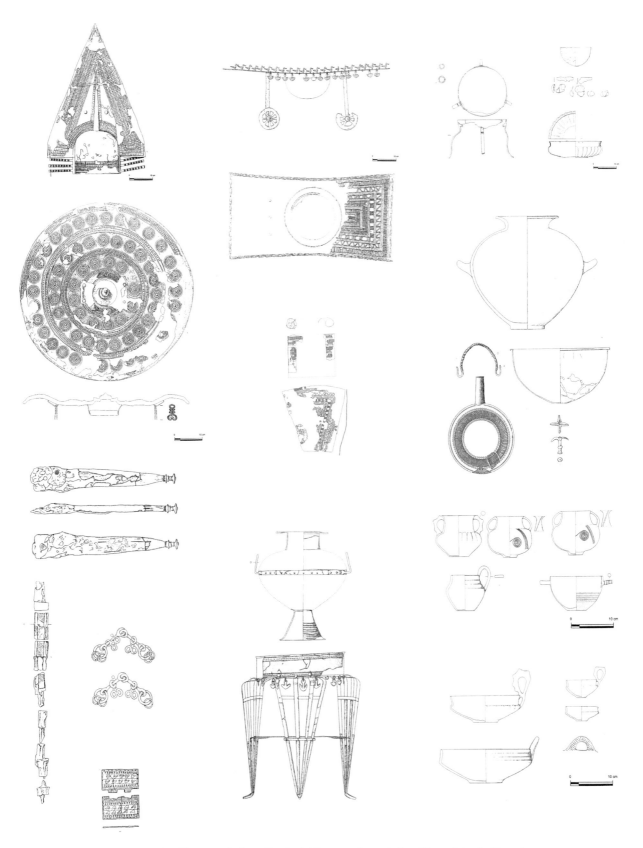

FIGURE 6.7. Grave goods from Casale del Fosso male tomb 871. (Copyright: L. Drago)

Tomb 1036 at Casale del Fosso (fig. 6.6:C) constitutes an *unicum* at Veii due to the presence of some highly significant objects and has been suggestively attributed to King Morrius,[38] mentioned above together with Numa in reference to the introduction of the cult of the Salii. Indeed, among the burial goods was preserved a club, which can be imagined to have been used to beat the *ancilia*, sacred lobed shields—also present in the tomb—laid over the body during the sacred ceremony of this priestly group.[39]

Approximately twenty years later, tomb 871 (fig. 6.7)[40] (alongside the princely tomb of a woman, tomb 872) represents a sovereign fully entitled to be included within the circles of the wealthiest aristocrats of the Mediterranean in the ancient Orientalizing period.[41] The burial is distinguished by the monumental configuration of the *fossa*, which had a burial recess for the deposition of the body, anticipating the idea of an individual chamber tomb. The tomb stands out also for its funerary goods and emblems of power, modeled on those of the Eastern dynasties.[42] The male buried was young, between fifteen and eighteen years of age, and may not have actually held a royal position; nonetheless, he surely belonged to a family with such a status.

Dionysios described Veii at this time, in the account of the last war of Romulus against the Etruscan town of Veii at the end of his reign, as "the most powerful city of the Tyrrhenians . . . as big as Athens."[43] According to Dionysios, one hundred years of peace followed that war, and it was precisely at this time—and particularly from the middle of the following century—that reoccupation of the Veientine territory occurred.[44] The terrain of the necropoleis increased, and in the final decades of the eighth century BCE they expanded over the hills and along the streets throughout the territory, ensuring widespread control and allowing easier and more direct communications with the major surrounding towns. When the conflict with Rome reignited in the second half of the seventh century BCE, Veii lost the primacy it had built and maintained over its closed region and far beyond in the Tyrrhenian Sea for the entire eighth century BCE.

NOTES

1. See chapter 5.

2. Colonna 1991.

3. On the problematic name "Propetrius" or "Propertius," see chapter 7.

4. See chapters 7 and 8.

5. Schiappelli 2014:334.

6. See chapter 7.

7. Cifani 2013.

8. *Contra* the theories convincingly proposed by Tabolli (2012 and 2013:485–508). See also chapter 7.

9. On these aspects, see Bartoloni 1986, 1991; Colonna 1986; Torelli 1990:52; Bartoloni 2001.

10. Livy 1.33.2 and 9; Dionysios of Halikarnassos 3.41.3.

11. Bartoloni 2007–2008.

12. See also chapter 1.

13. For excavations before the Veii Project, see Stefani 1922: 390–404, 1944.

14. Colonna 2004.

15. D'Alessio 2001.

16. Fusco and Cerasuolo 2001.

17. Stefani 1953:41–42, 102–103; Colonna 2001:38; *Portonaccio* I, 146–147.

18. Ward-Perkins 1959; Murray Threipland 1963:23–44; *Formello*, 24–26; Cascino 2012.

19. Bartoloni and Delpino 1979:17–33; Bartoloni et al. 1994.

20. *QF* 1963, 1965, 1967, 1970, 1972, 1975:197; Toms 1986; Guidi 1992; Pacciarelli 2001.

21. Buranelli 1981; Buranelli, Drago, and Paolini 1997.

22. Berardinetti and Drago 1997. It is possible that the necropolis in the Casale del Fosso formed part of a single large cemetery with Grotta Gramiccia, since the separation between the two consists only of a creek (Fosso di Grotta Gramiccia).

23. For Valle La Fata, see Bartoloni and Delpino 1979; for Monte Campanile, see Raddatz 1985. The two groups of tombs can be considered a single cemetery on the top and slopes of the same elevated area.

24. L. Drago in Bartoloni et al. 1994:15–16.

25. Bartoloni and Delpino 1979:61, 81–83, table 19.2, plate 23, ill. 3; recently A. Berardinetti Insam in *Veio, Cerveteri, Vulci*, 93–94. On the relationship with Central European artisans, see Camporeale 1998:39–40; on the role of Veii in Villanovan metal technology see Strøm 2000.

26. L. Drago in Bartoloni et al. 1994:17.

27. The so-called New Archaeology paid particular attention to the social dimension of funerary ritual (see Binford 1971; Brown 1971; Chapman, Kinnes, and Randsborg 1981; O'Shea 1970, 1984; Bietti Sestieri 1986), partly criticized by the postprocessual approach (Hodder 1982a, 1982b, 1987; d'Agostino 1985; Morris 1987; Cuozzo 1996, 2000).

28. The only exception being the cup from the male tomb 491.

29. Finley 1955; Pitzalis 2011:260–261; Bartoloni and Pitzalis 2011: 138; 2016.

30. See note 20.

31. Bartoloni 2003a:87–93.

32. Pacciarelli 2001, 2010:31–32.

33. See notes 21 and 22.

34. A reference to the epic of Homer and Hesiod is given in Buranelli 1979:8 and Iaia 2006:194–197. As Odysseus narrates: "[195] Thereafter I cut away the leafy branches of the long-leafed olive, and, trimming the trunk from the root, I smoothed it around with the adze well and cunningly, and made it straight to the line, thus fashioning the bed-post; and I bored it all with the augur. Beginning with this I hewed out my bed, till I had finished it, [200] inlaying it with gold and silver and ivory, and I stretched on it a thong of ox-hide, bright with purple" (*Odyssey* 23.195–200, English translation by A. T. Murray, 1919).

35. Buranelli 1981:39–43.

36. De Santis 2005, 2012.

37. Hertz 1960:42–43.

38. Bartoloni 2003b:15–16.

39. This extremely wealthy funerary set also included two armor plates, a crested helmet, a scepter, two horses' bits, two hunting spears, a fire tong, fibulas, and bronze vases (some of Danubian origin).

40. A complete and thorough publication of the context can be found in Drago Troccoli 2005.

41. See chapter 8.

42. Besides the ceramic vases and the panoply (complete with a very high crested helmet, circular shield, sword, and spear), there is a *phiale* and a hemispherical silver cup (the oldest in Italy), both of Eastern import; a tripod basin; a Kurd *situla* (a kind of bucket); a ceremonial cart; a *flabellum* (fan); a footstool alluding to a throne; a scepter and fire tools; a flask; and a second cart.

43. Dionysios of Halikarnassos 2.54.3.

44. For a description of events during the reoccupation from the evidence dating back to the seventh century BCE, see the recent contribution by Arizza et al. (2013); for a new overview of the history of the Veientine territory, see De Cristofaro and Piergrosso 2016.

BIBLIOGRAPHY

Arizza, M., A. De Cristofaro, A. Piergrossi, and A. Rossi. 2013. "La tomba di un aristocratico *naukleros* dall'agro veientano: Il *kantharos* con scena di navigazione di via d'Avack." *ArchCl* 65:51–131.

Bartoloni, G. 1986. "I Latini e il Tevere." In *Il Tevere e le altre vie d'acqua del Lazio antico* (ArchLaz 7.2). *QuadAEI* 12:98–110.

———. 1991. "Veio e il Tevere: Considerazioni sul ruolo della comunità tiberina negli scambi tra Nord e Sud Italia durante la prima età del Ferro." *DialArch* 1–2:35–48.

———. 2001. "Le necropoli." In *Veio, Cerveteri, Vulci*, 89.

———. 2003a. *Le società dell'Italia primitiva: Lo studio delle necropoli e la nascita delle aristocrazie*. Rome.

———. 2003b. "Veio e Roma: Considerazioni alla luce dei recenti indagini." In *Formello*, 13–21.

———. 2007–2008. "La sepoltura al centro del pianoro di Piazza d'Armi–Veio." In *Sepolti tra i vivi*, 821–830.

Bartoloni, G., A. Berardinetti, A. De Santis, and L. Drago. 1994. "Veio tra IX e VI secolo a.C.: Primi risultati sull'analisi comparata delle necropoli veienti." *ArchCl* 46:1–46.

Bartoloni, G., and F. Delpino. 1979. *Veio* I: *Introduzione allo studio delle necropoli arcaiche di Veio: Il sepolcreto di Valle La Fata. MonAnt* 1. Rome.

Bartoloni, G., and F. Pitzalis. 2011. "Mogli e madri nella nascente aristocraziam tirrenica." In *Dalla nascita alla morte: Antropologia e archeologia a confronto. Atti del I Congresso Internazionale di Studi (Rome, 2010)*, ed. V. Nizzo, 137–160. Rome.

———. 2016. "Etruscan Marriage." In *Women in Antiquity: Real Women across the Ancient World*, ed. S. Budin and J. MacIntosh Turfa, 810–819. London.

Berardinetti, A., and L. Drago. 1997. "La necropoli di Grotta Gramiccia." In *Necropoli arcaiche*, 39–61.

Bietti Sestieri, A. M. 1986. "I dati archeologici di fronte alla teoria." *DialArch* 2:249–264.

Binford, L. R. 1971. "Mortuary Practices: Their Study and Their Potential." In Brown 1971:6–29.

Brown, J. A. 1971. *Approaches to the Social Dimension of Mortuary Practices*. Memoirs of the Society for American Archaeology 25. Washington, DC.

Buranelli, F. 1979. "Utensili per la lavorazione del legno in due tombe villanoviane." *ArchCl* 31:1–9.

———. 1981. "Proposta di interpretazione dello sviluppo topografico della necropoli di Casal del Fosso a Veio." In *Necropoli e usi funerari nell'età del Ferro*, ed. R. Peroni, 19–45. Bari.

Buranelli, F., L. Drago, and L. Paolini. 1997. "La necropoli di Casale del Fosso." In *Necropoli arcaiche*, 63–83.

Camporeale, G. 1998. "Dall'Europa transalpina all'Etruria: Facies villanoviana." In *Archäologische Untersuchungen zu den Beziehungen zwischen Altitalien und der Zone nordwärts der Alpen während der frühen Eisenzeit Alteuropas. Ergebnisse eines Kolloquiums in Regensburg (November 1994)*, 37–47. Regensburg.

Cascino, R. 2012. "La North-West Gate di Veio negli scavi della British School at Rome." In *MAV*, 51–56.

Chapman, R., I. Kinnes, and K. Randsborg. 1981. *The Archaeology of Death*. Cambridge.

Cifani, G. 2013. "Per una definizione storica dei Falisci, tra identità, cultura e territorio." In *Tra Roma e l'Etruria: Cultura, identità e territorio dei Falisci*, ed. G. Cifani, 1–53. Rome.

Colonna, G. 1986. "Il Tevere e gli Etruschi." In *Il Tevere e le altre vie d'acqua del Lazio antico* (ArchLaz 7.2). *QuadAEI* 12: 90–97.

———. 1991. "Gli scudi bilobati dell'Italia centrale e l'ancile dei Salii." *ArchCl* 43:55–122.

———. 2001. "Portonaccio." In *Veio, Cerveteri, Vulci*, 37–44.

———. 2004. "I santuari di Veio: Ricerche e scavi su Piano di Comunità." In *Bridging the Tiber*, 205–221.

Cuozzo, M. 1996. "Prospettive teoriche e metodologiche nell'interpretazione delle necropoli: La Post-Processual Archaeology." *AnnAStorAnt*, n.s. 3:1–38.

———. 2000. "Orizzonti teorici e interpretativi tra post-processual archaeology e tendenze italiane." In *Archeologia teorica. X ciclo di lezioni sulla ricerca applicata in Archeologia, Certosa di Pontignano (Siena), 1999*, 323–360. Florence.

d'Agostino, B. 1985. "Società dei vivi, comunità dei morti: Un rapporto difficile." *DialArch* 1:47–58.

D'Alessio, M. T. 2001. "Macchiagrande–Vignacce." In *Veio, Cerveteri, Vulci*, 17–18.

De Cristofaro, A., and A. Piergrossi. 2016. "*Ripa Veientana*: Per una storia del territorio tra Veio e Roma dal'VIII al IV seculo a.C." *Mediterranea* 12–13:31–76.

De Santis, A. 2005. "Da capi guerrieri a principi: La strutturazione del potere politico nell'Etruria protourbana." In *Dinamiche*, 615–631.

———. 2012. "I 're' di Veio." In *MAV*, 77–80.

Drago Troccoli, L. 2005. "Una coppia di principi nella necropoli di Casale del Fosso a Veio." In *Dinamiche*, 87–124.

Finley, M. I. 1955. "Marriage, Sale, and Gift in the Homeric World." *Revue Internationale des Droits de l'Antiquité* 2:167–194.

Fusco, U., and O. Cerasuolo. 2001. "Campetti." In *Veio, Cerveteri, Vulci*, 9–11.

Guidi, A. 1992. *La necropoli veiente dei Quattro Fontanili*. Florence.

Hertz, R. 1960. *Death and the Right Hand*. Aberdeen.

Hodder, I. 1982a. *Symbols in Action*. Cambridge.

———. 1982b. *Symbolic and Structural Archaeology*. Cambridge.

———. 1987. *The Archaeology of Contextual Meanings*. Cambridge.

Iaia, C. 2006. "Strumenti da lavoro nelle sepolture dell'età del Ferro italiana." In *Studi di protostoria in onore di Renato Peroni*, 190–201. Florence.

Morris, I. 1987. *Burial and Ancient Society*. Cambridge.

Murray Threipland, L. 1963. "Excavations beside the North-West Gate at Veii, 1957–1958." *PSBR* 31:23–73.

O'Shea, J. 1970. "Social Dimensions of Mortuary Practices." PhD diss., University of Michigan.

———. 1984. *Mortuary Variability: An Archaeological Investigation*. Orlando, FL.

Pacciarelli, M. 2001. "La necropoli di Quattro Fontanili a Veio e la trasformazione verso la società stratificata e l'assetto urbano nel corso del PF2." In M. Pacciarelli, *Dal villaggio alla città: La svolta protourbana del 1000 a.C. nell'Italia tirrenica*, 261–276. Florence.

———. 2010. "Forme di complessità sociale nelle comunità protourbane dell'Etruria meridionale." In *L'Etrurie et l'Ombrie avant Rome: Cité et territoire. Actes du colloque international, Louvain-la-Neuve (13–14 février 2004)*, ed. P. Fontaine, 17–33. Brussels.

Pitzalis, F. 2011. *La volontà meno apparente: Donne e società nell'Italia centrale tirrenica tra VIII e VII secolo a.C.* Rome.

Raddatz, K. 1985. "Grabfunde der Villanovakultur vom Monte Campanile in Veji Prov. Rom." In *Studi di Paletnologia in onore di Salvatore M. Puglisi*, ed. M. Liverani, A. Palmieri, and R. Peroni, 851–861. Rome.

Schiappelli, A. 2014. "Veii in the Protohistoric Period: A Topographical and Territorial Analysis." In *Novità*, 327–341.

Stefani, E. 1922. "Esplorazioni dentro l'area dell'antica città di Veio." *NSc* 1922:379–404.

———. 1944. "Scavi archeologici a Veio in contrada Piazza d'Armi." *MonAnt* 11:177–290.

———. 1953. "Veio—Tempio detto dell'Apollo: Esplorazione e sistemazione del santuario." *NSc* 1953:29–112.

Strøm, I. 2000. "A Fragment of an Early Etruscan Bronze Throne in Olympia." *ProcDanInstAth* 3:67–95.

Tabolli, J. 2012. "Memoria nell'identità a Narce durante la prima età del Ferro." *ArchCl* 52:485–508.

———. 2013. *Narce tra la prima età del Ferro e l'Orientalizzante antico: L'abitato, I Tufi e La Petrina*. Mediterranea 9; Civiltà arcaica dei Sabini nella Valle del Tevere 5. Pisa-Rome.

Toms, J. 1986. "The Relative Chronology of the Villanovan Cemetery of Quattro Fontanili at Veii." *AION* 8:41–97.

Torelli, M. 1990. *Storia degli Etruschi*. Rome.

Ward-Perkins, J. B. 1959. "Excavations beside the North-West Gate at Veii, 1957–58." *PSBR* 27:38–79.

CHAPTER 7

VEII AND THE OTHERS

Closest Neighbors

JACOPO TABOLLI

The long process of transformation of the political landscape northwest of the Lower Tiber Valley, which began in the Middle Bronze Age (MBA) and continued through a rapid succession of events until the end of the Final Bronze Age (FBA), resulted in the birth of Veii. This process can be considered to have been fully completed only at the beginning of the Early Iron Age (EIA).[1] Data from the settlement and the necropoleis demonstrate that Veii functioned as the hub of a new system. The dialogue between this center and its territory, its peripheries, and the closest neighbors outside its borders, especially between the eleventh and the early seventh century BCE, corresponded to a continuous and vibrant transformation. From small villages to the proto-urban settlement, from a widespread occupation of the land (MBA) to its almost complete abandonment (FBA–EIA 1) and later to its reoccupation/new occupation (EIA 2), the usage of the territory around Veii changed several times.

These revolutions did not occur only in the area around Veii and cannot be considered an internal phenomenon, since the entire region of central Tyrrhenian Italy was at that time in flux as a consequence of the creation of the proto-urban settlements in southern Etruria and of the continuous movements of social groups, mainly of Italic origin, along the Tiber and especially from the Apennines to the Tyrrhenian Sea.

PROBLEMATIC BORDERS

Even if the borders between Veii and its closest neighbors can be generally defined (*map 1*) — Rome and Latium to the east, the Tyrrhenian Sea to the south, Caere to the west, and, from the eighth century BCE, the Ager Faliscus and Ager Capenas to the north (*map 5*) — at the beginning of the first millennium BCE, we should not imagine fixed borders and well-defined political interactions. Fluid frontiers and rapid exchanges of land seem to have characterized these early phases, when different areas were probably disputed. At the same time, the control wielded by Veii over the different parts of its territory was not the same in every region, as demonstrated by the differences in the locations of the few surviving sites on its borders since the Early Iron Age.[2]

DIFFERENT METHODOLOGIES, DIFFERENT TERRITORIES, AND DIFFERENT NEIGHBORS?

Evidence for this vibrant early network of transformations and developing cultural definitions of autonomous entities has generated a lively dialogue among contemporary scholars. In fact, the dimensions of the territory of Veii and its earliest interactions with nearby communities are some of the most disputed topics of pre-Roman archaeology among different traditions of studies. On the one hand, the border of the Arrone River and Lake Bracciano is generally accepted as dividing the areas under the control of Veii and Caere, as well as the control of part of the Tyrrhenian coasts to the south, and especially the region of the Salinae (*map 1: no. 24*)[3] (despite the absence in both cases of significant published data). On the other hand, the northern and the eastern frontiers have been widely disputed.

In fact, the question of the border with Rome resulted in a quarrel mainly among Etruscologists, classical archaeologists, and Roman historians concerning the existence and especially the character of the small Iron Age settlements between Veii and Rome, given the tradition of the Septem Pagi (the Seven Villages, as in *map 1*) and the concepts of the Ager Romanus Antiquus and the so-called Ager Veientanus.[4] At the same time, the identification of the northern border, complicated by the problem of the Faliscans and the Capenates, resulted in a conflict mainly between protohistorians and Etruscologists.[5]

IS THE AGER FALISCUS PART OF THE TERRITORY OF VEII?

Based on the evidence of the earliest Thiessen polygons applied to southern Etruria, the balance in proportion between the territories of Vulci, Tarquinia, and Caere (which appear to have been similar in their extension) and the apparently smaller territory of Veii led R. Peroni and F. di Gennaro to suggest that the areas of the Ager Faliscus and the Ager Capenas (*map 5*), as well as most of the territory on the western bank of the Tiber, were part of the territory of Veii.[6]

Most scholars accept that Veii controlled all the territories—almost empty—north of the city to the Tiber,[7] but in regard to the beginning of the Early Iron Age, a major disagreement concerns the eighth century BCE. Protohistorians have suggested that in the eighth century BCE Veii promoted a reoccupation of the sites—mainly Falerii, Narce, and Nepi—that were abandoned at the end of the Final Bronze Age by those communities that had joined the synoecist process at Veii.[8] Classical archaeologists have also accepted this hypothesis. For example, G. Cifani has theorized a later development of the Ager Faliscus and of the Ager Capenas as independent and autonomous political entities, which might have been mainly under the political control of Veii until the siege of that city.[9] On the contrary, the tradition of a non-Etruscan origin of the Iron Age Faliscan and Capenate communities has been supported mainly by Etruscologists.[10]

This debate on the extension of the earliest territory of Veii results from the completely different approaches scholars use to read the existence of the different ethnic groups in the transition from protohistory to history. On the one hand, G. Colonna, among others, has stressed that the Final Bronze Age (the so-called Proto-Villanovan phase) should be considered the moment in which the principal *ethne*, such as the Etruscans and the Latins, completed their formation.[11] On the other hand, the tradition of the school of protohistory of Rome, and mainly the students of R. Peroni, denies any possible ethnic-based analysis of the transformations between the Final Bronze Age and the Early Iron Age, describing the Villanovan phenomenon as a matter of style and not of *ethnos*.[12]

Following on these premises, it is interesting to focus on the dynamics of interaction between Veii and its closest neighbors, working along the borders of Veii from west to east. This journey reveals that the fluid borders of the EIA I phase tended to become firmer during the second half of the eighth century BCE. Despite the power of Veii during the Early Iron Age and the Early Orientalizing period, the town seems to lose control over its peripheral areas together with the consolidation of its center.

THE WESTERN NEIGHBORS

The significant absence of modern publications on the EIA necropoleis of Caere has been repeatedly emphasized in scholarship. Based on the available data, the EIA material culture and funerary ideology of Caere (especially in the necropolis of Il Sorbo)[13] appears significantly different from that of Veii, while similarities with the area of Latium and Rome have been stressed (e.g., the circulation of reticulated jars—*ollette a rete*).

In addition, the presence of settlements, such as Sasso di Furbara, that exhibit direct continuity between the Final Bronze Age and the Early Iron Age[14] has led to a different perception of the territory of Caere. Following a movement from the area of the coast to the hinterland, Caere seems to have conquered and strengthened its control over its territory during the Early Iron Age.[15] This movement toward the north culminates in the favored interaction with the Faliscans, which began at least in the early seventh century BCE.[16]

THE KEY ROLE OF MONTE SANT'ANGELO AND TREVIGNANO

At the frontier between Veii and Caere—where, as mentioned above, Lake Bracciano played a fundamental role in simultaneously connecting and separating the two territories—two sites reveal a strong mixture of elements in their material culture: Monte Sant'Angelo (*map 5: no. 9*) for the ninth century BCE and Trevignano Romano (*map 5: no. 13*) for the eighth and seventh centuries BCE.[17]

Concerning the continuity between the Final Bronze Age and the Early Iron Age at Monte Sant'Angelo—at the center of an ancient system of lakes (fig. 7.1)—scholars have debated a possible re-foundation of this site promoted by Veii after the conclusion of the proto-urban formation process.[18] Despite this possible identification, it is interesting to observe that, within a vibrant network of interactions that also connected this site with the area of Bologna, the tomb-groups at Monte Sant'Angelo contain elements characteristic of both Caere and Veii (fig. 7.2), revealing close connections between the two. Among other details, double cordons in relief, typical of Caere, occur on locally made biconical urns, with close comparisons to types well known at Veii.[19]

Trevignano Romano probably was a foundation of Veii in the second half of the eighth century BCE, following a decrease in importance of the site of Monte Sant'Angelo and possibly the need to strengthen the frontier of Veii toward the north (fortifying a liminal space that was previously identified through the finds at Vicarello [*map 5: no. 15*]).[20] Trevignano Romano revealed mixed characteristics in its material culture, demonstrating a strong influence from Caere (especially in the Orientalizing painted pottery and some types of bucchero, such as the caryatid chalices) and from Veii (in particular in funerary ideology). However, the location of Trevignano appears to be a natural answer to the new consolidation of power of the Faliscans in the area of the Treja Valley, similarly to other frontier sites, such as Poggio Montano, near Lake Vico,

FIGURE 7.1. The settlement of Monte Sant'Angelo (circled) amid the ancient system of lakes. (Copyright: J. Tabolli)

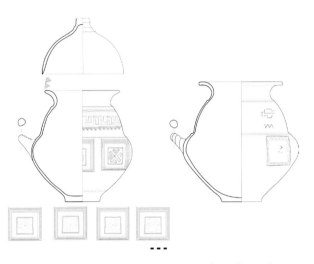

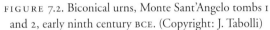

FIGURE 7.2. Biconical urns, Monte Sant'Angelo tombs 1 and 2, early ninth century BCE. (Copyright: J. Tabolli)

whose foundation by Tarquinia has been recently connected to the new presence of the Faliscans.[21]

BORDER WITH THE FALISCANS

As already mentioned, it is interesting to note that Caere surpassed Veii in influence on the material culture of the Faliscans at the end of the eighth century BCE, as has been recently demonstrated, especially, through the study of the Orientalizing pottery at Falerii.[22] Veii appears at that point to have been almost surrounded by a trade circuit directly linking Caere and Falerii. The presence of a border with the Faliscans, north of the volcanic caldera of Baccano near the

FIGURE 7.3. The Treja River and the waterfalls of
Monte Gelato. (Copyright: J. Tabolli)

springs of the Treja, is exemplified also by the necropolis of Piano del Pavone,[23] dating to the seventh century BCE, which, in analogy with Trevignano, demonstrates the mixed characteristics of this frontier, linking elements from Narce and Nepi, Caere and Veii.[24]

THE NORTHERN NEIGHBORS

Moving to the north, the Treja River (fig. 7.3) constitutes the "spine" of the ancient Ager Faliscus and a natural passage between the territory of Veii and the Tiber. It is important to stress that two main towns, Falerii and Narce, both sit on this river. In these two cities, which in the first millennium BCE would become the most important towns of the Faliscans, a system of "settlement with related necropolis" was already present during the Final Bronze Age.[25] In contrast, in the area of Capena, with a few exceptions, the abandonment of the sites seems to have occurred earlier, during the Recent Bronze Age, partially anticipating the complete abandonment of the territory preceding the proto-urban formation of Veii.

Following di Gennaro, B. Barbaro has suggested the existence of a territorial entity focused on Falerii during the Final Bronze Age, which would have also included the area around Veii (meaning that Isola Farnese and the necropolis of Pozzuolo [*map 4:V*] would have been part of it). If we postulate the existence of a Faliscan self-identity during the Final Bronze Age, we could argue that in the movement toward Veii the Faliscan

groups had maintained their original identity and then preserved it on the plateau for at least one century; after this period the groups would have returned to Faliscan territory. Nevertheless, despite the power and survival of memory, this overall picture of all these straightforward movements appears to be far too simplistic.

In fact, despite the similarity in the location of the settlements of Falerii and Narce during the Bronze Age and in the Iron Age, it is impossible to confirm that these Bronze Age communities were already Faliscan.

NARCE IN THE FINAL BRONZE AGE

Moving to Narce (*map 5*), to the south, recent surveys have demonstrated the presence of Middle to Final Bronze Age settlements on the different hills, and especially on the conical hill of Narce. In the late 1960s the British School at Rome excavated for five years in the foothills of Narce, discovering along the eastern bank of the Treja River traces of a village dating from the Middle Bronze Age to the Final Bronze Age.[26] R. Mengarelli collected similar data in 1933, in a small excavation on the top of the hill of Narce.[27] A general abandonment of the site occurred at the end of the Final Bronze Age, with a very limited number of pottery fragments that might be dated to the early Iron Age.[28]

Bronze Age evidence was also discovered at Narce, in the necropolis of I Tufi excavated in 1894.[29] Tomb 15 (XII) (fig. 7.4:a–b), a female burial in a simple stone sarcophagus, was part of the northern group of tombs in the necropolis. The chronology of the entire tomb-group dates to the second quarter of the eighth century BCE, but two special artifacts were discovered inside the trench: a jug and an *askos* (a type of jar with a handle that extends in an arc to join the back of the jar) dating to the Final Bronze Age. The presence of earlier material in tombs of the eighth century BCE, with at least two hundred years' separation in date, is not an isolated phenomenon in this necropolis. An FBA jug decorated with incisions (fig. 7.4:c) was also found in the southern sector of the necropolis, which consisted entirely of cremation burials. Tomb 3 dates to the beginning of the eighth century BCE. In the section of tomb 3 drawn by F. Benedetti, the jug is shown not inside the stone container, but outside, in the fill-

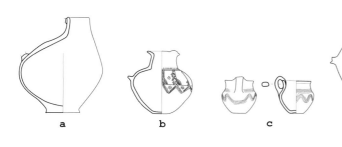

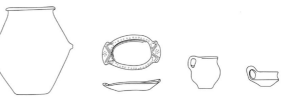

FIGURE 7.5. Objects from tomb 2, Falerii, necropolis of Montarano South, eleventh century BCE. (Copyright: J. Tabolli, based on Cozza and Pasqui 1981)

FIGURE 7.4. FBA objects from tombs 3 (c) and 15 (XII) (a, b), Narce, necropolis of I Tufi, eleventh century BCE. (Copyright: J. Tabolli)

ing of the well.[30] This peculiar evidence does not seem to reflect phenomena of preservation of earlier Bronze Age material in later Iron Age tombs. On the contrary, it has been possible to propose that when the "new" Iron Age community of Narce excavated the pits for its tombs during the eighth century BCE, they probably disturbed the previous Bronze Age burials (eleventh–tenth century BCE) and somehow respected them by preserving the artifacts in the filling of their tombs (but not inside the container for cremations or the sarcophagi, which strictly belonged to the individual sphere of the dead).[31]

FALERII IN THE FINAL BRONZE AGE

At Falerii (*map 5*), four tombs dating to the Final Bronze Age were discovered in the locality of Montarano, in the area of the later sanctuary of Juno Curitis, during the surveys for the Carta Archeologica d'Italia (archaeological map of Italy).[32] These tombs testify to the consistent use of cremation in the necropolis. Tomb 2 contained the most significant tomb-group (fig. 7.5). It is interesting to compare it with the only FBA tomb discovered at Veii in the later necropolis of Quattro Fontanili (tomb 838; *fig. 4.2:E*).[33] The assemblages of these two tomb-groups as well as the types of artifacts reveal a significant resemblance between the two sites during FBA 3B. Looking at funerary ideology and material culture, it is possible therefore to conclude that during the Final Bronze Age, no significant distinction existed between Falerii and Veii. To carry this assumption to the extreme, if we assume, following Colonna, that during the Final Bronze Age the

identities of the principal ethnic groups of the region were already formed, we may say that the communities that lived at Falerii and Narce during the Final Bronze Age could perceive themselves to be Etruscans. This perception could be confirmed by the fact that Falerii and Narce joined the new proto-urban settlement of Veii, led by the site of Isola Farnese, the closest to the main plateau.[34]

REREADING THE MYTH OF HALESOS

The myth of Halesos—descendant of Neptunus and the mythical Agamemnon,[35] founder of Falerii and at the same time ancestor of the Veientine king Morrius—seems to directly link Falerii and Veii.[36] From this perspective, the FBA evidence from Falerii and the abandonment of the site in favor of the establishment of Veii seems to be reflected in the myth, recalling a certain priority of Falerii.

THE ABANDONMENT OF THE AGER FALISCUS DURING EIA I

More than a century after the abandonment of the Final Bronze Age villages, within the first half of the eighth century BCE, new communities settled down in the Ager Faliscus and in the Ager Capenas. New Iron Age sites were found mainly in correspondence with most of the previous FBA sites, such as Falerii and Narce.[37] The type of settlement at Falerii, Narce, and Capena during the eighth century BCE appears to have been polycentric. The settlements spread onto different hills with different necropoleis. This model of occupation recalls the sites on the opposite bank of the Tiber (Latium Vetus and Sabina Tiberina). Of these three cities, only Falerii would develop into an urban center, but much later than the Early Iron Age, while the others would preserve a polycentric character at least until the fifth century BCE.[38]

These foundations during the eighth century BCE should be considered exceptional, given that, throughout the rest of its territory, Veii promoted a reoccupation of the previous FBA sites starting from the end of the eighth century BCE and especially in the early seventh century BCE, probably in relation to conflicts with Rome.[39] At the same time, the sites that Veii founded in the seventh century BCE were extremely small settlements, mainly formed on a single hill, and none reached the dimensions of Falerii, Narce, or Capena.[40] In the eighth century BCE the presence of new sites only in the historical region of the Faliscans, and immediately after of the Capenates, probably reflects the arrival of new populations.

MISUNDERSTANDING THE FOUNDATION OF CAPENA

Many scholars have wrongly viewed the foundation of Capena as being promoted by Veii, because of a misunderstanding in the reading of the historical sources. In fact, it is not the city of Capena but the interregional sanctuary of Lucus Feroniae (*map 5*) that was founded by Veii.[41] M. Di Fazio has stressed that the foundation of the sanctuary appears to have been the result of a combination of mixed origins, in a liminal space such as the *lucus*, that is, a sacred wood.[42] In the legend, the king of Veii, Propertius, sent its young men, *iuvenes*, to Capena to found the sanctuary.[43] Despite here being called "king of Veii," Propertius is not an Etruscan name, because the etymology relates to central Italy, implying Umbrian or Sabine origins.[44]

WITH OR WITHOUT VEII?

We cannot assume that the new occupation of the Faliscan and Capenate territories could have taken place without the control and/or the permission of Veii. In fact, at the end of the ninth century BCE (Veii IC) and at the beginning of the eighth century BCE (Veii IIA), Veii appears to have been at its apogee.[45] This

strong power hardly would have lost territories to the north. As early as 1986, Colonna pointed out that the depopulation of the territories at the end of the Bronze Age, despite the political control of Veii, could have attracted the interests of social groups from the central regions, such as Sabines and Latins.[46] However, the circumstance that the entire region of Veii was extremely receptive also toward the interregional links, especially with Latium and Rome, can be recognized in the progressive shift from cremation to inhumation attested by the necropoleis of Veii.[47]

MIXED CULTURAL IDENTITIES FOR AN "OTHERNESS IDENTITY"

The new foundations by the Faliscans and the Capenates had mixed cultural identities, with a combination of Italic elements (Latium Vetus, Sabina, and Abruzzo) and elements from Veii.[48] Strong cultural traits, for example, link Narce to the Tiber and especially Latium Vetus (such as Crustumerium, *map 1*) but also with the inland road, which headed toward Campania, as exemplified by the bowls with the decorative motif of the Master of Horses (fig. 7.6).[49] At the same time, the local debt the Ager Faliscus and the Ager Capenas owed Veii is exemplified by their inheritance of peculiar Veiian forms, such as the ceramic stand, and their local reinterpretation as *holmoi*, a distinctive characteristic of the Faliscans and Capenates, which does not appear in the necropoleis of Veii (fig. 7.7).[50] These examples illustrate the progressive formation of an "otherness identity" different from Veii, both in the Ager Faliscus and in the Ager Capenas, that would be strengthened during the seventh century BCE.[51]

Similar trends can be observed in funerary ideology, which from the earliest stages of the new foundations strongly differentiates Veii from the Faliscans and the Capenates. For the eighth century BCE, Falerii and Narce followed an almost identical yet peculiar system of burials that differed from the trends at Veii.[52] For example, the use of the sarcophagus at Veii only for infant burials could be contrasted with its exclusive use for adults at Narce and Falerii.[53] At Capena, the presence of a consistent number of trench tombs

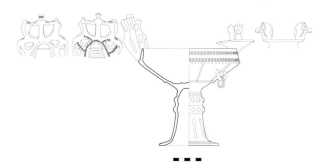

FIGURE 7.6. Footed bowl with the Master of Horses from Narce, necropolis of La Petrina. Ca. 730 BCE. (Copyright: J. Tabolli)

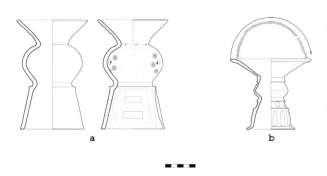

FIGURE 7.7. Finds from Narce, necropolis of La Petrina, 750–730 BCE. a. Tomb A15 (XXII), ceramic stand resembling a type from Veii; b. Tomb A11 (VII), earliest *holmos* of the Ager Faliscus. (Copyright: J. Tabolli)

for cremation reveals strong autonomous funerary customs differing from those of Veii.[54] Despite such differences, Veii did play an important role in spreading funerary customs, as illustrated by the origin of the niche (*loculus*) tombs at Veii and their widespread use in the northern territories.[55] Following this line of thought, S. Neri has stressed that from the end of the seventh century BCE, the composition of the tombgroups within the necropoleis of Capena reveals an Italic presence, based on the deposition of weapons in the burials.[56]

The strengthening of the autonomous territories of the Faliscans and the Capenates to the north in the second half of the eighth and especially in the first half of the seventh century BCE corresponds to a reduced extension of the territory of Veii, in a manner analogous to the trends that characterized the eastern border, within the framework of the conflicts between Veii and Rome.

THE EASTERN NEIGHBORS

The course of the Tiber within its lower valley constituted a true melting pot for all the cultural groups on both its banks. The inherent characteristics of being at once a barrier and an "osmosis area" are reflected in the interactions of Veii with nearby sites on the opposite bank.

SABINA TIBERINA AND LATIUM

Proceeding from the north, close interactions occurred between Veii and the lower sites of the Sabina Tiberina (Eretum and Cures, *map 5*) and the upper sites of the Latins, especially Crustumerium and Fidenae (*map 5*). Fidenae in particular was located at the junction between the Cremera and the Tiber Rivers, a strategic point recalling the location of Ficana (*map 1*) at the exit of the Fosso di Galeria and the Tiber to the south. The location of these two Latin sites at the access point to the major waterways of the territory of Veii demonstrates a sort of encirclement, similar to the position of Falerii near the junction between the Treja River and the Tiber, but on the opposite bank.[57] The close proximity of Fidenae to Veii corresponded to an impressive similarity of material culture, and it functioned as a litmus test for most of the events of the shared history with Veii.

ROME AND THE PROBLEM OF THE AGER ROMANUS ANTIQUUS

Finally, the theme of the close interaction between Veii and Rome appears in most of the chapters of this volume,[58] a consequence of the parallel lives of the two sister cities from the time of the Early Iron Age to the Archaic period, and until the Roman conquest of Veii in 396 BCE. In the ancient sources (mainly Greek ones) the conflicts between the two towns were inaugurated by the conquest by Romulus of the Septem Pagi, corresponding to seven villages of the territory of Veii on the western bank of the Tiber.[59]

Concerning the Early Iron Age and the Orientalizing period, a lengthy debate has addressed the political and cultural definition of the western bank of the Tiber. In particular, the complex definition of the Ager Romanus Antiquus has been strongly debated, in terms of historical existence, chronology, and real extension.[60] The critical approach by A. Ziołkowski, who denied its early existence, especially in relation to the frontier sanctuaries, has proved to be fundamental. Recently A. De Cristoforo and A. Piergrossi reconsidered the historical and archaeological sources and described the entire western bank of the Tiber not as part of the Ager Romanus Antiquus but as the Ripa Veiens, the "Veientine bank."[61] The reconstruction of the pattern of distribution of the small satellite sites moved from the earliest proposal by A. De Santis and resulted in the clear understanding of a system of sites occupying the closest hills in coincidence with the later consular road and the existence of a "buffer zone" between Veii and Rome.[62] In contrast with many earlier theories, all these satellite sites date after the beginning of the seventh century BCE, while no EIA evidence (or Early Orientalizing) was identified in the entire area. This evidence suggests a much later phenomenon of systematic reoccupation of the territory promoted by Veii in comparison with the other proto-urban centers (such as Caere, Tarquinia, and Vulci) and allows for a different origin of the early occupation of the new Faliscan and Capenate sites almost a century before.

CONCLUSIONS

Moving away from schematic models, we can see that between the Final Bronze Age and the Early Iron Age the close interactions between Veii and its closest neighbors resulted in a dynamic definition of physical, cultural, and political borders, with a progressive redefinition of the peripheral territories in a continuous evolution. Only after the seventh century BCE did the borders of the territory of Veii become relatively stable, holding until the Roman conquest of 396 BCE.

NOTES

1. See chapters 4 and 5.
2. See chapter 5.
3. See chapter 5.
4. See chapter 6. In addition, De Cristofaro and Piergrossi 2016, with bibliography.
5. Tabolli 2012, with bibliography.
6. di Gennaro 1982, 1986.
7. See chapter 5.
8. Iaia 1996, with bibliography. See also chapters 4 and 5.
9. Cifani 2003, 2005, and 2013.
10. After Baglione 1986. See in particular Baglione and De Lucia Brolli 1997; De Lucia Brolli and Baglione 1997.
11. Colonna 1986, 1988; most recently, Bartoloni forthcoming.
12. Peroni 1989. See chapter 4.
13. Personal communication, L. Arancio and O. Cerasuolo, 2012.
14. Barbaro 2010, with bibliography.
15. Cerasuolo 2012.
16. See below.
17. Tabolli 2015 and forthcoming.
18. See chapter 5.
19. Tabolli 2015.
20. Tabolli forthcoming and chapter 5.
21. Piergrossi 2002 and forthcoming.
22. Biella 2014.
23. Ceccarelli and Stoddart 2013:218.
24. Michetti 2009.
25. *Repertorio*; Barbaro 2010; Tabolli 2016.
26. Peroni and Fugazzola 1969; Potter 1976.
27. Tabolli 2013.
28. See also the different opinions by F. di Gennaro and F. Biagi in chapters 4 and 5.
29. di Gennaro 1986; Baglione and De Lucia Brolli 1990; Tabolli 2012, 2013, 2016.
30. Tabolli 2012.
31. Tabolli 2016.
32. After Cozza and Pasqui 1981; more recently, *Repertorio* and Barbaro 2010.
33. See chapters 4 and 5, with bibliography.
34. On Isola Farnese see especially chapter 4.
35. Ovid *Amores* 3.13.31; *Fasti* 4.74; Servius *ad Verg. Aen.* 7.695, 723; Silius Italicus 8.76.
36. On Halesos, Carandini 1997; Cifani 2005; Tabolli 2012. On the links between Haleus and Campania, Briquel 1994.
37. Iaia 1996, with bibliography; Cifani 2013; Tabolli 2012, 2016.
38. Tabolli 2016.
39. See below.
40. Most recently Biella 2014.
41. See chapter 6.
42. Di Fazio 2012:391–392.
43. Cato fr. 16, from Servius *ad Verg. Aen.* 7.697.
44. S. Neri in Tabolli and Neri 2017.

45. See chapter 6.

46. Colonna 1986, 1988.

47. After Bartoloni et al. 1994.

48. Tabolli 2013; Tabolli and Neri forthcoming.

49. Babbi 2008:291; Tabolli 2013.

50. After Benedettini 1999.

51. De Lucia Brolli and Tabolli 2013, 2016.

52. Tabolli 2016.

53. Pitzalis 2011; Tabolli 2012. See also chapter 6.

54. After Stefani 1958.

55. di Gennaro 2007.

56. S. Neri in Tabolli and Neri forthcoming.

57. On all these aspects see chapter 9.

58. This topic is especially addressed in chapter 6.

59. Livy 1.15.1–5; Dionysios of Halikarnassos 2.55.5; Plutarch *Romulus* 25.1–5.

60. For the theory of the Ager Romanus extended on the western bank of the Tiber see Capanna 2005, with bibliography. The history of the research is discussed in De Cristofaro and Piergrossi 2016, with bibliography.

61. De Cristofaro and Piergrossi 2016, with bibliography.

62. De Santis 1997; see also chapter 9.

BIBLIOGRAPHY

Acconcia, V. 2012. "La sistemazione della strada secondaria e la struttura B." In *Veio* II, 29–32.

Babbi, A. 2008. *La piccola plastica fittile antropomorfa dell'Italia antica dal Bronzo Finale all'Orientalizzante. Mediterranea*, suppl. 1. Pisa.

Baglione, M. P. 1986. "Il Tevere e i Falisci." In *Il Tevere e le altre vie d'acqua del Lazio antico. Atti del VII Incontro di Studio del Comitato per l'Archeologia Laziale*, 124–142. QuadAEI 12. Rome.

Baglione, M. P., and M. A. De Lucia Brolli. 1990. "Nuovi dati sulla necropoli de 'I Tufi' di Narce." In *La civiltà dei Falisci. Atti del XV Convegno di Studi Etruschi e Italici (Civita Castellana 1987)*, 61–102. Florence.

———. 1997. "Veio e i Falisci." In *Necropoli arcaiche*, 145–171.

Barbaro, B. 2010. *Insediamenti, aree funerarie ed entità territoriali in Etruria meridionale nel Bronzo finale.* Florence.

Bartoloni, G. Forthcoming. "Veii and the Tiber." In *Frontiers of the European Age, with a Regional Focus on Central Italy. Proceedings of an International Conference (Cambridge 2013)*, ed. S. Stoddart, and L. Ceccarelli. Cambridge.

Bartoloni, G., A. Berardinetti, A. De Santis, and L. Drago. 1994. "Veio tra IX e VI secolo a.C.: Primi risultati sull'analisi comparata delle necropoli veienti." *ArchCl* 46:1–46.

Benedettini, G. 1999. "Note sulla produzione dei sostegni fittili nell'Agro falisco." *StEtr* 43:3–73.

Biella, M. C. 2014. "I Falisci e i Capenati: Una prospettiva archeological." In *Entre archéologie et histoire: Dialogues sur divers peuples de l'Italie préromaine*, ed. M. Aberson, M. C. Biella, M. Di Fazio, and M. Wullschleger, 65–84. E pluribus unum? L'Italia dalla diversità preromana all'unità augustea 1; Etudes genevoises sur l'Antiquité 2. Bern.

Briquel, D. 1994. "Haleso, eroe campano (Virgilio, Eneide 7, 723–730) e i Falisci, coloni calcidiesi (Giustino 20, 1, 13)." *Hesperìa: Studi sulla Grecità di Occidente* 4:83–94.

Capanna, C. 2005. "Dall'ager Antiquus alle espansioni di Roma in età regia." *Workshop di Archeologia Classica: Paesaggi, Costruzioni, Reperti* 2:173–188.

Carandini, A. 1997. *La nascita di Roma: Dèi, lari, eroi e uomini all'alba di una civiltà.* Turin.

Ceccarelli, L., and S. Stoddart. 2013. "Nepi, nuovi dati dallo scavo in area urbana." In Cifani 2013:217–230.

Cerasuolo, O. 2012. "L'organizzazione del territorio di Cerveteri e dei Monti della Tolfa a confronto con l'agro tarquiniese (prima età del Ferro-età alto arcaica)." In *Il ruolo degli oppida e la difesa del territorio in Etruria: Casi di studio e prospettive di ricerca*, ed. F. Cambi, 121–172. Rome.

Cifani, G., ed. 2003. *Storia di una frontiera: Dinamiche territoriali e gruppi etnici nella Media Valle Tiberina dalla prima età del Ferro alla conquista romana.* Rome.

———. 2005. "I confini settentrionali del territorio veiente." In *Dinamiche*, 151–161.

———. 2013. *Tra Roma e l'Etruria: Cultura, identità e territorio dei Falisci.* Rome.

Colonna, G. 1986. "Il Tevere e gli Etruschi." In *Il Tevere e le altre vie d'acqua del Lazio antico. Atti del VII Incontro di Studio del Comitato per l'Archeologia Laziale*, 90–97. QuadAEI 12. Rome.

———. 1988. "I Capenati." In *Italia omnium terrarum alumna*, ed. G. Pugliese Carratelli, 512–522. Milan.

Cozza, L., and A. Pasqui. 1981. *Carta Archeologica d'Italia (1881–1897): Materiali per l'Agro Falisco.* Forma Italiae ser. II, doc. 2. Florence.

De Cristofaro, A., and A. Piergrossi. 2016. "Ripa Veientana: Per una storia del territorio tra Veio e Roma dall'VIII al IV secolo a.C." *Mediterranea* 12–13:31–76.

De Lucia Brolli, M. A., and M. P. Baglione. 1997. "I Falisci: Il caso di Narce." In *Nomen Latinum. Atti del Convegno Internazionale (Rome, 24–26 October 1995). Eutopia* 4.2:53–94.

De Lucia Brolli, M. A., and J. Tabolli. 2013. "The Etruscans and the Faliscans." In *The Etruscan World*, ed. J. MacIntosh Turfa, 259–280. London.

———. 2016. "The Ager Faliscus and Its Women." In *Women in Antiquity: Real Women across the Ancient World*, ed. S. Budin and J. MacIntosh Turfa. London.

De Santis, A. 1997. "Alcune considerazioni sul territorio veiente in età orientalizzante e arcaica." In *Necropoli arcaiche*, 101–141.

Di Fazio, M. 2012. "I luoghi di culto di Feronia: Ubicazioni e funzioni." In *Il Fanum Voltumnae e i santuari comunitari dell'Italia antica. Atti del XIX Convegno Internazionale di Studi sulla Storia e l'Archeologia dell'Etruria (Orvieto 2011)*, ed. G. M. della Fina, 379–408. Annali Fondazione Museo Claudio Faina 19. Rome.

di Gennaro, F. 1982. "Organizzazione del territorio nell'Etruria meridionale protostorica." *DialArch* 2:102–137.

———. 1986. *Forme di insediamento tra Tevere e Fiora dal Bronzo finale al principio dell'età del Ferro.* Florence.

———. 2007. "Le tombe a loculo di età orientalizzante di Crustumerium." In *Tusculum: Storia archeologia cultura e arte di Tuscolo e del Tuscolano. Atti del primo incontro di studi (Grottaferrata 2000)*, ed. F. Arietti and A. Pasqualini, 163–176. Rome.

Iaia, C. 1996. "Le origini dell'urbanizzazione nell'Agro Falisco e Capenate: Osservazioni e ipotesi." *Informazioni* 5:25–35.

Michetti, L. M. 2009. "Note su un'anfora orientalizzante dal tumulo di Monte Aguzzo a Veio." In *Etruria e Italia preromana. Studi in onore di Giovannangelo Camporeale*, ed. S. Bruni, 607–615. Pisa.

Peroni, R. 1989. *Protostoria dell'Italia continentale: La penisola italiana nelle età del Bronzo e del Ferro.* Rome.

Peroni, R., and M. A. Fugazzola. 1969. "Ricerche preistoriche a Narce." *BPI* 78:79–145.

Piergrossi, A. 2002. "Una comunità di frontiera: Poggio Montano." *ArchCl* 53:1–63.

———. Forthcoming. "Poggio Montano, a Frontier Site in Southern Internal Etruria: Landscape History and Cultural Interactions at the Turn of the Orientalizing Period." In *Frontiers of the European Age, with a Regional Focus on Central Italy. Proceedings of an International Conference (Cambridge 2013)*, ed. S. Stoddart and L. Ceccarelli. Cambridge.

Pitzalis, F. 2011. *La volontà meno apparente: Donne e società nell'Italia centrale tirrenica durante l'Orientalizzante antico.* Rome.

Potter, T. W. 1976. *A Faliscan Town in South Etruria: Excavations at Narce, 1966–71.* London.

Stefani, E. 1958. *Capena: Scoperte archeologiche nell'agro capenate. Ricerche archeologiche nella contrada "Le Saliere."* *MonAnt* 44. Rome.

Tabolli, J. 2012. "Memoria nell'identità a Narce durante la prima età del Ferro." *ArchCl* 63:485–507.

———. 2013. *Narce tra la prima età del Ferro e l'Orientalizzante antico: L'abitato, I Tufi e La Petrina.* Mediterranea 9; Civiltà arcaica dei Sabini nella Valle del Tevere 5. Pisa-Rome.

———. 2015. "Nuovi dati sulle necropoli di Monte Sant'Angelo: Rileggendo lo scavo del 1892." In *Novità*, 157–160.

———. 2016. "All'origine dell'Agro Falisco." *Ostraka* 2013-2014:173–195.

———. Forthcoming. "Living and Dying within the Frontier(s): Between Material Culture and Funerary Ideology at Narce." In *Frontiers of the European Age, with a Regional Focus on Central Italy. Proceedings of an International Conference (Cambridge 2013)*, ed. S. Stoddart and L. Ceccarelli. Cambridge.

Tabolli, J., and S. Neri. 2017. "The Faliscans and the Capenates." In *Peoples of Ancient Italy*, ed. G. Bradley and G. D. Farney, 567–586. Boston.

Ziołkowski, A. 2009. "Frontier Sanctuaries of the Ager Romanus Antiquus: Did They Exist?" *Palamedes* 4.1:91–130.

CHAPTER 8

THE ORIENTALIZING PERIOD

ORLANDO CERASUOLO

In Etruscan archaeology, the period between about 720 and 575 BCE is usually called "Orientalizing." This label acknowledges the strong Near Eastern influence evident in the culture and style of the Etruscans.[1] During this period, the society of Veii underwent great changes in almost every aspect of life and death: habitations evolved from simple huts into masonry buildings; the burial landscape saw the appearance of monumental mounds—the so-called *tumuli*—and family chamber tombs, sometimes with wall paintings; the material culture shifted to mass production; and the political organization became more complex, with the development of political roles that might be associated with early magistrates, similarly to the Roman monarchy. These changes occurred gradually over the entire period, so that archaeologists customarily divide the Etruscan Orientalizing into three main phases:[2]

- Early Orientalizing, about 720 to 675 BCE (so-called Veii IIIA)
- Middle Orientalizing, about 675 to 630 BCE (so-called Veii IIIB)
- Late Orientalizing, about 630 to 575 BCE (so-called Veii IV)

EARLY ORIENTALIZING PHASE

All over the entire plateau of Veii, finds from surveys show strong continuity in the life of the settlement, but with a higher density of buildings, especially in the northern part of the city.[3] This increase in evidence is also detected in the flat areas and is marked along the main roads and close to the gates.[4]

During the Early Orientalizing period, a gradual shift to rectangular timber buildings is attested, although in some areas, such as Macchiagrande (*maps 3 and 4:M*),[5] the coexistence of rectangular and elliptical huts is evident. One of the best-known examples of a rectangular hut has been excavated by the British School at Rome at the North-West Gate (*map 4:F*).[6] This building consisted of two squared rooms and a front porch (*see fig. 1.1:A*).

In Campetti South-West (*map 4:O*), a complex sequence of buildings has been identified:[7] from the second half of the eighth century[8] there are a few elliptical huts and one rectangular one;[9] in the first half of the seventh century,[10] a general reorganization of the area was accompanied by the foundation of a large rectangular building that seems to have had a special character.

In the wide fields of Comunità (*map 4:W*), in the southern part of the plateau, at least seven areas reveal evidence of pottery production.[11]

The Early Orientalizing workshops of Veii developed some new types of vessels (globular amphoras, high-footed cups, *kyathoi*, and basins) and introduced at Veii the Orientalizing brown impasto pottery and painted fine ware. The rise of a new system of serial production is a typical phenomenon of this period.

From the literary sources we know that in the same period, the king Numa Pompilius established in Rome some associations of crafts and activities.[12] The reign of Numa in Rome (ca. 715–673 BCE) corresponds to the Early Orientalizing period; at this time, peaceful relations between the two cities seem to have existed. What is traditionally known about Numa reveals some interesting clues regarding the society of that time.[13] As king he was chosen by the senators and hailed by the people.[14] He built the temple of Vesta and the temple of Janus as well as the Regia.[15] To reinforce the stability of Roman society he introduced reforms and fostered several institutions, mostly religious. Under his reign a number of social orders were established,[16] including the Curiates, the Flamini, the Celeres, the Vestals, the Augures, the Salii, and the Pontefices. The Pontefices, in particular, held sway over public and private morality and religious activities.[17] Numa also introduced a new lunar calendar and legislation about ritual sacrifices.[18]

We can identify very little of all of that at the coeval Veii. Evidence of its institutions and social practices are gone, and archaeology gives only hints of the ancient sociocultural order. At Piazza d'Armi (*map 4:Y*), a large earth altar allowed the continuation of ritual activity related to the burials, while the *heroon* was rebuilt as a squared chapel with antae. In at least thirteen areas of the city traces of cult activities have been identified,[19] making clear the richness and complexity of social and religious life at Veii. Such a large community required an advanced level of organization and coordination, in both the religious and the social spheres.

Characteristics of the society of Veii can be deduced through the funerary data. First of all, it is important to look at the location of the burial grounds (*map 3*). From the Early Iron Age, the necropolis of Grotta Gramiccia[20] was located and organized along the ancient road leading to the north (Ager Faliscus and Nepi); the necropoleis of Casale del Fosso[21] and Riserva del Bagno lay along the roads toward Caere. The tombs of Pozzuolo,[22] Oliveto Grande, and Quaranta Rubbie were linked to the route toward the lower Tiber region; finally, Vaccareccia[23] and Monte Michele[24] were associated with the road leading to Capena. The necropolis of Picazzano[25] came into use during this phase, along a northwest road. The necropolis of Quattro Fontanili was located on a northeast road. Casalaccio,[26] Monte Campanile, and Macchia della Comunità[27] are associated with roads toward Fidenae and Rome.

The locations of different burial grounds did not depend only on the landscape but seem to be related especially to the ownership of land, which would have been in the hands of the aristocratic families. In this context it is useful to recall the Roman tradition that attributes to Numa the definition of the boundaries of private and public landholdings, under the auspices of Juppiter Terminalis, that is, "Jupiter of the borders."[28]

Early Orientalizing tombs are attested at Vaccareccia[29] and Picazzano; around seventy tombs have been excavated at Casale del Fosso,[30] but only a few at Grotta Gramiccia and Macchia della Comunità.[31] So far, no single large burial ground at Veii, such as that of the Esquiline necropolis in Rome, has been identified.

The common characteristics of the tombs from Macchia della Comunità are quite different from those of the northern necropoleis. Since they are very simple and lacking in luxury goods, they have been considered to belong to the people living in the artisans' district of Comunità.[32]

The richest tombs of the Early Orientalizing period belong to different architectural types. The clustering of tombs is a common phenomenon, with a progressive emergence of one or two monumental burials within each group. The necropolis of Casale del Fosso provides a consistent sequence of burials.[33] Tombs 871 and 872 (ca. 730/720 BCE, fig. 8.1: no. 3; *see also fig. 6.7*) are trench tombs with burial in the *loculus*, consisting of a lateral niche. In the contemporary tombs 816 and 821, a chariot was placed in the *loculus* (fig. 8.1: nos. 2 and 4). Tombs 1089 and 1090, also dating to this period, were chamber tombs (fig. 8.1: no. 5).[34] During the first half of the seventh century BCE, the monumental chamber tombs 809 and 868 had long entrance corridors (fig. 8.1: nos. 14 and 13, respectively). Similar trends can be observed at the necropoleis of Riserva del Bagno (i.e., monumental tomb V[35] and the Tomb of the Ducks,[36] fig. 8.1: nos. 15 and 7, respectively) and at Monte Michele (i.e., the Campana Tomb [fig. 8.1: no. 18] and a few others[37]). This process likely represents the emergence of aristocratic leaders among their social groups.

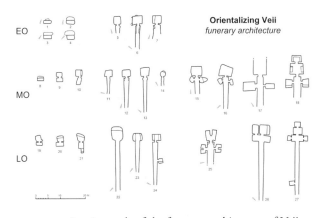

FIGURE 8.1. A sample of the funerary architecture of Veii during the Orientalizing period. 1. Casale del Fosso tomb 672; 2. Casale del Fosso tomb 816; 3. Casale del Fosso tomb 871; 4. Casale del Fosso tomb 821; 5. Casal del Fosso tomb 1090; 6. Tomb of the Roaring Lions; 7. Tomb of the Ducks; 8. Casalaccio tomb I; 9. Casalaccio tomb II; 10. Casalaccio tomb III; 11. Pantano di Grano tomb 2; 12. Pantano di Grano tomb 1; 13. Casale del Fosso tomb 868; 14. Casale del Fosso tomb 809; 15. Riserva del Bagno tomb V; 16. Monte Michele tomb 5; 17. Monte Aguzzo; 18. Campana Tomb; 19. Casalaccio tomb VI; 20. Casalaccio tomb V; 21. Casalaccio tomb IV; 22. Monte Michele tomb 2; 23. Monte Michele tomb 6; 24. Osteria del Fosso; 25. Oliveto Grande; 26. Monte Michele, tomb 9; 27. Vaccareccia. Nos. 17, 18, and 27 have tumuli; *marks tombs with wall paintings. (Copyright: O. Cerasuolo)

In contrast to the evidence at Caere,[38] the architecture of the earliest chamber tombs at Veii is less developed, perhaps as a consequence of the quality of the local geology.[39] Nonetheless, during the Orientalizing period several types of burials developed at Veii (fig. 8.1), from the shaft tombs with *loculus* to the chamber room with one to five rooms. Furthermore, it is at Veii that the earliest funerary wall paintings were created, in order to embellish the final dwelling of the leaders ruling the city. Exceptional cases are the Tomb of the Roaring Lions (fig. 8.1: no. 6; *map 4:A*), the Tomb of the Ducks (fig. 8.1: no. 7; *map 4:J*); and the later Campana Tomb (fig. 8.1: no. 18; *map 4:C*).[40] In these rich burials fine Proto-Corinthian pottery has been unearthed, together with locally produced, elaborate vessels and some luxury goods.

Early Orientalizing tombs also reflect ritual values. A fragmentary statue coming from Picazzano necropo-

lis (*map 3*) represented a noble seated on a throne.[41] This was likely an object of devotion placed in an accessible recess of a particular tomb, as in the case of the Tomb of the Statues at Ceri.[42]

In addition, there is a limited group of tombs with benches at the end of the corridors. These could have been used by the most important persons attending the funerary procession, or perhaps were where replicas of the ancestors might be placed during rituals.

MIDDLE ORIENTALIZING PHASE

According to the literary sources, a new period of struggles against Rome marked the beginning of the Middle Orientalizing phase, contemporary with the reign there of Tullus Hostilius (ca. 673–642 BCE).[43] The resolution of this antagonism brought a new victory to Rome, whose territory, after the conquest of the Septem Pagi and the Salinae on the north banks of the Tiber as well as the settlement of Ficana (*map 1*), now was larger than the Veientine lands.[44]

Perhaps as a result of the unfortunate historical condition of Veii, or simply because of scarce archaeological evidence, the Middle Orientalizing settlement of Veii is relatively little known. The survey data clearly show an increase in the amount of occupied urban areas, although a gap in the central area continues to be attested.[45]

The excavations at Piazza d'Armi (*map 4:Y; see fig. 1.2*) have revealed the most interesting remains to date. A semi-subterranean hut found within Structure A of Area I dates to the early part of the period. The discovery of several objects connected to aristocratic banqueting practice permits the attribution of this building to people of high rank.[46]

Around the mid-seventh century BCE, Area I was reorganized. A neat urban plan now overlay the earlier settlement of scattered clusters of huts, establishing the basis for the earliest orthogonal road system, which lasted for centuries.[47] Before the east–west road was laid, a pair of channels was dug to define the proper track, with a distance apart of about 5 meters (fig. 8.2; *see also fig. 1.5*). That this activity involved a foundation ritual is affirmed by the deposition of a jar and a chal-

FIGURE 8.2. The road and the channels of
Piazza d'Armi. (Copyright: G. Bartoloni)

ice.[48] Thus, the new urban layout acquired a sacred significance. A new rectangular structure was located along the road, in an area in front of the later *oikos* building.[49]

At Campetti South-West during the late Middle Orientalizing,[50] a few substantial changes confirm the contemporary renovation of the city. An isolated rectangular building was replaced by a new one featuring numerous large posts; the construction of massive terracing made out of tufa blocks and timber poles provided a leveled and optimized area upon which to build.

During the Middle Orientalizing period, at the North-West Gate (*map 4:F*) previous timber structures were replaced with new buildings that had foundations made of tufa blocks, wattle-and-daub walls, and tiled roofs.[51] Two distinct architectural phases can be identified on the basis of the quality of the tufa blocks.

Looking at the entire plateau, we see that the evidence from the surveys still shows continuity in the location of the cult areas.[52] Excavation revealed a formal religious area and votive pottery at Portonaccio (*map 4:S*), dating to around the mid-seventh century BCE, that existed in the area of the future sanctuary before any tufa building was built.[53] A more uncertain situation involved the above-mentioned rectangular buildings of Campetti South-West, which occupied the exact geometric center of the later sacred precinct. Unfortunately no significant finds at Campetti can help us in defining the function of this complex.

Field surveys have established the continuity of pottery production at Comunità (*map 4:W*).[54] Some archaeologists have called this area the potters' quarters of Veii, given the density of production activity.[55] Recent excavations brought to light some kilns and very large quantities of wasters. A new utilitarian ware was developed then, a coarse cream-colored ware with a sandy composition. Other new products of these workshops were ribbed globular jars, chalices, and dippers in brown impasto, sometimes with incised decoration (mostly lotus flowers and Phoenician palm trees). The Veientine production of bucchero first appears during the second quarter of the seventh century BCE. It is mostly attested in the funerary sets, such as tomb V at Monte Michele or tombs 863 and 867 at Casale del Fosso. High-footed chalices and globular amphoras are the most common vases, while the decoration consists of incisions and impressed patterns, such as the so-called fans. At the same time, bucchero has been found in the stratigraphic sequences of the settlement, as in phase I.4 of Campetti South-West (first half of the century), at a time when there also appear the earliest examples of Proto-Corinthian pottery in the houses (mainly Middle II and Late).

Recently at Piazza d'Armi a fragment of Italo-geometric pottery ascribed to the workshop of the Crane Painter was found.[56] This find is the first of this workshop that comes from a residential context, and it contributes to the debate about the transfer of the workshop from Caere, where the earliest of its products have been found, to Veii. Here the Crane Painter could have worked for the court of the rich aristocracies settled at Piazza d'Armi.

The funerary landscape at this time includes the necropoleis of Casale del Fosso, Grotta Gramiccia,[57] Quattro Fontanili, Vaccareccia, Picazzano,[58] Monte Michele,[59] Macchia della Comunità, Casalaccio,[60] Pozzuolo, and Riserva del Bagno. The most remarkable innovation is the building of monumental burial mounds (tumuli). The tumulus of Monte Aguzzo (*map 2: no. 1*), whose earliest burial has been pinpointed to the late Middle Orientalizing period, has a diameter at the base of 60 meters.[61] The burials at Monte Aguzzo and at Quaranta Rubbie[62] were very rich. A group of notable burials is located at Monte Michele, where tomb 5 is the earliest to be used, soon followed by a group of Late Orientalizing tombs, all of them belonging to high-ranking individuals. The deposition of the cremated bones of the male burial in tomb 5 at Monte Michele occurred within a lithic box covered by bronze sheets.[63] The material culture typical of these tombs shows some connections with the Ager Faliscus and Caere,[64] giving some hints of the commercial interests of these aristocrats.

LATE ORIENTALIZING PHASE

For the Late Orientalizing period the different surveys revealed a decisive increase in the number of sites and finds, to such an extent that it can be said the city was at its apogee at this time.[65] The gradual occupation of the plateau resulted from the more complex community and economy, as well as a likely substantial increase in population.

The huts were now completely transformed into buildings with foundations of tufa blocks and tiled roofs. In this phase a number of areas can be identified as sites of prestigious buildings, as evidenced by the finds from the highest point of Comunità, from the eastern part of Macchiagrande, and from central Campetti.

At Campetti South-West (*map 4:O*), between several tufa buildings, a new large precinct was built (ca. 25 × 29 meters, fig. 8.3). It is oriented east–west and is centered on the area previously occupied by the rectangular timber building.[66] Inside the precinct there were probably a few chapels and statues (one of Hercle);[67] outside, some votive deposits have been discovered.[68]

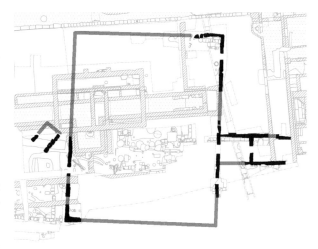

FIGURE 8.3. The Etruscan precinct found at Campetti South-West below the buildings of Roman age. (Copyright: O. Cerasuolo)

Among the various Etruscan inscriptions coming from this area, one refers to Tinia-Zeus.[69]

Piazza d'Armi again offers a good range of evidence. The most renowned is the *oikos*, a public structure with sacred functions, decorated with the earliest examples of roof terracottas (ca. 600 BCE);[70] themes such as the departure of the warrior, with a chariot followed by armed knights, appear on these pieces.[71] Near the *oikos* a tripartite building with a large porticoed piazza has been excavated (*see fig. 1.6*). This building finds comparisons with the so-called palace of area F at Acquarossa[72] and has characteristics of an aristocratic residential system, with diversified spaces devoted to public and sacral function, intended to exalt the aristocratic clan and legitimize its power.

Not far from this residence, in central area I, at the end of the seventh century BCE,[73] a compound was created within tufa walls. Some of the delineated areas were occupied not by actual buildings, but by functional areas and cooking pits.[74] A house-tower with a cistern in sector V dates in the first half of the sixth century.[75] Associated finds of rich terracotta reliefs have led this building to be considered a gentilicial one.

At the northern limit of Piazza d'Armi, ruins of multiroom buildings have been unearthed, together with a hypogeal cistern, built in tufa blocks with a corbeled roof. The cistern (fig. 8.4) is interesting for

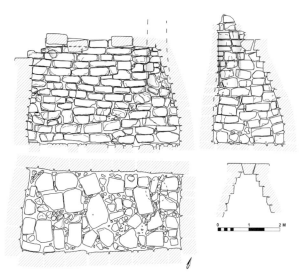

FIGURE 8.4. The hypogeal cistern at Piazza d'Armi.
(Copyright: O. Cerasuolo)

its covering technique, a line of blocks at the top inserted as wedges and functionally working as an arch;
it is an experimental solution that prefigures the creation of the true vault. The building technique of the
cistern, dating back to around 600 BCE, matches that
used at the same time to reinforce the entrance wall
of the Campana Tomb,[76] indicating that contemporary technology was more advanced than previously
believed. For this period there is a little evidence that
Piazza d'Armi was connected to the rest of the city by
a wooden bridge. Support for this possibility comes
from the tradition naming the Roman king Ancus
Marcius (ca. 641–616 BCE) as the builder of the Pons
Sublicius, the first bridge on the Tiber River.[77]

Other literary references, especially related to Rome
under the reign of Lucius Tarquinius Priscus (ca. 616–
579 BCE), help us in imagining the development of a
civilized Late Orientalizing city. The king of a large
city such as Rome or Veii was in charge of providing all
the infrastructure necessary to its social and economic
life. The Etruscan Tarquinius provided Rome with
new defensive walls,[78] built the Circus Maximus for
horse races,[79] and started construction of the sewage
system—the Cloaca Maxima[80]—and of the Temple
of Capitoline Jupiter.[81] Tarquinius Priscus also expanded the equestrian order, the centuriate assembly,
and the senate.[82] He held sumptuous triumphs[83] and

introduced royal etiquette modeled on Etruscan style,
in sacrificial rituals, divination, music during public
events (in particular with trumpets), and scepters and
other symbols of power.[84]

Tarquinius called to Rome the famous Veientine craftsman Vulca to create the statue of Capitoline Jupiter.[85] Surveys and excavations undertaken in
the area of Comunità have uncovered a high density
of pottery production (mainly bucchero, Etrusco-
Corinthian, and fine ware), suggesting that his workshop was located there.[86]

Most of the necropoleis of Veii were in use during
the Late Orientalizing: Casale del Fosso, Grotta Gramiccia, Quattro Fontanili, Vaccareccia, Picazzano,
Monte Michele, Macchia della Comunità, Casalaccio,
Pozzuolo, Oliveto Grande, Riserva del Bagno, Monte
Campanile,[87] and a few tombs near Monte Aguzzo.[88]
Most of the monumental tumuli belong to this period
(*see fig. 9.1*).[89] The abundant funerary evidence allows archaeologists to divide the Late Orientalizing into three
subphases: phase IVA1 (ca. 630–620 BCE); phase IVA2
(ca. 610–590 BCE); and phase IVB (ca. 590–575 BCE).[90]

The southwestern necropoleis lack any monumental characteristic.[91] On the contrary, among the richest
tombs of the phase stands the tumulus of Vaccareccia
(*map 4:N*). It has a complex architectural plan (fig. 8.1:
no. 27), with four chambers, all painted in red.[92] The
depositions were at least three: two inhumations and
one cremation, one belonging to a male accompanied
by a sword, an exceptional item in this period. The rich
tomb-group included a two-wheeled chariot. Another
tomb indicative of high rank is the one found at Oliveto Grande (*map 4:U*), which contained a large set
of vases, including incised bucchero and a sealed amphora, together with the remains of wooden furniture
covered with richly decorated bronze sheets (fig. 8.5).[93]

The discovery of a pair of clay models of boats from
the main chamber of tomb 1 at Monte Oliviero (*map 2:
no. 10*)[94] underlines the interest of the aristocracy of
Veii in the river trade.[95] Literary sources in fact mention the failed attempt of some Veientine rulers to re-
conquer the territory of the Septem Pagi (*map 1*) during the reign of Ancus Marcius. At the same time,
Rome founded the colony of Ostia, taking control of
the mouth of the Tiber.

FIGURE 8.5. Details of the bronze plaques with embossed decoration from the Oliveto Grande tomb. (Copyright: O. Cerasuolo)

During the reign of Lucius Tarquinius Priscus, the battles between Romans and Etruscans of Veii and Caere lasted for seven years, ending with the victory of Rome at the Battle of Eretum. To indicate their capitulation the defeated Etruscans offered to Tarquinius the symbols of power of their cities, *fasces littores* (a bundle of wooden rods bound around an axe with its blade emerging, used to represent the power of magistrates) and *sellae curulis* (a stool with two pairs of crossed, arched legs, an emblem of kingly power later used by Roman senators).[96]

CONCLUSIONS

The rich and complex archaeological evidence, significantly increased by recent discoveries, makes the Orientalizing period one of the best known in Veientine history, allowing for a detailed reconstruction of the city and its necropoleis during a crucial time span of almost one hundred years. In these years the earliest Veientine epigraphic texts appeared, and a number of references from Latin literary sources shed light on the tangled relationship with Rome and provide useful comparisons to illuminate the social and political life of the Etruscan city, information that is not visible in the archaeological data.

NOTES

1. For a general overview of the Etruscan Orientalizing period, see Haynes 2000:47–134, and Sannibale 2013. Concerning Veii during this period, see Boitani 2008 and chapters 10 and 11.

2. The division was proposed first by Pallottino (1939). Veii IIIA is discussed in Close-Brooks 1965.

3. Rendeli and Sansoni 2004:16, figs. 3–4; Cascino et al. in *Survey*, 345–347.

4. The main roads, clearly visible in aerial photographs and via geophysical analysis (see chapter 3), were likely constructed during the first half of the sixth century, but they replaced earlier tracks with similar orientation (Guaitoli 2015:85).

5. D'Alessio 2015:29.

6. Ward-Perkins 1959; *Formello*, 24–26.

7. The final publication of the area of Campetti South-West is currently in process. The references here to site periodization use the label "site phase" plus the relevant number. For a preliminary description of the phases at Campetti South-West see Fusco and Maras 2016:333.

8. Campetti South-West, site phase I.3a.

9. Cerasuolo, Bruno, and Gori 2004.

10. Campetti South-West, site phase I.4.

11. Rendeli et al. in *Survey*, fig. 6.12; the evidence of production in this period is based on finds of wasters of Italo-geometric pottery.

12. Plutarch, *Numa* 17.3.

13. We refer here to the traditional dates for the seven kings of Rome, as accepted by the majority of scholars. Nonetheless, many aspects of the historical timeline, as well as the mythical character of these kings and their institutions, are still a matter of debate. For a comprehensive introduction to the topic see Cornell 1995:118–150.

14. Plutarch *Numa* 7.1. Numa accepted only after the proper auspices were received from the gods, as Romulus had done (Dionysios of Halikarnassos 2.5.1–2).

15. Dionysios of Halikarnassos 2.65.5; Plutarch, *Numa* 14.1, 20.1–3.

16. Dionysios of Halikarnassos 2.63.4.

17. Plutarch, *Numa* 7.4.

18. Eutropius, *Breviarium ab urbe condita* 1.3.

19. In *Survey*, fig. 6.12.

20. Berardinetti and Drago 1997.

21. Colini 1919; Stefani 1929; Buranelli 1981; Buranelli, Drago, and Paolini 1997.

22. Colini 1919:7; Ward-Perkins 1961:42–43.

23. Lanciani 1889:154–158 and 238–239; Stefani 1935:329; Palm 1952; Ward-Perkins 1961:43–46; Papi 1988; De Santis 2003b:84–98.

24. Mengarelli 1901; Ward-Perkins 1961:46; Cristofani 1969; Boitani 1982, 1985, 2003:81–84.

25. Lanciani 1889:10–12, 29–30, and 60–62; Palm 1952; Ward-Perkins 1961:46–47.

26. Vighi 1935:40; Ward-Perkins 1961:43.

27. Colini 1919:7; Adriani 1930:46; Ward-Perkins 1961:43; Galante 2003.

28. Dionysios of Halikarnassos 2.74.1–4. Numa also initiated the festivals of the Terminalia.

29. See tombs IV and XIV (phase IIIA2, early seventh century): Cristofani 1969:67–70.

30. Buranelli, Drago, and Paolini 1997:77–82.

31. A high-ranking female burial has been published by Galante (2003).

32. Bartoloni 2009:10.

33. Buranelli, Drago, and Paolini 1997:69; Drago Troccoli 2005. The *loculus* of this tomb suggests the idea of a chamber tomb.

34. Buranelli, Drago, and Paolini 1997:77.

35. Buranelli 1982:91.

36. Dating to 680–670 BCE: Medoro 2003; Brocato 2012.

37. Brocato 2012:22–23; tomb B (phase IIIA2, early seventh century BCE): Cristofani 1969:67–70.

38. Cerasuolo 2016.

39. At Veii architectural details are rendered only rarely: the roof decoration of tomb V at Riserva del Bagno (Buranelli 1982); engravings and paintings at Vaccareccia (Stefani 1935). As at Caere, the entrance of the main tombs is arched (Tomb of the Roaring Lions, Tomb of the Ducks, and Campana Tomb).

40. See Boitani 2010 and chapter 21.

41. See chapter 22.

42. Cerasuolo 2016.

43. Eutropius, *Breviarium ab urbe condita* 1.4.

44. For a recent and comprehensive analysis of the southern part of the territory of Veii between the eighth and the fourth centuries BCE see De Cristofaro and Piergrossi 2015–2016. See also chapters 9 and 11.

45. In *Survey*, 347. It is not clear how much such a gap could be related to postdepositional factors or to the actual ancient situation. The common opinion is that the entire plateau was densely inhabited from the mid-seventh century BCE: Guaitoli 2015:88 and 90.

46. Bartoloni 2003a:59–67.

47. Acconcia 2012:15.

48. Piazza d'Armi: site subphase IIIA.

49. Neri and Pitzalis 2015:7, fig. 1.1.1.5.

50. Campetti South-West: site phase I.5.

51. See *Formello*, 24–26.

52. See *Survey*, figs. 6, 13.

53. See chapter 13.

54. Rendeli et al. 2012: fig. 6.13; Cascino 2008; Belelli Marchesini and Cascino 2011–2012.

55. See chapter 23 with references to the comparison with the Kerameikos (potters' quarter) of Athens.

56. Cerasuolo and Pulcinelli 2015: fig. 1.1.3.11.

57. See, for example, tombs 863 and 867, Berardinetti and Drago 1997:62 n. 74.

58. See, for example, tombs XVIII, XXA, and XXB, in Cristofani 1969:67–70.

59. See, for example, tomb C (ca. 660–630 BCE), in Cristofani 1969:67–70; tomb V (ca. 670–650 BCE), in Boitani 1982, 1985; Tomb Buranelli V (ca. 675–650 BCE); tombs 1, 2, and 3 (ca. 635–625 BCE).

60. See, for example, tombs I, II (supposed to be the earliest), and III, in Cristofani 1969:67–70.

61. Ghirardini 1882:291; Ward-Perkins 1961:47; Colonna 1986:421; Della Ratta Rinaldi 1998; Michetti and van Kampen 2014. A reconstruction of this tomb is on view at the archaeological museum in Florence.

62. Stefani 1929:329–330; Adriani 1930:57–66; Inglieri 1930:69–71; Rizzo 1990:43–48; Bartoloni et al. 1994:33, 35.

63. Boitani 1985.

64. Medoro 2003:74.

65. *Survey*, 347–349, figs. 6, 14–15.

66. Fusco 2015:43, fig. 1.4.2.2.

67. Fusco 2011.

68. Cerasuolo and Di Sarcina 2015.

69. Fusco and Maras 2016.

70. See chapter 24.

71. Bartoloni 2009:11.

72. Neri and Pitzalis 2015:8, fig. 1.1.1.6.

73. Piazza d'Armi: site subphase IIIc, structure A.

74. Acconcia 2012:16–18.

75. Bartoloni 2003b:99–122.

76. Cerasuolo and Pulcinelli 2015:19–20.

77. Florus, *Epitomae de Tito Livio Bellorum omnium annorum DCC* 1.4.2.

78. Livy, *Periochae ab urbe condita libri* 1.19 and 1.37.

79. Eutropius, *Breviarium ab urbe condita* 1.6.

80. Livy, *Periochae ab urbe condita libri* 1.19 and 1.37.

81. Eutropius, *Breviarium ab urbe condita* 1.6.

82. Livy, *Periochae ab urbe condita libri* 1.37.

83. Florus, *Epitomae de Tito Livio Bellorum omnium annorum DCC* 1.5.6.

84. Strabo, *Geography* 5.2.2; Florus, *Epitomae de Tito Livio Bellorum omnium annorum DCC* 1.5.6.

85. Pliny, *Nat. Hist.* 35.157. See chapter 13.

86. Rendeli et al. 2012:349, fig. 6.14; see also chapters 21 and 23.

87. Colini 1919:7; Ward-Perkins 1961:43.

88. Five or six scattered tombs: Della Ratta Rinaldi 1998: 37–51.

89. See chapter 9.

90. The following are the typical tombs of each subphase. For phase IVA1: Monte Michele tombs B, D, 2, 6, 7, 8, and 9 (Boitani 1982); Picazzano XI and XII; Casalaccio IV, V, VI, and VIII (Cristofani 1969:67–70); Vaccareccia tumulus (Stefani 1935; Naso 1996:19–21; De Santis 2003b:84–89); a tomb at Quaranta Rubbie (Adriani 1930:57); Oliveto Grande (Boitani and Cerasuolo 2015). Phase IVA2: Monte Michele E and F; Picazzano XIII, XV, XVI, and XVIII (Cristofani 1969:67–70); the dromos tomb of Vaccareccia tumulus (De Santis 2003b:87); Casalaccio VII (Brocato [2012] considers it a Middle Orientalizing tomb with later intrusions); Formello (Stefani 1922:215); the first depositions of the Campana Tomb (Cristofani and Zevi 1965; Rizzo 1989:109–111). Phase IVB: the last depositions of the Campana Tomb (Cristofani 1969:67–70). Phase IV generic: tumuli Olgiata, Via Veientana, and Pisciacavallo (Monte Tondo) (Ward-Perkins 1961:47); tomb north of Casale di Osteria del Fosso, with a 16-meter corridor (Stefani 1929:325–328).

91. Ward-Perkins 1961:47; Bartoloni et al. 1994:30–31; Brocato 2012:19.

92. De Santis 2003b:85.

93. Boitani and Cerasuolo 2015.

94. Stefani 1928; Ward-Perkins 1961:47; De Santis 2003b:88.

95. Arizza et al. 2013.

96. Dionysios of Halikarnassos 3.57.4–62.

BIBLIOGRAPHY

Acconcia, V. 2012. "Lo scavo dell'area 1: Periodi III e I." In *Veio* II, 15–86.

Adriani, A. 1930. "Macchia della Comunità; Tomba a camera in contrada Quaranta Rubbie." *NSc* 1930:46–56, 57–66.

Arizza, M., A. De Cristofaro, A. Piergrossi, and D. Rossi. 2013. "La tomba di un aristocratico *naukleros* dall'agro veientano: Il *kantharos* con scena di navigazione di via d'Avack." *ArchCl* 64:51–131.

Bartoloni, G. 2003a. "Veio–Piazza d'Armi: Un'abitazione in capanna." In *Formello*, 57–67.

———. 2003b. "Veio–Piazza d'Armi: Una casa con tetto di tegole." In *Formello*, 99–102.

———. 2009. "Introduzione." In *Veio* I, 7–14.

Bartoloni, G., A. Berardinetti, L. Drago, and A. De Santis. 1994. "Veio tra il IX e il VI secolo a.C.: Primi risultati sull'analisi comparata delle necropoli veienti." *ArchCl* 46:1–46.

Belelli Marchesini, B., and R. Cascino. 2011–2012. "Veio, Comunità." In *Atlante dei siti di produzione ceramica (Toscana, Lazio, Campania e Sicilia)*, ed. G. Olcese, 215–217. Rome.

Berardinetti, A., and L. Drago. 1997. "La necropoli di Grotta Gramiccia." In *Necropoli arcaiche*, 39–64.

Boitani, F. 1982. "Veio: Nuovi ritrovamenti nella necropoli di Monte Michele." In *Archeologia nella Tuscia* I, 95–103. Rome.

———. 1985. "Veio: La tomba 'principesca' della necropoli di Monte Michele." *StEtr* 51:535–556.

———. 2003. "Necropoli di Monte Michele, la tomba principesca." In *Formello*, 81–84.

———. 2008. "Veio: Profilo storico-topografico." In *Etruschi: Le antiche necropoli del Lazio*, ed. M. Torelli and A. M. Moretti Sgubini, 46–63. Rome.

———. 2010. "Veio, la tomba dei Leoni Ruggenti: Dati preliminari." *Daidalos* 10:23–47.

Boitani, F., and O. Cerasuolo. 2015. "Novità del tardo orientalizzante veiente dalla necropoli di Oliveto Grande." In *Novità*, 133–141.

Brocato, P. 2012. *La tomba delle Anatre di Veio*. Rossano.

Buranelli, F. 1981. "Proposta di interpretazione dello sviluppo topografico della necropoli di Casale del Fosso a Veio." In *Necropoli e usi funerari nell'età del Ferro*, ed. R. Peroni, 19–45. Bari.

———. 1982. "Un'iscrizione etrusca arcaica dalla tomba V di Riserva del Bagno a Veio." *StEtr* 50:91–102.

Buranelli, F., L. Drago, and L. Paolini. 1997. "La necropoli di Casale del Fosso." In *Necropoli arcaiche*, 63–83.

Cascino, R. 2008. "Attività produttive ceramiche a Veio." *MÉFRA* 120:5–19.

Cerasuolo, O. 2016. "The Orientalizing Period at Caere: Material and Cultural Connections." In *Caere*, ed. N. de Grummond and L. Pieraccini, 118–152. Austin.

Cerasuolo, O., A. Bruno, and M. Gori. 2004. "Scavi nel complesso archeologico di Campetti a Veio: Materiali e contesti dell'età del Ferro." In *Preistoria e protostoria in Etruria. Atti del Sesto Incontro di Studi*, 593–598. Milan.

Cerasuolo, O., and M. T. Di Sarcina. 2015. "Depositi votivi e attività cultuali a Campetti, area SO." In *Novità*, 180–182.

Cerasuolo, O., and L. Pulcinelli. 2015. "Le mura occidentali e il quartiere presso le mura settentrionali." In *Novità*, 15–21.

Close-Brooks, J. 1965. "Proposta per una suddivisione in fasi." *NSc* 1965:53–64.

Colini, G. A. 1919. "Veio: Scavi nell'area della città e della necropoli." *NSc* 1919:3–19.

Colonna, G. 1986. "Urbanistica e architettura." In *Rasenna*, ed. G. Pugliese Carratelli, 369–530. Rome.

Colonna, G., and D. Maras. 2006. *Corpus Inscriptionum Etruscarum II, 1, 5., Add. II 2,b1.* Pisa.

Cornell, T. J. 1995. *The Beginnings of Rome.* London.

Cristofani, M. 1969. *Le tombe di Monte Michele nel Museo Archeologico di Firenze.* Florence.

Cristofani, M., and F. Zevi. 1965. "La tomba Campana di Veio: Il corredo." *ArchCl* 17:1–35, 284–285.

D'Alessio, M. T. 2015. "Macchia Grande: Il paesaggio urbano tra l'età del ferro e la tarda età imperiale." In *Novita*, 27–34.

De Cristoforo, A., and A. Piergrossi. 2015–2016. *"Ripa veientana*: Per una storia del territorio tra Veio e Roma dall'VIII al IV secolo a.C." *Mediterranea* 12–13:31–66.

Della Ratta Rinaldi, F. 1998. "Rinvenimenti funerari dall'area di Monte Aguzzo: Il Tumulo Chigi." In *Per un Museo dell'Agro Veientano: Dalla tutela del patrimonio archeologico alla sua valorizzazione*, ed. F. Della Ratta Rinaldi and F. Boanelli, 35–51. Rome.

De Santis, A. 2003a. "La rappresentazione e l'architetto." In *Rappresentazione e architettura: Linguaggi per il rilievo ed il progetto*, ed. A. Testa and A. De Santis, 119–162. Rome.

———. 2003b. "Necropoli di Vaccareccia, il tumulo." In *Formello*, 84–99.

Drago Troccoli, L. 2005. "Una coppia di principi nella necropoli di Casale del Fosso a Veio." In *Dinamiche*, 87–124.

Fusco, U. 2011. "Il culto di Ercole presso il complesso archeologico di Campetti, area S-O, a Veio testimonianze dall'età etrusca a quella romana." *ArchCl* 62, n.s. 1:379–412.

———. 2015. "I santuari presso Campetti, area SO." *NSc* 2015: 40–48.

Fusco, U., and D. Maras. 2016. "Veii: Campetti, area sud-ovest." *StEtr* 77:332–333, 341–345.

Galante, G. 2003. "Necropoli di Macchia della Comunità, tomba 7." In *Formello*, 67–73.

Ghirardini, G. 1882. "Formello." *NSc* 1882:291–300.

Guaitoli, M. 2015. "Veio: Osservazioni sulla topografia della città." *NSc* 2015:83–90.

Haynes, S. 2000. *Etruscan Civilization: A Cultural History.* Los Angeles.

Inglieri, U. 1930. "Sepolcreti villanoviani in località Picazzano e tombe a camera in tenuta Oliveto Grande." *NSc* 1930: 67–71.

Lanciani, R. 1889. "Veio: Scoperte nell'area della città e nella necropoli veientana." *NSc* 1889:10–12, 29–30, 60–62, 154–158, and 238–239.

MacIntosh Turfa, J., ed. 2013. *The Etruscan World.* New York.

Medoro, A. 2003. "Necropoli di Riserva del Bagno, tomba delle Anatre." In *Formello*, 73–81.

Mengarelli, R. 1901. "Veio (territorio di Formello): Nuove indagini nell'area della necropoli veientana." *NSc* 1901:238–246.

Michetti, M. L., and I. van Kampen. 2014. *Il Tumulo di Monte Aguzzo a Veio e la collezione Chigi: Ricostruzione del contesto dell'Olpe Chigi e note sulla formazione della collezione archeologica della famiglia Chigi a Formello. MonAnt* 16. Rome.

Naso, A. 1996. *Architetture dipinte: Decorazioni parietali non figurate nelle tombe a camera dell'Etruria meridionale nel VII sec. a.C.* Rome.

Neri, S., and F. Pitzalis. 2015. "Le più antiche fasi di occupazione e le residenze." In *Novità*, 3–9.

Pallottino, M. 1939. "Sulle facies culturali arcaiche dell'Etruria." *StEtr* 13:85–129.

Palm, J. 1952. "Veian Tomb Groups in the Museo Preistorico, Rome." *OpArch* 7:50–86.

Papi, R. 1988. "Materiali sporadici dalla necropoli della Vaccareccia di Veio." In *Quaderni dell'Istituto di archeologia e storia antica* 4:87–144.

Rendeli, M., and M. Sansoni. 2004. "Etruscan Veii." In *Bridging the Tiber*, 15–18.

Rizzo, M. A., ed. 1989. *Pittura etrusca al Museo di Villa Giulia.* Rome.

———. 1990. *Le anfore da trasporto e il commercio etrusco arcaico* I: *I complessi tombali dell'Etruria meridionale.* Rome.

Sannibale, M. 2013. "Orientalizing Etruria." In MacIntosh Turfa 2013:99–133.

Stefani, E. 1922. "Scoperta di antichi sepolcri nel territorio del comune di Formello." *NSc* 1922:215–219.

———. 1928. "Veio: Scoperta di antichi sepolcri nella tenuta di Monte Oliviero." *NSc* 1928:95–105.

———. 1929. "Veio: Saggi e scoperte fortuite nella necropoli." *NSc* 1929:325–351.

———. 1935. "Veio: Esplorazione del tumulo di Vaccareccia." *NSc* 1935:329–361.

Vighi, R. 1935. "Veio: Scavi nella necropoli degli alunni dell'anno 1927–28 del Corso di Topografia dell'Italia Antica della r. Università di Roma." *NSc* 1935:39–68.

Ward-Perkins, J. B. 1959. "Excavations beside the North-West Gate at Veii, 1957–58." *PBSR* 27:38–79.

———. 1961. "Veii: The Historical Topography of the Ancient City." *PBSR* 29:1–123.

CHAPTER 9

VEII DURING THE SEVENTH AND SIXTH CENTURIES BCE

Political Structure and Organization of the Territory

GILDA BARTOLONI AND ANNA DE SANTIS

During the Orientalizing period, the two main regions on the opposite banks of the Tiber, Etruria and Latium Vetus, showed a strong ethnic and cultural differentiation, which had already been defined at the end of the Bronze Age. This differentiation was probably regulated by political agreements and treaties.

For the area between the Arrone River, the Tiber, and the sea, the archaeological evidence reveals a well-defined organization of the different settlements within a hierarchical system centered on Veii. At least from the eighth century BCE onward, Veii constituted the political and economic core of this system, according to the literary ancient sources, which referred to the western bank of the Tiber as the Ripa Etrusca (the Etruscan bank), and especially as the Ripa Veientana (the Veientine bank).[1]

THE TUMULI AROUND THE PLATEAU

During the Orientalizing period, the necropoleis had a more complex articulation than it did in the eighth century BCE.[2] The northern cemeteries (Grotta Gramiccia, Casale del Fosso, and Quattro Fontanili; *map 3*) continued to be used only by gentilicial groups. Starting from the Late Orientalizing period, the earliest tumuli were built by, and represented the highest expression of, the aristocratic elites.[3] The monumental tumuli at Veii total only nine or ten, if we count also the tumulus that probably covered the Campana Tomb, as suggested by M. A. Rizzo (*map 4:C*).[4] All were located near the most important roads, at a cer-

tain distance from the town center, and in prominent positions, in order to be visible from far away and to emphasize the prestige of their owners. Based on their distance from the town, these tumuli can be divided into two different groups:

(a) the tumuli located at less than one kilometer from the plateau near previous or contemporary necropoleis marked family links with the earliest burials, such as the tumuli of Vaccareccia (fig. 9.1; *map 2: no. 8*), Grotta Gramiccia (*map 2: no. 4*), Oliveto Grande (*map 2: nos. 6–7*), and, probably, the Campana Tomb (*map 4:C*); and

(b) the tumuli located outside the necropoleis, including Monte Aguzzo, at 5 kilometers (*map 2: no. 1*), Monticchio-Olgiata, at ca. 3 kilometers (*map 2: no. 3*), Pisciacavallo, at 2 kilometers (*map 2: no. 2*), and the via Veientana one, at 1 kilometer from the plateau (*map 2: no. 9*). These probably were intended to stress the family links with the control of parts of the land (*ager*).[5]

Both groups of tumuli reflected a common funerary ideology aimed at representing, to the entire society, the strength of the aristocratic groups and their links with the land. The location of the tumuli along the most important roads, besides emphasizing a link with agricultural exploitation, referred to the aristocratic control of trade along the contemporary commercial circuits.

FIGURE 9.1. The Vaccareccia tumulus.
(Copyright: A. De Santis)

FIGURE 9.2. The Monte Oliviero tumulus.
(Copyright: A. De Santis)

The burial structures underneath the tumuli had distinctive and complex plans, especially as compared to the earliest and the contemporary chamber tombs. Chamber tombs are located, in small groups, north of the plateau at Casale del Fosso,[6] Riserva del Bagno,[7] and Monte Michele[8] (*map 3*). South of the plateau, chamber tombs had simpler plans, such as those at Macchia della Comunità,[9] Monte Campanile,[10] Casalaccio,[11] and Pozzuolo[12] (*map 3*).

On the contrary, several different rooms, often aligned to each other and gradually decreasing in size, comprise the chamber tombs inside the tumuli. The Campana Tomb had this type of plan,[13] thus suggesting the onetime presence of a tumulus on top of it. In addition, at Veii the chamber tombs were never on axis with the physical center of the tumulus.

Excavation reports are preserved in the cases of only four tumuli: Monte Aguzzo,[14] Vaccareccia,[15] Monte Oliviero (fig. 9.2),[16] and Oliveto Grande, recently investigated.[17] Rodolfo Lanciani mentioned the discovery of a tumulus at the junction between the Formello–Veii and the Rome–Cesano roads[18]—this probably corresponds to the tumulus of Grotta Gramiccia—but he had no access to the excavation reports of this tumulus.[19] Enrico Stefani mentions in one of his notebooks (preserved at the Biblioteca Apostolica Vaticana) his visit to the excavation of the tumulus of Pisciacavallo, directed by G. Q. Giglioli, which was suspended because no important finds had been discovered.[20]

THE ORGANIZATION
OF THE TERRITORY

The strong link between the aristocrats and their land was probably the main reason for the reoccupation of the territory that began in the first half of the seventh century BCE. The Orientalizing and Early Archaic territory of Veii, between the Arrone River, the Tiber, and the sea, seems to have been organized into three different but interconnected systems.[21] Veii organized these three systems according to a consistent plan. They were characterized by precise patterns (fig. 9.3):

(a) The first system includes the sites located at the most critical defensive borders, in the farthest areas of the territory of Veii. These settlements occupied hills near the Tiber at regular intervals from each other (6–7 kilometers).

(b) The second system includes small-size settlements on top of isolated plateaus, which controlled internal roads and waterways.

(c) The third system includes all the sites that densely occupied the countryside. Small aristocratic nuclei slowly developed into larger rural sites, widely distributed in the territory, especially during the Archaic period.

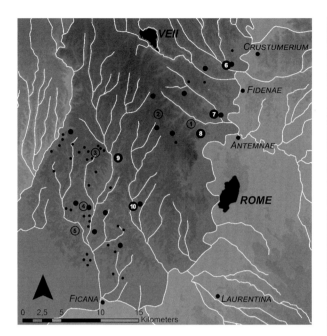

FIGURE 9.3. Settlements in the territory of Veii between the Arrone and Tiber Rivers. Secondary sites on plateau: I. Acqua Traversa; 2. Poggio Verde (Fosso dell'Acqua Traversa); 3. Santa Rufina; 4. Monte Roncione; 5. Pantano di Grano (Fosso Galeria). Sites on the border: 6. Prima Porta (Fosso di Prima Porta); 7. Monte delle Grotte; 8. Colle Sant'Agata; 9. Boccea–Casalotti; 10. Acquafredda. Small dots correspond to rural settlements. (Copyright: O. Cerasuolo and J. Tabolli)

FIGURE 9.4. Aerial view of part of the necropolis of the fortified settlement between via Boccea and via di Casalotti. (Copyright: A. De Santis)

THE FIRST SYSTEM

The most important sites belonging to the first system were Torre di Prima Porta (fig. 9.3: no. 6), near the via Tiberina;[22] Colle Sant'Agata (fig. 9.3: no. 8) on the via Triumphalis;[23] Acquafredda (fig. 9.3: no. 10), at the junction between the Fosso della Maglianella and the via Aurelia;[24] and Marmo Nuovo, in a more internal position along the via Triumphalis.[25] The recently discovered and excavated settlement near via Boccea and via di Casalotti (figs. 9.3: no. 9) belongs probably to this first system (fig. 9.4).[26] These settlements have similar characteristics: (a) their frequentation began around the mid-seventh century BCE and continued throughout the entire Archaic period, and in some case afterward; (b) they were all located on tufa hills not particularly high or naturally defended, requiring the construction of deep ditches around each settlement;

and (c) underground drainage systems with tunneling and *cuniculi* occurred at each, these mainly consisting of wells and tunnels that provided the water supply.

The locations of all these settlements, which had the same material culture as Veii and reflected its funerary architecture (especially Colle Sant'Agata and via Boccea–via Casalotti), attest the necessity for Veii to control this territory. These peripheral areas were in fact at that time under a constant pressure from Rome, which on several occasions attempted to expand on the western bank of the Tiber.[27]

THE SECOND SYSTEM

In the second system, it is evident that the sites followed a single scheme. These sites occupied (or reoccupied) isolated small plateaus along the most important rivers going north to south, such as the Fosso della Maglianella, the Fosso Galeria, and the Arrone, and especially their junctions with the most important roads of the region, the via Aurelia, the via Cornelia, and the via Triumphalis. The land they occupied rarely exceeded one hectare. The distribution of these sites with their necropoleis reveals the extensive utilization of the surrounding land and the effort to exert control throughout the territory. The most significant settlements are S. Rufina[28] and Monte Roncione[29] near the intersections between the Fosso Galeria and the via Cornelia and via Aurelia; and Poggio Verde on the via Triumphalis (fig. 9.3: no. 2).[30]

Monte Roncione is an example of these satellite sites of Veii during the Orientalizing and Archaic periods. The settlement was located on a small triangular tufa plateau (less than one hectare), which had steep vertical cliffs and dominated the Fosso Galeria, near the via Aurelia. In order to protect its northwestern side, a large ditch and a rampart were built (only a small part has been excavated). The morphology of the site (a plateau surrounded by steep walls) and its dominant location overlooking a river valley (implying the possibility of controlling a large portion of land) also inspired the Middle and Late Bronze Age settlement on the same site. The absence of a phase of this site dating to the Early Iron Age is an effect of the general abandonment of the territory during the formation of the proto-urban settlement of Veii.[31] The site was reoccupied in the first half of the seventh century BCE and continued to be inhabited for a long period, as evidenced by the Orientalizing, Archaic, Republican, Imperial, and medieval finds collected on its plateau and its western slopes.

Poggio Verde was a similar type of settlement, located in the eastern part of the territory of Veii along

FIGURE 9.5. *Kantharos* from the necropolis of via d'Avack, tomb 3. (Copyright: D. Rossi)

the via Triumphalis. Twenty-six chamber tombs have been excavated in its necropolis. The entrance corridors (*dromoi*) of the tombs were aligned in part to the via Triumphalis and in part to a secondary street that departed from the via Triumphalis and climbed the hill to reach the settlement. The tombs date from the Middle Orientalizing period to the beginning of the fifth century BCE. All the chamber tombs had small dimensions and were characterized by funerary benches and open-air *dromoi*. Inhumation was the funerary ritual in all the tombs. The tomb-groups reflect a middle-class community, as in most of the other Orientalizing burials at Veii and in the territory.

The small group of tombs discovered in modern via d'Avack probably belonged to a satellite site similar to the others in this second system of settlements. The site of via d'Avack is located along the ancient via Veientana, 4 kilometers distant from Piazza d'Armi. Seven chamber tombs with *dromoi* date to the Orientalizing period. Among the discoveries, most worthy of mention is the remarkable drinking cup (*kantharos*) from tomb 3, with complex incised decoration representing two cargo ships (fig. 9.5).[32] These ships, with long rudders, are shown amid Near Eastern mo-

tifs, with animals, human figures, and transport amphoras distributed in two different registers. The type
of amphoras represented here recall some of the finds
from the same necropolis, thus stressing the realistic
connection between the dead and ownership of trade
cargo. In fact, among the different characters, the representation of the figure of the ship-owner stands out.
This scene may be a confirmation of the connection of
Veii with sea trade that has always been suggested but
never proved by the archaeological record. It is fascinating to recall the words of Dionysios of Halikarnassos (2.55.4), describing the rich ships of Veii with their
precious goods: "and likewise their boats, which were
laden with great store of provisions."[33]

THE THIRD SYSTEM

From the seventh century BCE onward, all over southern Etruria, a widespread occupation of the countryside took place and continued through the later periods. In the territory of Veii, sporadic remains of groups
of finds attest the progressive and intensive occupation
of the land during the Orientalizing and Archaic periods. Cooking pots and other fragments of pottery used
in daily life testify to a widespread occupation of very
small sites. The tombs were organized in a gentilicial
scale, as shown by the chamber tombs discovered in
the area, especially at Pantano di Grano,[34] Prati Madonna,[35] and Cava ESI (*see map 1*).[36] During the sixth
century BCE, a continuous and systematic increase in
the numbers of groups repopulating the countryside is
evident in the numerous finds, indicating the presence
of settlements uniformly distributed throughout the
territory.[37] This colonization of the *ager* is probably to
be connected to the rise of rural communities, which
in the Archaic period consisted of domestic production facilities, real farms, and a new production system
organized on a larger scale, promoted and controlled
by the city of Veii.

The small necropolis of Pantano di Grano presents
all the characteristics of this type of settlement.[38] Excavations in 1983–1985 uncovered two chamber tombs
and two trench tombs dating to the Middle Orientalizing period (second half of the seventh century BCE)

FIGURE 9.6. Necropolis of Pantano di Grano, tomb 2
during excavation. (Copyright: A. De Santis)

and to the Archaic period (second half of the sixth
century BCE) (fig. 9.6). The spatial link between these
tombs and the consistency in the types of finds suggest
that they formed a single-family group, likely belonging to the aristocracy. These tombs confirm the conclusion of the process of consolidation of an aristocratic
class related to land ownership. The settlement would
have been located in the immediate vicinity, probably
on the same plateau from which comes domestic material that dates generally to the Orientalizing and Archaic periods.

Another small group of chamber tombs, dating to
the second half of the seventh century BCE, was discovered in 1986 on the hill located between the Fosso
di Volusia and the Fosso dell'Impiccato (modern via
Bracciano). These tombs can be linked to another rural
settlement.[39] Thanks to the discovery of an inscription

incised on an *aryballos*, the names and the status of the families living in the area are preserved, including Venel Satiu, who was considered to be a *homo novus*, "a new man."[40]

CONCLUSIONS

Taking into account all this evidence, the valley of the Fosso Galeria (with its tributaries), where most of the settlements were located, seems to have played a large role in the gradual occupation of the territory. All the settlements were located along the two banks of the river, within just a few kilometers of each other: Santa Rufina (fig. 9.3: no. 3), Quarto della Vipera, Monte Roncione (fig. 9.3: no. 4), Prati Madonna, Pantano di Grano (fig. 9.3: no. 5), and Monte Ficone. The reason lies probably in the economic role played by the river at this time. The Fosso Galeria flows into the Tiber at a spot where the Latin settlement of Ficana was located, on the opposite bank. Trade moved along this waterway in order to reach Latium Vetus (therefore somehow skipping Rome) and, from Ficana, reached Castel di Decima and then the coast, toward Lavinium, Ardea, Satricum, and Antium. The small settlements between Ficana and Decima, along the Fosso di Malafede (another important waterway), such as Casal Brunori, Torrino, and Colle S. Ciriaco,[41] dating between the end of the eighth and seventh centuries BCE, should be also related to this route. These sites controlled trade through economic and social exchanges among the leaders of the different communities.

The second-most important waterway corresponded to the valley of Cremera, which meets the Tiber in front of another Latin settlement, Fidenae. In this case as well, in the corresponding territory on the Latin bank of the Tiber, a number of sites are attested.[42]

All the evidence allows us to recognize in the territory of Veii, during the Orientalizing and the Archaic periods, a type of occupation of the land based on forms of distribution of the population, complementary to but also different from the contemporary internal organization of the town. The small villages were located in defensible and dominant positions, with different functions determined by their locations, and small settlements with their necropoleis, in which we can recognize the different stages of the development of the rural population, belonged to a political structure of the landscape depending entirely on Veii.

NOTES

1. De Santis 1997. See also chapters 6 and 7.
2. During the eighth century BCE the formation of "aristocratic" and "gentilicial" groups in the necropoleis occurred together with a societal transformation in which power started to be inherited among the different families (Bartoloni 2003). The leaders of the aristocratic families held a kind of "regal" power (De Santis 2005; see also chapter 7).
3. Bartoloni 2012.
4. Rizzo 1989; and see below.
5. Zifferero 2006.
6. Zifferero 2006.
7. Buranelli 1982.
8. Boitani 2003.
9. Adriani 1930.
10. Colini 1919:7.
11. Vighi 1935.
12. Colini 1919:7.
13. Delpino 2012.
14. Michetti and van Kampen 2014.
15. Stefani 1935; De Santis 2003.
16. Stefani 1928.
17. Boitani and Cerasuolo 2015.
18. Biblioteca dell'Istituto Nazionale di Archeologia e Storia dell'Arte: Manoscritti Lanciani 79: Bartoloni and Delpino 1979:19, pl. VI.
19. De Santis 1994:35 n. 5.
20. Biblioteca Apostolica Vaticana, *Carte Stefani* 21:54.
21. De Santis 1997.
22. Messineo 1987.
23. Caprino 1954; De Rossi 1981.
24. Damiani and Pacciarelli 2006.
25. De Santis 1997:102.
26. Unpublished excavation by A. De Santis and C. Sforzini. This settlement appears to have the characteristics of sites of the first system. Funerary architecture and ritual confirm that this site belongs to the territory of Veii.
27. De Santis 1997.
28. Brunetti Nardi 1972.
29. Cardarelli et al. 1984:34–40; De Santis 1997:104–107.
30. De Cristofaro and Santolini Giordani 2005.
31. See chapters 5, 6, 7, and 8.
32. Arizza et al. 2013.
33. Translation by the authors. Bartoloni forthcoming. See also chapter 8.
34. De Santis 1997.

35. Radmilli 1951–1952.

36. Unpublished excavation by A. P. Anzidei.

37. De Cristofaro and Rossi 2008.

38. De Santis 1997:108–141.

39. Carbonara, Messineo, and Pellegrino 1996.

40. Maras 2007.

41. Pisani Sartorio and Quilici Gigli 1984; Bedini 1985; Quilici Gigli 1986; Bedini 1988–1989.

42. Quilici and Quilici Gigli 1980:278–285; 1986:368–388.

BIBLIOGRAPHY

Adriani, A. 1930. "Veio. Macchia della Comunità." *NSc* 1930: 46–56.

Arizza, M., A. De Cristofaro, A. Piergrossi, and D. Rossi. 2013. "La tomba di un aristocratico *naukleros* dall'agro veientano: Il *kantharos* con scena di navigazione di via d'Avack." *ArchCl* 64:51–131.

Bartoloni, G. 2003. *Le società dell'Italia primitiva: Lo studio delle necropoli e la nascita delle aristocrazie.* Rome.

———. 2012. "Il tumulo Chigi e gli altri tumuli veienti." In *L'Olpe Chigi: Storia di un agalma. Atti del Convegno Internazionale (Salerno 2010)*, ed. E. Mugione, 19–27. Ergasteria 2. Salerno.

———. Forthcoming. "The Tiber between Latins and Etruscans." In *Frontiers in the Iron Age Archaeology of Europe. Cambridge, 20–22 September 2013.*

Bartoloni, G., A. Berardinetti, L. Drago, and A. De Santis. "Veio tra IX e VI secolo a.C.: Primi risultati sull'analisi comparata delle necropoli veienti." *ArchCl* 46:29–40.

Bartoloni, G., and F. Delpino. 1979. *Veio* I: *Introduzione allo studio delle necropoli arcaiche di Veio: Il sepolcreto di Valle La Fata. MonAnt* 1. Rome.

Bedini, A. 1985. "Tre corredi protostorici dal Torrino: Osservazioni sull'affermarsi e la funzione delle aristocrazie terriere dell'VIII secolo a. C. nel Lazio." *Archeologia Laziale* 7:44–63. *QuadAEI* 11.

———. 1988–1989. "Tor de' Cenci (Roma): Tombe protostoriche." *NSc* 1988–89:221–282.

Boitani, F. 2003. "Necropoli di Monte Michele, la tomba principesca." In *Formello*, 81–84.

Boitani, F., and O. Cerasuolo. 2015. "Novità sull'orientalizzante veiente dalla necropoli di Oliveto Grande." In *Novità*, 133–141.

Brunetti Nardi, G. 1972. *Repertorio degli scavi e delle scoperte archeologiche nell'Etruria meridionale (1966–1970).* Rome.

Buranelli, F. 1982. "Un'iscrizione etrusca arcaica dalla tomba V di Riserva del Bagno a Veio." *StEtr* 50:91–102.

Caprino, C. 1954. "Roma (Via Trionfale): I ritrovamenti di Innocenzo dall'Osso sul colle S. Agata a Monte Mario." *NSc* 1954:195–268.

Carbonara, A., G. Messineo, and A. Pellegrino. 1996. *La necropoli etrusca di Volusia.* Rome.

Cardarelli, A., I. Damiani, M. Pacciarelli, and A. C. Saltini. 1984. "Ricognizioni di superficie F. 22 N." In *Preistoria e Protostoria nel territorio di Roma*, ed. A. M. Bietti Sestieri, 34–46. Rome.

Colini, G. A. 1919. "Veio: Scavi nell'area della città e della necropoli." *NSc* 1919:3–12.

Damiani, I., and M. Pacciarelli. 2006. "L'insediamento di Acquafredda e l'occupazione rurale del territorio tra Roma, Caere e Veio dal primo Ferro all'età arcaica." In *La Fattoria e la villa dell'Auditorium nel quartiere Flaminio di Roma*, ed. A. Carandini, M. T. D'Alessio, and H. Di Giuseppe, 511–556. Bulletino della Commissione archeologica comunale di Roma 14. Rome.

De Cristofaro, A., and D. Rossi. 2008. "Dagli Etruschi ai Romani (VII–I secolo a.C.)." In *Archeologia a Massimina: Frammenti di storia del suburbio romano da un quartiere sulla via Aurelia*, ed. D. Rossi Diana and A. Piergrossi, 51–58. Rome.

De Cristofaro, A., and R. Santolini Giordani. 2005. "Roma, località Poggioverde: Una necropoli etrusca sulla via Trionfale." In *Dinamiche*, 164–172.

Delpino, F. 2012. "La tomba Campana e la sua scoperta." In *MAV*, 97–102.

De Rossi, G. 1981. "Topografia antica di Monte Mario." *ArchCl* 33:31–37.

De Santis, A. 1997. "Alcune considerazioni sul territorio veiente in età orientalizzante e arcaica." In *Necropoli arcaiche*, 101–141.

———. 2003. "Necropoli di Vaccareccia, il tumulo." In *Formello*, 84–99.

———. 2005. "Da capi guerrieri a principi: La strutturazione del potere politico nell'Etruria proto urbana." In *Dinamiche*, 615–631.

Drago Troccoli, L. 2009. "Veio tra villanoviano e tardo arcaismo: Appunti sulla necropoli di Casale del Fosso." In *Etruria e Italia preromana. Studi in onore di Giovannangelo Camporeale*, ed. S. Bruni, 327–370. Studia Erudita 4. Pisa.

Maras, D. F. 2007. "Note in margine a *CIE* II,1,5." *StEtr* 73: 237–247.

Messineo, G. 1987. "La torre di Prima Porta." *Archeologia Laziale* 8:130–134. *QuadAEI* 14.

Michetti, L., and I. van Kampen, eds. 2014. *Il Tumulo di Monte Aguzzo a Veio e la collezione Chigi: Ricostruzione del contesto dell'Olpe Chigi e note sulla formazione della Collezione Archeologica della famiglia Chigi a Formello. MonAnt* 16. Rome.

Pisani Sartorio, G., and S. Quilici Gigli. 1984. "Trovamenti arcaici nel territorio Laurentino: Annotazioni di topografia e prospettive di ricerca." *BullCom* 89.1:9–26.

Quilici, L., and S. Quilici Gigli. 1980. *Crustumerium.* Rome.

———. 1986. *Fidenae.* Rome.

Quilici Gigli, S. 1986. "Scali e traghetti sul Tevere in epoca arcaica." In *Il Tevere e le altre vie d'acqua del Lazio antico. Archeologia Laziale* 7.2:71–89. *QuadAEI* 12.

Radmilli, A. M. 1951–1952. "Prati Madonna—Via Aurelia." *BPI* 8:78–79.

Rizzo, M. A. 1989. "Veio: Tomba Campana." In *Pittura etrusca al Museo di Villa Giulia* (exh. cat.), ed. M. A. Rizzo, 109–111. Rome.

Stefani, E. 1928. "Veio: Scoperta di antichi sepolcri nella tenuta di Monte Oliviero presso Prima Porta." *NSc* 1928:95–105.

———. 1935. "Veio: Esplorazione del tumulo di Vaccareccia." *NSc* 1935:329–361.

Vighi, R. 1935. "Veio: Scavi nella necropoli degli alunni dell'anno 1927–28 del Corso di Topografia dell'Italia Antica della R. Università di Roma." *NSc* 1935:39–68.

Zifferero, A. 2006. "Circoli di pietre, tumuli e culto funerario: La formazione dello spazio consacrato in Etruria settentrionale tra età del Ferro e alto arcaismo." *MÉFRA* 118:117–213.

CHAPTER 10

VEII AND THE GREEKS

FRANCESCA BOITANI

THE EARLIEST CONTACTS

The discovery of thousands of trench tombs and well-tombs (*tombe a pozzo*) in the Villanovan necropoleis of Veii has brought to light an impressive amount of brown impasto pottery decorated with incised and impressed motifs. From the beginning of the eighth century BCE, in some of these tombs fine ware and wheel-made pottery with geometric decorations are present. Double-handled cups (*skyphoi*) were the earliest shapes, decorated with semicircles or with short vertical tracks (chevrons). Later cups, still dating within the eighth century BCE, had a decoration consisting of birds and lozenges (the "one-bird *skyphoi*"; fig. 10.1).

These Middle and Late Geometric vases, produced mainly on the Greek island of Euboea, were first imported to Veii and then reached Rome and the area of Latium Vetus closest to the Tiber. Their arrival dates before 770 BCE, when the Euboean colony of Ischia (Pithekoussai) was founded. Right after this date, these vessels appeared in most of central Tyrrhenian Italy, at Caere, Tarquinia, and Pontecagnano.[1]

Veii, like Rome, was favored by its fortunate location in the region of the Tiber and was involved in the earliest trade activities. Sailors from Euboea and the Cyclades—competing with the more expert Phoenician merchants, who had been sailing in this sea since the end of the ninth century BCE—moved west, probably seeking the abundant raw metals that came from mines in the Tyrrhenian area. Local craftsmen soon began to imitate new ceramic techniques, including the use of the pottery wheel. This phenomenon demonstrates that the communities of Veii and of southern Etruria in general were ready to receive innovative cultural input from abroad. They also learned new metal-working and goldsmithing technologies from foreign artisans, who probably had permanently settled in Etruria. New cultural trends, which were to have a great success in later periods, slowly appeared. The above-mentioned Geometric cups were used in ceremonial drinking of wine, which was a distinctive custom of the Etruscan aristocracy. These cups are evidence that the high-status members of the community quickly imitated the Greek habit of the *symposium* ("drinking together"), in which participants acknowledged their membership in the same social group and aimed to establish solidarity bonds. These cups, according to some scholars, might also have appeared in Etruria and Latium Vetus with the introduction of Greek wine, a substitute for the local protohistoric beverage (*temetum*) made from wild vines.[2]

ORIENTALIZING MERCHANTS

During the Orientalizing period, in the last decades of the eighth and the beginning of the seventh century BCE, a large number of settlers from Chalcis moved to southern Italy and eastern Sicily. The continuous and frequent contacts with Hellenic cultural models, which had been re-elaborated from sumptuous Near Eastern customs, transformed the lifestyle and funerary customs of Etruscan aristocratic families, which attained high social status and political prestige at this time.

FIGURE 10.1. One-bird *skyphos*, Casal del Fosso,
tomb 983. Civita Castellana, Museo archeologico dell'Agro
Falisco, inv. 37055. (Copyright: F. Boitani)

Veii was a prosperous center during this period but did not reach the same level of opulence that characterized other southern Etruscan towns, such as Caere.[3] In the first half of the seventh century BCE, the prestigious burials at Veii contained Etruscan Geometric pottery, produced by artisans trained by Greek masters who settled in the Euboean colonies in the Gulf of Naples.[4]

THE NARCE PAINTER, A VEIENTINE WORKSHOP

An important personality among this group of craftsmen was the Narce Painter, named for early discoveries of his productions in the nearby Ager Faliscus.[5] More than forty masterpieces (some of them only recently attributed to this artist) derived from his workshop, in which many other craftsmen probably were active. The style of these vases allows us to date their production between 700 and 660 BCE. They included many amphoras and jars (*ollae*), the most common shapes of pottery, and some plates, a *pyxis*, a *kotyle*, and even a rare ram's-headed jug, endowed with a filter to purify wine, now displayed at the British Museum in London.[6] The figures represented in the decorations and the numerous geometric patterns were derived from Greece and imitate the Attic Late Geometric style. The most common figures were lions with wide-open jaws, horses with rich manes, deer with small tails, and long lines of fowls with curvy bodies and heart-shaped heads.

A jar on which a "monster-lion" was painted—probably an early production of this master (*plate 4*)—

was found in the Tomb of the Roaring Lions, which is the earliest-known example of funerary painting in Etruria (*map 4:A*).[7] The same iconography is attested in the painted decoration of this tomb. Two other jars come from a slightly later painted tomb, the Tomb of the Ducks (*map 4:J*), and show lines of fowls (*plate 9*), which have been attributed to a more recent phase of production of the same workshop.[8] Although these similar motifs are recognized in different mediums, we cannot assume that the ceramists painted the two large wall paintings as well.[9]

THE CRANE PAINTER

Recently, many new examples of Orientalizing ceramic production were discovered at Veii, in a great number of different styles and forms. Among them, the vases attributed to the Crane Painter are of particular interest.[10] This artist excelled in pottery production at Caere from the beginning of the seventh century BCE. It is easy to recognize his hand in at least three examples at Veii, as they show the two distinctive elements of his ways of painting: the winged griffin and the large tree with lush, leafy branches. Vases attributed to his workshop date to the mid-seventh century BCE or a little later, suggesting that some artisans moved from the workshop in Caere to Veii, in order to meet increasing demands of local customers.[11]

A GIFT FROM CORINTH IN THE TUMULUS OF MONTE AGUZZO

From the mid-seventh century BCE and for about one hundred years, Corinthian pottery prevailed over other Greek imported ceramics in Etruria. Proto-Corinthian pottery had already been circulating from Euboea, especially around 650 BCE, a situation that calls to mind the well-known story of the merchant Demaratus. He was a member of a noble Corinthian family and later the father of a king of Rome, Tarquinius Priscus. According to Pliny,[12] Demaratus settled in Tarquinia, bringing with him a team of three artisans (whose names seem allegorical rather than specific to real historical persons) expert in crafts (Eucheir), in painting (Eugrammos), and in architecture (Diopos).[13]

Proto-Corinthian imports were quite rare at Veii, but a masterpiece of this production, dating to 640 BCE, was found in the princely tumulus of Monte Aguzzo. This is one of the largest tumuli ever discovered in Etruria (*map 2: no. 1*) and was excavated in 1882 by Rodolfo Lanciani. According to recent studies, it belonged to the Pepuna family; this name occurs on some vases discovered in the tomb.[14] The impressive dimensions of its mound (more than 60 meters in diameter) made it a landmark visible from most of the territory of Veii, more than three miles from the urban town. The tumulus was the burial place of an important nucleus of the Veientine aristocracy, which probably lived nearby and controlled a large portion of the land and trade along the valley. Inside the tumulus, a large chamber built of massive squared tufa blocks consisted of two cells and a long *dromos*.[15] The earliest burial within the tumulus dates immediately after the mid-seventh century BCE.

The famous Chigi Vase, preserved and displayed at the Villa Giulia museum, has been assigned to this earlier burial.[16] This exceptional vase is an *olpe* ("jug"; *plate 5*) decorated with various friezes, one immediately above the other. It was painted very skillfully in miniature style in the polychrome technique. The contours and details of the figures were defined by fine engraved lines, and the colors were painted over one another to achieve different effects.

The decorative scheme of the vase includes themes of high symbolic value to Corinthian elites. The most recent readings of the jug recognize the lifestyle of Corinthian aristocrats in the different scenes painted on the three registers.[17] The younger members of the elite (*epheboi*) are shown learning to hunt hare and fox in the lower register. In the middle register the figures are engaged in lion hunting, an activity associated with kingship in the Near East. Finally, warriors fighting in a battle—reflecting the emergence of hoplites—are shown in the upper register (*plate 6*). The mythical episode of the judgment of Paris also appears in the middle register, a reference to another "challenge"—that is, marriage—that constituted as fundamental a rite of passage for aristocrats as hunting and fighting in war.

The Chigi Vase would have been used to pour wine into cups during banquets, and it was almost certainly meant for Greek customers. It was probably given as a gift during a funerary ceremony in the tumulus in honor of the Etruscan prince buried there. That individual might have recognized aspects of his own political, social, and cultural beliefs in the images of this vase.

THE HOUNDS PAINTER AT QUARANTA RUBBIE

A slightly earlier *olpe* by the Hounds Painter (ca. 650 BCE) is also a fine late Proto-Corinthian import.[18] An uncommon "black-polychrome" technique was used to decorate this vase. The image on the shoulder is a lion biting a bull, rendered in white and purple painting on a black background. This jug was found in 1926 in a rich tomb, with multiple burials, excavated at Quaranta Rubbie, north of Veii. In this tomb, several transport containers—including two Attic "sos" amphoras for oil and an East Greek amphora, which rarely appeared at Veii—were found together with another Late Proto-Corinthian jug. The earliest local imitations of these peculiar Corinthian productions were found in this tomb as well.

These vases were made by the Castellani Master in Veii between 630 and 620 BCE.[19] He was a local ceramicist who used the polychrome technique for small vases, such as *aryballoi* for perfumed oils (fig. 10.2). He opened a promising workshop, producing *olpai* with complex decorations in scales that were common in Latium Vetus and in the Ager Faliscus. With his brilliant works, this master began a systematic imitation of Corinthian pottery and contributed to the beginning of the massive production of Etrusco-Corinthian ceramics in southern Etruria, with the most important workshop in Vulci. Thousands of vases were produced on an industrial scale, up until the middle of the sixth century BCE. All of them have been recently classified according to the different craftsmen and workshops.[20]

THE *DOKANON* OF OLIVETO GRANDE

A unique masterpiece, dating between the end of the seventh and the beginning of the sixth century BCE,

FIGURE 10.2. *Aryballos* painted
by the Castellani Master.
(Copyright: F. Boitani)

FIGURE 10.3. Fragment of the *dokanon*, representing
a rooster, discovered in the tomb of Oliveto Grande.
(Copyright: F. Boitani and O. Cerasuolo)

was recently found in a rich hypogeum beside the tumulus of Oliveto Grande (*map 2: nos. 6–7*). It is an extraordinary funerary altar—*dokanon*—made of more than ten bronze plates very finely decorated in repoussé with figures and ornamental patterns (*fig. 8.5*). It was also decorated with elements in the shape of a horse-headed man and a rooster (fig. 10.3). That altar represented—together with the contemporary famous paintings in the Campana Tomb (*map 4:C*)—one of the final products of the Late Orientalizing style in Veii, which imitates prototypes from Corinth and follows the Greek Orientalizing style.[21]

FROM ARCHAIC GREECE TO VEII

In the sixth century BCE, the finest vases from the Kerameikos (Potters' Quarter) of Athens, along with more rare East Greek, Laconian, and Chalcidian vases, were imported to Etruria through the harbors of Vulci, Caere, and Tarquinia. Traders first from Ionia, and at

the end of that century from the island of Aegina, reached those ports, taking part in the important trade between Greece and the West. The trade routes do not seem to have reached Veii during the Archaic and Classical periods. In fact, the city of Veii reveals in its burials, like Rome, a widespread austerity because of the Archaic funerary laws.[22] That is very likely to have reduced the demand for imported pottery coming from the most prestigious Attic workshops, since people could not exhibit such objects in their burials. From now on these vases occur only in the sanctuaries.

In the famous sanctuary of Portonaccio (*map 4:S*), sacred to Menerva—where the large temple and its statues can be compared to the sanctuary of Delphi—three large Attic vases for wine consumption were discovered among the votive offerings. These date to the last two decades of the sixth century BCE. A black-figure *dinos* by the Antimenes Painter was decorated with images of two warships inside the vase rim. These ships were painted in such a manner as to create the illusion that they were moving among the waves when the vase was filled with wine and water, according to the Greek tradition. A second red-figure *dinos*, attributed to the Pan Painter, and a huge spiral-shaped crater with red figures, by the Nikoxenos Painter, were discovered in the same votive deposit.[23] All of these vessels are displayed at the Villa Giulia museum and represent the most important imports to reach Veii from Greece during the Archaic and Classical periods.

During the fifth century BCE, the exceptional role of Veii as a center of art and craft production suffered because of its continuous wars with Rome. The direct and indirect interactions with the Greeks that characterized this town from the time of the Early Iron Age began to decrease and ended completely at the time of the Roman conquest in 396 BCE.

NOTES

1. Boitani 2005:319; Rizzo 2005:333; D'Agostino 1999:13.
2. Bartoloni, Acconcia, and ten Kortenaar 2012:201.
3. Martelli 2008:121; Torelli 2000:141.
4. Neri 2010.
5. See most recently Bonadies et al. 2015; Conti and Giuliani 2016.
6. Williams 2009: fig. 1.
7. See chapter 21.
8. Drago et al. 2014:7.
9. Colonna 1989:19; Martelli 2008:14; Drago et al. 2014:48.
10. On the Crane Painter see Neri 2010:244–252.
11. Boitani, Biagi, and Neri 2014:69–80. The only fragment by the Crane Painter discovered in the urban area of Veii was found during the excavation around the walls of Piazza d'Armi.
12. Pliny, *Nat. Hist.* 35.43.153.
13. Torelli and Menichetti 1997:625.
14. *CIE* II, 1.5, 6672. See Maras 2007.
15. Michetti and van Kampen 2014.
16. D'Acunto 2013; Torelli 2007:64.
17. D'Acunto 2013.
18. Rizzo 1990:43–44.
19. Martelli 1987:269.
20. Szilàgyi 1992, 1998.
21. Boitani and Cerasuolo 2015:133.
22. See chapter 12.
23. Baglione 2011:95.

BIBLIOGRAPHY

Baglione, M. P. 2011. "Funzione dei grandi donari attici di Veio-Portonaccio." In *Corollari. Scritti di antichità etrusche ed italiche in omaggio all'opera di Giovanni Colonna*, ed. D. Maras, 95–101. Pisa.

Bartoloni, G., V. Acconcia, and S. ten Kortenaar. 2012. "Viticoltura e consumo del vino in Etruria: La cultura materiale tra la fine dell'età del Ferro e l'Orientalizzante Antico." In *Archeologia della vite e del vino in Toscana e nel Lazio: Dalle tecniche dell'indagine archeologica alle prospettive della biologia molecolare*, ed. A. Ciacci, P. Rendine, and A. Zifferero, 201–275. Florence.

Boitani, F. 2005. "Le più antiche ceramiche greche e di tipo greco a Veio." In *Oriente e Occidente: Metodi e discipline a confronto. Riflessioni sulla cronologia dell'età del Ferro in Italia. Atti dell'incontro di studi, Roma, 2003*, ed. G. Bartoloni and F. Delpino, 319–332. Mediterranea 1. Pisa.

Boitani, F., F. Biagi, and S. Neri. 2014. "Amphores de table étrusco-géométriques d'époque orientalisante à Véies." In *Les potiers d'Étrurie et leur monde: Contacts, échanges, transferts. Hommage à M. A. Del Chiaro*, ed. L. Ambrosini and V. Jolivet, 69–80. Paris.

Boitani, F., and O. Cerasuolo. 2015. "Novità del tardo-orientalizzante veiente dalla necropoli di Oliveto Grande." In *Novità*, 133–141.

Bonadies, M., A. Carapellucci, L. Drago, L. Paolini, and C. Predan. 2015. "Novità sul Pittore di Narce a Veio." In *Novità*, 193–195.

Colonna, G. 1989. "Gli Etruschi e l''invenzione' della pittura." In *Pittura etrusca al Museo di Villa Giulia nelle foto di Takashi Okamura*, ed. M. A. Rizzo, 18–25. Rome.

Conti, A., and B. Giuliani. 2016. "Rileggendo un holmos in 'white-on-red' da Narce: Suggestioni tiberine." In *I Falisci attraverso lo specchio*, ed. M. C. Biella and J. Tabolli, 93–116. Officina Etruscologia 13. Rome.

D'Acunto, M. 2013. *Il mondo del vaso Chigi: Pittura, guerra e società a Corinto alla metà del VII secolo a.C.* Berlin.

D'Agostino, B. 1999. "La ceramica greca e di tipo greco dalle necropoli della Prima Età del Ferro di Pontecagnano." In *Prima di Pithecusa: I più antichi materiali greci del Golfo di Salerno* (exh. cat.), ed. G. Bailo Modesti and P. Gastaldi, 13–24. Naples.

Drago, L., M. Bonadies, A. Carapellucci, and C. Predan. 2014. "Il Pittore di Narce e i suoi epigoni a Veio." *ArchCl* 45:7–58.

Maras, D. F. 2007. "Note in margine al *CIE* II, 1, 5." *StEtr* 73: 237–247.

Martelli, M., ed. 1987. *La ceramica degli Etruschi*. Novara.

———. 2008. "Il fasto delle metropoli dell'Etruria meridionale: Importazioni, imitazioni e arte suntuaria." In *Etruschi: Le antiche metropoli del Lazio* (exh. cat.), ed. M. Torelli and A. M. Moretti Sgubini, 121–139. Verona.

Michetti, L. M., and I. van Kampen, eds. 2014. *Il Tumulo di Monte Aguzzo a Veio e la Collezione Chigi. Ricostruzione del contesto dell'olpe Chigi e note sulla formazione della Collezione archeologica della famiglia Chigi a Formello.* MonAnt 16. Rome.

Neri, S. 2010. *Il tornio e il pennello: Ceramica depurata di tradizione geometrica di epoca orientalizzante in Etruria meridionale (Veio, Cerveteri, Tarquinia, Vulci).* Officina Etruscologia 2. Rome.

Rizzo, M. A. 1990. *Le anfore da trasporto e il commercio etrusco arcaico, 1: Complessi tombali dall'Etruria meridionale.* Rome.

———. 2005. "Ceramica geometrica greca e di tipo greco da Cerveteri (dalla necropoli del Laghetto e dall'abitato)." In *Oriente e Occidente: Metodi e discipline a confronto. Riflessioni sulla cronologia dell'età del Ferro italiana, (Atti Convegno Roma 2003)*, ed. G. Bartoloni and F. Delpino, 333–378. Mediterranea 1. Pisa.

Szilàgyi, J. G. 1992. *Ceramica etrusco-corinzia figurata, 1: 630–580 a.C.* Florence.

———. 1998. *Ceramica etrusco-corinzia figurata, 2: 590/580–550 a.C.* Florence.

Torelli, M. 2000. "L'ellenizzazione della società e della cultura etrusca." In *Gli Etruschi* (exh. cat.), ed. M. Torelli, 141–155. Milan.

———. 2007. *Le strategie di Kleitias: Composizione e programma figurativo del vaso François.* Milan.

Torelli, M., and M. Menichetti, eds. 1997. "Attorno a Demarato." In *Corinto e l'Occidente. Atti XXXIV Convegno di Studi sulla Magna Grecia (Taranto 1994)*, ed. G. De Sensi Sestito and M. Intrieri, 625–654. Taranto.

Williams, D. 2009. "The Ridgway Ram Vase." In *Etruscan by Definition. Studies in Honour of Sybille Haynes*, ed. J. Swaddling and P. Perkins, 21–24. London.

CHAPTER 11

VEII AND THE NEAR EAST

ANNETTE RATHJE

Veii has long awaited a comprehensive analysis of its cross-cultural connections. Other Etruscan cities have been given a prominent position in the scientific dialogue, but new evidence put forward by the Veii Project along with a reconsideration of older finds has given us quite a different view of this important site in the Orientalizing period, a time when Veii had a small royal Etruscan court.[1] The Orientalizing phenomenon is not a sudden event, as we are dealing with a long period, from at least the ninth century BCE onward, when there were long-distance connections involving multinational entrepreneurial expansion.[2]

VEII AND TRANSMARINE TRADE AND EXCHANGE

It is rightly stressed by the scholars who published the *kantharos* from the necropolis of via d'Avack in the territory of Veii that its representation of the figure of the shipowner must lead to a revision of our perception of Veii and the sea in the period in question (*see fig. 9.5*).[3] It is commonly believed that Veii controlled the Lower Tiber Valley in the Iron Age, as various finds suggest. The Ripa Veientana would have been an important borderline, too, as it controlled access to the salt-pans at the mouth of the Tiber.[4]

Efforts must be made to find some traces of the ancient harbor site belonging to Veii. This will be a difficult endeavor, because there may be very little permanent material evidence, as boats and ships could simply be drawn up onto the beach. We can imagine a

Veientine counterbalance to the Latin town of Ficana (*map 1*). It does not need to be a settlement and could indeed even be a market connected to a sanctuary. Knowledge of the harbor location will be an important addition to our understanding, because Veii had a first-hand, active role in maritime exchange and the interactions of aristocrats, sailors, traders, and artisans. It is telling that representations of ships have been found in the same number at Veii as at Tarquinia and Vulci.[5]

We know that our archaeological finds represent only a small fraction of what once existed and that we have mostly only circumstantial evidence provided by finds of goods that circulated in the Mediterranean, such as textiles (whether garments or utilitarian items), wooden objects (like furniture), solid food and foodstuffs, liquids (wine, oils, and perfumes), spices and incense, and live animals (exotic specimens and horses). These items, animals, and substances were critical components of Mediterranean trade and the chains of gift exchange.[6]

IMPORTS AT VEII

From tombs of this period at Veii we have evidence of the movements of goods, ideas, and technologies and of people. Actual imports start with Egypto-Phoenician amulets and small figures of faïence.[7] These have been compared to Venetian glass beads in the colonial trade of the seventeenth century CE, although we are not sure of their significance. Do they represent an affection for the exotic or a transforma-

FIGURE 11.1. Lion-headed bronze vessel from the Casale del Fosso necropolis, eighth century BCE. Museo di Villa Giulia, Rome. (Photo courtesy of the Soprintendenza Archeologia per i Beni Archeologici dell'Etruria Meridionale)

tion and construction of new tradition? Removed from their original religious context, were they used at Veii as mere ornaments?

ASSYRIAN GOODS

Most significant for this discussion is an Assyrian beaker or bucket from the Casale del Fosso necropolis (*map 3*), unfortunately with no exact provenience. It is made of double-walled bronze, and the bottom has the shape of a roaring lion's head (fig. 11.1).[8] We know of this bucket type from the royal tombs at Gordion,[9] and close analysis of the wall decoration of the palace of Sargon II (722–705 BCE) at Khorsabad shows at least two different kinds of lion-headed vessels as well as members of the Assyrian elite who are seen sitting (dignitaries) or standing (rulers) and raising lion-headed beakers in the banquet scenes of rooms II and VII.[10] The Assyrian king is never seen drinking from this kind of vessel, but eunuch attendants are carrying buckets to the king in room VI and on façade L;[11] each person carries two such vessels, one pointing up and one down, as the left arm is outstretched and the right arm is bent. In the doorway to room II attendants are seen scooping a beverage from a large cauldron.[12] On a relief from Khorsabad now in Baghdad (fig. 11.2)[13] a

FIGURE 11.2. Decoration in the palace of Sargon II (722–705 BCE) at Khorsabad. (After Deller 1985: pl. 30)

eunuch carries a lion-headed vessel with both hands, covering part of it with his right hand, as if to protect its contents.

We presume that this Assyrian bronze vessel found at Veii was transferred to the west together with other items as a result of the connections between Phoenician artisans and traders and the Assyrian court.

CUPS FOR DRINKING AMONG THE ELITE

Similar to these vessels are the hemispherical bowls that are carried in both the right and the left hands of foreign tributaries at Khorsabad.[14] These hemispheri-

FIGURE 11.3. Silver bowl, from Casale del Fosso tomb 804, eighth century BCE. Museo di Villa Giulia, Rome. (Copyright: L. Drago)

cal cups are made of various materials, including precious metal, bronze, glass, and ostrich egg, and they are imitated in bronze as well as clay in different ceramic classes.[15] At Veii they have been found in two princely tombs from the end of the eighth century or beginning of the seventh century BCE at the Casale del Fosso necropolis (fig. 11.3).[16] Tomb 804 was found disturbed when excavated in 1915, and although only fragments have survived, it is quite clear that it belonged to a highly important lady, who was lavishly dressed with clothing embroidered and ornamented with beads of glass and gold foil when she was carried to her last destination to be interred.[17] The rich finds evoke a comparison with the famous Regolini-Galassi Tomb at Caere, now magnificently exhibited in the Vatican Museums in Rome.[18]

The other tomb, 871,[19] is one of a pair and contained the inhumation of a young man who also belonged to the upper echelons of society. It has been noted that many of these cups were connected to prominent females in central Italy,[20] but they occur with both sexes. In the Near East, kings, queens, and courtiers are represented holding them at parties and ceremonies, and they also appear in scenes at Khorsabad, carried as tribute by male foreigners.[21] At the very end of the Orientalizing period, we find them on the banquet scene from Murlo, Poggio Civitate,[22] where the hemispherical bowls are held by male participants.

A SYMBOL OF INTERACTION

Tomb 871 also contained bronze *paterae*, that is, ribbed or fluted bowls[23]—which are another symbol of interaction among the various cultures of the Mediterranean. F. Sciacca has contributed much to our understanding with his monograph on this metal vessel type that circulated from Luristan (in western Iran) to Iberia and had a great impact in Italy.[24] The type was widely imported and imitated in both metal and clay, indicating that the craftspeople had a direct knowledge of the prototypes. The *patera* from tomb 871 at Casale del Fosso is considered to be of Assyrian production and is one of the oldest imports to Italy. Originally there were two examples, evidently found in separate locations in that tomb.

The central role of Assyria regarding the form and ideology around this vessel type has been confirmed. But the artistic and cultural relations of the production area to the Near East are far from understood, including such questions as the formation of taste at the Assyrian court; these circulated objects are often the spoils of war or plunder, rather than being reflective of aesthetic choices. In addition, some of these vessels are considered to be Near Eastern products or even invented by Phoenician immigrants. The Neo-Assyrian period (900–612 BCE) shows an integration of non-Assyrians from throughout the empire into all levels of Assyrian society and an adoption of rites and costumes.

TRACKING INTERACTIONS

Two more items from tomb 871 should be mentioned here. Although they are not imports, they illustrate the impact and importance at Veii of signs of rank and power.[25] The first is a fan in sheet bronze of Etruscan manufacture.[26] The late Pia Guldager analyzed fans from central Italy, stressing the important role of Veii, from which we have some of the earliest items of the eighth century BCE.[27] The fan has a long life in the Near East, the Middle East, and Egypt. This object could be used to cool an individual, to waft incense around kings, to keep away flies, and in connection with purifying rituals.[28] Representations show such instruments being carried and used by attendants to circulate air around either persons or solid food and liquids, at both secular and ritual events.

The next item is a footstool decorated with sheet bronze.[29] Although it is now in fragments, there can be no doubt about its form and function. Once again we are dealing with a well-known object used by kings, queens, and elites in the Near East, and it is highly significant to find such items in Italy in the so-called princely tombs. It is equally notable that an early sculpture type in Etruria resembles statues from the Neo-Hittite area (northern Syria) representing persons sitting on thrones with their feet placed on footstools.[30] A fragment of such a statue has been found in the Picazzano necropolis of Veii (*see fig. 22.1*), and once again we can recall the later representation on the reliefs from Murlo.[31] We are not able to tell if the person represented at Veii was male or female, but the fragment suggests an honorific context for an important individual.

FEASTING AND THE IMPACT OF THE NEAR EAST

The objects mentioned above point to the ambitions, demands, and desires of local elites, who accepted technical changes as social capital and made aesthetic adjustments to their symbols of prestige. The imports stress the importance of feasting and celebrating together using foreign utensils at events—whether secular or religious—and they represent practices of consumption and manifestation of rituals.

From annals, letters, and other documents we learn that the Assyrian kings were famous for their collections of objects (ivory furniture, metal, glass and stone vessels) and living entities such as plants and animals. This collecting behavior is represented on the stone reliefs that adorned their palaces, where the kings were "symbolically magnifying their power."[32]

ACCEPTANCE AND SELECTION

We have no evidence of what the Etruscans may have written about themselves; we are left to decipher the function and meanings of objects and to decode their nonverbal communications. New finds from Veii and publication of the old finds will help us to achieve a much clearer understanding of the acceptance, selection, and hybridism that took place in the networks of the Mediterranean. In Etruria cultural symbols were needed to hold power; the elite surrounded themselves with objects that were associated with power, and constructed it from the ideas of locals and Etruscans who traveled, as well as foreign visitors and immigrants. No doubt practices of cooking, drinking, and feasting were an important aspect of societal interactions. We must not forget, however, that objects could often be multifunctional; it requires great skill to understand the image left to us, an image that contained a contextual meaning when produced as well as a meaning in the mind of the viewers.

NOTES

1. Sciacca 2005:316; van Kampen 2012; De Santis 2012; Drago 2005:95. Cf. Hesiod, *Theogony* 1011–1016.

2. D'Agostino 2010:78; Rathje 2010. See also chapter 8.

3. Arizza et al. 2013:115–119. See also chapter 9.

4. See chapters 6 and 7.

5. Arizza et al. 2013:116.

6. As can be learned from written sources like Ezekiel 27; for a critical position regarding Near Eastern trade, see Fletcher 2012.

7. Sciacca 2010a:55–57.

8. Sciacca 2003; Drago 2005:119.

9. Radner 2013.

10. Albenda 1986: pl. 121 (room II), pls. 88–89 (room VII); Álvarez-Mon 2008; Gaspa (2014:25–33) has collected useful evidence for the terminology surrounding these important vessels.

11. Albenda 1986: pl. 66 (room VI), pl. 47 (façade L).

12. Albenda 1986: pl. 123.

13. Iraq Museum 72126; Deller 1985: pl. 30b. Gaspa (2014: 30) suggests that it represents a third type of vessel; I am not convinced.

14. Albenda 1986:66–73, pl. 24 (façade N), pls. 27–30 (room 10), pl. 67 (room 6).

15. Rathje 1997; Sciacca 2010a:47–50 and 2010b:9, 11–16.

16. Drago 2013:32–33, figs. 31–32 and 33–34. The two cups are of nearly the same size. The two burials have been amply discussed by Drago (2005 [tomb 871] and 2013 [tomb 804]); we look forward to her final publication of the tombs.

17. Drago 2013:39–41.

18. Sannibale 2012 and 2013:109–115; as for the monumentality of the Regolini-Galassi Tomb, see Tuck 2012:45–46, unconvincingly arguing for three burials in the tomb.

19. Drago Troccoli 2005:95. See also chapter 20.

20. Drago Troccoli 2013:40 n. 42.

21. Cf. note 13.

22. Rathje 2007: fig. 3.

23. Drago Troccoli 2005:98, 102 n. 76.

24. Sciacca 2005.

25. Rathje 2010:25, table 1.

26. Drago Troccoli 2005: fig. 12.2.

27. Guldager Bilde 1994:20.

28. Petersen 2014.

29. Drago Troccoli 2005: fig. 12.1.

30. van Kampen 2012. See also chapter 22.

31. Rathje 2007: fig. 4.

32. Thomason 2005:215.

BIBLIOGRAPHY

Albenda, P. 1986. *The Palace of Sargon, King of Assyria: Monumental Wall Reliefs at Dur-Sharrukin, from Original Drawings Made at the Time of Their Discovery in 1843–1844 by Botta and Flandin.* Paris.

Álvarez-Mon, J. 2008. "'Give to drink, o cup-bearer!': The Arjan Beaker in the Context of Lion-Headed Drinking Vessels in the Ancient Near East." *Iranica Antiqua* 43:127–152.

Arizza, M., A. De Cristofaro, A. Piergrossi, and D. Rossi. 2013. "La tomba di un aristocratico *naukleros* dall'agro Veientano: Il *kantharos* con scena di navigazione di via d'Avack." *ArchCl* 64:51–131.

D'Agostino, B. 2010. "Osservazioni al convegno." *Bollettino di Archeologia On Line* 2010.1, F/F2/6:77–82.

Deller, K. 1985. "SAG.DU Ur.MAH: 'Löwenkopf-situla, Löwenkopf-becher." *BaM* 16:327–346.

De Santis, A. 2012. "I 're' di Veio." In *MAV*, 77–80.

Drago Troccoli, L. 2005. "Una coppia di principi nella necropoli di Casale del Fosso a Veio." In *Dinamiche*, 87–124.

———. 2013. "Aspetti dell'Orientalizzante antico a Veio." In *Dall'Italia omaggio a Barbro Santillo Frizell*, ed. A. Capodiferro, L. D'Amelio, and S. Renzetti, 19–44. Rome.

Fletcher, R. N. 2012. "Opening the Mediterranean: Assyria, the Levant, and the Transformation of Early Iron Age Trade." *Antiquity* 86:211–220.

Gaspa, S. 2014. *Contenitori neoassiri: Studi per un repertorio lessicale. Philippika* 67. Wiesbaden.

Guldager Bilde, P. 1994. "Ritual and Power: The Fan as a Sign of Rank in Central Italian Society." *ARID* 22:7–34.

Petersen, N. 2014. "The Fan, a Central Italian Elite Utensil." *Acta Hyperborea* 14:303–330.

Radner, K. 2013. "Tabal and Phrygia: Problem Neighbours in the West." Assyrian Empire Builders: www.ucl.ac.uk/sargon/essentials/countries/tabalandphrygia/.

Rathje, A. 1997. "Gli Etruschi e gli altri: Il caso di Veio." In *Necropoli arcaiche*, 201–205.

———. 2007. "Murlo, Images, and Archaeology." *Etruscan Studies* 10:175–184.

———. 2010. "Tracking Down the Orientalizing." *Bollettino di Archaeologia On Line* 2010.1, F/F2/2:23–30.

Sannibale, M. 2012. "The Etruscan Princess of the Regolini-Galassi Tomb." In *"Princesses" of the Mediterranean in the Dawn of History*, ed. N. C. Stampolides, 306–321. Athens.

———. 2013. "Orientalizing Etruria." In *The Etruscan World*, ed. J. MacIntosh Turfa, 99–133. New York.

Sciacca, F. 2003. "Nota sul rhyton a protome di leone da Veio: Confronti e produzione." *ArchCl* 54:301–319.

———. 2005. *Patere baccellate in bronzo: Oriente, Grecia, Italia in età orientalizzante.* Rome.

———. 2010a. "Commerci fenici nel Tirreno orientale: uno sguardo dalle grandi necropoli." *Bollettino di Archaeologia On Line* 2010.1, F/F2/5:45–61.

———. 2010b. "Veio: La metallotecnica orientalizzante e i rapporti con l'Oriente." *Bollettino di Archaeologia On Line* 2010.1, F/F7/2:5–19.

Thomason, A. Karmel. 2005. *Luxury and Legitimation: Royal Collecting in Ancient Mesopotamia.* Aldershot.

Tuck, A. 2012. "Monumentality, Burial Practice, and Community Identity in Central Italy's Urbanizing Period." In *Monumentality in Etruscan and Early Roman Architecture: Ideology and Innovation*, ed. M. L. Thomas and G. E. Meyers, 41–60. Austin.

van Kampen, I. 2012. "La statua di un principe da Veio-Picazzano." In *MAV*, 81–83.

CHAPTER 12

VEII DURING THE ARCHAIC PERIOD (SIXTH AND FIFTH CENTURIES BCE)

GILDA BARTOLONI AND LAURA M. MICHETTI

THE HISTORICAL BACKGROUND

At the end of the seventh century BCE, the founding of the Tarquin monarchy at Rome resulted in the stabilization of political interactions between Veii and Rome, and the two cities were now interdependent.

The arrival in Rome of two brothers from Vulci, Aulus and Caelius Vibenna, was certainly mediated by Veii. After a confusing period of conflicts, Veii contributed to the events that brought Mastarna/Servius Tullius to power. According to the Annales historians, a new war between Veii and Rome coincided with the beginning of the reign of Servius Tullius.[1] The ancient sources tell us that, alongside the friendly political relations between the two towns, Tarquinius Priscus and Tarquinius Superbus requested that a master craftsman named Vulca come to Rome from Veii.[2]

Veii also supported Tarquinius Superbus when he was exiled from Rome. This occurred before the defeat at the Prata Aesuvia, near the Silva Arsia, in an area under the control of Rome, when free passage was guaranteed to Porsenna in his expedition against Rome. Nevertheless, any expectations regarding the attack of Porsenna on Rome vanished when he restored to the Romans the Septem Pagi and the region of the western bank of the Tiber, which he had taken from them for only a short period of time. This return was carried out so that Porsenna would receive the help of the Romans in his war against the Latin League, in a moment of heavy conflicts between patricians and plebeians and during the constant attacks of the Volscians, Equi, and Sabines against Rome.

The Roman senate allowed the family of the Fabii and their entire *gens* to conduct a war against Veii. The rural tribe of the Fabii was in fact based in an area not far from the point where the Cremera flows into the Tiber, near the tribe Romilia. The consequences of the war were disastrous for the Romans: the Fabii were all killed and the armies of Veii reached the walls of Rome (477 BCE).

A truce was declared in 474 BCE, but it was broken almost immediately, in 473, when the Latin settlement of Fidenae was taken over by Veii. The Romans accused Lars Tolumnius, the king of Veii, of the murder of the ambassadors whom Rome had sent to Veii to inquire into the matter. In the following war Lars Tolumnius was killed in a duel. The Etruscan League refused to help Veii, and, despite help being provided to them by the Faliscans, the city was defeated. A new truce was decided and lasted until shortly before the siege of Veii. After ten years of siege, Veii was conquered in 396 BCE by the dictator M. Furius Camillus.[3]

Recent excavations at the Campetti Bastion, near one of the gates of the town, have revealed evidence of the conflicts in the first quarter of the fifth century BCE (reflecting the famous Battle of the Cremera fought by the Fabii in 477 BCE?) and the final conquest of Veii in the early fourth century BCE. The archaeological evidence revealed by the Veii Project therefore strongly supports the historical narrative by Livy concerning the defeat of Veii.[4]

THE SETTLEMENT: TOWN WALLS, STREETS, HOUSES, AND RESIDENCES

At the beginning of the sixth century BCE, a building fervor overtook Veii. A massive fortification wall in squared blocks (*opus quadratum*), uncovered in the area of Campetti (*map 4:G*), replaced the ramparts made of tufa chips and wooden posts.[5] Rich architectural terracottas showing Eastern influence decorated the contemporary aristocratic residence at Piazza d'Armi (*map 4:Y*), emphasizing the status of its owners.[6] All over the plateau sturdy houses replaced the earlier huts. At Piazza d'Armi, the mid-seventh-century BCE articulation of main and secondary roads was extended, along with the creation of large compounds, and a huge circular cistern was built at the center of the small plateau. The main street of Piazza d'Armi was paved with tufa slabs.[7]

At Piano di Comunità (*map 4:W*), the construction of the complex potters' quarter dates to the Late Orientalizing period. Here the excavations have revealed furnaces and kilns, making it possible to identify elements of the process of producing highly specialized pottery, such as bucchero and Etrusco-Corinthian vases.[8]

DOMESTIC ARCHITECTURE IN TRANSFORMATION

Before the end of the seventh century BCE a radical transformation in the civic and domestic architecture of Veii occurred. The foundations and plinths of the buildings were now made of squared blocks that came from the local quarries. The rest of the walls were made mainly of mud bricks or in the *opus craticium* technique, in which a wooden framework is filled with irregular stones. In most cases, the walls would have been plastered and painted.

The plan of the houses shows a lateral arrangement consisting of two or three rooms and often a portico. The single rooms did not intercommunicate but opened onto a courtyard or a corridor. In the rare cases where the room in the middle was open to the lateral ones, it may have functioned as a vestibule. At the North-West Gate,[9] houses consisting of only two rooms have been

FIGURE 12.1. Tuscania, necropolis of Peschiera. (Copyright: J. Tabolli)

excavated by the British School at Rome, and at Macchiagrande (*map 4:M*), similar two-room structures have been discovered by the Veii Project.[10] Contemporary models of houses, used as ossuaries, give us an image of how these structures may have looked.

At the same time, two rock-cut tombs at Tuscania represent clearly the exterior of contemporary houses. In the necropolis of Peschiera, a tomb of the sixth century BCE replicates a house divided into three rooms and having a gabled roof (fig. 12.1). A triangular gable appears on both the short sides, where the single beams supporting the roof truss were left visible. In the necropolis of Pian di Mola, a tomb with portico had its roof decorated with *cippi* (standing stones), sculptures, and other elements, including statues of sphinxes and lions and disk-shaped acroteria. This tomb offers a precise match for the aristocratic residence recently discovered in the citadel of Piazza d'Armi (*see fig. 1.6*).[11]

NEW ROOFS

A great novelty in this period was the use of terracotta tiles for the roofs of buildings. The system adopted was a mix of the Laconian and Corinthian formats, consisting of plain rectangular tiles connected by semicylindrical tiles, all placed on a framework of wooden beams. These elements attest the introduction of complex carpentry.

The roofs, mostly gabled, were surmounted by a ridge covered with roof tiles that sometimes sup-

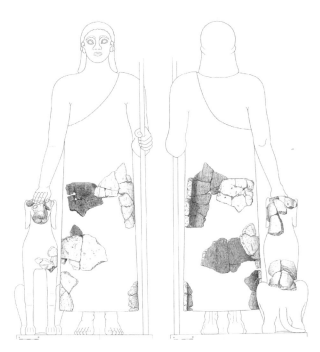

FIGURE 12.2. Piazza d'Armi, acroterion representing a man with his dog. (Copyright: G. Bartoloni and S. Barberini)

ported acroteria. These acroteria, mostly consisting of various human figures, recall the custom of the bifurcated poles or primitive figures that were placed on top of huts, as evidenced by Early Iron Age hut-shaped urns. Roof tiles ended in terracotta antefixes, gutters, or slabs that covered the beams, painted or decorated in relief. Of particular interest is an acroterion representing a standing figure of a lord accompanied by his dog, which probably decorated the residence of Piazza d'Armi (figs. 12.2–12.3).[12]

THE SANCTUARIES AND THE VOTIVE OFFERINGS

The sanctuaries discovered in the town and in the hinterland of Veii are the most significant archaeological evidence from this period (*see fig. 14.1*). The location of the polyadic temple of Juno Regina (i.e., the Etruscan goddess Uni as queen) mentioned by Livy is still uncertain.[13] One possibility is that this temple was built on the summit of Comunità (*map 4:W*), which probably functioned as the acropolis at the time of the Roman conquest. Its presence has been hypothesized because of architectural terracottas dating to the sec-

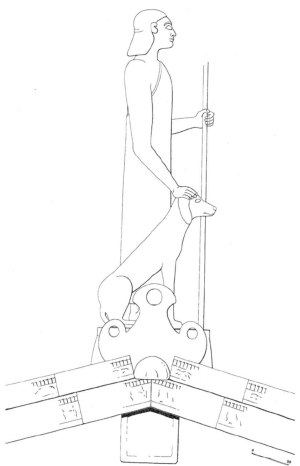

FIGURE 12.3. Acroterion representing a man with his dog, from the right side. (Copyright: G. Bartoloni and S. Barberini)

ond half of the sixth century BCE discovered in this area during the surveys of the British School at Rome and the Veii Project excavations.[14]

SCHOOL OF COROPLASTIC AND VOTIVE OFFERINGS IN THE SANCTUARY OF PORTONACCIO

The sub-urban sanctuary of Portonaccio (*map 4:S*) undoubtedly played a major role not only within the city but also internationally, as visits would have been made to this shrine by high-status persons and sometimes even kings from Veii, the rest of Etruria, and Latium Vetus.[15]

A corpus of important epigraphic evidence consists

of inscriptions in a local alphabet incised on pottery offerings and especially on ambitious bucchero vessels apparently specifically made for the cult.[16]

In addition, an extraordinary school of coroplastic art worked for this sanctuary during the sixth century and part of the fifth century BCE, creating architectural and votive masterpieces. The sculptor Vulca was certainly the most important among these masters. His name has survived in the literary sources, and he is linked to the decoration of the Roman temple of the Capitoline Triad.[17] Members of the elite often commissioned important votive groups and single statues.

The eastern area of the sanctuary was sacred to Menerva. Excavation of this area has revealed an extremely rich votive deposit—one of the earliest in Etruria—consisting mainly of ornaments, bronze figurines, locally made pottery, and small bucchero figures representing nude youths, rams, horses, and other animals. Such items occurred also in other ceremonial contexts of the town (Piazza d'Armi, Comunità, Macchiagrande, and Campetti).[18]

Among the Etrusco-Corinthian pottery was a large *phiale* that has been attributed to the workshop of the Rosoni Painter. On this phiale occurs the signature of a ceramicist, Velthur Ancinies, who was probably a Veientine craftsman working in the area of Comunità.[19] Only a few Attic vases have been discovered in the sanctuary, yet these represent highly specialized types, such as a black-figured *dinos* from the group of the Antimenes Painter, a red-figured *dinos* attributed to the Pan Painter, and a volute crater made by the Nikoxenos Painter.[20] The black-figured *dinos* is one of a group of twelve vases bearing the representation of a ship on their internal rim; these were found in Sicily, the Aeolian islands, and Campania, and, on the northern border of this distribution area, at Veii, Falerii, and Orvieto.[21] Their findspots in the area of the Tiber indicate that this type of vase circulated in significant sanctuary or funerary contexts.[22]

THE SANCTUARIES OF CAMPETTI

Different sanctuaries are attested within the urban area, especially in the northwestern part of the plateau, in the area of Campetti (*map 4:K, I, and O*).[23]

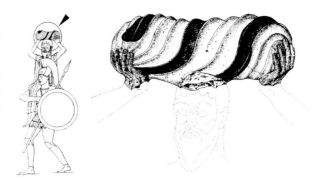

FIGURE 12.4. Statue of Aeneas and Anchises, from the sanctuary of Campetti South. (Copyright: G. Colonna and S. Barberini)

The sanctuary of Campetti South (excavations by A. Carandini and U. Fusco) is located near the town walls (*map 4:O*), and it has been identified as a public thermal and therapeutic complex, probably related to Hercle.[24] Between the end of the sixth and the beginning of the fifth century BCE, statues and other exceptional, although fragmentary, fictile groups appeared in this sanctuary. G. Colonna recently proposed the identification of a statue of Aeneas, carrying on his shoulders Anchises and the sacred symbols of the city (fig. 12.4).[25] This group can be attributed to the workshop of the Master of Aplu (Apollo), who decorated the temple of Portonaccio.[26]

The cult of Aeneas was already attested, as evidenced by small terracotta figurines, in the sanctuaries of Portonaccio and Campetti North. The hero may have been worshiped as a founder of Veii, a reflection of the city's close cultural interactions with Rome and the Latins. Other fragments of terracotta statues come from the same sanctuary of Campetti South, and were viewed by U. Fusco as part of a contemporary group representing Hercle in a fight against the river god Achelöos.[27] Thus at Veii there is a clear relation between the hero and water in the sanctuaries of both Campetti and Portonaccio.[28]

Another great—but unfortunately mostly unpublished—temple was located on the central part of the plateau of Campetti (*map 4:I*) and had foundations in squared blocks and a Tuscan temple plan. This temple was probably destroyed immediately after the siege of Veii.[29] Its location—along the main road of Veii, in a dominant position—made this large structure visible from far away. According to G. Colonna, this temple probably was sacred to Vei, the eponymous goddess of the city, considering the exceptional votive offerings discovered in the sanctuary, especially a headless terracotta statue, dating to ca. 400 BCE, representing a kneeling worshiper.[30]

All the other sacred areas of the city seem to have lacked significant monumental structures and probably functioned only for the immediately surrounding community. The sanctuary of Campetti North (*map 4:H*) (excavated by M. Santangelo) was located not far from the one on the central area of the plateau. It was near the foothills of the northeastern part of the plateau of Veii, in a marginal position only 20 meters from the town walls. It was probably founded in 530 BCE and was sacred to a chthonic deity, likely Demeter-Vei. It consisted of an artificial grotto in which a bust of the deity was displayed.[31] The typology of the ex votos accumulated outside the grotto, together with its plan, which recalls the *thesmophoria* sanctuaries of Sicily, suggests other possible links with Demeter.[32] As with other sanctuaries in the hinterland of Veii, this sacred area seems to have been in use until the fourth or third century BCE, when Roman settlers would have assimilated this cult to one of Ceres.

The presence of two other sanctuaries at Campetti (Campetti North and North-West) has been surmised, based on the evidence of past excavations, not entirely taken into account until recently. This new information contributes to a clearer understanding of this particular part of the plateau, where at least three sanctuaries were located along the road coming from the North-West Gate of the town.[33]

THE SANCTUARIES AT THE CAERE GATE AND MACCHIAGRANDE

Other sanctuaries were closely linked to the main gates of the city, as in the cases of Campetti-Caere Gate (*map 4:K*) and Macchiagrande (*map 4:P*). The votive deposit discovered at the Caere Gate (excavations by M. Torelli and I. Pohl)[34] appears to have been similar to the larger one discovered on the southern slopes of Piano di Comunità, the so-called Stipe Lanciani, which was

FIGURE 12.5. Necropolis of Grotta Gramiccia, tomb 426. (Drawing by N. Malavolta; copyright: G. Bartoloni)

only recently published. This votive deposit attests the long-term dedicatory practice in the area between the early fifth and the mid-second century BCE.[35]

Finally, evidence of another important sanctuary was excavated in the area of Macchiagrande (by M. Santangelo), but unfortunately scholars cannot identify its exact position. It seems to have been aligned with the rock-cut road heading toward the Caere Gate. Here a temple dating to the second quarter of the fifth century BCE was discovered together with antefixes representing women carrying vases, which have been connected to the saga of Hercle/Herakles.[36]

THE FUNERARY RECORD DURING THE ARCHAIC PERIOD

Between ca. 580 BCE and the siege of Veii, in contrast to the richness displayed in the sanctuaries and especially at Portonaccio, a drastic reduction in the cost of funerary goods and architecture occurred in the necropoleis. Both the tumuli and the chamber tombs were no longer used, with the single exception of the Tomb of the Pillars, dating to the late fifth century BCE.[37] The so-called vestibule tombs began to be the most common type, housing cremations in niches or *loculi* carved into the walls (fig. 12.5).[38] Regardless of the origin or the significance of these tombs, the political decision to invest all expressions of richness and power in the public sphere is clear. The private luxury that characterized the rich Orientalizing tombs seems to have been banned.

THE ROLE OF FUNERARY LAWS

Numerous scholars have tried to analyze the reasons behind these dramatic changes, which appear in the archaeological record to have been even more drastic than the evidence of the Twelve Tables in Rome, described by Cicero, would imply. G. Colonna has stressed that the new laws among the Latins presupposed an early consistency between practical and ideological religion, and a complete desecration of the rite, which had a direct connection to the Greek world.[39] C. Ampolo has suggested that the rules of Greek funeral ritual in the Archaic period constituted a fundamental political tool for each town at the time of its definition, which coincided with the search for an isonomic balance among the members of the new elite.[40] This new ideology was certainly linked to the central power of the town, which was now able to actualize it.

It has been stressed also that the sixth-century BCE funerary laws should be linked to contemporary *nomothetes* (legislators) and tyrants: the fights against luxury and wealth were an important component of the nomothetic phase of the Greek poleis, and the laws against funerary excesses were mostly directed against previous aristocracies, affecting both the life and the death of the richest citizens. From the end of the seventh and during the sixth century BCE, the crisis of the old aristocracy occurred together with the emergence of new powers and personalities. Conflicts and disagreements certainly arose among the aristocratic families, and the "winner of those conflicts could have been also a person belonging to the old dominant group."[41] In the tombs there was undoubtedly a strong limitation of indicators of a luxurious lifestyle, involving mainly the funeral display, the clothing, and the funerary ritual.[42]

The tenth passage in the sixth of the Twelve Tables mentions the ritual of the *circumpotatio*, which probably corresponded to a ceremony connected to the consumption of wine: "*Haec praeterea sunt in legibus . . . .: servilis unctura tollitur omnisque circumpotatio . . . ne sumptuosa respersio, ne longae coronae, ne acerrae* [And still the following rules can be found in the laws: the anointing of the bodies by the slaves is to be banned and there should be no round of wine,[43] no

expensive sprinkling, no crowns, and no incense containers]." The practice of anointing the dead was abolished, as well as the drinking of wine.

At Rome and Veii, ethical and cultural reasons would have contributed to the suppression, in a more drastic way than in Greece, of these exuberant drinking activities, which were attested in many of the Orientalizing funerary contexts. The number of the participants had to be consistent. The aristocratic clan perceived the funeral as an occasion to demonstrate its continuity and cohesion, at a time in history when the polis was not entirely yet formed and the dominant class of the aristocracy still firmly held power.

SIXTH-CENTURY FUNERARY RIGOR VERSUS FIFTH-CENTURY NEW RICHNESS

During the sixth century BCE, the contraction of the funerary ritual resulted in the sole deposition of the container for the ashes (in terracotta or stone). A few tombs constituted an exception to this rigor. The presence of a limited but significant number of artifacts in these tombs probably reflects the idea of stressing the status of the dead, despite the funerary laws, probably through a kind of religious privilege.

At the end of the sixth and throughout the fifth century BCE, while the traditional funeral rites and the same types of burial structures continued to be used, tomb-groups began to show new forms of richness. Compared to the sixth century BCE, this significant break occurred together with sociocultural changes among the aristocratic class of the Etruscan city.[44] Accompanying the ossuaries or beside the buried bodies, a few but significant vases recall, on a smaller scale, the aristocratic tradition of the funerary banquet.

In addition, objects connected to the personal sphere of the dead—such as mirrors, jewels, perfumes, and toilet articles—are attested in the female tombs, while the male tombs were characterized by strigils and perfumes. Despite the unchanged rigor established in the previous century, the ruling classes, with the deposition of these personal objects, managed to continue to allude to their *virtutes*. In the funerary sphere the upper-class adherence to new and Hellenizing aristocratic ideals required, in the case of men, an association of the dead with athletics and, in the case of women, a reference to the beauty and values of the *mundus muliebris* (the world of the women). Significantly, at the same time, the absence of weapons in the male graves was certainly not without reason.

THE TERRITORY AND ITS FARMS

Archaeological evidence, especially from the recent intensive surveys, demonstrates that a drastic change occurred in the organization of rural settlements at the end of the seventh and beginning of the sixth century BCE. Finds on the small tufa plateaus in the territory reveal a dense constellation of small-size settlements, indicated by concentrations of domestic pottery fragments and especially of building materials. Unfortunately, without excavation, it is impossible to define the exact chronology and the specific nature of all these rural sites. In some cases, the recovered building materials could have belonged not to houses, but to ditches, pavements, or simple dumping areas, which would at any rate suggest proximity to a small settlement. The large quantity of terracotta tiles indicates the number of rural sites with houses covered by roofs incorporating them.

The presence of numerous rural settlements is confirmed also by the wide distribution of tombs. Small groups of chamber tombs occur at many of these sites. In the cases in which the tomb-groups were properly excavated, we can determine that most of these tombs were used beginning from the Late Orientalizing period.[45]

It was mainly during the high Archaic period (575–500 BCE) that the occupation of the countryside intensified. In fact, most of the data from the rural sites of the territory of Veii belong to the second half of the sixth century BCE. The location of the sites in the countryside reflects the need to create and control new roads, which Veii must have planned beginning in the late seventh century BCE.[46] In the area of the northwestern territory of the modern municipality of Rome, different "units" have been discovered, most having an elliptical or rectangular plan, made of different rooms, and covered by roofs with reddish brown impasto or cream coarse-ware terracotta tiles. The areas surrounding these units were characterized by deep cuts into the natural tufa bedrock: small channels, grain stores, and complex systems of water drainage and water collection into large moats, *cuniculi*, and wells.[47]

All this evidence testifies to the creation of a system of isolated and autonomous farms dependent on agricultural exploitation. Data from surveys and excavations reveal the cultivation of cereals, fruits, and produce, while infertile fields were left for brush and pasture.[48] It is not clear if this organization of farms in the Archaic period represented the results of land allocation to clients by the aristocracy or if we should imagine the existence of private properties. At Rome, which followed a very similar urban evolution,[49] Servius Tullius promoted in the mid-sixth century BCE the reorganization of the *ager* (according to Varro and Dionysius),[50] which consisted of a diffused occupation of the territory in an attempt to populate the countryside at the expense of the smaller towns that were controlled by the *gentes*. This policy was in full accord with the anti-sumptuary laws promoted by the same king.[51]

NOTES

L. M. Michetti wrote the section of this chapter entitled "The Sanctuaries and the Votive Offerings"; G. Bartoloni wrote all others.

1. Livy 1.42.2; Dionysios of Halikarnassos 4.27.2 and 6.
2. See chapters 13 and 24.
3. See chapter 25.
4. Unpublished excavations directed by G. Bartoloni.
5. Boitani 2008. See also chapter 16.
6. G. Bartoloni, in Bartoloni et al. 2013–2014. See also chapter 2.
7. V. Acconcia, in Bartoloni and Acconcia 2012:16–20.
8. Belelli Marchesini 2015. See also chapter 23.
9. R. Cascino, in *Novità*.
10. M. T. D'Alessio, in *Novità*.
11. G. Bartoloni, in Bartoloni et al. 2013–2014.
12. Bartoloni et al. 2012. See also chapter 1.
13. Livy 5.21.1–4 and 10. For a complete discussion see chapter 14.
14. Torelli 1982; B. Belelli Marchesini, in Bartoloni and Benedettini 2011:769–771.
15. See chapter 13, where the sanctuary of Portonaccio and especially the temple of Aplu (neither mentioned here) are diachronically described.

16. Michetti 2001:45–46, I.F.1.1; *Portonaccio* I, 176–178, figs. XXXIX–XLI, LXXVII, figs. 15, 29–30; Michetti 2002:233; Maras 2002, 2009:405–427; L. M. Michetti, in Carlucci and Michetti 2014; Michetti 2017.

17. Pliny, *Nat. Hist.* 35.157. Colonna 1987a, 1987b, 2001: 39–43, 65–68, 2008:53–63; Baglione 2001:69–77. See also chapter 13.

18. Concerning the votive deposit near the altar: Michetti 2001; *Portonaccio* I. A list of the figured bucchero appears in M. G. Benedettini, in Bartoloni and Benedettini 2011:702–703.

19. Colonna 2006.

20. Baglione 2001:77–78; 2011 (to this list can be added an example from Orvieto-Campo della Fiera: Bizzarri 2012: 83–84, 94–95 nn. 12–14, figs. 13–15). See also Baglione 1989–1990:656.

21. *CVA* Boston 2, figs. 65–66.

22. See also chapter 10.

23. For a detailed analysis see chapter 14.

24. Fusco 2001, 2011.

25. Colonna 2009.

26. See chapters 13 and 25.

27. Fusco 2011; see also Colonna 2015b:94.

28. On the cult of water, see chapter 13.

29. Cf. A. M. Jaia, in Reggi and Turchetti 2010:62, and Colonna 2015b:63.

30. Colonna 2015b:63.

31. For an interesting comparison with the sanctuary discovered at Macchia delle Valli in the territory of Vetralla see Scapaticci 2010.

32. Vagnetti 1971; Comella 1981:771–773; Comella and Stefani 1990; Carosi 2002; Colonna 2015b:61–69.

33. Colonna 2015b:68–69. The site is also discussed in chapter 14.

34. Torelli and Pohl 1973. See also the description in chapter 14.

35. Bartoloni and Benedettini 2011.

36. Colonna 2015b:80–94.

37. Colonna 1986:494, fig. 353.

38. Drago Troccoli 1997.

39. Colonna 1977, 1981.

40. Ampolo 1984.

41. Mazzarino 1989:193.

42. Bartoloni 2010. Historical and epigraphical sources do not refer to rich burials at this time, and the aristocracies could maintain their visibility only by continuing to bury their dead in the earlier chamber tombs. Even during the Middle Ages, sumptuary laws forbade funeral robes lined with fur, wider than ten arm-lengths at the level of the feet, or, especially, adorned by precious embroidery; see Muzzarelli 2002. At Sparta, Lycurgus prohibited the burial of any goods together with the deceased: the body could only been wrapped in "purple bandages and between olive leaves" (Plutarch, *Lycurgus* 27). In the rest of Greece and in the colonies, the funerary laws mainly required a reduction in the amount of goods deposited in the burials. The Ioulis law at Keos, which was incised on a white marble stele in the late fifth century BCE, apart from its limit of three articles of clothing to cover the body (side A, line 10), allowed "no more than three *choes* of wine on the tomb, no more than one of oil, and all the vases should be brought back." In another passage (lines 13–14), the need to "bring back home, from the tomb, the *kline* and the clothes" recalls scenes represented on the Attic *pinakes*. This textual evidence seems to explain the absence of grave goods in Late Archaic and Classical burials. The rest of this law referred to the *ekphora*, which should have been silent and composed, with demonstrations of sympathy limited strictly to the family. See Frisone 2000:57–102.

43. *Circumpotatio* has also been translated as "funerary banquet."

44. Drago Troccoli 1997.

45. Pacciarelli and Damiani 2006.

46. Pacciarelli and Damiani 2006.

47. Rossi and Iorio 2009.

48. Rossi 2006; Rossi and Iorio 2009:563.

49. Colonna 2006; Bartoloni 2010.

50. The papyrus Oxyrhynchus 2088 allows an attribution to Servius Tullius of the distribution of the *pagi* to the rustic tribes (Traina 1987).

51. Colonna 2006.

BIBLIOGRAPHY

Ampolo, C. 1984. "Il lusso funerario e la città antica." In *Aspetti dell'ideologia funeraria nel mondo romano. AIONArchStAnt* 6:71–102.

Anathema = *Regime delle offerte e vita dei santuari nel Mediterraneo antico. Atti del convegno internazionale (Rome 1989)* (*ScAnt* 3–4 [1989–1990])

Baglione, M. P. 1989–1990. "Considerazioni sui santuari di Pyrgi e di Veio-Portonaccio." In *Anathema*, 651–667.

———. 2001. "Le statue ed altri oggetti votivi." In *Veio, Cerveteri, Vulci*, 69–78.

———. 2008. "Il santuario dell'Apollo: La plastica votiva tarda." In *Etruschi*, 64–69.

———. 2011. "Funzione dei grandi donari attici di Veio-Portonaccio." In *Corollari. Scritti di antichità in omaggio all'opera di Giovanni Colonna*, ed. D. F. Maras, 95–101. Studia Erudita 14. Rome.

Bartoloni, G. 2010. "Il cambiamento delle pratiche funerarie nell'età dei Tarquini." *AnnFaina* 27:159–185.

Bartoloni, G., V. Acconcia, F. Biagi, B. Boitani, U. Fusco, and S. Neri. 2013–2014. "Le ricerche dell'Università di Roma 'La Sapienza' a Veio." *RendPontAcc* 86:1–82.

Bartoloni, G., V. Acconcia, E. Biancifiori, C. Mottolese, D. Sarracino, and V. Basilissi. 2012. "Veio, Piazza d'Armi: La fossa del cane." *ArchCl* 63:55–126.

Bartoloni, G., and M. G. Benedettini. 2011. *Veio: Il deposito votivo di Comunità (scavi 1889–2005)*. Rome.

Belelli Marchesini, B. 2015. "Comunità. La funzione del distretto: Strutture e infrastrutture produttive." In *Novità*, 21–27.

Bizzarri, C. 2012. "Gli inizi del santuario di Campo della Fiera: La ceramica greca." In *Il Fanum Voltumnae e i santuari comunitari dell'Italia antica. AnnFaina* 19:77–114.

Boitani, F. 2008. "Nuove indagini sulle mura di Veio nei pressi della porta Nord-Ovest," with an appendix by S. Neri and F. Biagi. In *Città murata*, 135–154.

Carlucci, C., and L. M. Michetti. 2014. "Il santuario di Portonaccio a Veio tra committenza pubblica e committenza privata." In *Artisti, committenti e fruitori in Etruria tra VIII e V secolo a.C. AnnFaina* 21:501–530.

Carosi, S. 2002. "Nuovi dati sul santuario di Campetti a Veio." *ArchCl* 53:355–377.

———. "Culti demetriaci in Etruria e nel Lazio dall'età tardo-arcaica a quella medio-repubblicana: Il caso di Vei." *AIANews* 3:11–12.

Colonna, G. 1977. "Un aspetto oscuro del Lazio antico: Le tombe del VI–V secolo a.C." In *Lazio arcaico e mondo greco. PP* 32:131–165.

———. 1981. "L'ideologia funeraria e il conflitto delle culture." *Archeologia Laziale* 4:229–232.

———. 1986. "Urbanistica e architettura." In *Rasenna: Storia e civiltà degli Etruschi*, 371–532. Milan.

———. 1987a. "Note preliminari sui culti del santuario di Portonaccio a Veio." *ScAnt* 1:419–446.

———. 1987b. "Il Maestro dell'Ercole e della Minerva: Nuova luce sull'attività dell'officina veiente." *OpRom* 16:7–41.

———. 2001. "Portonaccio"; "Torso di statua virile raffigurante probabilmente Ercole." In *Veio, Cerveteri, Vulci*, 37–44, 65–68.

———. 2006. "Un pittore veiente del ciclo dei Rosoni: Velthur Ancinies." In *Tarquinia e le civiltà del Mediterraneo. Atti del convegno internazionale (Milano 2004)*, ed. M. Bonghi Jovino, 163–175. Milan.

———. 2008. "L'officina veiente: Vulca e gli altri maestri di statuaria arcaica in terracotta." In *Etruschi*, 53–63.

———. 2009. "Il mito di Enea tra Veio e Roma." In *Gli Etruschi e Roma: Fasi monarchica e alto-repubblicana. AnnFaina* 16:51–92.

———. 2015a. "Novità sugli scavi Santangelo a Veio." In *Novità*, 111–132.

———. 2015b. "Gli Scavi Santangelo nell'Area Urbana di Veio (1945–1952)." *ArchCl* 65:59–101.

Colonna, G., and D. F. Maras. 2006. *Corpus Inscriptionum Etruscarum. II, 1, 5 (Tituli 6325–6723), et addit. vol. II, 2, 1 (Tituli 8881–8927) (Inscriptiones Veiis et in agro veientano, nepesino sutrinoque repertae, additis illis in agro capenate et falisco in-*

ventis, quae in fasciculo CIE II, 2, 1 desunt, nec non illis perpaucis in finitimis sabinis repertis). Rome.

Comella, A. 1981. "Tipologia e diffusione dei complessi votivi in Italia in epoca medio- e tardo-repubblicana (contributo alla storia dell'artigianato antico)." *MÉFRA* 93:717–803.

Comella, A., and G. Stefani. 1990. *Materiali votivi del santuario di Campetti a Veio: Scavi 1947 e 1969*. Rome.

Drago Troccoli, L. 1997. "Le tombe 419 e 426 del sepolcreto di Grotta Gramiccia a Veio: Contributo alla conoscenza di strutture tombali e ideologia funeraria a Veio tra il VI e il V secolo a.C." In *Etrusca et Italica. Scritti in ricordo di Massimo Pallottino*, 239–280. Pisa.

Etruschi = M. Torelli and A. M. Moretti Sgubini, eds., *Etruschi: Le antiche metropoli del Lazio* (exh. cat.) (Rome, 2008)

Frisone, F. 2000. *Leggi e regolamenti funerari nel mondo greco, 1: Le fonti epigrafiche*. Scuola di Specializzazione in Archeologia Classica e Medioevale. Lecce.

Fusco, U. 2001. "Nuovi reperti dall'area archeologica di Campetti a Veio." *ArchCl* 52:255–278.

———. 2011. "Il culto di Ercole presso il complesso archeologico di Campetti, area S-O, a Veio: Testimonianze dall'età etrusca a quella romana." *ArchCl* 52:379–412.

Guaitoli, M. 1995. "Lavinium: Nuovi dati dalle necropoli." *Archeologia Laziale* 12:551–562. *QuadAEI* 23–24.

Maras, D. F. 2002. "Appendice II: Le iscrizioni." In *Portonaccio* I, 261–273.

———. 2009. *Il dono votivo: Gli dei e il sacro nelle iscrizioni etrusche di culto*. Biblioteca di Studi Etruschi 46. Rome.

Mazzarino, S. 1989. *Fra Oriente ed Occidente*. Milan.

Michetti, L. M. 2001. "Gli scavi di Massimo Pallottino nella zona dell'altare (1939–1940)." In *Veio, Cerveteri, Vulci*, 45–56.

———. 2002. "Considerazioni sui materiali; Note conclusive." In *Portonaccio* I, 229–250.

———. 2010. "Produzioni artigianali tra Veio e il Lazio nell'età dei Tarquini." In *La grande Roma dei Tarquini. AnnFaina* 17:133–158.

———. 2011. "Gli dei sul tetto. Le basi acroteriali del tempio di Veio-Portonaccio: Struttura e apparato decorativo." In *Deliciae Fictiles* 4: *Images of Gods, Monsters, and Heroes. Proceedings of the Fourth International Conference on Architectural Terracottas from Ancient Italy (Rome and Syracuse, 21–25 October 2009)*, ed. P. S. Lulof and C. Rescigno, 96–106. Oxford.

———. 2017. "Veio nell'età di Tarquinio il Superbo: Appunti sulle produzioni artigianali." In *The Age of Tarquinius Superbus: Central Italy in the Late Sixth Century. Atti del convegno internazionale (Roma 2013)*, ed. C. Smith and P. Lulof, 177–186. Leuven.

Muzzarelli, M. G., ed. 2002. *La legislazione suntuaria, secoli XIII–XVI: Emilia-Romagna*. Rome.

Pacciarelli, M., and I. Damiani. 2006. "L'insediamento di Acquafredda e l'occupazione rurale del territorio tra Roma,

Caere e Veio dal primo Ferro all'età arcaica." In *La fattoria e la villa dell'Auditorium*, ed. A. Carandini, M. T. D'Alessio, and H. Di Giuseppe, 511–556. *Bollettino della Commissione Archeologica Comunale* suppl. 14. Rome.

Reggi, A., and R. Turchetti. 2010. *Guida archeologica del Parco di Veio*. Rome.

Rossi, D. 2006. "Municipio XVI Ovest: Terre di frontiera fra Etruschi e Romani." In *Roma: Memorie dal sottosuolo. Ritrovamenti archeologici 1980/2006*, ed. M. A. Tomei, 523–525. Rome.

Rossi, D., and V. Iorio. 2009. "Nuovi dati dal nord-ovest di Roma." In *Suburbium* II: *Il suburbio di Roma dalla fine dell'età monarchica alla nascita del sistema delle ville (V-II secolo a.C.)*, ed. V. Jolivet, C. Pavolini, M. A. Tomei, and R. Volpe, 557–572. Rome.

Scapaticci, M. G. 2010. "Vetralla: Un santuario a Macchia delle Valli." In *Archeologia nella Tuscia. Atti dell'Incontro di studio (Viterbo 2007)*, ed. P. A. Gianfrotta and A. M. Moretti. *Daidalos* 10:101–127.

Torelli, M. 1982. "Veio, la città, l'*arx* e il culto di Giunone Regina." In *Miscellanea Archaeologica Tobias Dohrn Dedicata*, ed. H. Blanck and S. Steingräber, 117–128. Rome.

Torelli, M., and I. Pohl. 1973. "Veio—Scoperta di un piccolo santuario etrusco in località Campetti." *NSc* 1973:40–258.

Traina, G. 1987. "Il papiro di Servio Tullio." *Annali Scuola Normale Superiore di Pisa* 17:389–406.

Vagnetti, L. 1971. *Il deposito votivo di Campetti a Veio (Materiale degli scavi 1937–1938)*. Florence.

CHAPTER 13

THE SANCTUARY OF PORTONACCIO

GIOVANNI COLONNA

Although it is not mentioned in the ancient Greek and Roman sources, and little monumental evidence survives, the sanctuary of Portonaccio clearly stood out not only among the sanctuaries at Veii but also among the sanctuaries of all Etruria.[1]

The sanctuary was located in a sub-urban area, on a natural terrace (originally quite irregular) immediately under the cliff dominated by the monumental town walls (*map 4:S*). Vertical natural cliffs, raging waters, and lush forests characterized this sacred landscape. The terrace of Portonaccio, to the south, faced a natural precipice over the gorge of the Fosso della Mola (Piordo River). Despite its proximity to one of the gates of Veii, which opened onto a road coming from the sea coast and the Salinae region, the sanctuary was secluded. A secondary road reached the area from the west and crossed the entire terrace.[2]

THE DISCOVERY AND THE EXCAVATIONS AT PORTONACCIO

Because the terrace is located halfway up the plateau's cliff, the sanctuary was soon covered by a great mass of soil washed down from the top of the plateau. In addition, the partial collapse of the Archaic substructure wall of the terrace allowed a large quantity of the soil filling the wall to fall into the lower valley of Cannetaccio (*map 4:T*). This filling, like the "Persian debris" of the Athenian Acropolis, held numerous votives and architectural terracottas, which had been piled near the wall during the second half of the sixth century BCE, at the time of the remodeling of the sanctuary.[3]

The random exposure by erosion of some of these terracottas in the outcrop along the stream resulted in 1914 in the launch of the first archaeological excavations by E. Gabrici, which brought to light the first exceptional discoveries. In the two following years, G. Q. Giglioli moved the excavation up onto the terrace of Portonaccio. The famous statue of Aplu (Apollo), the remains of other acroteria, the Roman road, the walls of the pool, and the temple were rapidly identified.[4]

Between 1917 and 1921, E. Stefani excavated the pool and the temple and discovered also the large altar in the eastern sector, which was associated with a shrine (the *sacellum*) and porticos.[5] In 1939–1940 M. Pallottino excavated the deepest layers in the area of the altar and found an earlier Archaic altar as well as a terracotta statue of the goddess with a baby and a large male torso in terracotta. Between 1944 and 1950, M. Santangelo discovered the cistern facing the temple and the precinct wall, together with the torso of Hercle and other remains of acroteria.[6] Pallottino ordered the construction of a shelter covering the altar and directed the process of anastylosis of the foundations of the temple, which had partially collapsed due to the presence of an underground quarry opened during Imperial times. At the end of the 1950s a new and final exploration was conducted in the valley of Cannetaccio, but with no relevant discoveries.

In 1993, a courageous reconstruction of the temple was achieved using a lightweight structure sitting directly on top of the existing walls (fig. 13.1).[7] At the same time, a new display was organized at the Villa Giulia museum.

FIGURE 13.1. Portonaccio, reconstruction of the temple, from the northeast. (Copyright: J. Tabolli)

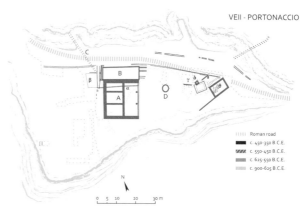

FIGURE 13.2. Portonaccio, plan of the sanctuary. A. Temple; B. Pool; C. *Cuniculus*; D. Cistern; α. Remains of the Regia (?); β. *Hestiatorion*; γ. Portico; δ. Altar of Menerva; θ. *Sacellum* of Menerva. (Copyright: O. Cerasuolo and J. Tabolli)

In 1996, with the beginning of the Veii Project, new excavations were carried out at the sanctuary. In particular, between 1996 and 1997 the area behind the temple, only partially known, was explored. At the same time, in the other test trenches, archaeologists uncovered the "Santangelo Cistern," the tunnels underneath the altar, and the stratigraphy of the Roman road.[8]

Together with the long process of restoration of the acroteria, new research was conducted on the unpublished finds from the early excavations at the sanctuary, preserved in the storerooms of the Villa Giulia. This resulted in the complete publication of Pallottino's excavations in the area of the altar and in a revision of the plan of the sanctuary previously published by Stefani.[9]

THE OPEN-AIR CULT (FIRST PHASE OF THE SANCTUARY)

The excavation of the lower layers near the altar, which E. Stefani had begun and later M. Pallottino continued in a more scientific way, was extremely important for our understanding of the original morphology of the site and the earliest evidence of the cult. In fact, the entire area of the terrace had been flattened only in a later period (fourth phase). Originally, a difference in level existed between the ridge where the altar was and the hollow where the *sacellum* was located (fig. 13.2). A small road went from this hollow toward the town.

Excavation of the earliest layers found by Stefani and Pallottino revealed that the cult began in the first half of the seventh century BCE. During the second half of that century (or at the end of it), minor construction is attested in the area. Early Iron Age huts on the ridge were leveled and covered, creating an almost flat area. This area was also bounded, to the north, by a substructure wall in *cappellaccio* tufa. In the area of the later *sacellum*, an irregular platform was made—also in *cappellaccio*—and formed the basis for a small *aedicula*.

A large amount of votive offerings were piled in the open-air space near this structure, mainly pottery vessels (Etrusco-Corinthian and bucchero). Earlier offerings in metal, contemporary with the above-mentioned offerings, were deposited at a later time in the foundation core of the large altar.[10] This Late Orientalizing/Archaic deposit constitutes the most important contemporary votive deposit of this period in Etruria. The types of offerings suggest that the deity worshiped was female. Numerous inscriptions on the vases include the name Menerva.[11] A fragment of pottery contained a dedication to the god Rath,[12] a deity who has been associated with Aplu. The appearance of the gentilicial name Ratumenna—which was the name of the unlucky charioteer after whom a Capitolium gate onto the via Triumphalis was named—confirms the link between Veii and Rath.[13] Notable among the terracotta votives are a "canopic"-type bust with stylized head; various figurines, including an Orientalizing figure of a "lord" seated on a throne;[14] and full-length statues, in poor and fragmentary condition because of their deposition in the open-air space. A male statue of greater than life-size dimensions, reminding us of the *Hercules fictilis* made in Rome by Vulca, was later offered in the same deposit.[15]

The oracular cult was connected to Menerva (Minerva)—as evidenced by the small cleromantic box (*arca*) made of bucchero to contain the lots dedicated to this goddess[16]—but also to Hercle[17] and to Rath (in his aspect of *haruspex* connected to divination); both gods probably played a secondary role compared to Menerva. The presence of a powerful oracle attracted people from other towns, such as Caere, Vulci, and Castro. The authors of the dedications can be identified as high-ranking members of the aristocracies of Veii and elsewhere, including a Tulumne (see fig. 13.5) and a Vipienna. These personages probably went to Portonaccio to receive particular responses and not for a "federal" political reason, as has been suggested.

The presence of inscriptions of various types indicates the existence of a local scriptorium (school for writing) managed by the sanctuary.[18] The "sigma" in the form of a cross and the use of syllabic punctuation are two of the characteristics of the local tradition of writing.[19] The principal duties of the scribes would have been to write the *sortes* (responses) and the dedications of the faithful. The scribal profession probably passed from father to son, resulting in the creation of a powerful gentilicial group.

The scribes worked in a semi-subterranean room with a square plan, in a dominant position in the western area of the sanctuary. Based on the votive evidence discovered here, this room existed simultaneously with the above-mentioned eastern area and continuously functioned as a habitation and a *hestiatorion* (lodging for visitors), where a great number of animals were sacrificed and then consumed, as revealed by analysis of the animal bones. This room, whose access was from the south, was a sort of tower.[20] The roof had a covering of tiles, and its simas were decorated by hollowed triangles.[21] Between the first and the second quarter of the sixth century BCE, this building was decorated with a frieze showing pacing felines, resembling the decorative scheme of the Regia in Rome in its third period.[22]

THE EARLIEST MONUMENTAL EVIDENCE (SECOND PHASE)

The second phase of the sanctuary at Portonaccio dates from 540–530 to 510–500 BCE and constitutes the first monumentalization of the sanctuary. At this time, the long terrace wall along the side of the precipice was built, of blocks of red tufa. The small *sacellum* (called "room G" by Stefani), which was an *oikos* with a rectangular plan, was also built at this time. This structure faced west-southwest, similarly to temples sacred to Menerva, Uni, and other female deities.[23]

The pavement was leveled around the top of the former ridge, and its foundation deposit was filled with the earlier votives from the *cappellaccio* structure nearby. A very small terracotta votive model with its front door not set perfectly in the middle of the wall suggests the actual appearance of this *sacellum*.[24] Similar to the *sacella* of the Southern area of the sanctuary of Pyrgi at Caere, this peculiar structure has the characteristics of a secret place. The decorations consisted of lateral simas with sphinxes in relief[25] and most probably of a frontal sima with painted *anthemion*.[26]

A squared altar faced the *sacellum* but was not on axis with it. M. Pallottino discovered this early altar underneath the platform of the later altar (fourth phase).[27] A large conduit crossed this structure and reached bedrock, suggesting a sacred pit, even if it was sealed off.[28] This element implies a chthonic cult, with the same characteristics as the ones at Pyrgi (area C and altar *iota* in the Southern area) and at Punta della Vipera, where Menerva was worshiped in her oracular aspect.[29] A portico fenced off the area of the *sacellum* and the altar, and some steps permitted access from the road, which ran at a lower elevation. Pallottino discovered the greater portion of the ex-votos near the base of the steps.

In the western area of the sanctuary, around the foundation of the earlier tower, which at this time was demolished, the first monumental building of the sanctuary was erected. Only its northern wall survived in subsequent reconstructions, and it was oriented east to southeast, like the later tripartite temple.[30] Most probably this building was an *oikos*, with a narrow rectangular plan. A large cistern in the middle of the two areas of the sanctuary, with its sides covered by clay, should be connected with this *oikos*.[31]

Terracottas of the so-called first phase decorated this *oikos*, as indicated by discoveries in this area.[32] In particular, friezes with scenes of processions and chariots, also pulled by winged horses, and of symposia, the "divine assembly," and the apotheosis of Hercle[33] recall the series of friezes referred to as "Veii-Rome-Velletri" and date to 530 BCE.[34] The friezes were connected to some beautiful antefixes, without nimbus, of an Ionic-Attic style.[35] The iconography represented in the friezes suggests that this building functioned as a kind of Regia, used by the *gens* that inherited power over the sanctuary, and especially over the oracle of Menerva, from the earlier priest-scribes.

Unfortunately no votive deposit has been found in association with this large *oikos*; such a cache would be of great help in identifying the cult practiced in this building. Only a series of terracotta statues have been attributed to the *oikos*: two *kouroi* in Ionic style, fully dressed with shoes, and a third for which only one leg was found; a statue of Turms (Hermes) at three-quarters life size, for which the torso is the only remaining part;[36] the figure of a hunter, which may represent Hercle in his Hyperborean costume;[37] and the earliest group of Hercle and Menerva, half life-size, which corresponded to the most standard *tripedanea* (of three feet length) measure (fig. 13.3).[38] Hercle here wears a tunic and appears in triumphal form, similar to his apotheosis (in much smaller scale) on the bronze tripod from Vulci discovered on the acropolis of Athens.[39] This appearance of Hercle is the first suggestion of tyrannical ambitions within the society of Veii.

THE APOGEE OF THE SANCTUARY, AT THE TIME OF THE MASTERS OF TERRACOTTA (THIRD PHASE)

At the end of the sixth century BCE, a radical restructuring of the sanctuary gave this sacred place its well-known monumental aspect. A royal authority certainly promoted this transformation, putting an end to the excesses of the gentilicial power of the previous groups. The "private" residence was destroyed and a

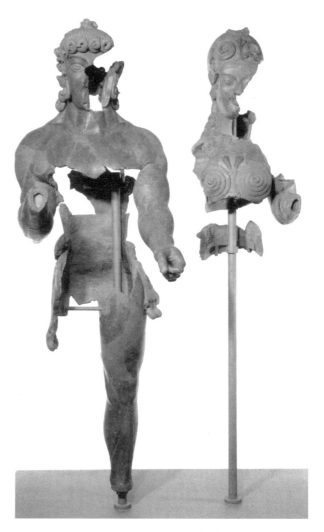

FIGURE 13.3. Terracotta statues of Hercle and Menerva. (Copyright: G. Colonna)

new medium-size temple was built and connected to a rectangular pool. This pool was plastered with clay and received water from a small tunnel coming from the entrance to the sanctuary (fig. 13.2).

The plan of the temple was designed using a module of three Attic feet (0.89 m), coinciding with the height of the podium, the lower diameter of the column, and the lower thickness of the walls. In addition, the platform of the temple measured 62 Attic feet per side and the elevation of the temple was 60 feet; the *pronaos* was 24 feet long; the three cellas were 30 feet long (the central was 18 feet wide, and the lateral ones 15 feet wide). The pronaos had two tufa columns *in antis*, measuring 21 feet high[40] (6.22 m).

The use of this module recalls the Servian temple of S. Omobono[41] in Rome and, probably, the temple at Velletri. The temple in the Portonaccio sanctuary at Veii represents the earliest example in Etruria of the "Tuscanic plan" (*Tuscanicae dispositiones*) mentioned by Vitruvius. In the same way, the terracottas decorating this temple, together with the ones of temple B of Pyrgi, represent the first evidence of the second phase in architectural terracottas in Etruria and Latium Vetus. It was an architectural jewel, characterized by exuberance and extreme care in its decoration, which make it unique in Etruria and comparable with the most sophisticated Greek Archaic monuments, such as the Siphnian Treasury at Delphi. The master designer (a real *epistates*—superintendent) was able to combine the harmonious supporting structure and the complex terracotta decorations.

All the components of temple were numbered using a refined system of syllabic symbols, following the excellent tradition of the Veientine scribes,[42] and revealing the Etruscan spirit of the entire project. The large repertoire of statues and statuettes in the round, heads, and high- and low-relief sculptures, in most cases modeled by hand, demonstrates the exceptional capacities of the masters in coroplastic art and technique at Veii. Vulca had inaugurated this tradition in the previous phase, during the final years of the reign of Tarquinius Priscus.

The most original part of the design was the adornment of the structure with multiple acroteria. Judging from the number of bases discovered, twelve statues were lined up on the ridge pole (*columen*) and eight on the two frontal slopes of the roof. All these acroteria were life-size (or a bit more) and their positions were organized according to a mythical narrative, in groupings of two or three. Despite being created by different masters, all the acroteria convey a sense of movement, their volume clearly depicted and the drapery in its formal conception emphasizing dynamism and vitality.

These productions are attributed to the "Master of Apollo," the Veientine expert in coroplastic art from whom Tarquinius Superbus, before 509 BCE, commissioned the chariot of Jupiter for the famous temple on the Roman Capitolium.[43] The statues stood on

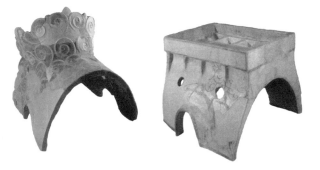

FIGURE 13.4. Acroteria bases from the temple of Portonaccio. (Copyright: G. Colonna)

trapezoidal bases, which were fixed onto the principal cover tile over the ridge pole and onto the cover tiles that were placed at the terminals of the tile gables (fig. 13.4). Unfortunately, we are missing the statue that was placed on the summit of the pediment of the temple, which sat directly on the principal cover tile, on a throne surrounded by brilliant clouds.[44]

Among the different votives of this phase, a group with Hercle and Menerva (three-quarters life-size) was found near the *sacellum* of Menerva. The master who created these two statues belonged to a different school and was more careful in the representation of anatomical details. This group—especially the presence of Hercle—highlights once again the presence of a tyrannical ideology and appears to have been the ex-voto of someone who was at that time ruling the city as a king, similar to Thefarie Velianas at Caere, as shown by temple B at Pyrgi.[45]

Numerous restorations and replacements of the reliefs and the antefixes occurred during the last quarter of the sixth century BCE (*see plate 14*), confirming the central importance of this temple for the citizens of Veii, which would have justified the expenditures that were certainly required for maintaining and improving it. This phenomenon contrasts with the policies of the patrician government of Rome in the same years.

Immediately after 470 BCE, an entire cycle of paintings on terracotta plaques formed the new decoration of the walls of the pronaos. Among the various obscure themes, it has been possible to identify a warrior dance with young girls.[46]

A small altar was built in front of the temple,[47] and a precinct wall fenced the area behind the temple. Excavation has revealed that this area remained substantially empty, with a few remains of cult practices[48] during the subsequent phases of the sanctuary, before its partial destruction during its use as a mid-Republican quarry. This area could have appeared as a sacred grove (*lucus*) in close proximity to the nearby temple.[49]

The identity of the deity or deities worshiped in the temple is still uncertain, since no specific votive deposit has been found that is linked directly to this temple. Menerva appears to have played a secondary role within it, associated only with Hercle.[50] Moreover, Hercle and Aplu appear at least two times in the groups of acroteria (*see plates 11–12*). In particular, Hercle appears in the episode of his fight with the Lernaean Hydra, while Aplu is represented as an infant in the arms of his mother, Leto, in the foundation myth of the oracle at Delphi, in which he fought against the snake Python.[51] However in the main episode, the adult Aplu, as a Delphic and Hyperborean god, rushes toward Hercle to reclaim the hind sacred to his sister Artumes (Artemis), which Hercle had killed in another of his labors. Turms (Hermes) also took part in this episode, judging from the beautiful head—part of another acroterion—that is another masterpiece of the Master of Apollo. The messenger god, with his superior and provocative mocking expression, was opposed to the two contenders, and represented the real star of the scene, while facing the wrath of Aplu with his back to the snarling Hercle, who jumps on his prey like a wild beast.[52]

Tinia (Zeus) probably sat on the summit of the frontal pediment, surrounded by shining clouds; on the rear pediment, he may have been standing, facing the entrance of the sanctuary. A hand holding a scepter or a thunderbolt and two shod feet might be assigned to this second statue, thought to be more than two meters in height.

Several votive terracottas have been connected both to Aplu (and Rath) and to Hercle and testify to their cult within the sanctuary.[53] The central presence of these two deities, in the representation of the conflict for the tripod, not only reveals, as an *exemplum*, the divine protection of the hero but also suggests that they were the dedicatees of this temple, together with their father, Tinia. The three cellas of the temple can

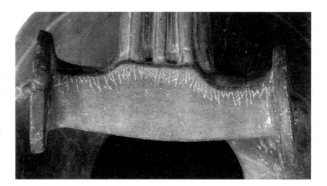

FIGURE 13.5. Detail of the rim of an *oinochoe* with inscription engraved on the handle referring to Karkuna Tulumne. (Copyright: G. Colonna)

be assigned to these three gods, who would have been welcomed in the sanctuary of Menerva.

The construction of the temple and of the pool highlighted the nature of the prophetic divination of the Veientine oracle, which appears to have been modeled on that at Delphi. Preliminary rites of purification would have taken place in the sacred wood and in the large pool. This connection of temple and pool occurs also at Falerii, in the temple of Scasato I, which was sacred to Aplu as mantic and *haruspex*.[54]

The link of Veii to Delphi follows similar close connections already promoted by Caere and Rome during the monarchy of the Tarquinii.[55] The echo of this religious link with Delphi characterizes also the famous black-figure and red-figure *dinoi* and column-craters, which, starting from this moment, exceeded in number the previous imports of Etrusco-Corinthian *phialai*, and especially the bucchero chalices and the monumental *oinochoe* (fig. 13.5). These new shapes recall the tradition of the golden crater that Furius Camillus sent to Delphi as a tithe of the booty of Veii.[56]

The cult of Hercle in Etruria also had particular oracular connotations, and it involved the ritual use of water. The importance of water in the sanctuary of Portonaccio is emphasized by the series of antefixes representing the river god Acheloos,[57] and by the pair of dolphins that appear on the angular *mutules* and are painted on the bases of the acroteria. In addition, the hundreds of subterranean *cuniculi* and water infrastructure excavated in the territory of Veii imply the participation of the same royal authority that built the temple.

THE RETURN OF MENERVA (FOURTH PHASE)

Immediately after the mid-fifth century BCE, while no more evidence of transformation and restoration of the temple has been found (part of its roof was also removed), the eastern part of the sanctuary was completely transformed. The *sacellum* of Menerva was demolished, and on top of its ruins a new enclosure was created, functioning as another entrance to the shrine. The group of Hercle and Menerva, together with other statues, was buried during the leveling of the ground. In fact, at this time the level of this sector reached the height of the open area and of the temple, while the stairs were covered and the altar was transformed into a larger and monumental structure. The form of this new altar, with two *antae*, is very similar to the famous altars of Lavinium. A selection of the ex-votos of the first phase of the sanctuary, which previously had been stored within the *sacellum*, was moved into the inner space of the altar. The entire area around the altar was paved, with the exception of the mouth of the sacred pit, which was kept open. The portico was rebuilt, with a higher podium, and was enlarged with a second portico. The evidence of this second portico is a column set close to the new wall.

All these new activities in the eastern part of the sanctuary resulted finally in the unification of its two main areas, which until this phase had always been physically separated. A peculiar ritual occurred during this reunification: the acroterion of Leto, with the baby Aplu, was buried, together with some of the open-work cornices of the frontal sima and the large male torso mentioned above. All these statues had probably been damaged before this ritual burial. Attic pottery, coming from the pavement, dates this action around 450–440 BCE.

This new phase of the sanctuary continued also after the siege of Veii, and numerous statues in Classical style, representing young boys and girls, testify to this new beginning. The famous "Malavolta head" (fig.

FIGURE 13.6. Classical-style sculpture at Portonaccio: the so-called Testa Malavolta. (Copyright: G. Colonna)

13.6), together with other votive heads and figurines, representing Aplu and enthroned women, in some cases holding a baby on their lap, reveals an impressively high artistic quality of this period.[58]

This evidence suggests the "return of Menerva," no longer as an oracular deity but as the protectress of births, of the *iuventus*, and of the initiations of young pupils. A new dedication to Menerva on a kylix by the Veii Painter, dating to the mid-fifth century BCE, with two ephebes conversing in the center medallion was discovered, significantly, near the pool.

In terms of historic value, this transformation of the sanctuary is particularly meaningful, since it may testify to the end of the tyrannical regime during which the temple was built together with the exaltation of the figure of Hercle and the strengthening of the cult of Aplu, following the Delphic model. The return to the origins of the sanctuary represented by the cult of Menerva may possibly have demonstrated that the aristocracy of the town had regained possession of the sanctuary and restarted the cult on behalf of the whole community.

NOTES

1. In *Arezzo*, 99–109.

2. Ward-Perkins 1961:36; Fontaine 1993:222.

3. Colonna 1987a:33–39.

4. Giglioli 1919, 1923.

5. Stefani 1953; Baglione 1987.

6. Santangelo 1952.

7. The project was designed by G. Colonna, with the help of G. Foglia and E. Ceschi, under the supervision of F. Boitani. See Boitani and Ceschi 1995.

8. Colonna 1998:139–141.

9. Stefani 1953: fig. 4; *Portonaccio* I; Colonna 1998: fig. 1. The incomplete plan by Stefani resulted in several misunderstandings, e.g., Ward-Perkins 1961:39.

10. Stefani 1953:81–87; Ward-Perkins 1961:30; G. Colonna, in *Portonaccio* I.

11. Colonna 1987b:420–428.

12. Colonna 1987b:433–435.

13. Colonna 1996:363n41.

14. Colonna and von Hase 1984:48 n. 96, pl. 16:c.

15. See chapter 24.

16. Colonna 1987b:423.

17. Champeaux 1982:63.

18. Colonna 1976:18; Cristofani 1978:10.

19. See chapter 15.

20. Similarly to the bridge of San Giovenale: Colonna and Backe Forsberg 1999:78, with bibliography.

21. Stefani 1953:104; Baglione 1987:410 n. 34.

22. Andrén 1974:4 n. 21.

23. Prayon 1991.

24. In *Arezzo*, 107, 5.1.G.1.

25. The reconstruction was promoted by F. Melis: see *Arezzo*, 101, 5.1.B.1.

26. Stefani 1953:54, fig. 29.

27. G. Colonna, in *Portonaccio* I.

28. Stefani 1953:43, fig. 20.

29. Torelli 1968.

30. Stefani 1953:103, fig. 70B; Baglione 1987:408, fig. 22.

31. The cistern was terribly damaged by the mid-Republican quarry. Only the bottom part of the structure survived to this destruction.

32. See chapter 24.

33. Torelli 1992, although without mention of Portonaccio.

34. Stefani 1953:56–59, fig. 32, a–i, m–p, r–s; Gantz 1975: figs. 33–42.

35. In *Arezzo*, 101, 5.1.B.2; Colonna 1987a:28, fig. 65.

36. Colonna 1987a:32, figs. 64 and 76; Colonna 1987b:423, fig. 5.

37. Mastrocinque 1993.

38. The first evidence occurs in the tomb of Isis at Vulci (Pliny, *Nat. Hist.* 34.24); see Roncalli 1982.

39. Riis 1997:62, fig. 60; Colonna 2000.

40. Colonna 1998:139.

41. Colonna 1991.

42. De Vita De Angelis 1968; Pandolfini and Prosdocimi 1990:185.

43. See chapter 24.

44. Stefani 1946.

45. Colonna 2000.

46. Stefani 1953:67–80; Colonna 1987b:444.

47. The altar was completely ruined during the mid-Republican period, when the entire square was destroyed for the opening of a quarry.

48. Colonna and Belelli Marchesini 1998.

49. Colonna 1998:141.

50. According to D'Agostino 2000.

51. Several paintings in the pronaos referred to this myth; see Colonna 1987b:444.

52. For the iconography of the myth, see D'Agostino 2000: pl. I, 1.

53. Colonna 1987b:431–441.

54. This aspect of Apollo made him different from the Faliscan Soranus, whose temple was situated on the plateau of Vignale; see *Arezzo*, 87; Comella 1993:147–149.

55. Coarelli 1993.

56. Livy 5.25.10, 28.2.

57. Ward-Perkins 1961:48, 51.

58. In *Arezzo*, 5.1.G.3–5.

BIBLIOGRAPHY

Andrén, A. 1974. "Osservazioni sulle terrecotte architettoniche etrusco-italiche." *OpRom* 8:1–16.

Arezzo = G. Colonna, ed., *Santuari d'Etruria* (Milan, 1985)

Baglione, M. P. 1987. "Il santuario di Portonaccio a Veio: Precisazioni sugli scavi Stefani." *ScAnt* 1:381–417.

Boitani, F., and F. Ceschi. 1995. "La rievocazione del tempio dell'Apollo a Veio." In *I siti archeologici: Un problema di musealizzazione all'aperto*, ed. B. Amendolea, 88–97. Rome.

Champeaux, J. 1982. *Fortuna: Recherches sur le culte de la Fortune à Rome et dans le monde romain des origines à la mort de César*, 1: *Fortuna dans la religiuons archaïque*. Rome.

Coarelli, F. 1993. "I Tarquini e Delfi." In *I grandi santuari della Grecia e l'Occidente*, ed. A. Mastrocinque, 31–42. Trento.

Colonna, G., 1976. "Il sistema alfabetico." In *L'Etrusco arcaico*, 7–24. Florence.

———. 1987a. "Il Maestro dell'Ercole e della Minerva: Nuova luce sull'attività dell'officina veiente." *OpRom* 16:7–41.

———. 1987b. "Note preliminari sui culti del santuario di Portonaccio a Veio." *ScAnt* 1:419–446.

———. 1991. "Le due fasi del tempio arcaico di S. Omobono." In *Stips votiva*, ed. M. Gnade, 51–59. Amsterdam.

———. 1996. "L'Apollo di Pyrgi." In *Magna Grecia, Etruschi, Fenici*, 345–375. Naples.

———. 1998. "Veio: I santuari di Portonaccio e Piano della Comunità." *Scavi e ricerche archeologiche dell'Università di Roma "La Sapienza,"* ed. L. Drago, 139–143. Rome.

———. 2000. "Il santuario di Pyrgi dalle origini mitistoriche agli altorilievi frontonali dei Sette e Leucotea." *ScAnt* 10: 251–336.

Colonna, G., and Y. Backe Forsberg. 1999. "Le iscrizioni del 'sacello' del ponte di San Giovenale." *OpRom* 24:63–81.

Colonna, G., and B. Belelli Marchesini. 1998. "Veii." *StEtr* 44: 422–427.

Colonna, G., and F. W. von Hase. 1984. "Alle origini della statuaria etrusca: La tomba delle Statue di Ceri." *StEtr* 52: 13–59.

Comella, A. 1993. *Le terrecotte architettoniche del Santuario dello Scasato a Falerii: Scavi 1886–1887*. Naples.

Cristofani, M. 1978. "Rapporto sulla diffusione della scrittura nell'Italia antica." *Scrittura e Civiltà* 2:5–33.

D'Agostino, B. 2000. "Iconografia e contesto: Qualche annotazione sul Santuario di Portonaccio." In *Damarato. Studi di antichità classica offerti a Paola Pelagatti*, ed. I. Berlingò, H. Blanck, F. Cordano, P. G. Guzzo, and M. C. Lentini, 99–103. Milan.

De Vita De Angelis, G. 1968. "Contrassegni alfabetici e di altro tipo su elementi del rivestimento fittile dal tempio dell'Apollo a Portonaccio." *StEtr* 36:403–449.

Fontaine, P. 1993. "Véies: Les remparts et la porte de la Piazza d'Armi." *MÉFRA* 105:221–239.

Gantz, T. 1975. "Terracotta Figured Friezes from the Workshop of Vulca." *OpRom* 10:1–9.

Giglioli, G. Q. 1919. "Veio. Scavi nell'area urbana della città e della necropoli: Statue fittili di età arcaica." *NotSc* 1919:13–37.

———. 1923. "Veio. Ritrovamenti sporadici." *NotSc* 1923: 163–173.

Mastrocinque, A., ed. 1993. *I grandi santuari della Grecia e l'Occidente*. Trento.

Pandolfini, M., and A. L. Prosdocimi. 1990. *Alfabetari e insegnamento della scrittura in Etruria e nell'Italia antica*. Florence.

Prayon, F. 1991. "Deorum sede: Sull'orientamento dei templi etrusco-italici." In *Miscellanea etrusca e italica in onore di Massimo Pallottino. ArchCl* 43:1285–1295.

Riis, P. J. 1997. *Vulcentia Vetustiora: A Study of Archaic Vulcian Bronzes*. Copenhagen.

Roncalli, F. 1982. "Un bronzo etrusco della collezione Carpegna nel Museo profano della Biblioteca Vaticana." In *Miscellanea Archaeologica Tobias Dohrn Dedicata*, ed. H. Blanck and S. Steingräber, 89–96. Rome.

Santangelo, M. 1952. "Veio, santuario 'di Apollo': Scavi fra il 1944 e il 1949." *BdA* 37:147–172.

Stefani, E. 1946. "Veio. Basi di statue fittili scoperte nel santuario dell'Apollo." *NotSc* 1946:36–59.

———. 1953. "Veio. Tempio detto dell'Apollo: Esplorazione e sistemazione del santuario." *NotSc* 1953:29–112.

Torelli, M. 1968. Appendix to A. La Regina and M. Torelli, "Due sortes preromane." *ArchCl* 20:227–229.

———. 1992. "I fregi figurati delle *regiae* latine ed etrusche: Immaginario del potere arcaico." *Ostraka* 1:249–274.

Ward-Perkins, J. 1961. "Veii: The Historical Topography of the Ancient City." *PBSR* 29:1–123.

CHAPTER 14

CULT EVIDENCE FROM THE URBAN SANCTUARIES AT VEII

INGRID EDLUND-BERRY

The Etruscan city of Veii has been much admired for reasons reminiscent of a backhanded compliment: only because the city was so great did it become an enemy worthy of her closest neighbor, Rome, and the target of that city's aggressive politics. As a result, according to Livy's famous account, the final event that brought Veii down in 396 BCE was the Roman attack on the temple of Juno on the citadel, and the cult of that goddess was transferred to Rome.[1] Livy's chilling description of the fall of Veii has continued to influence our view of the city and has been reinforced by statements such as those by George Dennis, author of *The Cities and Cemeteries of Etruria*, who comments, "He who would make the tour of Veii must not expect to see numerous monuments of the past. . . . Veii lives in the page of history rather than in extant monuments."[2]

Thanks to recent excavations and ongoing research, we are today in a much better position to evaluate the cultural identity and status of Veii.[3] My contribution here aims at highlighting the urban cult places of Veii, and how their location and history contributed to the profile of the city as a major player in all of Etruria, equal to, if not surpassing, her neighbors to the north, including Caere and Tarquinia, and south, including Rome.[4]

TEMPLE OF JUNO (ETRUSCAN UNI)

It may seem ironic that the temple we know best from the historical sources is also the most elusive in terms of its location and appearance. According to

Livy (5.21), the temple was located on the citadel of Veii (*in Veientana arce*), and it could be reached from within through a tunnel (*cuniculus*) that allowed the Roman soldiers to enter the sanctuary, where a priest pronounced a prophecy while the king was performing sacrifices (*inmolante rege Veientium vocem haruspicis. . . . exauditam*).

The scenery thus described would fit well with the landscape of ancient Veii, known for its *cuniculi* that penetrate the volcanic rock of the city plateau, and the location of a major temple on a high point of the city compares well with the pattern known from many Etruscan cities. Like other Etruscan temples it could have been built in the Tuscan style, serving as the home for the cult statue, and it would in all likelihood have been decorated with brightly colored architectural terracottas. The rituals performed at the sanctuary would have included processions with sacrifices and prayers and offerings of votive pottery or figurines.

To date, however, the exact location of this important temple cannot be established with certainty. The identification of Piano di Comunità (fig. 14.1:J; *map 4:W*)[5] as the optimal location for the temple of Juno is based on a number of factors, including its elevation in relation to the surrounding plateau, the discoveries by Lanciani in 1889, and the continuity of building activity.[6] Fragments of architectural terracottas indicate that an important building (or buildings) existed here as early as the late seventh century BCE,[7] and the type of cult is suggested by the presence of an architectural terracotta antefix of a helmeted female, identified as Uni/Juno (fig. 14.2).[8] Since the layout of the temple

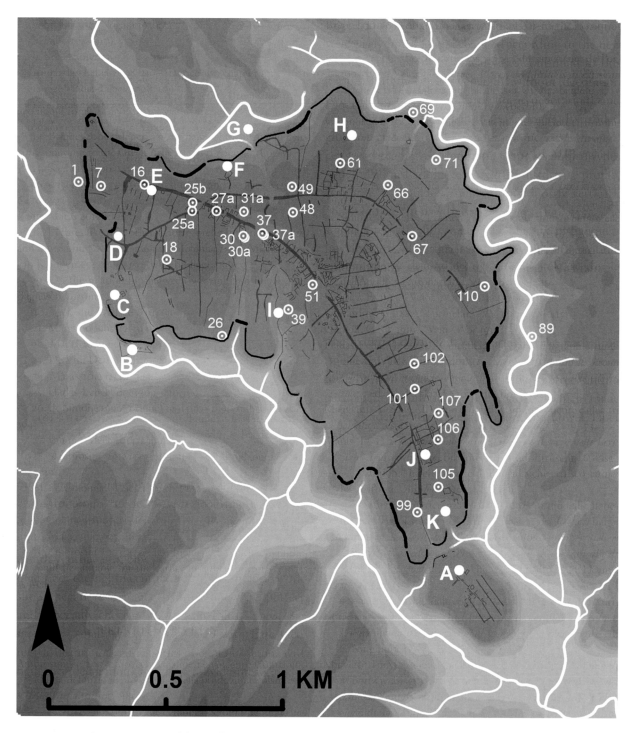

FIGURE 14.1. Sanctuaries at Veii (the numbers recall those used in *Survey*). Empty dots correspond to ritual sites identified by survey, while filled dots correspond to excavated sanctuaries. A. Piazza d'Armi, *oikos*; B. Portonaccio; C. Campetti South-West; D. Caere Gate; E. Campetti, Central Area; F. West of Formello Gate; G. Outside Formello Gate; H. Capena Gate; I. Vignacce Postern; J. Piano di Comunità; K. Stipe Lanciani. (Copyright: O. Cerasuolo and J. Tabolli)

FIGURE 14.2. Terracotta head of Uni/Juno from Piano di Comunità. Roma, Museo Nazionale di Villa Giulia, inv. 61406. (© MiBACT, Museo Nazionale Etrusco di Villa Giulia)

publication by G. Bartoloni and G. Benedettini that we can begin to evaluate its full significance.[11] Of the fifteen categories of votives included in the deposit, the main ones are fragmentary terracotta statues, terracotta heads and figurines, animal statuettes, anatomical votives, and votive pottery, as well as a few architectural terracottas.[12]

While a few of the objects may date from the sixth century BCE, the peak of use seems to have been from the late fourth century BCE until the second century BCE. The types of votives, ranging from representations of the offerants or of the deity to anatomical votives, suggest a cult to a female deity. The early material (for example, terracotta figurines of a female seated on a throne) may be connected with a cult to Uni/Juno, whereas the later votives indicate a transformation from the Etruscan cult to a more generic Etrusco-Roman cult of a female deity.[13]

If then we accept that the main temple at Veii was located at Piano di Comunità (in spite of the absence of a *cuniculus*), and assume that Uni/Juno was worshiped there as the principal goddess, there is also evidence that the city housed many other cults at sanctuaries on the city plateau and *arx*. Due to the different find circumstances and the long excavation history of Veii, each sanctuary preserves varying elements of evidence for reconstructing its appearance and function, ranging from roofed structures and open-air spaces to votives and inscriptions as evidence of the cults practiced during Veii's Etruscan and later history.[14]

VEII'S ETRUSCAN AND LATER HISTORY

ROOFED STRUCTURES AND OPEN-AIR SPACES

With the exception of the extramural Portonaccio temple (discussed in chapter 13), the structures connected with sanctuaries at Veii represent a variety of forms, and it is the context rather than the specific plan that would indicate that they had a sacred use.[15]

The best-known example from Veii of an early roofed structure is the so-called *oikos* at Piazza d'Armi (fig. 14.1:A; *map 4:Y*), which in the earlier literature

of Juno cannot be reconstructed, we can only suggest that it was built as a Tuscan temple with one or more rooms and a porch supported by columns, like the Portonaccio temple,[9] or that it followed the plan of the so-called *oikos* at Piazza d'Armi, discussed below.

In addition to scattered votive objects, the area can also be linked to the so-called Stipe Lanciani, that is, the votive deposit found on the slopes of the plateau to the south, facing Piazza d'Armi (fig. 14.1:K; *map 4:X*).[10] According to the early reports, this votive deposit was the largest of all those found at Veii, but like so many other discoveries of this kind, many of the objects from this closed group have since been scattered, lost, or stolen, and it is only thanks to the recent

was often identified as the temple of Juno.[16] The foundation walls belonged to a rectangular structure, ca.
8.07 × 15.35 meters, oriented northeast to southwest.[17]
Abundant finds of architectural terracottas indicate
that the structure was elaborately decorated with revetment plaques, antefixes, and painted eaves tiles, dating
to 580 BCE and later.[18]

Recent and ongoing excavations have shown that
the *oikos* is one product of a stretch of continuous
building activity on Piazza d'Armi, beginning with Iron
Age huts and developing into a monumental building
with an open courtyard that in all likelihood served as
a residence.[19] While it seems clear that the *oikos* was an
important building that may have had several political and religious functions, its sacred nature has been
debated, given that the evidence for rituals or votive
offerings is somewhat ambiguous.[20]

The architectural forms of the preserved structures
at other locations vary in layout and function. Recent
excavations at the location known as Campetti South-
West (fig. 14.1:C; *map 4:O*), at the western edge of the
city, north of the Portonaccio Gate (fig. 14.1:B; *map
4:S*), have revealed a large open-air precinct, 25 × 29
meters, oriented east–west with an entrance from the
south (fig. 14.3:A).[21] Remains of wells and a cistern,
as well as a variety of votives, suggest that this was a
sanctuary associated with water cults, dating from the
late seventh century BCE.[22] Over time other structures
were added, and fragments of architectural terracottas
indicate that roofed buildings already existed here in
the early and late sixth century BCE.[23]

As for the cults active at this sanctuary, there is evidence for Tin (Jupiter) on an inscribed sherd,[24] and
fragments of terracotta statues have been reconstructed
to represent a group with Aeneas and Anchises (*see fig.
12.4*) and a statue of Hercules.[25] The continuity of use
of the site as a water sanctuary is further documented
by a dedicatory inscription to Hercules and the Fontes
(Springs), dated to the second century CE.[26]

Further to the north, on the western edge of the
city plateau, at Caere Gate (fig. 14.1:D; *map 4:K*), a
votive deposit was discovered in a complex including a cistern (*pozzo*) and a basin (*vasca*) with a curved
back wall, which imply the presence of a sanctuary.[27]
The cistern and basin are placed some 8 meters apart,

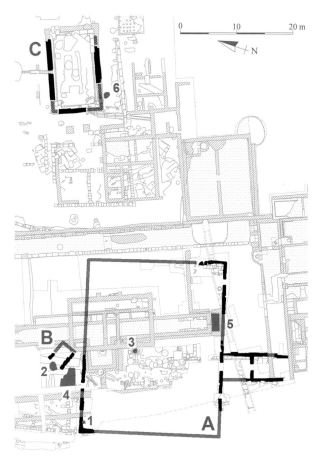

FIGURE 14.3. Plan of the sanctuary of Campetti South-West.
1–6. Votive deposits; A. Large open-air precinct; B. Small
chapel; C. *Sacellum* (?). (Copyright: O. Cerasuolo)

and within a paved precinct defined by a wall to the
east (fig. 14.4). The complex would have been entered
from the south, that is, from the Caere Gate. Well-
preserved architectural terracottas include a *silenus*, a
female head, and revetment plaques, dated to 500–
450 BCE, suggesting that a building (sacred? temple?)
existed somewhere in the vicinity of the presumably
open-air precinct.[28] The stratigraphy and pottery indicate that the sanctuary was in use as early as the sixth
century BCE and that the cult continued well into the
second century BCE. In addition to terracotta male and
female heads and anatomical votives, there was a statuette of a seated Menerva, who may have been the deity
venerated at this sanctuary.[29]

Features such as an enclosed open area and votives
also appear in the so-called Campetti North sanctuary, located to the west of the Formello Gate (figs.

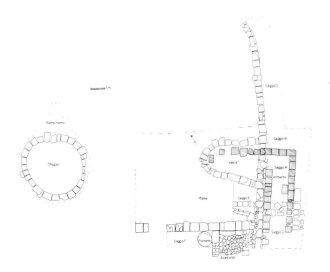

FIGURE 14.4. Plan of Caere Gate sanctuary.
(From Torelli and Pohl 1973: fig. 3)

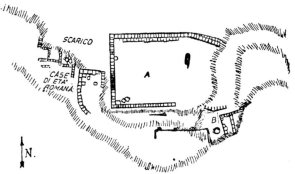

FIGURE 14.5. Plan of Campetti North sanctuary. (From
Pallottino 1938: fig. 1; reproduced by permission for the
Ministero per i Beni e le Attività Culturali e del Turismo)

14.1:F, 14.5; *map 4:H*).[30] Although unfortunately the remains of buildings are no longer visible, the published plan[31] includes a rectangular structure, labeled A, that measures 20 × 17 meters. Because of the size of the walls and the lack of interior supports, this structure has been interpreted as an open-air precinct. Next to the precinct, there is a second structure, labeled B, of which only the northwest corner was uncovered (fig. 14.5). In the vicinity of these structures was also an artificial cave (*grotta*) that seems to have played an important role in the rituals performed at the sanctuary.[32] Remains of Roman buildings have been interpreted as houses, but could perhaps also be connected with the later use of the sanctuary.[33]

Fragments of architectural terracottas, including antefixes and revetment plaques, signal the presence of a roofed building at the sanctuary but cannot be linked to either of the identified structures. The earliest examples date from around 500 BCE and have been compared to similar material from the Portonaccio temple.[34]

As indicated in the two main publications of the finds from Campetti North, thousands of votive objects were recovered from all areas of the sanctuary, both within the structures and inside the cave, some in seemingly closed deposits, while others were scattered. Of the twelve categories of votives, the main types include male and female votive heads and figu-rines, anatomical votives, and pottery ranging from impasto and bucchero to fragments of Greek black-and red-figure vases.[35] Although the earliest votive offerings can be dated to the sixth century BCE, the peaks of activity seem to have occurred in the fifth century BCE, and in the fourth and third centuries BCE.[36] The deity worshiped here may have been Vei, an Etruscan counterpart of the Roman Ceres, documented in a Latin inscription,[37] and represented by votive offerings of seated female figures or standing figures holding a piglet.[38] In addition to various forms of male and female figurines, the best-known type is a statuette representing Aeneas and Anchises, a popular motif in both Etruscan and Roman iconography, and, in the case of Veii, also thought to have been represented at the Campetti South-West sanctuary.[39]

Located further east, and closer to a gate, the Capena Gate, or North-East Gate of the city plateau (fig. 14.1:H), is the Macchiagrande sanctuary.[40] It consists of two main components: a structure with five small rooms aligned from east to west (fig. 14.6), and a deposit consisting of building elements such as tufa blocks and roof tiles as well as votive objects, including terracotta veiled heads and anatomical votives and a set of altars, inscribed in Latin to deities such as Apollo, Minerva, Victoria, Pitumnus, Iupiter Libertas (?), and the Gods and Goddesses.[41]

While the five-room structure has been interpreted

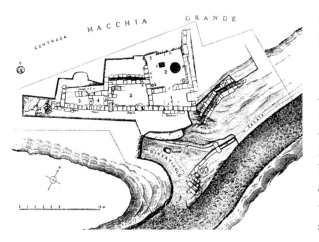

FIGURE 14.6. Plan of Macchiagrande sanctuary.
(From Stefani 1922: fig. 2)

as an early Etruscan dwelling, the deposit is dated to the fourth century BCE and is seen as an indication that cults of a Roman origin were introduced into the conquered Etruscan city.[42] The remains of blocks and architectural terracottas[43] would suggest that the sanctuary originally contained a roofed building with an open-air precinct for the rituals connected with the altars.

Considering the location of the so-called Etruscan houses and the deposit along the road toward the Capena Gate, it would seem likely that some form of cult place existed here already in Etruscan Veii.[44] Remains of water channels along the road may indicate that water played an important part in cult activities here as at other urban sanctuaries (Campetti South-West).

Finally, three sites that are referred to in current studies of Veii as temples are Campetti, Central Area (fig. 14.1:E; *map 4:I*),[45] Casale Caprioli (fig. 14.1: area 110; *map 4:L*),[46] and Macchiagrande (*map 4:M*).[47] Of these, the identification of Casale Caprioli seems to be based primarily on the discovery of early architectural terracottas, whereas at Campetti, Central Area, remains of *opus quadratum* walls have been identified as belonging to a temple, adorned with architectural terracottas found in a nearby cistern.[48] Archival documentation from early excavations and remains of walls and a kiln, in addition to architectural terracottas, may indicate the presence of a sanctuary at a location that

corresponds with areas 65 and 66 at Macchiagrande (fig. 14.1: area 66).

As indicated by the above discussion of sanctuaries, there is evidence that open-air precincts were used in connection with the rituals surrounding votive offerings. While foundation walls may indicate roofed buildings, the primary evidence for such structures comes from architectural terracottas that represent the remains (often modest) of once-existing roofing systems.

In addition to the excavated sites, organized surveys as well as surface finds provide evidence for potential roofed structures, decorated with architectural terracottas.[49] While there is no proof, without further evidence of religious practices, that such structures had a sacred function, they reinforce an overall image of Veii's impressive cityscape, dominated by urban architecture.[50]

While the remains of structures, whether open-air or roofed, combined with the presence of architectural terracottas provide a useful starting point from which to identify the urban sanctuaries at Veii, evidence of cults and rituals is necessary to verify the sacred nature of such spaces. Because of the vicissitudes of early discoveries of votive deposits—such objects were sometimes discarded or sold—it is unfortunately not possible to establish the complete set of data necessary to evaluate typologies and changes in the function of the sanctuaries. Also, where the findspots and original contexts of votive objects are uncertain, it is not possible to differentiate between true sealed deposits and a seemingly random scatter.

VOTIVE OFFERINGS AND DEPOSITS

In addition to the multitude of votive objects found at sites such as Campetti North, Macchiagrande, and the slopes of Comunità (the Lanciani deposit), recent studies based on the surveys initiated by the British School at Rome in the 1960s have provided much new information on sites and objects, clarifying both the typology of the material and the chronology. The cult places located by the surveys are sometimes identified on the evidence of one or a few objects considered to be votive in nature,[51] but more often by a considerable amount of material, sometimes in locations in the vicinity of excavated sanctuaries.[52]

Votive offerings may range in type depending on the context in which they appear. While votive deposits (whether occurring scattered or in a defined receptacle) could contain objects used in daily life, such as plain pottery or coins, it is the specific types and the way in which they were presented that allow us to identify cults and rituals. Thus, especially fine pottery or distinctive forms, such as miniature vessels, may be considered part of the votive repertoire, as would figurines in bronze or terracotta portraying deities or offerants and terracotta heads, anatomical votives, and animal figurines. Depending on the type and quantity of offerings, votives are then interpreted to identify the cults practiced at any given sanctuary.

In the excavated sanctuaries such as Campetti North, Caere Gate, and Macchiagrande, the emphasis of the votives is on representations of individuals, presumably offerants, portrayed as figurines or heads. The anatomical votives may be interpreted as requests for healing or else as an expression of appreciation for restored health,[53] but overall the votive offerings do not seem to be tied exclusively to one named cult over another, except for the notable predominance of female votives. Therefore, it seems prudent to assume that the presence of isolated representations of deities such as Menerva at Caere Gate, Aplu in the Lanciani deposit, or Aeneas/Anchises at Campetti North should be regarded mainly as indications of a specific cult presence amidst the general context of votive offerings to any deity, named or unnamed.

INSCRIPTIONS

In addition to the votive material that can be linked to a specific deity, there are also a few inscriptions found at the urban sanctuaries.

A fragmentary early Etruscan inscription to Tin comes from Campetti South-West,[54] and the same site preserves another fragmentary inscription, dated to the late seventh or early sixth century BCE, that may provide the Etruscan equivalent of Pater Indiges.[55] The continuity of the cult is shown there by Roman Imperial Latin inscriptions to Hercules, Fontes, Aesculapius (?) and Hygieia, and Diana.[56] The extent to which names of Etruscan deities can be equated in terms of the cult to corresponding Roman ones, or vice versa, is debatable, but the dedicatory Latin inscription by L. Tolonios to Crere—that is, Latin Ceres—has been one of the key elements in associating the Campetti North sanctuary with Vei, the Etruscan equivalent of Demeter/Ceres.[57]

The Macchiagrande sanctuary presents the largest number of names of deities inscribed in Latin on individual altars that are dated to the third century BCE. As noted, these include Apollo, Minerva, Victoria, Pitumnus, Iupiter Libertas (?), and the generic Gods and Goddesses.[58] Although deities such as Apollo and Minerva were already familiar to the Veiians, it is not clear why this particular set was chosen or how the cult practices corresponded with earlier traditions.

THE LOCATION OF
URBAN SANCTUARIES

While allowing for all the uncertainties of preservation and interpretation of evidence for urban sanctuaries, certain patterns can be established. First, their location seems to be closely connected with roads and gates, or with elevated topographical points. In particular, the sanctuary areas documented by the British School surveys reinforce the already recognized ties between sanctuaries and city gates/walls, and the close connection between roads and votive offerings, whether isolated or as part of sanctuaries.[59] Second, the cult buildings at the urban sanctuaries—with the possible hypothetical exception of the temple of Juno—consist of open-air structures or roofed buildings of varying plans but probably small in size. Third, the evidence of votives suggests a variety of cults, some geared specifically to a particular aspect of the inhabitants (healing, women, etc.), whereas others are common to a wide variety of cults, but not necessarily to a named deity.

Although each sanctuary site seems to have had a

specific function, based on its layout and votive offerings, it would seem that it is ultimately the location that determined its role for the citizens of Veii. Many sanctuaries display a continuity of cults from the Archaic period to the time when Veii contained a mixture of Etruscan and Latin speakers, and it would seem that the location of a sanctuary was the one stable factor within a changing society.

CONCLUSIONS

With the exception of the impressive remains at the Portonaccio sanctuary, it may seem difficult to evaluate the religious activities at Etruscan Veii. As I have tried to show in this brief overview, there is strong evidence for a number of well-defined sanctuaries, as well as scattered cult places. Although the presence of roofs with architectural terracotta decoration does not automatically identify the type or use of a building, it would seem that the intra-mural sanctuaries placed around the city plateau of Veii contained roofed structures, unroofed areas, and objects defining the rituals practiced there, such as votive items or altars. While the roofed buildings may be considered "sacred" because of their context, they cannot be regarded as "temples" in an architectural sense. Because of the location of these sanctuaries, I would interpret their purpose as serving primarily the local population of the city, together with the urban temple to Uni/Juno, probably located in the Comunità area, whereas the major extra-mural sanctuary at Portonaccio provided opportunities for Veii to share ritual practices with its neighbors.

With the possible exception of the Macchiagrande sanctuary, the sanctuaries and cult places at Veii suggest a continuity of cults, of which only a small number can be attributed to named deities.[60] Starting in the seventh century BCE, votive offerings were made throughout the sacred places, and regardless of the political or cultural affiliation of the worshipers, Etruscan and/or Roman, the deities continued to be honored well into the second century BCE, or even later, as evident at the Campetti South-West sanctuary.

NOTES

I am grateful to Professor Gilda Bartoloni and her colleagues, Dr. Orlando Cerasuolo and Dr. Jacopo Tabolli, for their important work in the Veii Project and for inviting me to participate in this volume on Etruscan Veii. Bibliographical assistance was kindly provided by Shiela Winchester and staff at the University of Texas at Austin Libraries and by Astrid Capoferro and staff at the Library of the Swedish Institute in Rome. Jean M. Turfa provided valuable comments and suggestions for improving the text. Jessica Trelogan mapped the excavated sanctuaries and surveyed sites (fig. 14.1) to illustrate the concentration of locations at the city gates and along the roads, thus highlighting the density of sanctuaries at important points.

1. Livy 5.16–22. For an analysis of the historical events, see also chapters 6, 10, 12, and 25 in this volume and Murray 2011.

2. Dennis 1907:83.

3. For earlier explorations and surveys, see Ward-Perkins 1961.

4. As I will discuss in the following presentation of the sanctuaries and cults at Veii, it is important first of all to define the different types of evidence for cults and to connect structures and objects to the specific findspots in relation to the city plateau and the adjoining *arx*, Piazza d'Armi (see fig. 14.1:A). The focus here is thus sanctuaries that were located within the city proper, or directly connected with the city wall and gates, thus excluding the extra-mural sanctuaries such as the Portonaccio temple, discussed by Giovanni Colonna in chapter 13. Because of its extra-mural location, and the specific forms of the cults practiced there, I would argue that it, as well as other sanctuaries located off the main plateau and *arx*, included functions that connected to the territory of Veii and its boundaries, and that therefore they were not directly tied to the city proper. For discussions of the importance of the location of sanctuaries, see Colonna 1985 and Edlund 1987.

5. The names of specific locations on the city plateau vary in the different publications. Without attempting absolute consistency I have used the names that seem most common and easy to identify. The site of Comunità is referred to as Piano or Quarto di Comunità; see Colonna and Maras 2006; Gaultier 2010; *Culto degli Antenati*, pl. I. As for the Campetti sites, Colonna identifies the areas by location and excavator as follows: Campetti Sud (scavi Carandini-Carafa-Fusco), Campetti Porta Caere (scavi Torelli-Pohl), Campetti Area Centrale (scavi Fenelli-Iaia), and Campetti North (Pallottino) (Colonna 2014: 61).

6. For up-to-date summaries of the history of excavations and new discoveries, see, among others, Torelli 1982; Belelli Marchesini 2001; Colonna 2004; and Belelli Marchesini 2011.

7. See Belelli Marchesini 2001, 2009, 2011.

8. Rome, Museo di Villa Giulia inv. 61406. Carlucci 2004; Winter 2009:350, 5.C.4 (530–520 BCE).

9. See chapter 12.

10. According to Bartoloni and Benedettini (2011:790) the location of the cult, at least as it was practiced in the third and second centuries BCE, was extra-mural. Its earlier ties, however, seem to have been with the cult of Juno, which was definitely urban.

11. Bartoloni and Benedettini 2011. Also, Bartoloni 2000.

12. While the architectural terracottas suggest the presence of a roofed building in the early phase of the deposit, the cult may later have been practiced in an open-air space; see Bartoloni and Benedettini 2011:789.

13. Bartoloni and Benedettini 2011:779–790.

14. On the inscriptions see chapter 15.

15. Definitions of what constitutes a sacred area or "sanctuary" vary a great deal. Ideally, such a space would be identifiable by a recognizable "temple" (in the Tuscan style), altars, votive objects, inscriptions, and evidence of rituals. While the presence of architectural terracottas used to be considered evidence of a sacred building (Andrén 1940), Nancy Winter has demonstrated beyond doubt that this is not the case (Winter 2009). We should also realize that even where such terracottas were present on a sacred building, the iconography may not necessarily indicate the cult practiced. And, the multitude of so-called votive objects found at Veii, ranging from miniature vases to anatomical body parts, while suggesting cult activities, are not necessarily connected with the specific location where they appear, especially as isolated examples.

16. Dennis 1907:86–88. Concerning the *oikos* in the sequence of the periods of Piazza d'Armi, see above, chapter 1.

17. Stefani 1944; Winter 2009:224.

18. Bartoloni et al. 2006; Winter 2009:224–228, roof 4-1. See also chapter 24.

19. For some recent references, see Bartoloni 2004; Bartoloni et al. 2006; Bartoloni 2009:17–62; *Culto degli Antenati*, 7–10; Acconcia et al. 2012; Bartoloni et al. 2012, 2013. See also chapters 1 and 12.

20. See, for example, Bartoloni et al. 2011:118; Damgaard Andersen 1998:148; Winter 2009:568 (tentatively reconstructed as a courtyard building).

21. Fusco and Cerasuolo 2001; Fusco 2006–2007, 2011a, 2011b; Fusco, Maggi, and Latini 2015:40–48. See also chapter 12.

22. Cerasuolo and Di Sarcina 2013. For the overall importance of water at Veientine sanctuaries, including the rural sanctuary at Casale Pian Roseto, see Torelli 2001.

23. Fusco and Cerasuolo 2001:14–15, I.B.18 (Winter, ArchTerr DB 1695 [580–570 BCE]), I.B.19 (Winter, ArchTerr DB 1696 [530 BCE]); and Winter 2009:331, 5.A.1.c.

24. Fusco, communication (June 16, 2015). I am grateful to Dr. Fusco for sharing information from his manuscript on the Campetti area SO with me.

25. Colonna 2009; Fusco 2009, 2011.

26. Fusco 2009, 2011b:401 and fig. 26.

27. Torelli and Pohl 1973.

28. Torelli 1970 (female head); Torelli and Pohl 1973:58–63, figs. 28–30; Winter, ArchTerr DB 6499, 6504/6508, 6507/6509.

29. Torelli and Pohl 1973:248–249, fig. 127.

30. Pallottino 1938; Vagnetti 1971; Comella and Stefani 1990; Colonna 2014:61–69, 2015:112–113. For the votive deposit outside the Formello Gate (fig. 14.1:G), see Murray Threipland 1969. The location of the votive deposit is described as "on the low ground below the Veii escarpment, south of the Cremera, adjacent to the line of the Ponte San Silvestro (Formello) Etruscan road as it wound up to the gate." The finds consisted of bucchero and coarse-ware sherds, and a fragment of a votive figurine, but no architectural terracottas or remains of walls have been recorded. The deposit dates from the late sixth to the fifth century BCE.

31. Vagnetti 1971:16–17, fig. 1; Comella and Stefani 1990:195–203.

32. Comella and Stefani 1990:198–199; Carosi 2002; Colonna 2014:65–66.

33. Although it may be historically correct to refer to any event or archaeological remains at Veii after 396 BCE as "Roman," it would seem that the transition from clearly Etruscan to identifiably Roman was fluid and may have lasted for several generations.

34. Vagnetti 1971:26–30. See Winter, ArchTerr DB 6501 (late sixth–early fifth century BCE); 6500 (500–480 BCE); 6502 (500–450 BC); 6503 (500–300 BCE); 6505 (475–450 BCE); 6506 (no date). According to Colonna, one fragment may be as early as 530 BCE (2014: fig. 2; Comella and Stefani 1990: pl. 42, fig. d N10). Additional finds of architectural terracottas and pottery from the Campetti area have led Colonna to postulate the existence of two more sanctuaries, labeled Campetti North-East and Campetti North-West (Colonna 2014:69).

35. Vagnetti 1971; Gentili 1985; Comella and Stefani 1990. As pointed out by Colonna (2014:67–69, 2015:112–113), to the number of published votives should be added the material discovered by M. Santangelo in 1947.

36. Comella and Stefani 1990:202.

37. See below, page 137. For the cult of Vei, see most recently Carosi 2008 and Bellelli 2012.

38. See, for example, Comella and Stefani 1990:114–115, L 1 (bronze statuette with piglet). The interpretation of the cult is discussed by Comella and Stefani (1990:201–216).

39. Vagnetti 1970:88 and 181, fig. 48; Colonna 2009.

40. Stefani 1922; Olivieri 2005.

41. Stefani 1922; Olivieri 2005.

42. Torelli 1982; Olivieri 2005.

43. Olivieri 2005:183–184, pl. IVb. The example illustrated by Olivieri may be the one referred by Stefani (1922:389) as dating from the fifth century BCE, that is, while Veii was still an Etruscan city.

44. Early cult practices in the contrada Macchiagrande have been documented by the British School surveys, for which see, for example, area 61, in *Survey*, 59–60.

45. See Colonna 2009:81, no. 7; Gaultier 2010:117, no. 5; Bartoloni 2011:22, no. 5; Colonna 2014:61, fig. 1: no. 4.

46. See Colonna 2006: fig. 4: no. 5; Colonna 2009:81, no. 11; Gaultier 2010:117, no. 11; Bartoloni 2011:22, no. 12. The site is mentioned by Guaitoli (1981:81); Colonna and Maras (2006: 13); Colonna (2009: fig. 1); and Gaultier (2010:118–119); and in *Survey*, area 110. Most recently, see Colonna 2014:80 and fig. 1: no. 9.

47. Colonna 2014:80–94, 2015:113–116.

48. Fenelli 1998:138; Jaia and Cella 2015:37–38; Colonna 2014:63.

49. See *Survey*, 299–306, 309; Carlucci 2015:183–185. For other types of remains interpreted as sanctuaries, see, for example, *Survey*, 306–309.

50. Findspots of isolated architectural terracottas include the road leading to the North-West Gate (fig. 14.1: area 16), at Vignacce (fig. 14.1:I), west of the Vignacce Postern (fig. 14.1: area 26), at Campetti-Vignacce, at intersection between major roads (fig. 14.1: areas 30 and 30a). Of the findspots of two terracotta frieze plaques, both labeled Macchiagrande-Vignacce, one is located in the center of the city plateau (Colonna 2014:80, fig. 1.8), d'Alessio 2001:20–21, I.C.8 (Winter, ArchTerr DB 1697 [Archaic]) and I.C.9 (Winter, ArchTerr DB 1698 [580 BCE]), and the other may correspond with Gaultier map 6 (survey areas 30–31?) or Bartoloni map 9 (area 39?) (Giglioli 1923: pl. III.2 [Winter, ArchTerr DB 6497 (530 BCE)] and Giglioli 1923: pl. III.1 [Winter, ArchTerr DB 6498 (530 BCE)]). Other sites preserve features interpreted as evidence of a sacred building, such as a podium (Vignacce, south of main road: fig. 14.1: area 51; Ward-Perkins 1961:69, fig. 18; *Survey*, 56).

51. *Survey*, for example, area 1 (northwest hillslope), area 16 (along road leading to the North-West Gate), area 66 (Macchiagrande, along road toward North-East Gate), area 69 (northeast of Macchiagrande, inside or outside city wall), and area 89 (extramural site, along bank of Vaccareccia).

52. *Survey*, for example, area 7 (Campetti, inside city wall) and area 106 (site east of major north–south road, at highest point of plateau).

53. See, for example, Turfa 2006, 2013.

54. Fusco, communication (June 16, 2015). The inscription will be published by D. Maras.

55. The preserved letters are: ha. *CIE* 6342; Colonna 2009:54 n. 19; Fusco 2011b:384 n. 18.

56. Fusco 2001, 2009.

57. Vagnetti 1971:176–177; Comella and Stefani 1990:204–205; Fusco 2011b:384–385; Bellelli 2012; Giontella 2012:178–186.

58. Stefani 1922; Torelli 1982:26, 1988, 1999:25–29; Olivieri 2005.

59. *Survey*, for example, area 18 (along road toward Portonaccio), area 25a (Campetti, along road toward the North-West Gate), area 27a (Campetti, along road toward the North-West Gate), area 31a (Campetti, at intersection between major roads), area 37 (Vignacce, at intersection of major roads), area 48 (Macchiagrande, east of intersection of major roads), area 49 (Macchiagrande, north of east–west road), area 61 (Macchiagrande, north of east–west road), area 67 (Macchiagrande, west of Casale Caprioli), area 71 (south of North-East Gate on road toward Capena), area 99 (at edge of plateau, facing Piazza d'Armi, west of major north–south road), area 101 (site along major north–south road), area 102 (site east of major north–south road, north of Lanciani deposit), area 105 (site east of major north–south road, on slopes of plateau, north of South-East Gate), area 107 (site east of major north–south road, north of area 106), and area 110 (site located at highest point on east side of plateau, in the proximity of the Vaccareccia Gate).

60. For an important analysis of the cults at Veii, see Benedettini 2012. The degree to which cults were reinstated or strengthened after Veii politically became subject to Rome is difficult to determine.

BIBLIOGRAPHY

Acconcia, V., G. Bartoloni, M. Milletti, S. Neri, and F. Pitzalis. 2012. "Le ricerche a Piazza d'Armi." In *MAV*, 57–63.

Ambrosini, L., B. Belelli Marchesini, G. Colantoni, B. Giuliani, M. R. Lucidi, M. Merlo, and A. Celant. 2009. "Il contributo degli scavi di Piano di Comunità alla conoscenza dell'abitato di Veio: materiali dal riempimento di un pozzo sul pianoro sommitale." In *Veio* I, 65–123.

Andrén, A. 1940. *Architectural Terracottas from Etrusco-Italic Temples*. Lund.

Bartoloni, G. 2000. "Il deposito votivo rinvenuto a Veio negli scavi del 1889." In *Depositi votivi e culti dell'Italia antica dall'età arcaica a quella tardo-repubblicana. Atti del Convegno di Studi Perugia, 1–4 giugno 2000*, ed. A. Comella and S. Mele, 171–178. Bari.

———. 2004. "Veio-Piazza d'Armi: Campagne di scavo 1996-7." In *Bridging the Tiber*, 191–203.

Bartoloni, G., V. Acconcia, B. Belelli Marchesini, F. Biagi, O. Cerasuolo, S. Neri, F. Pitzalis, L. Pulcinelli, and D. Sarracino. 2013. "Progetto Veio: Novità dalle ultime campagne di scavo." *ScAnt* 19:133–156.

Bartoloni, G., V. Acconcia, E. Biancifiori, C. Mottolese, D. Sarracino, and V. Basilissi. 2012. "Veio, Piazza d'Armi: La fossa del cane." *ArchCl* 63:55–126.

Bartoloni, G., V. Acconcia, A. Piergrossi, S. ten Kortenaar, and I. van Kampen. 2006. "Veio: L'abitato di Piazza d'Armi: Le terrecotte architettoniche." In *Deliciae Fictiles* III: *Architectural Terracottas in Ancient Italy: New Discoveries and Interpretations*, ed. I. Edlund-Berry, G. Greco, and J. Kenfield, 50–76. Oxford.

———. 2011. "Veio, Piazza d'Armi: Riconsiderazioni e novità." In *Tetti di terracotta*, 116–174.

Bartoloni, G., and M. G. Benedettini. 2011. *Veio: Il deposito votivo di Comunità (scavi 1889–2005)*. Rome.

Bellelli, V. 2012. "*Vei*: Nome, competenze e particolarità cultuali di una divinità etrusca." In *Antropologia e archeologia a confronto: Rappresentazioni e pratiche del sacro. Atti dell'Secondo Incontro Internazionale Roma, Museo Preistorico Etnografico "Luigi Pigorini" 20–21 Maggio 2011*, ed. V. Nizzo and L. La Rocca, 455–478. Rome.

Belelli Marchesini, B. 2001. "Comunità." In *Veio, Cerveteri, Vulci*, 23–28.

———. 2009. "Materiali edilizi." In Ambrosini et al. 2009: 115–123.

———. 2011. "Veio: Un frontoncino da Piano di Comunità." In *Tetti di terracotta*, 175–183.

Benedettini, G. 2012. "Contesti sacrali Veienti." In *MAV*, 137–139.

Bouma, J. W. 1996. *Religio Votiva: The Archaeology of Latial Votive Religion. The Fifth-to-Third-Century BC Votive Deposit Southwest of the Main Temple at Satricum (Borgo Le Ferriere)*. Groningen.

Carlucci, C. 2004. "L'antefissa a testa di dea elmata." In Colonna 2004:218–219.

———. 2015. "La decorazione fittile architettonica a Veio tra la fine del VI e il V sec. a.C." In *Novità*, 183–185.

Carosi, S. 2002. "Nuovi dati sul Santuario di Campetti a Veio." *ArchCl* 53, n.s. 3:355–377.

———. 2008. "Veio, Roma ed il culto di Demetra/Cerere." In *Symposium Cumanum* 2008. www.centrumlatinitatis.org/cle_it/cuma/simona_carosi.pdf (accessed July 28, 2014).

Cerasuolo, O., and M. T. Di Sarcina. 2015. "Depositi votivi e attività cultuali a Campetti Area S-O." In *Novità*, 180–182.

Colonna, G. 1985. *Santuari d'Etruria*. Milan.

———. 2004. "I santuari di Veio: Ricerche e scavi su Piano di Comunità." In *Bridging the Tiber*, 206–221.

———. 2009. "Il mito di Enea tra Veio e Roma." In *Gli Etruschi e Roma: Fasi monarchica e altorepubblicana. Atti del XVI Convegno internazionale di studi sulla storia e l'archeologia dell'Etruria*, ed. G. Della Fina, 51–92. Rome.

———. 2014. "Gli scavi Santangelo nell'Area Urbana di Veio (1945–1952)." *ArchCl* 65:59–101.

———. 2015. "Novità sugli scavi Santangelo a Veio." In *Novità*, 111–132.

Colonna, G., and D. F. Maras. 2006. *Corpus Inscriptionum Etruscarum*, vol. 2, sect. 1, fasc. 5. Pisa.

Comella, A., and G. Stefani. 1990. *Materiali votivi del santuario di Campetti a Veio: Scavi 1947 e 1969*. Rome.

d'Alessio, M. T. 2011. "Macchiagrande–Vignacce." In *Veio, Cerveteri, Vulci*, 17–22. Rome.

Damgaard Andersen, H. 1998. "Etruscan Architecture from the Late Orientalizing to the Archaic Period (c. 640–480 BC)." PhD diss. University of Copenhagen. http://frontpage.cbs.dk/staff/hda/phd/ (accessed July 30, 2014).

Dennis, G. 1907. *The Cities and Cemeteries of Etruria*. London.

Edlund, I. E. M. 1987. *The Gods and the Place: Location and Function of Sanctuaries in the Countryside of Etruria and Magna Graecia (700–400 B.C.)*. Stockholm.

Fenelli, M. 1998. "Veio: Topografia generale e cartografia." In *Scavi e ricerche archeologiche dell'Università di Roma "La Sapienza,"* ed. L. Drago Troccoli, 137–138. Roma.

Fusco, U. 2001. "Nuovi reperti dall'area archeologica di Campetti a Veio." *ArchCl* 52:255–278.

———. 2006-2007. *Il complesso archeologico di Campetti a Veio e i luoghi di culto collegati alle acque (santuari alla sorgente, complessi termali/terapeutici/cultuali) dell'Italia centrale in età romana: tipologie monumentali e considerazioni storiche* (Diss. Università degli Studi di Pisa).

———. 2009. "Iscrizioni votive ad Ercole, alle Fonti, e a Diana dal sito di Campetti a Veio: ulteriori elementi per l'interpretazione archeologica." In *RendPontAcc* 81: 443–500.

———. 2011a. "Il complesso archeologico di Campetti, area S-O." In *Culto degli Antenati*, 11–15.

———. 2011b. "Il culto di Ercole presso il complesso archeologico di Campetti, area S-O, a Veio: Testimonianze dall'età etrusca a quella romana." *ArchCl* 72:379–412.

Fusco, U., and O. Cerasuolo. 2001. "Veio–Campetti." In *Veio, Cerveteri, Vulci*, 9–15.

Fusco, U., M. Maggi, and T. Latini. 2015. "I santuari presso Campetti, area SO." In *Novità*, 40–48.

Gaultier, F. 2010. "Sanctuaries et territoire en pays étrusque: Le cas de Véies." In *Les sanctuaires et leur rayonnement dans le monde méditerranéen de l'antiquité à l'époque moderne. Actes*, ed. J. de La Genière, A. Vauchez, and J. Leclant, 115–139. Paris.

Gentili, M. D. 1985. "Il deposito votivo di Campetti a Veio." In *Civiltà degli Etruschi*, ed. M. Cristofani, 279–280. Milan.

Giglioli, G. Q. 1923. "Veio. Ritrovamenti sporadici." *NSc* 1923: 163–173.

Giontella, C. 2012. *"Nullus enim fons non sacer . . .": Culti idrici di epoca preromana e romana (Regiones VI–VII)*. Pisa.

Guaitoli, M. 1981. "Notizie preliminari su recenti ricognizioni svolte in seminari dell'Istituto." *QITA* 9:79–82.

Jaia, A. M., and E. Cella. 2015. "Campetti–Paesaggi urbani a Veio. Saggi di scavo della sezione topografia antica della Sapienza." In *Novità*, 34–40.

Murray, C. 2011. "Constructions of Authority through Ritual: Considering Transformations in Ritual Space as Reflecting Society in Iron Age Etruria." In *State Formation in Italy and Greece: Questioning the Neoevolutionist Paradigm*, ed. D. Haggis and N. Terrenato, 199–216. Oxford.

Murray Threipland, L. 1969. "Veii: A Deposit of Votive Pottery." *PBSR* 37:1–13.

Olivieri, V. 2005. "Attorno al deposito votivo di Macchiagrande a Veio." In *Depositi votivi e culti dell'Italia antica dall'età arcaica a quella tardo-repubblicana. Atti del Convegno di Studi Perugia, 1–4 giugno 2000*, ed. A. Comella and S. Mele, 179–187. Bari.

Pallottino, M. 1938. "Scavo di un'area sacra a Veio." *Le Arti* 1:402–403.

Stefani, E. 1922. "Veio. Esplorazioni dentro l'area dell'antica città." *NSc* 1922:379–404.

———. 1944. "Scavi archeologici a Veio in contrada Piazza d'Armi." *MonAnt* 40:177–290.

Torelli, M. 1970. "Veio." In *Nuovi tesori dell'antica Tuscia*, ed. G. Colonna, 50–51. Viterbo.

———. 1982. "Veio, la città, l'*arx* e il culto di Giunone Regina." In *Miscellanea Archaeologica Tobias Dohrn Dedicata*, ed. H. Blanck and S. Steingräber, 117–128. Rome.

———. 1988. "Aspetti ideologici della colonizzazione romana più antica." *DialArch* 6:65–72.

———. 1998 (2001). "Stata Mater in agro Veientano: La 'risco-perta' di un santuario rurale veiente in loc. Casale Pian Roseto." *StEtr* 64:117–134.

———. 1999. *Tota Italia: Essays in the Cultural Formation of Roman Italy*. Oxford.

Torelli, M., and I. Pohl. 1973. "Scoperta di un piccolo santuario etrusco in località Campetti." *NSc* 1973:40–258.

Turfa, J. M. 2006. "Votive Offerings in Etruscan Religion." In *The Religion of the Etruscans*, ed. N. T. de Grummond and E. Simon, 90–115. Austin.

———. 2013. "Review of Bartoloni, G., and M. G. Benedettini. 2011. *Veio: Il deposito votivo di Comunità (scavi 1889–2005)*. Archaeologica 162. Rome." *BABESCH* 88:258–259.

Vagnetti, L. 1971. *Il deposito votivo di Campetti a Veio: Materiali degli scavi 1937–1938*. Florence.

Ward-Perkins, J. 1961. "Veii: The Historical Topography of the Ancient City." *PBSR* 29:1–123.

Winter, N. A. 2009. *Symbols of Wealth and Power: Architectural Terracotta Decoration in Etruria and Central Italy, 640–510 B.C.* Ann Arbor.

———. ArchTerr DB. "Etruscan and Central Italian Architectural Terracottas Online Database." University of Oxford, Classical Research Centre and the Beazley Archive. www.beazley.ox.ac.uk/databases/terracottas.htm (accessed July 29, 2014).

CHAPTER 15

THE EPIGRAPHICAL EVIDENCE

DANIELE FEDERICO MARAS

The discovery of Etruscan epigraphical texts at Veii occurred relatively late, in the twentieth century. Only a few inscriptions were known before then, and there were doubts regarding their provenience; this is the case, for instance, with the small bucchero flask of *piana plenianas*,[1] the bucchero horse statuette of *mamarce vel[—]nśnaś*,[2] and a mirror engraved with a scene of Peleus and Thetis.[3]

The epigraphical muteness of the Etruscan town was striking, especially when compared to the abundant inscriptional evidence from Caere and Tarquinia, and made it difficult for new finds to be accepted by scholars as Veientine. In fact, the very first Etruscan inscription found in context, coming from a regular excavation directed by Rodolfo Lanciani in 1882, was the small bucchero amphora inscribed with an *abecedarium* and a gift-text found together with the famous Chigi Vase in the tumulus of Monte Aguzzo (*map 2: no. 1; plates 5–6*).[4] The amphora, published almost immediately, a few months after the discovery, was cheered by the academic world as precious evidence of the literacy of Veii.[5] But the real birth of an Etruscan epigraphy of the town came only after the discovery of an impressive number of votive inscriptions in the sanctuary of Portonaccio by Ettore Gabrici and Giulio Quirino Giglioli (in 1914 and 1916),[6] Enrico Stefani (in 1917–1921),[7] and, later, Massimo Pallottino (in 1939–1940),[8] which suddenly filled the quantitative gap between Veii and the other towns of southern Etruria (*maps 4:S–T*).

The epigraphic record of Veii at the time of the publication of the relevant volume of the *Corpus Inscriptionum Etruscarum* (2006; *CIE*) amounted to 468 inscriptions, marks, single letters, and graffiti, the majority of them (at least 268) coming from Portonaccio.[9] This apparent preference for sacred places as contexts for inscriptions is unparalleled in the rest of Archaic Etruria, where this phenomenon may be observed only from the late sixth century onward. In the Orientalizing period at Caere, Tarquinia, and Vulci, tombs were the most frequent context for epigraphic finds; on the contrary, not more than twenty-three inscriptions of the same period come from funerary contexts at Veii.

This situation has been hypothetically attributed to the existence of sumptuary laws that restricted the display of luxury in tombs goods;[10] but although this could be a factor in a later period,[11] several funerary contexts of the seventh and sixth centuries can be rightfully considered luxurious, and it has still to be demonstrated to what extent the use of writing was considered "luxury" in the same sense as the display of bronzes, clothes, or arrays of banquet vessels.

On the other hand, it is worth noting that having an epigraphic record that is fuller in sanctuaries than in tombs is a feature shared by Late Orientalizing Veii with the contemporary cities of Greece and Magna Graecia. This is undoubtedly the sign of a precocious Hellenization of the use of writing in the Etruscan town that anticipates the writing tradition of the coastal sanctuaries of southern Etruria, such as Pyrgi and Graviscae, frequented by Greek worshipers from the second half of the sixth century BCE and after.[12]

This anomaly in the epigraphic record of Veii is re-

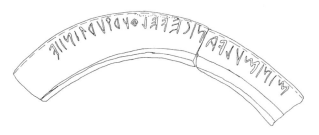

FIGURE 15.1. Etruscan gift-inscription (*CIE* 6451) painted on a fragmentary Etrusco-Corinthian cup, first half of the sixth century BCE. Reading from right to left: *mini mulvanice velϑur qurtiniie*. (Copyright: D. F. Maras)

flected in all the genres it encompasses. A large number of the longer inscriptions consistently refer to gift practices, both in funerary and in sacred contexts. Most frequently gift-texts with the verb *muluvanice* (and variants) are represented, recalling the Etruscan system of gift-exchange among people of high rank in the Orientalizing period.[13]

The standard formula of this kind of inscription has the object speaking in the first person, with the name of the donor (or offerer) and the verb in the past tense: for example, *CIE* 6451: *mini mulvanice velϑur qurtiniie*, "Velthur Qurtiniie gave me" (from Portonaccio, first half of the sixth century BCE [fig. 15.1]); and *CIE* 6713: *mini muluvanice tetana velkasnas veleliiasi*, "Tetana Velkasnas gave me to Velelia" (of unknown provenience, late seventh century BCE).

Also well attested are ownership inscriptions, which at times could even imply a situation of gifting; in this case the standard formula has the first-person pronoun and the name of the owner in genitive: for example, *CIE* 6676: *mi larisal pataras*, "I [am] of Laris Pataras" (on a bucchero patera from Casale Pian Roseto [*map 1: no. 5*], late sixth century BCE); and *CIE* 6710: *mi aviles aukanas qutumuza*, "I [am] the small jug of Avile Aukanas" (on a small impasto oinochoe of unknown provenience, early seventh century BCE).

At times the formulas are combined, such as in the case of *CIE* 6703b: *mi ϑanacvilus kanzina(ia) venel muluva(ni)ce setiu*, "I [belong to] Thanacvil Kanzinai. Venel Setiu gave [me to her]" (from Volusia [*map 1: no. 37*], late seventh century BCE). In some cases a eulogistic expression is added to the formula, praising the beauty and nobility both of the object and of the re-

cipient of the gift: for example, *CIE* 6405: *mini ϑanirsiie turice hvuluves mi mlaχ mlakas*, "Thanirsie Fuluves gave me. I [am] a beautiful [gift] for a beautiful/noble [person]" (from Portonaccio [*map 4:S*], early sixth century BCE).

These simple formulaic expressions, related to the ceremonial practice of gift-giving among peers in the Orientalizing aristocratic courts of southern Etruria, were extended for the first time in Veii to votive-offering practices in sacred contexts. Gift formulas were used for offerings to the gods, and ownership formulas declared the possession of an object by a deity: for example, *CIE* 6436: *laris velkasna[s mini muluvanice* (vel sim.)*] menervas*, "Laris Velkasnas gave me to Menerva," and *CIE* 6446: *[mi?] menarv[as]*, "[I am] of Menerva" (both from Portonaccio, early sixth century BCE).[14] A primary role in this shift was probably played by a scribal school in the sanctuary of Portonaccio that operated between the mid-seventh and the late sixth century BCE.[15]

Only one monumental funerary inscription is currently known, and that is sculpted on the wall of a tomb in the necropolis of Riserva del Bagno (*map 3*). It preserves only the name of the deceased in the form of an ownership formula: *CIE* 6661: *mi aranϑ mula* [—], "I (am) Aranth Mula . . ." (late seventh century BCE). Much later in date is a sculpted inscription (*CIE* 6707) recording the name of a local magistrate responsible for the construction or restoration of a road cut into the rock, the so-called Cavetta, at Monte Sant'Angelo in the countryside (*map 1: no. 19*).

Further epigraphic evidence from Veii not falling in the above-mentioned categories is mainly constituted by *sigla*, marks of trade and production such as single letters, syllables, and graffiti, which are very useful for understanding the spread of literacy and the history of writing systems, as we will see in the following pages. Having special relevance in this context are *abecedaria*, which have been found in surprisingly high numbers in Veii, either complete, such as *CIE* 6670 and 6673–6674, or partial, such as *CIE* 6467, 6669, and 6678–6681.

Also belonging to the milieu of production is a group of signatures[16] that most probably record, in an Early Archaic context, the names of the aristocratic owners of the workshops, rather than of the crafts-men, given their use of nomenclature indicating high status.[17] This is the case of *CIE* 6449: *mi zinace velϑ[ur a]ncinies*, "I, Velthur Ancinies, made [this]."[18] A com-bination of different formulas occurs occasionally, such as in *CIE* 6449 and 6673, which bear both a gift inscription and a signature.

A few chronological issues are pertinent here. Veii shares with Tarquinia the distinction of preserving written documents from as early as the late eighth cen-tury BCE: these are impasto spools (*rocchetti*), marked either with the letter *a* (*CIE* 6662–6667) or with the nu-meral sign *V* (identical to a letter *u*, *CIE* 6671*bis*), found in tombs. Almost as early is a fragment of a portable stove (*fornello*) marked with the numeral *XV* (*CIE* 6351), found near the Caere Gate (*map 4:K*). Of course, these are not properly called inscriptions; however, they do provide evidence for the early presence of a certain de-gree of literacy in some productive environments.

Most probably writing was at first included among the technical skills of high-level craftsmen of both gen-ders in weaving as well as in pottery making.[19] Although we have no opportunity to study inscriptions on cloth, there is ample evidence of the literacy of potters.[20]

In the early seventh century BCE, a small number of proper inscriptions demonstrate the use of writing for marking ownership (*CIE* 6668, 6710) and, in one case, for an *abecedarium* (*CIE* 6669). Only from the second half of the seventh century BCE is there enough ma-terial to analyze the writing systems of Veii. It appears that two different alphabets were used in the same period, corresponding to different contexts.

Alphabet A (fig. 15.2:A) has been detected primarily in inscriptions found in the sanctuary of Portonaccio, which date from the late seventh to the mid-sixth cen-tury BCE. The main features of this alphabet are the forms of *zeta* and *tau* (with the bars cutting across the vertical line), *pi* (with an open loop), and especially the use of a cross-shaped sign for a sibilant.

Alphabet B (fig. 15.2:B) appears in a smaller number of inscriptions found mainly in the town and in funer-ary contexts, and is only sparsely present at Portonac-cio; its chronology does not exceed the beginning of the sixth century BCE. The main features of this alpha-bet are *zeta*, *het*, and *tau* with horizontal bars at the

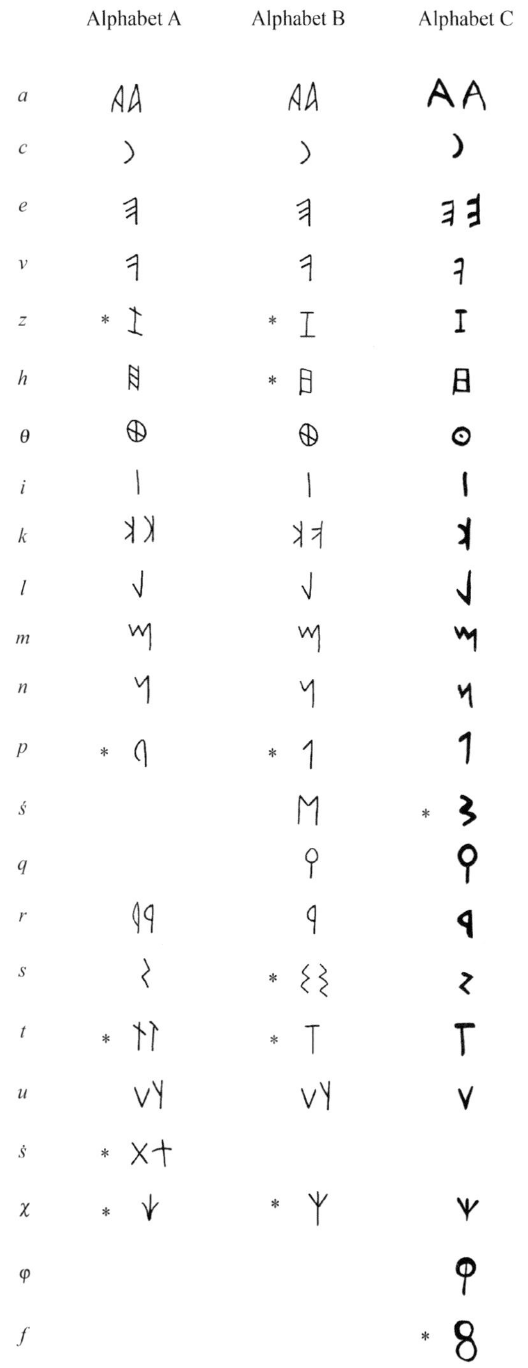

	Alphabet A	Alphabet B	Alphabet C
a	ΑΑ	ΑΑ	ΑΑ
c	⟩	⟩	⟩
e	∃	∃	∃ E
v	⅂	⅂	⅂
z	* ⊥	* I	I
h	目	* 日	日
θ	⊕	⊕	⊙
i	l	l	l
k	⋊ ⋉	⋊ ⊦	⋊
l	∨	∨	∨
m	⋀	⋀	⋀
n	⋏	⋏	⋏
p	* ⌐	* ⌐	⌐
ś		Μ	* Ƨ
q		φ	φ
r	⊲⊳	⊳	⊲
s	⟩	* ⟩⟨	⟩
t	* ⋔	* Τ	Τ
u	∨⋎	∨⋎	∨
ṣ	* ⨯†		
χ	* ⋎	* Υ	Υ
φ			φ
f			* 8

FIGURE 15.2. Alphabets of archaic Veii: A. Mainly attested in the sanctuary of Portonaccio from the late seventh to the mid-sixth century BCE; B. Mainly attested in the town and in the necropolis from the early seventh to the beginning of the sixth century BCE; C. Alphabetic series extracted from the syllabic marks painted on the terracotta pieces of the roof decoration of the temple of Portonaccio, ca. 510 BCE. (Note: the asterisks mark the distinctive features of the alphabets.) (Copyright: D. F. Maras)

end of the vertical line, hooked *pi*, and multibar *sigma*. Most probably, these two alphabets were the distinctive features of two different writing schools present in Veii, with the former being related to the priestly caste of the sanctuary of Portonaccio, who curated the majority of the votive inscriptions locally offered.

Interestingly enough, the same discrepancies that distinguish these two alphabets can be detected in the two earliest Latin texts of Rome: respectively the *cippus* of the Lapis Niger (*CIL* I², 1) and the vase of Duenos (*CIL* I², 4). Apparently, in early Rome the distinction between an official writing system and a "cursive" alphabet, customary in private contexts, retraced the writing tradition of the neighboring Veii, whose cultural influence was fully operating in the age of the Tarquins.[21]

In the second half of the sixth century, the epigraphic material of Veii decreases abruptly, preventing us from following the further developments of the earlier writing systems. It is possible, however, to observe the sporadic introduction of the M-shaped sign (*tsade*) alternating with *sigma* for transcribing the two sibilants (/ś/ and /s/, respectively pronounced as in "shame" and "same"). The new letter occurs in inscriptions on bucchero vessels, such as *CIE* 6703 (late seventh century BCE), 6410, 6714 (early sixth century BCE), and 6677 (late sixth century BCE), and a later black-gloss bowl, *CIE* 6337 (early third century BCE). On the grounds of this sparse documentation, it seems that Veii was at first influenced by the north Etruscan rule of sibilants (with *tsade* for /s/ and *sigma* for /ś/), but in the recent period adopted the opposite, south Etruscan, rule.[22]

Nonetheless, the letter *tsade* is missing in the most complete alphabetic series of Veii, deduced from the syllabic marks painted on the terracotta pieces of the roof decoration of the temple of Portonaccio, which date from the last decade of the sixth century BCE (*CIE* 6480–6639). These marks were a reckoning system based upon the alphabetic order of open syllables (such as *ca-ce-ci-cu* and so on), which allows us to reconstruct the complete sequence (fig. 15.2:C).[23]

Interestingly enough, instead of the *tsade* or the cross-shaped sign (by then forgotten), we find a four-bar *sigma* beside the normal three-bar *sigma*. Since such a feature matches with the contemporary writing system of Caere, this phenomenon could cast some light on the intellectual relationship between the two Etruscan towns in the Late Archaic period.[24]

As we have seen, the epigraphy of Veii is ill documented for the period following the end of the sixth century BCE, which is generally lacking in both number and variety of inscriptions, even though the independent history of the town as it existed before the Roman conquest continued until the early fourth century BCE. In this context an important indicator is the sparseness of funerary inscriptions, which is in line with the poverty of funerary goods in this period;[25] in addition, the epigraphic production of the sanctuary of Portonaccio ceases in the second half of the sixth century BCE, with a few exceptions, although the cult flourished until the Roman period.

Cult places such as Campetti, Macchiagrande, Vignacce (*maps 3 and 4:H, M, O, and P*), and, in the countryside, Casale Pian Roseto (*map 1: no. 5*) still remained the preferred places for displaying literacy, but the number of inscriptions is never comparable with the earlier documentation of Portonaccio, and the epigraphic evidence is mostly constituted by single letters and graffiti, rarely containing names or words.

In this context, an engraved mirror has a certain relevance. Its figure labels (*CIE* 6715) have graphic features matching the alphabet of Veii, the aforementioned official inscription sculpted in the rock (*CIE* 6707), and several graffiti on Attic pottery (*CIE* 6386, 6394, 6398, and 6401)—providing evidence for the use of writing at a high level in the fifth century BCE.

Just a few Etruscan inscriptions have been preserved that postdate the Roman conquest, traditionally dating to 396 BCE. These testify to the persistence of the local population during the mid-Republican period, especially in the context of the sanctuaries of Campetti (*CIE* 6337–6338 and 6341) and Portonaccio (*CIE* 6479). Significantly, contemporary inscriptions in Latin have been found in the same cult places, including the twin dedications to Ceres and Minerva by a L(ucio) Tolonio, whose Etruscan origin is apparent in his name (as it recalls the Tulumnes royal family)

FIGURE 15.3. Latin inscription scratched on a miniature jug from the sanctuary of Portonaccio, third century BCE: *Paco*. (Copyright: D. F. Maras)

(*CIL* I², 2908–2909),²⁶ and the inscription of a Musonio (*CIE ad* 6397–6398), whose name might correspond to the Etruscan *muśni* (*CIE* 443) and *musunia* (*CIE* 4708).²⁷

In this regard, it is worth mentioning the word *paco* inscribed in Latin on a small jug found at Portonaccio that dates to the third century BCE (fig. 15.3). As a matter of fact, rather than its being an unlikely abbreviation of a gentilicium *Paco(nius)*,²⁸ I propose to interpret the word as a Latinization of the Etruscan *paχa* (or, better, **paχe* in the masculine form), corresponding to the Greek *bakkhós* and defining an initiate to the mysteries of Bacchus/Dionysus. All considered, the earliest testimonies of the Latin language at Veii have a good possibility of being associated with Etruscan residents who evidently changed their language after the Roman conquest of the town.

Finally, it is important to note Veientine inscriptions found outside of Veii that shed light on cultural contacts and exchanges, such as the gift inscriptions on bucchero vases found in Vulci (*CIE* 11258–11259) and Lavinium (*CIE* 8612), whose donors are among the devotees of the sanctuary of Portonaccio.

In this category probably belongs the name of a *ϑanur<sa>sie* inscribed in the Tomb of the Graffiti Inscriptions at Caere, as early as 530–520 BCE.²⁹ The person bearing this name was probably a foreigner in Caere, as well as the Faliscan Mama.³⁰ They both took part in the funerary ritual for Larice Veliinas, to whom they were bound as companions (Lat. *sodales*) by personal links.³¹

Another Veientine inscription was found in the necropolis of Crocifisso del Tufo at Volsinii (Orvieto), where the tomb of a Larth Cupures was marked by an inscribed cippus shaped in the form of the helmeted

head of a warrior (*CIE* 5000). The deceased was most probably a military chief or a mercenary of Italic origin who migrated from Veii to Volsinii in the late sixth century BCE.³²

Finally, a bronze mirror in Providence, Rhode Island—dating from the early fourth century BCE and engraved with the figure of Artemis riding a pair of hinds—bears a caption (*CIE* 10722) whose features are compatible with the alphabets of Veii and Caere, although it was produced in Volsinii. It is likely, therefore, that the object was inscribed by an immigrant craftsman, who probably left Veii after the Roman conquest in 396 BCE.³³

To sum up, we have seen that the Etruscan city of Veii had a peculiar relationship with writing and literacy throughout the centuries. Veii has produced some of the earliest written attestations in Etruria, and its epigraphic evidence, precociously following a contemporary Greek trend, was linked to sacred places as early as the Orientalizing period.

The sanctuaries of Veii played a special role in spreading literacy and adapting gift formulas to sacred contexts. Therefore, they remained favorite places for inscriptions even when the number of attestations shrank as a consequence of a different epigraphic tradition, and even after the Romans conquered the city and the language of the inscriptions changed to Latin. Finally, as we have seen, the peculiar, conservative alphabetic tradition of Veii makes it easy for us to recognize Veientine inscriptions even in unexpected contexts, such as other Etruscan cities.

NOTES

1. *CIE* 8870, said to have been found in Chiusi or in Campania: Maras 2012b:47.
2. *CIE* 6714, believed to be a fake: Morandi 1989:585–588.
3. *CIE* 6715, said to have been found in Città della Pieve. See below, note 33.
4. *CIE* 6673.
5. See, for instance, Ghirardini 1882:410–412 and Mommsen 1882.
6. Gabrici 1913; Giglioli 1919.

7. Stefani and Nogara 1930.

8. Pallottino 1939.

9. See chapter 13.

10. Hadas-Lebel 2008:210–212. See also chapter 12.

11. See Hadas-Lebel 2008:209–210.

12. Maras 2009a:50–51.

13. Maras 2009a:20–24.

14. Briquel 2009. Minerva is the name of the Etruscan deity corresponding to the Greek Athena and the Latin Minerva.

15. See below, pp. 141–142.

16. *CIE* 6449, 6475, 6673, 6675, 6703, and perhaps 6325 and 6476.

17. Maras 2012b:52.

18. In cases like this, other scholars prefer integrating *mi(ni)* and translating "X made me"; see Colonna 2006; Michetti and van Kampen 2014:149–150 (with bibliography).

19. On the relationship between weaving and literacy, see Bagnasco Gianni 1999.

20. Tuck and Wallace 2011:196–197.

21. Maras 2009b:312–313.

22. Maras 2012a:341–342.

23. De Vita De Angelis 1968:411–420.

24. Maras 2012a:342–343.

25. Hadas-Lebel 2008:209–210.

26. de Simone 1990; Briquel 1991:197–199; Ambrosini 2012: 364.

27. van der Meer 2014:299 n. 49.

28. Ambrosini 2012:347 and 364; see also Nonnis 2010: 127–129.

29. G. Colonna, "Caere," *StEtr* 71 (2007): 183 n. 33.

30. G. Colonna, "Caere," *StEtr* 71 (2007): 180 n. 29.

31. Colonna 2007:13–16.

32. Maggiani 2005:46–47.

33. Ambrosini 2003:420–421. Incidentally, such a hypothesis could be suitable for the earlier inscribed mirror *CIE* 6715 as well.

BIBLIOGRAPHY

Ambrosini, L. 2003. "Specchi volsiniesi e vulcenti: Contributo ad una definizione preliminare della produzione volsiniese." *AnnFaina* 10:407–481.

———. 2012. "Le olpette in ceramica acroma depurata nei contesti votivi: Il caso del santuario di Portonaccio a Veio." *MÉFRA* 124:345–376.

Bagnasco Gianni, G. 1999. "L'acquisizione della scrittura in Etruria: Materiali a confronto per la ricostruzione del quadro storico e culturale." In *Scritture mediterranee tra il IX e il VII secolo a.C. Proceedings of the Seminar (Milan, 1998)*, ed. G. Bagnasco Gianni and F. Cordano, 85–106. Milan.

Briquel, D. 1991. "Entre Rome et Véies: Le destin de la *gens Tolumnia*." *ArchCl* 43:193–208.

———. 2009. "Les inscriptions votives du sanctuaire de Portonaccio à Véies." In *Votives, Places, and Rituals in Etruscan Religion*, ed. M. Gleba and H. Becker, 43–67. Leiden.

CIL = *Corpus Inscriptionum Latinarum* (Berlin).

Colonna, G. 2006. "Un pittore veiente del Ciclo dei Rosoni: *Velthur Ancinies*." In *Tarquinia e le civiltà del Mediterraneo. Proceedings of the Congress (Milan, 2004)*, ed. M. Bonghi Jovino, 163–185. Milan.

———. 2007. "Novità su Thefarie Velianas." *AnnFaina* 14: 9–24.

de Simone, C. 1990. "Etrusco *Tulumne(s)*: Latino *Tolonio(s)* e le formazioni etrusche in *-me-na*." *AION-Ling* 11:197–206.

De Vita De Angelis, G. 1968. "Contrassegni alfabetici e di altro tipo su elementi del rivestimento fittile dal tempio dell'Apollo a Portonaccio." *StEtr* 36:403–449.

Gabrici, E. 1913. "Veio." *NSc* 1913:164–169.

Ghirardini, G. 1882. "Formello." *NSc* 1882:408–417.

Giglioli, G. Q. 1919. "Veio." *NSc* 1919:13–37.

Hadas-Lebel, J. 2008. "Considérations sur l'épigraphie funéraire de Véies." In *Écritures, cultures, sociétés dans les nécropoles d'Italie ancienne. Proceedings of the Round Table (Paris, 2007)*, ed. M.-L. Haack, 203–216. Bordeaux.

Maggiani, A. 2005. "Il cippo di Larth Cupures veiente e gli altri *semata* a testa umana da Orvieto." *AnnFaina* 12:29–73.

Maras, D. F. 2009a. *Il dono votivo: Gli dei e il sacro nelle iscrizioni etrusche di culto.* Biblioteca di Studi Etruschi 46. Pisa.

———. 2009b. "Interferenze culturali arcaiche etrusco-latine: La scrittura." *AnnFaina* 16:309–331.

———. 2012a. "Interferenza e concorrenza di modelli alfabetici e sistemi scrittori nell'Etruria arcaica." In *Régler l'usage: Norme et standard dans l'Italie préromaine. Premier atelier: Langages. Proceedings of the Seminar at the École française de Rome (Rome, 2009)*, ed. L. Haumesser and J. van Heems. *MÉFRA* 124:331–344.

———. 2012b. "Materiale epigrafico dal Tumulo Chigi: Notizie su testi e contesti." In *L'Olpe Chigi: Storia di un agalma. Proceedings of the International Congress (Salerno, 2010)*, ed. E. Mugione, 47–54. Ergasteria 2. Naples.

Michetti, L. M., and I. van Kampen, eds. 2014. *Il tumulo di Monte Aguzzo a Veio e la collezione Chigi: Ricostruzione del contesto dell'Olpe Chigi e note sulla formazione della Collezione Archeologica della famiglia Chigi a Formello.* MonAnt 16. Rome.

Mommsen, Th. 1882. "Alfabeto greco-italico primitivo del vaso Chigi." *BdI* 1882:91–96.

Morandi, A. 1989. "Note di epigrafia etrusca veiente." *MÉFRA* 101:581–596.

Nonnis, D. 2010. "Le iscrizioni vascolari latine da Populonia e da contesti sacri dell'Etruria tra media e tarda repubblica."

In *Scavi e reperti dalla città e dal territorio: Archeometria e archeologia delle decorazioni in pietra dell'acropoli. Le stoviglie di Calvio: Vita e lavoro degli Etruschi di Populonia. Atti della giornata di studi (Milan, 2009)*, ed. G. Baratti and F. Fabiani, 123–142. Materiali per Populonia 9. Pisa.

Pallottino, M. 1939. "Rivista di epigrafia etrusca: Veii." *StEtr* 13:456–465.

Stefani, E., and B. Nogara. 1930. "Veio: Rinvenimento di alcune iscrizioni etrusche durante lo scavo del tempio scoperto in contrada Portonaccio, presso Isola Farnese." *NSc* 1930:302–334.

Tuck, A., and R. E. Wallace. 2011. "An Inscribed 'Rocchetto' from Poggio Civitate (Murlo)." *StEtr* 74:197–202.

van der Meer, L. B. 2014. "The Etruscan Bronze Lamp of Cortona, Its Cosmic Program, and Its Attached Inscription." *Latomus* 73:289–302.

CHAPTER 16

THE DEFENSIVE SYSTEM

LUCA PULCINELLI

DISCOVERING THE CITY WALLS OF VEII

With a circuit of more than 8 kilometers and several gates, the city walls are among the most imposing remains of ancient Veii, although most of them have now disappeared (*map 4*).

In 1647 F. Nardini provides the earliest description of some parts of the town walls. The first comprehensive presentation of the topography and the remains of the ancient city dates to the first decades of the nineteenth century, when several antiquarians promoted a new season of research.[1] At the dawn of modern archaeological research in this area, the remains of the city walls were among the few visible monuments on the plateau of Veii.[2] During the nineteenth century, several sections of these walls and the location of the main gates of the ancient town were studied and described. Since these early studies, no extensive excavations or surveys have been conducted, and many of these early observations remain very important to our understanding of the ancient topography.[3] In 1957, the British School at Rome, through test trenches and systematic surveys, uncovered the first evidence on which a chronology could be based, undertaking as well an architectural study of the city walls.[4]

In 2003, a new excavation began, with the goal of investigating the city walls; it was promoted by the Archaeological Superintendence and then carried out by the Sapienza University of Rome. This excavation allowed us to better understand how the walls were constructed and to outline the sequence of the various building phases. The most important result of this new investigation has been the identification of the earliest defensive walls, which date to the end of the tenth century BCE.[5] At the same time, new surveys and ongoing topographical studies have improved our knowledge of the circuit of the fortifications, since some new parts have been rediscovered and earlier reports have been revised.[6]

The chronological data deriving from recent studies are of the utmost importance. Earlier test trenches set out by the British archaeologists revealed a long and complex sequence of houses as well as drainage channels, all of which had been wiped out when the walls and the massive sustaining rampart (*agger*) were built. Various scholars initially believed that the walls were built in the mid-sixth century BCE, based on the evidence found in these first excavations,[7] but the 2003 fieldwork revealed a much more complex situation. The monumental tufa walls dating to the sixth century BCE replaced an earlier fortification consisting of a rampart made of large tufa chips that had been built during the first half of the eighth century BCE and restored many times in the following century. The rampart itself was preceded by an earlier and similar fortification, also reinforced several times, which overlaid a deep trench dug into the rock parallel to the edge of the plateau. These ancient fortifications appear to have been contemporary to the earliest settlement on the plateau of Veii, and date to the end of the Final Bronze Age, around the end of the tenth century BCE.[8]

The fortifications of Veii were abandoned between the end of the fourth and the beginning of the third century BCE, long after the Roman conquest. At that time, the ditch outside the fortifications was refilled and the walls were dismantled.[9] Sections of the city walls probably were still visible during the Imperial age,[10] given the epigraphic evidence detailing the division of citizens of the Augustan *municipium* into those living within the walls (*intramurani*) and those living outside of them (*extramurani*).

THE STRUCTURE OF THE CITY WALLS

The area investigated via test trenches in the most recent years is the best known of the entire perimeter of the walls, and is located at the northwestern edge of the plateau of Veii. This is the only part of the plateau that was not naturally defended by the steep tufa cliffs surrounding the settlement on the other sides. The existence of such early and strong fortifications can be explained by the fact that Veii had weak natural defenses in its northern part, making this area quite easily accessible. The rest of the perimeter is known only through surface surveys. A few segments of the walls are evident, consisting of fortifications of tufa blocks dating to the Archaic period.

The city walls of Veii followed the edge of the plateau, often set on a cliff at a slightly lower position so the structure might function as a retaining wall to prevent the natural progressive collapse of the edges (fig. 16.1: section 2). The line of the walls occasionally occupied a lower level in order to follow the contours of the small valleys.

The structure of the walls was solid, consisting of local tufa blocks placed as alternating headers and stretchers in regular courses. The wall foundations have some courses where blocks were placed more irregularly and were left with rougher surfaces. The wall segments that have been studied are between 1.5 and 2 meters thick; the blocks themselves have various dimensions.[11]

Topographic research through the years has revealed the existence of at least eleven ancient gates within the walls of Veii. These gates, which are hardly visible nowadays, have a direct correspondence with the early road system, still in use in Roman times, that

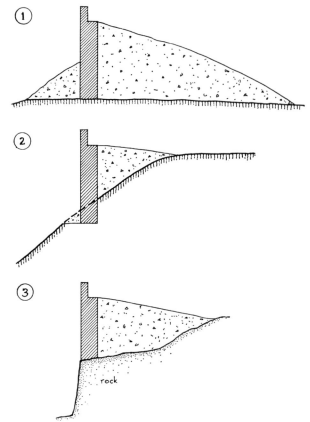

FIGURE 16.1. Hypothetical reconstruction of sections of the town walls of Veii: 1. On a flat area; 2. Sloping, functioning as an embankment; 3. On the tufa bedrock. (After Ward-Perkins 1961: fig. 9; by permission of the BSR Archive, Ward-Perkins Collection, South Etruria Survey Series)

connected the city with surrounding centers. Since no test trenches have ever focused specifically on an understanding of the main gates, their locations can be identified by looking at the ground level of the edges and the general topography of the area. This was the type of survey carried out during the nineteenth century, when it was possible to study a territory that had not undergone intensive agriculture and modern urbanization.[12]

THE NORTHERN WALLS

The northwestern part of the walls is the best known, and it is here, on the highest point of the saddle connecting the plateau with the surrounding hills, that the North-West Gate is located. We notice a deep rock-cut road that was still used in Roman times and by the current country track. Some tufa blocks at the roadside are the only evidence of the ancient structure.[13]

South of this area, recent excavations revealed a stretch of over 200 meters of the ancient walls, right inside the edge of the plateau. Only two or three courses of blocks are still preserved. About 200 meters south of that part, a very important discovery brought to light a small gateway opening directly beside a corner of the walls, in the so-called site of Campetti Bastion. The construction of this gate and this segment of the city walls can be dated to the Archaic Period. The passage, 1.9 meters wide, went straight to the outside, with no other outerworks for an advanced defense. It consisted of two parallel wings delimiting a sort of court or chamber on the inside part of the walls. The structure, which had at least three building phases, is still under study. It seems to have been closed during the fifth century BCE.[14]

Continuing southward, a small shallow depression has been recognized as the site of the Caere Gate. Unfortunately, there is no visible evidence of that structure today.

THE WESTERN WALLS

On the western end of the plateau near the temple of Portonaccio, a rock-cut road, dug into the tufa and 3.2 meters wide, suggests the presence of another gate. On its southern side, we can still observe an important segment of the walls, over 20 meters long, running halfway up the ridge and following its natural direction (fig. 16.2).

Unfortunately, nothing is still visible of the gate apart from the rock-cut road.[15] A narrow *cuniculus* draining part of the underlying valley, and making its crossing a little easier, might be related to the road departing from this gate.[16] About 200 meters to the southeast the walls seem to end, in coincidence with a re-entrant, a deep gorge known as Valloncello dei Campetti. At the beginning of the twentieth century, E. Stefani excavated in this area an important segment of the city walls, over 1.7 meters thick, with four courses of blocks preserved.[17]

South of this point there are no visible remains of

FIGURE 16.2. Part of the walls preserved near Portonaccio Gate, on the southern slope of the valley. (Copyright: L. Pulcinelli)

the walls, except alongside a small gorge at Vignacce, a site where the walls followed a narrow valley. Some parts of the walls are still visible here: a sort of retaining wall, almost at the bottom of the slope, has three superimposed courses of blocks.[18] Moving to the south, in a lower depression, another ancient gate, called the Vignacce Postern, is known, but there are no extant traces of it. Some blocks found at ground level and a tufa rock-cut road reveal the location of another ancient gate, called the Valle La Fata Gate, which is near a modern country house to the south. From this point on, up to the southern edge of the plateau, in front of the isolated elevation of Piazza d'Armi, the scarce remains of the walls still visible in the fairly recent past are now completely lost.[19]

FIGURE 16.3. Rock-cut road at the end of the valley, sloping toward the South-East Gate and probably corresponding to the ancient via Veientana. Photo from the plateau, looking south. (Copyright: L. Pulcinelli)

FIGURE 16.4. A particularly well preserved section of the walls near the so-called Valchetta Postern. (Photo: G. C. Duncan, 1959; by permission of the BSR Photographic Archive, Ward-Perkins Collection, South Etruria Survey Series)

THE SOUTHERN WALLS

The South-East Gate was associated with a deep depression separating the main plateau from Piazza d'Armi. All we observe today, a long rock-cut road that was widened in recent times, comes down from the settlement. An ancient road passed here and was still in use in Roman times. This road seems to continue toward the modern via Veientana (fig. 16.3). Many remains of the walls were also evident in the nineteenth century near the gate and along the ridge facing Piazza d'Armi.[20]

THE EASTERN WALLS

On the eastern side of the plateau, a long segment of the city wall was still visible in the 1950s, immediately beyond Piazza d'Armi,[21] but now has almost entirely disappeared or is covered with brambles. A particularly impressive part, maybe the best preserved of the entire perimeter, stands at the edge of a deep depression known as Valchetta Postern. The wall, which features a re-entrant with its sides facing the sides of the valley, was 2.7 meters wide and is preserved to at least sixteen courses[22] (fig. 16.4). Along the steep ridge of the Valchetta Valley, up to the northeastern end of the plateau, where one of the best-preserved gates of the ancient settlement opened—the North-East (or Capena) Gate—the wall perimeter was entirely mapped by the British surveys. The line of the fortification was regularly adapted to the winding of the hill, probably followed also by another ancient gate, the Vaccareccia Postern, which is also no longer visible.[23]

The North-East Gate opened near a tufa prominence, which had been modified in such a way as to make it form part of the fortifications. Some segments can still be seen on the upper edge of the plateau. The ancient road coming out here, headed toward the valley bottom, sunk in the tufa, was more than 300 meters long, 3.15 meters wide, and about 14 meters deep, in correspondence with the gate. This pathway was still used in Roman times, when the rock-cut road was deepened and cobbled to make it a paved road, still existing, and a bridge was built to cross the creek. The characteristic funerary niches dug outside the gate date to the Roman period.[24] In 1959, another exceptionally well-preserved part of the city walls was discovered. It is still visible and measures 2.2 meters wide at the base, and has twelve courses, about 3.95 meters high. The different treatment of the blocks of the foundation rows (at least six) is evident in this part, in contrast to the upper part of the walls, which appears to have been carefully finished.[25]

Further on, in the long stretch between the North-East and the North-West Gates, we can only rarely perceive the presence of the walls, because of the dense weeds and the damage caused by agricultural activities. The current condition of the wall contrasts with the nineteenth-century accounts, since at that time archaeologists could still see the city walls almost totally preserved in this area.[26] Two ancient gates probably opened in this region, one close to the large tunnel of Ponte Sodo[27]—which probably had the double function of draining the Valchetta Valley and facilitating the crossing of the creek[28]—and a second one, the Formello Gate, farther north, close to a natural hollow. There is no evidence left of either of them today, but a few blocks emerging from the edge of the plateau indicate how the walls lined up with the North-West Gate area.[29]

MEDIEVAL WALLS OF PIAZZA D'ARMI

The fortifications visible in Piazza d'Armi belonged to a completely different and separate system. Since the earliest surveys, the presence of segments of walls and structures connected with a gate have been recognized.[30] Most scholars believed that the walls of Piazza d'Armi dated to the beginning of the sixth century BCE[31] and that they were earlier than those of the main plateau, because of the substantial differences in building techniques and the lack of physical connections between the two systems.

Recent excavations, still in progress, have revealed, however, that these walls date between the ninth and the tenth—or eleventh—centuries CE, when Middle Age settlers occupied the area of Piazza d'Armi. These fortifications were mainly constructed of reused materials, and rested upon earlier structures. In general, it is not yet possible to confirm the existence of Etruscan walls on the Piazza d'Armi plateau.[32]

MILITARY ARCHITECTURE

From the point of view of military architecture, the Archaic city walls of Veii were strongly influenced by the morphology of the hills and their natural contours. Their remarkable extension and their strong connection with the natural topography, always used as a

natural defense, are peculiar characteristics of Greek and Etruscan military defense walls.[33]

The walls' line did not always follow the tactical edge of the hill. The walls were placed at a lower level in the valleys and where the cliff was not steep enough. Re-entrant segments of the walls overlying the depressions granted a sort of embryonal defense, with lateral salients in the weak points.

For the Archaic period, as far as we know, there were no other advanced defense devices such as towers or bastions that could grant warriors an adequate launch field, not even at the gates, which apparently opened directly from the walls. The most similar city walls are found at Tarquinia, dated to the mid-sixth century BCE,[34] and the Archaic walls of Rome, in their more recent "Servian" rebuilding, which seem to have had very similar building techniques.[35] The walls of Veii also have a simple appearance, clearly inspired only by the need for a defensive structure.

The methods of poliorcetics (siege warfare) in Etruscan-Italic and Roman areas during the Archaic period and up to the end of the fourth century BCE were essentially static. If the fortification was not overcome at the first assault, the only possible choice was to isolate the settlement with a long and dispersive siege aimed at defeating the enemy through starvation or desperation. The offensive devices available in this era—ladders and primitive battering rams—were in fact useless against the fortifications of a large settlement. A recourse to other stratagems, as sources sometimes mention, was quite exceptional.[36] At that time, when armies did not have consistent structures and logistic services, a battle on an open field between two deployed armies was the most common way to resolve wars.[37]

The very long duration—ten years—of the Roman siege of Veii at the beginning of the fourth century BCE is most probably merely one facet of a constructed narrative. Nevertheless, the difficulty of the siege and the final victory by means of a stratagem, a tunnel dug under the fortifications, certainly testifies to the high value of the city walls of Veii and the military strength of the Etruscan city.

NOTES

1. Delpino 1985:24, 65–68, 1999 (with further bibliography).

2. Dennis 1848:5.

3. Gell 1832:11–21; Canina 1846:105–106, 119–121; Gell 1846:436–456; Dennis 1848:7–17; Nibby 1849:424–425, 431–434; Ward-Perkins 1961:82–86.

4. Ward-Perkins 1959, 1961:3–20, 32–38; Murray Threipland 1963.

5. Boitani 2008; Bartoloni et al. 2013:137–139; Boitani, Neri, and Biagi 2013 (with further bibliography).

6. Cerasuolo and Pulcinelli 2007; Biagi et al. 2013.

7. Ward-Perkins 1959:43–44; Murray Threipland 1963: 54–63; Cascino 2012.

8. Bartoloni et al. 2013:137–138.

9. Boitani, Neri, and Biagi 2013:160.

10. Liverani 1987:91–92; Jaia and Cella 2013.

11. Ward-Perkins 1959:66–67, 1961:32–34; Boitani 2008: 137–138.

12. Gell 1832:11–27; Nibby 1849:431–434; Ward-Perkins 1961:3–4.

13. Ward-Perkins 1961:4–6.

14. Ward-Perkins 1961:6–8, 38; Boitani 2008:135–137; Bartoloni et al. 2013:139; Boitani, Biagi, and Neri 2014:304–308; Boitani, Neri, and Biagi 2016. See chapter 12 in this volume.

15. Cerasuolo and Pulcinelli 2007:103–105.

16. Judson and Kahane 1963:95; Cerasuolo and Pulcinelli 2007:99–100.

17. Stefani 1953:95; Cerasuolo and Pulcinelli 2007:102.

18. Gell 1832:24; Biagi et al. 2013:168.

19. Ward-Perkins 1961:13–14, 38.

20. Gell 1832:11; Dennis 1848:7, 11; Ward-Perkins 1961: 14–15.

21. Ward-Perkins 1961: fig. 6.

22. Canina 1846:119–121 and pl. 26; Ward-Perkins 1961:36 and fig. 11.

23. Ward-Perkins 1961:16.

24. Ward-Perkins 1961:16–19 and fig. 4.

25. Ward-Perkins 1959:79, 1961:34–35 and fig. 10.

26. Gell 1832:15–16, 18, 25–27; Dennis 1848:13–15.

27. Ward-Perkins 1961:49–50, see also fig. 14.

28. Judson and Kahane 1963:92–93; Quilici Gigli 1988.

29. Ward-Perkins 1961:19–20, 39.

30. Gell 1832:11–12, 25; Dennis 1848:10; Stefani 1922: 390–397.

31. Torelli 1982; Colonna 1986:432–433; Fontaine 1993.

32. Bartoloni et al. 2013:149–152; Cerasuolo and Pulcinelli 2013; Bartoloni and Pulcinelli 2016.

33. Winter 1971:111–114; Fontaine 2008:206–208, 2013: 276–277.

34. Fontaine 1994; Baratti, Cataldi, and Mordeglia 2008.

35. Cifani 2008:45–73, 256–260, 2013.

36. Napoli 2013:16–17.

37. Fontaine 1990:45–48; Napoli 2013:8–37.

BIBLIOGRAPHY

Baratti, G., M. Cataldi, and L. Mordeglia. 2008. "La cinta fortificata di Tarquinia alla luce della nuova documentazione." In *La città murata in Etruria*, 155–169. Pisa.

Bartoloni, G., V. Acconcia, B. Belelli Marchesini, F. Biagi, O. Cerasuolo, S. Neri, F. Pitzalis, L. Pulcinelli, and D. Sarracino. 2013. "Progetto Veio: Novità dalle ultime campagne di scavo." *ScAnt* 19:133–156.

Bartoloni, G., and L. Pulcinelli. 2016. "Veio. Le mura di Piazza d'Armi." In *Fortificazioni arcaiche del* Latium vetus *e dell'Etruria meridionale*, ed. P. Fontaine and S. Helas, 37–50. Brussels.

Biagi, F., O. Cerasuolo, S. Neri, and L. Pulcinelli. 2013. "Ricerche sulle mura di Veio." *ScAnt* 19:167–170.

Boitani, F. 2008. "Nuove indagini sulle mura di Veio nei pressi della porta Nord-Ovest," with an appendix by S. Neri and F. Biagi. In *La città murata*, 135–154.

Boitani, F., F. Biagi, and S. Neri. 2014. "Le fortificazioni a Veio: Novità dalle ricerche in atto." *RendPontAcc* 86:297–308.

Boitani, F., S. Neri, and F. Biagi. 2013. "Le più antiche fortificazioni di Veio (scavi 2003–2013)." *ScAnt* 19:160–162.

———. 2016. "Le fortificazioni a Veio tra Porta Nord-Ovest e Porta Caere." In *Le fortificazioni arcaiche del Latium vetus e dell'Etruria meridionale*, ed. P. Fontaine and S. Helas, 19–35. Brussels.

Canina, L. 1846. *L'antica Etruria marittima compresa nella dizione pontificia*. Vol. 1. Rome.

Cascino, R. 2012. "La North-West Gate di Veio negli scavi della British School at Rome." In *MAV*, 51–56.

Cerasuolo, O., and L. Pulcinelli. 2007. "Contributo allo studio dei dintorni di Portonaccio a Veio in epoca etrusca e romana: Documenti sulle mura urbiche, la porta e la viabilità." In *Atti del I Convegno Nazionale "Federico Halbherr" per i giovani archeologi*, ed. C. Pisu and A. Giuffrida, 83–114. Rome.

———. 2013. "Nuovi dati sulle mura di Piazza d'Armi." *ScAnt* 19:176–178.

Cifani, G. 2008. *L'architettura romana arcaica: Edilizia e società tra monarchia e repubblica*. Rome.

———. 2013. "Considerazioni sulle mura arcaiche e repubblicane a Roma." *ScAnt* 19:204–208.

Colonna, G. 1986. "Urbanistica e architettura." In *Rasenna: Storia e civiltà degli Etruschi*, 369–530. Milan.

Delpino, F. 1985. *Cronache veientane: Storia delle ricerche archeologiche a Veio*, I: *Dal XIV alla metà del XIX secolo*. Rome.

———. 1999. "La 'scoperta' di Veio etrusca." In *Ricerche ar-*

cheologiche in Etruria meridionale nel XIX secolo. Atti dell'incontro di studio, Tarquinia, 1996, ed. A. Mandolesi and A. Naso, 73–85. Florence.

Dennis, G. 1848. *The Cities and Cemeteries of Etruria*. Vol. 1. London.

Fontaine, P. 1990. *Cités et enceintes de l'Ombrie antique*. Brussels.

———. 1993. "Véies: Les remparts et la porte de la Piazza d'Armi." *MÉFRA* 105:221–239.

———. 1994. "Tarquinia: L'enceinte et la porte nord." *AA* 1994:73–86.

———. 2008. "Mura, arte fortificatoria e città in Etruria: Riflessioni sui dati archeologici." In *La città murata*, 203–220.

———. 2013. "Les enceintes préromaines de l'Italie centrale: Traditions régionales et influences extérieures (VIIIe–IIe s. av. J.-C.)." *ScAnt* 19:267–294.

Gell, W. 1832. "Gli avanzi di Veji." *Memorie dell'Instituto di Corrispondenza Archeologica* 1:3–29.

———. 1846. *The Topography of Rome and Its Vicinity*. 2nd ed. London.

Jaia, A. M., and E. Cella. 2013. "Tra continuità e cambiamento: Le mura del *Municipium Augustum Veiens*." *ScAnt* 19:213–215.

Judson, S., and A. Kahane. 1963. "Underground Drainageways in Southern Etruria and Northern Latium." *PBSR* 31:74–99.

Liverani, P. 1987. *Municipium Augustum Veiens: Veio in età imperiale attraverso gli scavi Giorgi (1811–1813)*. Rome.

Murray Threipland, L. 1963. "Excavations beside the North-West Gate at Veii, 1957–58. Part II: The Pottery." *PBSR* 31: 33–73.

Napoli, J. 2013. *Évolution de la poliorcétique romaine sous la République jusqu'au milieu du IIe siècle avant J.-C.* Brussels.

Nibby, A. 1849. *Analisi storico-topografico-antiquaria della carta de' dintorni di Roma*. Vol. 3. 2nd ed. Rome.

Quilici Gigli, S. 1988. "Osservazioni su Ponte Sodo a Veio." *ArchCl* 38–40:118–127.

Stefani, E. 1922. "Veio. Esplorazioni dentro l'area dell'antica città." *NSc* 1922:379–404.

———. 1953. "Veio. Tempio detto dell'Apollo: Esplorazione e sistemazione del santuario." *NSc* 1953:29–112.

Torelli, M. 1982. "Veio, la città, l'*arx* e il culto di Giunone Regina." In *Miscellanea Archaeologica Tobias Dohrn Dedicata*, ed. H. Blanck and S. Steingräber, 117–128. Rome.

Ward-Perkins, J. B. 1959. "Excavations beside the North-West Gate at Veii, 1957–58." *PBSR* 27:38–79.

———. 1961. "Veii: The Historical Topography of the Ancient City." *PBSR* 29:1–123.

Winter, F. E. 1971. *Greek Fortifications*. London.

PART III

MATERIAL CULTURE OF THE CITY

The third part of this volume presents an overview of the exceptional material culture of Veii. As in part II, we follow a chronological narrative. For the first time, the entire artistic production of Veii, especially pottery, is presented in one place, highlighting the trends of each period. In addition, new data on painting, stone sculpture, workshop areas, metal production, and architectural terracotta decoration are presented, this information derived from the latest discoveries and the results of studies of the daily life and death of the ancient Etruscans of Veii.

CHAPTER 17

EARLY IRON AGE POTTERY

SARA NERI

Our knowledge of Early Iron Age pottery at Veii increased greatly after the 1960s thanks to the excavation and resulting publication of six hundred tombs from the necropolis of Quattro Fontanili (*map 3*). These data supported new analyses focused both on the definition of a local sequence for the material culture and on the study of the complex network of external interactions of Veii.[1] The archaeological record deriving from funerary contexts was also expanded by the publication of the necropolis of Valle La Fata,[2] and of the different studies on Casale del Fosso[3] and Grotta Gramiccia[4] (*map 3*).

DATA FROM THE TOMBS AND THE SETTLEMENT

The data from the necropoleis appear to have been filtered by funerary ideology and ritual, which influenced the composition of the tomb-groups.[5] During phase IA (see the appendix to this volume), the extreme reduction of the assemblages to solely the cinerary urn and its covering bowl constitutes the most significant example of this selective process. Thus it is helpful to look at the parallel evidence coming from the settlement, more fragmentary but probably more representative. The most recent scientific excavations in different areas of the protohistoric settlement, at Piazza d'Armi (*map 4:Y*)[6] and Campetti (*map 4:G*),[7] have yielded an impressive amount of finds. This body of objects and especially its contextual connection to well-defined stratigraphical sequences have made possible a better understanding of the earliest phases of Veii and especially the character of its material culture.

BROWN IMPASTO

Until the mid-eighth century BCE, impasto (coarse ware) was the exclusive type of pottery at Veii (fig. 17.1). The characteristics of the clay used varied according to the function of the vases, from the cooking pots and tools, with thick sections and large inclusions, to elegant banquet vessels, with polished surfaces decorated by incisions and impressions. At the same time, the sections of the cup walls reached the extremely fine thickness of two millimeters. In the past, scholars have considered the production of this pottery to be mainly linked to single families and their huts, with only large vases being made in more specialized areas of production[8].

SPECIALIZATION IN THE EARLY IRON AGE AT VEII

The recent discoveries in the workshop area of Campetti reveal that, from the earliest phase, a large part of pottery production did not occur in the domestic areas, but was undertaken by specialized members of the community, experts in pottery production, who probably also operated next to workshops that produced metal objects.

At the site of Campetti, in an area located in a peripheral part of the settlement and of which only

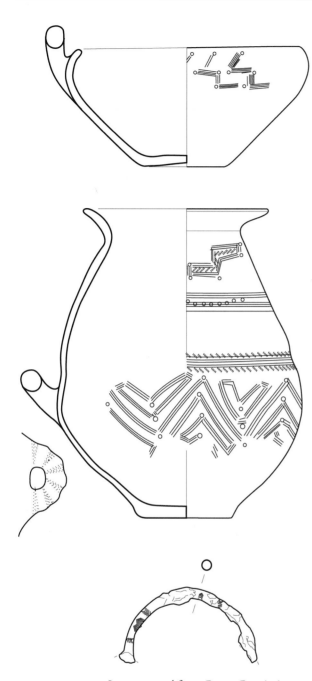

FIGURE 17.1. Impasto vessel from Grotta Gramiccia
tomb 94 (ninth century BCE). (Copyright: J. Tabolli)

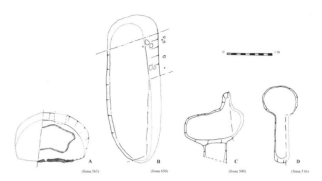

FIGURE 17.2. Kilns found at Campetti
(ninth century BCE). (Copyright: S. Neri)

THE EIA REPERTOIRE

During the Early Iron Age the repertoire of shapes
included large containers for food preservation, jars
of different dimensions, biconical vases, jugs, cups,
bowls, multiple vases, and plates. Objects made of clay
had many functions and included also filters, cooking-
stands, stands, and tools for spinning and weaving, as
well as hut-shaped urns and helmets.

The decorations of vases continued trends evident at the end of the Final Bronze Age: (a) the use
of the comb; (b) the impressions obtained by different
"tools," such as shells, fibula bows, twine, and various punches; (c) freehand incision; (d) applications of
clay with indentations, cords, and strips; and (e) applications in mixed materials with small bosses and
tin plaques (*lamellae*), fixed to the vases by natural
adhesives.

The use of paint was extremely rare, but on the examples we do have, it consisted of a reddish-brown
color placed on a thick layer of pure light clay, which
smoothed the surface of the impasto and created a bi-
chrome effect. This technique was inspired by Greek
painted pottery, probably of southern Italy, and its
earliest preserved occurrence is on a biconical urn discovered in tomb 11 at the necropolis of Valle La Fata
(fig. 17.3).[10] Between the mid-eighth and the early
seventh century BCE, painted impasto "red-on-white"
became more common.

The decorative motifs were mainly geometric—
angular shapes, meanders, swastikas—and more rarely
human figures, solar boats, and animal-shaped motifs
that derived from the Hallstatt tradition.[11] The syntax

twelve square meters have been excavated, during the
course of the ninth century BCE (Veii IA to IC), at least
ten different kilns were built on top of each other (fig.
17.2). They belonged to different types, from simple
areas of "firing on wood piles" to kilns with separate
firing and combustion chambers, with horizontal or
vertical alignment.[9]

FIGURE 17.3. Biconical urn painted in red on white, from Valle La Fata tomb II (late ninth century BCE). (Copyright: L. Drago)

network of connections with other Etruscan areas, such as Tarquinia[13] and Bologna,[14] and, to the south, with Sala Consilina and Pontecagnano.[15] Interactions with its closest neighbors appear to have been more consistent and continuous.[16]

During the earliest phase of the Early Iron Age (Veii I), as in the Final Bronze Age and in parallel to the lesser-known Caere,[17] Veii was part of a cultural area focusing on the Tiber that included the southern part of Etruria and nearby Latium Vetus. With Latium, relations were continuous but ambivalent, given that Veii controlled the Lower Tiber and was surrounded by Italic groups. Affinities with other ceramic traditions are evidenced by the presence at Veii of small reticulated jars, hut-shaped urns, jars with small plates on their rims, and different types of cups and decorations with single incised lines, as seen at Fidenae and Crustumerium (*map 1*).[18] During Veii IC and IIA, the focus of Veii on the Tiber area and Latium increased, as the circulation of amphora-craters demonstrates.[19]

THE MATERIAL CULTURE REVOLUTION IN THE EIGHTH CENTURY BCE

In the early eighth century BCE a clear rupture in the pottery sequence indicates the renovation of the entire ceramic repertoire. Contacts with the Greek world, and especially with the sites on the Bay of Naples, signal the beginning of a revolution also in craftwork. Technological innovations occurred together with the introduction of the fast pottery wheel and involved new techniques for preparing and firing the clay of fine wares. New shapes appeared in the ceramic repertoire, and many of these were connected to wine consumption, such as pitchers (*oinochoai*), small jugs (*olpai*), cups (*skyphoi* and *kotylai*), and plates. New decorative styles recalled the Euboean, Cycladic, Attic, and Boeotian traditions and anticipated the radical transformation of the entire pottery production during the Orientalizing period.

Veii appears to have been a pioneer center of these new trends. Small but significant fragments of Euboean *skyphoi* with pendant semicircles (fig. 17.4:A) have been controversially dated between the end of the

consisted of metopes or continuous friezes and emphasized the most significant parts of the vases, especially the shoulder, the neck (for the biconical vases), and the foot (for the conical heating-stands).

Apart from a standardized manufacture of vases connected to food preparation and cooking (jars, simple and large bowls, lids, cooking-stands, etc.), at Veii, as at other towns, the more refined pottery productions appear to have had local characteristics: among this the cups with curving profiles are particularly well attested, together with the biconical jars with pronounced shoulder and the bowls with extremely deep basins.[12]

REGIONAL CONNECTIONS

It is important to highlight the evidence for different aspects of Veii's cultural interactions with external productions. The material culture at Veii reveals a dense

FIGURE 17.4. Fine-ware *skyphoi*. A. *Skyphos* with pendant semicircles, Euboean production (from Quattro Fontanili tomb AAβγ); B. *Skyphos* with chevrons, Corinthian production (from Grotta Gramiccia tomb 779); C. One-bird *skyphos*, Euboean production (from Casale del Fosso tomb 983). (Copyright: F. Boitani)

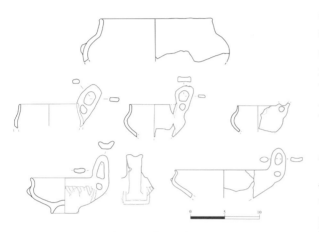

FIGURE 17.5. A selection of cups found at Piazza d'Armi (excavated 2000–2013). (Copyright: F. Biagi)

vases connected to funerary displays or to the banquet were easily updated and changed according to the new fashion. The use of biconical vases continued in this period, but they were generally without decoration (with some rare examples of linear decoration) and were covered by bowls and crest helmets. Expanded globular and lenticular (and in some cases footed) jars also became very common. Cups resembled types widespread in Latium Vetus, with a distinctive profile, compressed shoulders, smaller rims (mostly vertical), and handles often with saddle edges (fig. 17.5). The stands attest the diffusion of the practice of banqueting. These peculiar stands constituted the origin of the "monumental" *holmoi* in use during the Orientalizing period, which were not attested at Veii.[25]

The material culture of Veii dating to the Early Iron Age reveals the extraordinary capacity of the newborn town both to produce specialized local pottery and to participate in international exchanges, which made Veii a leader in the trade activity of the Lower Tiber Valley.

ninth and the mid-eighth century BCE.[20] A more precise chronology can be suggested for different *skyphoi* decorated with chevrons (fig. 17.4:B), imported from Corinth and Euboea from the second quarter of the eighth century BCE onward.[21] Starting from the third quarter of the eighth century BCE, different local workshops began to produce painted fine-ware pottery, and especially chevron *skyphoi*, one-bird *skyphoi* (fig. 17.4:C),[22] small *olpai*,[23] *amphoriskoi* with Late Geometric decoration, and a series of cooking-stands with figurative decoration, which were widespread also at Rome.[24]

NEW TRENDS AND CONSERVATIVE TENDENCIES

These new unusual products were at any rate limited in number, and everyday pottery continued to be made of impasto, following the earlier tradition. Conservative traditions attended utilitarian pottery, while the

NOTES

1. Close-Brooks 1965, 1967; Toms 1986; Guidi 1993; Babbi and Piergrossi 2005.
2. Bartoloni and Delpino 1979.
3. Buranelli 1981; Buranelli, Drago, and Paolini 1997; Drago 2005, 2009.
4. Berardinetti and Drago 1997; Galante, Piergrossi, and ten Kortenaar 2012.
5. Bartoloni et al. 1994.
6. See chapter 1.
7. Boitani 2008; Boitani, Neri, and Biagi 2008, 2009, and 2017; Boitani, Biagi, and Neri 2014.
8. Bietti Sestieri and Pulitani 1992.
9. Boitani, Neri, and Biagi 2009:29.
10. Bartoloni and Delpino 1979:53–54, 73, 96, pls. 10, XVIIc, XXVc; Berardinetti Insam 2001:92, I.G.2, pl. V.
11. Concerning the decoration on the pottery of the Villanovan tradition in southern Etruria, see De Angelis 2001; on the metope decoration at Veii, see Guidi 1980.
12. Biagi 2015.
13. Babbi and Piergrossi 2005.
14. Tabolli 2015:145; Biagi 2015.

15. Berardinetti Insam 1990:18–22.

16. See chapter 7.

17. Delpino 1987.

18. Berardinetti Insam 1990; di Gennaro et al. 2009; Di Gennaro, Schiappelli, and Amoroso 2004.

19. Babbi and Piergrossi 2005:297, 308.

20. Toms 1997, updated by Boitani (2005:319–320) and Rizzo (2005:334–339). See also chapter 10.

21. Boitani 2005.

22. Boitani 2005.

23. Bartoloni 1984:110.

24. Martelli 2008; Colonna 1977, 1980 concerning the evidence from Rome.

25. See also chapter 7.

BIBLIOGRAPHY

Acconcia, A., and G. Bartoloni. 2015. "La Piazza d'Armi." In Bartoloni et al. 2015:5–28.

Babbi, A., and A. Piergrossi. 2005. "Per una definizione della cronologia relativa ed assoluta del villanoviano veiente e tarquiniese (IC–IIB)." In *Oriente e Occidente: Metodi e discipline a confronto. Riflessioni sulla cronologia dell'età del Ferro in Italia. Atti dell'incontro di studi, Roma, 2003*, ed. G. Bartoloni and F. Delpino, 293–318. Mediterranea 1. Pisa.

Bartoloni, G. 1984. "Ancora sulla Metopengattung: Il biconico dipinto di Pitigliano." In *Studi in onore di Guglielmo Maetzke*, ed. M. G. Marzi Costagli and L. Tamagno Perna, 103–113. Rome.

———. 1989. "Veio nell'VIII secolo e le prime relazioni con l'ambiente greco." In *Atti del secondo Congresso internazionale Etrusco, Firenze, 1985*, 63–78. Rome.

———. 1991. "Veio e il Tevere. Considerazioni sul ruolo della comunità tiberina negli scambi tra nord e sud Italia durante la prima età del Ferro." *DialArch* 1–2:35–48.

———. 2012. "I primi abitanti di Veio: L'insediamento di Isola Farnese." In *MAV*, 47–49.

———. 2015. "Il Progetto Veio." In Bartoloni et al. 2015:2–4.

Bartoloni, G., V. Acconcia, B. Belelli Marchesini, F. Biagi, O. Cerasuolo, S. Neri, F. Pitzalis, L. Pulcinelli, and D. Sarracino. 2013. "Progetto Veio: Novità dalle ultime campagne di scavo." *ScAnt* 19:133–156.

Bartoloni, G., V. Acconcia, F. Biagi, F. Boitani, U. Fusco, and S. Neri. 2015. "Le ricerche dell'Università degli Studi di Roma La Sapienza a Veio." *RendAccPont* 86:1–82.

Bartoloni, G., V. Acconcia, A. Di Napoli, G. Galante, H. Marchetti, M. Milletti, V. Nizzo, A. Piergrossi, F. Pitzalis, F. Sciacca, F. Rossi, S. ten Kortenaar, and I. van Kampen. 2009. "Contesti abitativi da Veio-Piazza d'Armi a confronto: Materiali da una capanna e da una casa." In *Ceramica, abitati, territori nella bassa valle del Tevere e Latium Vetus. Atti dell'incontro di studi, Roma, 2003*, ed. M. Rendeli, 215–266. CÉFR 425. Rome.

Bartoloni, G., V. Acconcia, A. Piergrossi, S. ten Kortenaar, and I. van Kampen. 2011. "Veio, Piazza d'Armi: Riconsiderazioni e novità." In *Tetti di terracotta*, 116–174.

Bartoloni, G., A. Berardinetti, A. De Santis, and L. Drago. 1994. "Veio tra IX e VI secolo a.C.: Primi risultati dell'analisi comparata delle necropoli veienti." *ArchCl* 46:1–46.

———. "Le necropoli villanoviane di Veio: Parallelismi e differenze." In *Necropoli arcaiche*, 89–100.

Bartoloni, G., and F. Delpino. 1975. "Un tipo di orciolo a lamelle metalliche: Considerazioni sulla prima fase Villanoviana." *StEtr* 43:3–45.

———. 1979. *Veio I: Introduzione allo studio delle necropoli arcaiche di Veio: Il sepolcreto di Valle La Fata. MonAnt 1.* Rome.

Bartoloni, G., and M. L. Michetti, eds. 2013. *Mura di legno, mura di terra, mura di pietra: Fortificazioni nel Mediterraneo antico. Atti del convegno internazionale (Rome 2012). ScAnt 19.* Rome.

Bartoloni, G., S. Neri, and F. Pitzalis. Forthcoming. "Con il coltello e con il fuoco: Sacrificio e ritualità alle origini della comunità etrusca di Veio." In *Il sacrificio: Forme rituali, linguaggi e strutture sociali. Atti del Seminario di Storia e Archeologia Greca.* Rome.

Berardinetti, A., and L. Drago. 1997. "La necropoli di Grotta Gramiccia." In *Necropoli arcaiche*, 39–61.

Berardinetti Insam, A. 1990. "La fase iniziale della necropoli villanoviana di Quattro Fontanili: Rapporti con le comunità limitrofe." *DialArch* 1:5–28.

———. 2001. "Necropoli di Valle La Fata, tomba 11." In *Veio, Cerveteri, Vulci*, 92.

Biagi, F. 2015. "La prima età del Ferro a Veio: Seriazione della ceramica e cronologia relativa, alla luce dei nuovi dati dall'abitato." PhD diss., Sapienza University of Rome.

Biagi, F., O. Cerasuolo, S. Neri, and L. Pulcinelli. 2014. "Ricerche sulle mura di Veio." In Bartoloni and Michetti 2014:167–176.

Bietti Sestieri, A. M., and G. Pulitani. 1992. "Esperimento di riproduzione della ceramica d'impasto." In *La necropoli laziale di Osteria dell'Osa*, ed. A. M. Bietti Sestieri, 439–446. Rome.

Boitani, F. 2005. "Le più antiche ceramiche greche e di tipo greco a Veio." In *Oriente e Occidente: Metodi e discipline a confronto. Riflessioni sulla cronologia dell'età del Ferro in Italia*, ed. G. Bartoloni and F. Delpino, 319–332. Pisa.

———. 2008. "Nuove indagini sulle mura di Veio nei pressi di Porta Nord-Ovest, con Appendice. Elenco dei materiali di S. Neri, F. Biagi." In *Città murata*, 135–154.

Boitani, F., F. Biagi, and S. Neri. 2014. "Le fortificazioni a Veio: Novità dalle ricerche in atto." *RendPontAcc* 86:297–308.

Boitani, F., S. Neri, and F. Biagi. 2008. "La donna delle fornaci di Veio-Campetti." In *Sepolti tra i vivi*, 833–868.

———. 2009. "Novità dall'impianto produttivo della prima

età del Ferro di Veio-Campetti." In *I mestieri del fuoco: Officine e impianti artigianali nell'Italia preromana*, 23–42. Officina Etruscologia 1. Rome.

———. 2013. "Le più antiche fortificazioni di Veio (scavi 2003–2013)." *ScAnt* 19:160–162.

———. 2015. "Le fortificazioni di Veio: Novità dalle ricerche in atto." In Bartoloni et al. 2015:29–40.

———. 2017. "Le fortificazioni a Veio tra Porta Nord-Ovest e Porta Caere." In *Le fortificazioni arcaiche del Latium vetus e dell'Etruria meridionale (IX–VI sec. a.C.): Stratigrafia, cronologia e urbanizzazione*, ed. P. Fontaine and S. Helas, 19–35. Rome.

Buranelli, F. 1981. "Proposta di interpretazione dello sviluppo topografico della necropoli di Casale del Fosso a Veio." In *Necropoli e usi funerari nell'età del Ferro*, ed. R. Peroni, 19–45. Bari.

Buranelli, F., L. Drago, and L. Paolini. 1997. "La necropoli di Casale del Fosso." In *Necropoli arcaiche*, 63–83.

Close Brooks, J. 1965. "Proposta per una suddivisione in fasi della necropoli veiente di Quattro Fontanili." *NSc* 1965: 53–64.

———. 1967. "Considerazioni sulla cronologia delle facies arcaiche dell'Etruria." *StEtr* 35:323–329.

Colonna, G. 1977. "Un tripode fittile geometrico dal Foro Romano." *MÉFRA* 89:471–491.

———. 1980. "PARERGON: A proposito del frammento geometrico dl Foro." *MÉFRA* 92:591–605.

De Angelis, D. 2001. *La ceramica decorata di stile "villanoviano" in Etruria meridionale*. Soveria Mannelli.

Delpino, F. 1987. "Etruria e Lazio prima dei Tarquini: Le fasi protostoriche." In *Etruria e Lazio arcaico. Atti dell'incontro di studio, Roma, 1986*, ed. M. Cristofani, 9–36. Rome.

Di Gennaro, F., F. Bartoli, E. Foddai, B. Giorgetta, C. Iaia, M. Merlo, S. Pasquarelli, and S. ten Kortenaar. 2009. "Contesti e materiali della prima età del Ferro, di età orientalizzante, arcaica e tardo-arcaicada Fidenae." In *Ceramica, abitati, territorio nella basse valle del Tevere e Latium Vetus. Atti dell'incontro di studi, Roma, 2003*, ed. M. Rendeli, 137–210. Rome.

Di Gennaro, F., A. Schiappelli, and A. Amoroso. 2004. "Un confronto tra gli organismi proto statali delle due sponde del Tevere: Le prime fasi di Veio e Crustumerio." In *Bridging the Tiber*, 147–177.

Drago, L. 2005. "Una coppia di principi nella necropoli di Casale del Fosso a Veio." In *Dinamiche*, 87–124.

———. 2009. "Veio tra Villanoviano e tardo arcaismo: Appunti sulla necropoli di Casale del Fosso." In *Etruria e Italia preromana. Studi in onore di Giovannangelo Camporeale*, ed. S. Bruni, 327–370. Pisa.

Galante, G., A. Piergrossi, and S. ten Kortenaar. 2012. "Le necropoli veienti della prima età del ferro (IX–VIII secolo a.C.): Alcuni contesti da Grotta Gramiccia e Quattro fontanili." In *MAV*, 65–75.

Guidi, A. 1980. *Studi sulla decorazione metopale nella ceramica villanoviana*. Florence.

———. 1993. *La necropoli veiente dei Quattro Fontanili nel quadro della prima età del Ferro italiana*. Florence.

Martelli, M. 2008. "Variazioni sul tema etrusco-geometrico." *Prospettiva* 132:2–30.

Rizzo, M. A. 2005. "Ceramica greca e di tipo greco da Cerveteri (dalla necropoli del Laghetto e dall'abitato)." In *In Oriente e Occidente: Metodi e discipline a confronto. Riflessioni sulla cronologia dell'età del Ferro in Italia*, ed. G. Bartoloni and F. Delpino, 333–378. Pisa.

Tabolli, J. 2015. "Nuovi dati sulla necropolis di Monte Sant'Angelo." In *Novità*, 141–146, 157–160.

Toms, J. 1986. "The Relative Chronology of the Villanovan Cemetery of Quattro Fontanili at Veii." *AnnArchStorAnt* 8:41–97.

———. 1997. "La prima ceramica geometrica a Veio." In *Necropoli arcaiche*, 85–87.

CHAPTER 18

ORIENTALIZING POTTERY

SILVIA TEN KORTENAAR

The adoption of the ceremonial banquet in Etruria was certainly one of the most characteristic phenomena of the Orientalizing period and had significant effects on contemporary pottery production. In fact this new ceremony increased the demand for utensils and pottery used during the banquet, mainly when it became widespread not only among the aristocrats but also in other different social groups.[1] This all resulted in a progressive increase in production occurring alongside the final transition from family-based pottery-making activity to specialized workshops characterized by an impressive advance in technology.

At Veii this transformations is evident in both the diversification of production and the significant revitalization of the shapes in all the ceramic classes. In fact, during the Orientalizing period new models and shapes developed, were refined, and increased in the production of red impasto, brown impasto, and painted fine ware (already-existing ceramic classes), while at the end of the period a completely new production began: bucchero pottery. Concerning the shapes, the changes that had already started at the end of the Early Iron Age continued, with the adoption/imitation of shapes of either Greek origin (amphoras, *oinochoai*, *kylikes*, and *kotylai*) or a Levantine one (tripod bowls, Phoenician-Cypriot jugs, and fluted bowls). At the same time, a consistent selection of traditional Villanovan shapes accompanied a local adaptation of forms (jars, two-handled and single-handled cups, and small amphoras),[2] which showed great variety at the beginning of this period but tended toward standardization in later years.

The location of Veii, close to the Lower Tiber Valley, played a fundamental role in these innovations. The Tiber allowed both for the early reception of Greek pottery and Eastern models and for the circulation of a typological repertoire with distinctive local characteristics connected to the Faliscan and Capenate areas and with Rome and Latium Vetus. The link with Latium Vetus seems to have become stronger at the end of the Orientalizing period.[3] At the same time, consistent cross-connections with the material culture of the southern Etruscan city of Caere continued through the entire Orientalizing period.

FINE WARE OF GEOMETRIC TRADITION

THE EARLY ORIENTALIZING PERIOD

At Veii, the earliest examples of locally produced items in the Geometric style closely follow the first arrival of Euboean pottery (dating to the beginning of the eighth century BCE, Veii IIA).[4] In the Early Orientalizing period, local production adjusted to the Corinthian models, imitating the new shapes and reinventing Corinthian products according to indigenous tastes. The earliest workshop at Veii dates to the first quarter of the seventh century BCE and produced dotted-lozenge *kotylai* (cups) and *oinochoai* (pitchers).[5] Different elements point to Caere, especially the presence of incised and painted herons. The herons were characteristic of Caere and began to be autonomously reinterpreted at Veii on the model of a later Faliscan and Capenate series.[6]

FIGURE 18.1. Jar with geometric designs attributed to the Narce Painter, from the Tomb of the Ducks. (Copyright: S. Neri, after Neri 2010: pl. 19.3)

Dating to the last decades of the Early Orientalizing period at Veii, the workshop of the Narce Painter is associated with the sole individual master yet identified.[7] Many vases have been attributed to this painter (some of them in a red-on-white technique; fig. 18.1).

It has been suggested that the wall painting in the Tomb of the Roaring Lions (*map 4:A*) could be attributed to this master or to his entourage, and that a complex and fascinating interaction occurred between wall painting and ceramography.[8] Late Geometric Attic and Boeotian models were probably the inspiration for these decorations and would have reached Veii through the mediation of Pithekoussai, along the trade routes that linked Greece, the Gulf of Naples, and southern Etruria.[9] The evidence for local manufacture at this time is also confirmed by the recent studies of fragments coming from the furnaces close to Grotta Gramiccia and Quattro Fontanili (*map 3*).[10]

THE MIDDLE AND THE LATE ORIENTALIZING PERIODS

The large amount of evidence from the beginning of the Middle Orientalizing period suggests the existence of different local workshops. These workshops produced stamnoid jars (a storage type following Greek models) and plates decorated with herons, widely attested in southern Etruria and Latium Vetus. Amphoras resemble similar types made in Caere but soon developed into local variations.[11] The presence of the *spanti* plates (an Etruscan plate type with flat rim inspired by Levantine models), decorated with white-on-red triangles on their bases, demonstrates the continuous circulation of types that were common also to sites in Latium Vetus and in the Faliscan and Capenate areas.

Starting from the mid-seventh century BCE, the general adoption of widespread types (*oinochoai* with radial decoration, *skyphoi* with empty bands, and stamnoid jars, among which at least one group is locally made[12]) continued, especially in the Late Orientalizing, with standardization of the forms (jars with vertical rim, *situlae* with a bridge handle, and *kotylai* that imitated the Late Proto-Corinthian/Transitional models).[13]

RED IMPASTO

"Red impasto" is the name of a pottery production typical of southern Etruria, Latium Vetus, and the Faliscan area during the Orientalizing and Archaic periods. Its main feature is its more or less shiny red color, obtained by the use of a special kind of clay and specific firing techniques, and also by polishing the surfaces with purified clay (*ingobbio*) enriched with iron oxides and hydroxides. This technique has been traced to Phoenician Red Slip ware by way of Pithekoussai or, earlier, to the direct influence of Levantine craftsmen during precolonial contacts, now better understood than in the past.

The identification of a local production of red impasto vessels beginning 780–740 BCE (Veii IIB) confirms the importance of Veii in the experimentation in and development of different pottery productions.[14] During the Orientalizing period, this type of pottery is connected to wine consumption. The footed plates with handles on the rim[15] and the jars with vertical rims were probably locally produced together with other shapes that were common in the broader southern Etruscan repertory of plates and jars in the earliest

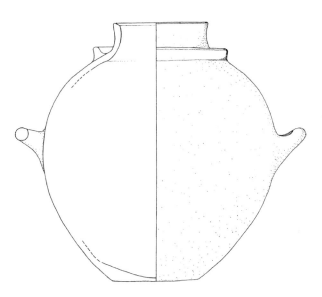

FIGURE 18.2. Red impasto jar, from Vaccareccia tomb VI. (Copyright: S. ten Kortenaar, after ten Kortenaar 2011: pl. 19, type 150 F 2)

period of this production, as in the numerous tomb-groups of the city and the territory (fig. 18.2).[16] The jars with vertical rim occurred also in white-on-red versions and in the aforementioned Geometric series (see fig. 18.1).[17]

The earliest connection of red impasto with Caere should be read especially from a functional perspective. In fact, the early adoption both in Veii and in Caere of the double-handled jars with plain surfaces occurred here before other regions. At the same time, a close interaction with the Faliscan region is reflected by the presence of shared forms such as the rim jars and different types of bowls and cups, whose morphological variety was extremely rich at Veii in the earliest phases.[18] Also for red impasto, in the Late Orientalizing period the standardization of shapes prevailed. Only a few new types were produced, such as the probably local small jars with conical neck and vertical handle on the shoulders.[19] A general increase in production is attested mainly for the domestic shapes, such as cylinder-ovoid jars and basins, which during the Archaic period competed with the most common variations in coarse ware or in creamy coarse ware, widespread not only in southern Etruria but also in Latium Vetus.[20]

BUCCHERO

Bucchero is a black, sometimes gray, earthenware, often shiny from polishing. The black color was achieved by firing pots in an atmosphere charged with carbon monoxide instead of oxygen (reduction process). It became common in central Italy between about the seventh and the early fifth centuries BCE. The earliest productions in bucchero are localized in Caere.

There is a lively debate among different scholars concerning the earliest bucchero pottery at Veii. Despite the fact that some researchers have suggested dating its earliest production at Veii to the second quarter of the seventh century BCE—immediately after the first evidence at Caere—recent studies have indicated that the bucchero of Veii dates before the third quarter of the seventh century BCE and was entirely imported from Caere.[21]

In general, study of the timeline for the presence of bucchero has proven the presence at Veii of imports from Caere through the entire Orientalizing period alongside the gradual development of local workshops. This conclusion is based on the occurrence of peculiar morphological and technological characteristics and on the diffusion of some specific shapes and types throughout all the necropoleis of Veii. The existence of a local production is also confirmed by the exceptional discovery of an artisanal area at Piano di Comunità, in use from the end of the seventh century BCE and producing Etrusco-Corinthian and bucchero pottery.[22]

The evidence for an earlier date of the local bucchero is based mostly on the princely tomb 5 of the necropolis of Monte Michele, whose burials date around 670 BCE.[23] The presence within the tomb-group of an *amphoriskos* in bucchero (type Rasmussen 1a)[24] confirms links with the production of Caere, while other elements appear locally made.[25] In particular, different artifacts show reinterpretations of traditional impasto vases, such as in the shapes of the footed carinated chalices, a carinated *kyathos* with vertical basin, a carinated cup, and a kantharos with vertical *biforae* handles.[26]

Similarly, a number of miniature vases discovered in the tumulus of Monte Aguzzo (*map 2: no. 1*; dating

FIGURE 18.3. Miniature bucchero *kyathoi* from Monte Aguzzo. (Copyright: L. M. Michetti and I. J. van Kampen, after Michetti and van Kampen 2014: pl. 5, nos. 55–57)

between the Middle Orientalizing period and the first twenty years of the sixth century BCE; fig. 18.3) seem to be connected to a local workshop that would have been active in the second and the third quarters of the seventh century BCE.[27]

Generally bucchero is not well attested in the tombs at Veii before the mid-seventh century BCE,[28] while the most common shapes in its necropoleis, definitely locally produced, can be dated between the end of the seventh and the first half of the sixth century BCE (the *oinochoai* Rasmussen 3a, the chalices Rasmussen 2 and 3, and the *kantharoi* Rasmussen 3a[29]), in light of the recent discovery of the artisanal area at Comunità (*map 4:W*). At this time a few examples of incised bucchero and probably chalices with figurative stands are also attested.[30]

ETRUSCO-CORINTHIAN PRODUCTIONS

The same workshop of Piano di Comunità (*map 4:W*) was also producing Etrusco-Corinthian pottery[31]— that is, an imitation of Corinthian pottery initiated by local Etruscan artisans—between 630 and 540 BCE. The main centers of production of this style were at Vulci, Caere, and Tarquinia.

The signature of the ceramist Velthur Ancinies has been identified on an Etrusco-Corinthian *phiale*.[32] According to G. Colonna, this individual was a pupil of the Rosoni Painter, who probably moved from Vulci to Veii and was responsible for the local production of the vases discovered in this sanctuary.[33] His products can be ascribed to a wide tradition of local workshops on the basis of specific elements of the decoration and distinctive morphological characteristics. For example, the amphoras discovered in the tumulus of Monte Aguzzo find many parallels in the territory

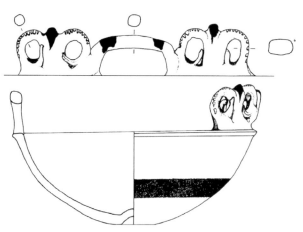

FIGURE 18.4. Etrusco-Corinthian *lebes* from Monte Aguzzo. (Copyright: L. M. Michetti and I. J. van Kampen, after Michetti and van Kampen 2014: pl. 6, no. 79)

of Veii and at Narce; these date to between the late seventh century and the first twenty years of the sixth century BCE.[34] In addition, we can refer to a group of *lebetes* with umbilicated basin and handles rising on top of the rim, decorated with lotus flowers or spirals and dating to the Late Orientalizing period (fig. 18.4). This type was probably produced by the same workshop and appears to have been widespread in the tomb-groups of the territory of Veii and occurred also in a tomb at Narce.[35]

NOTES

1. G. Bartoloni in Bartoloni, Acconcia, and ten Kortenaar 2012:201, 204–205.

2. On this phenomenon see Neri 2010:266; G. Bartoloni in Bartoloni, Acconcia, and ten Kortenaar 2012:205–206. A functional study of these shapes in relation to wine consumption during the Orientalizing period has been suggested by V. Acconcia and S. ten Kortenaar in Bartoloni, Acconcia, and ten Kortenaar 2012 (with the analysis of the tomb-groups dating to this period).

3. Michetti 2009:140–142.

4. Neri 2010:236; on the earliest local production see Boitani 2005. See also chapter 17.

5. Types Neri Bb2 and Aa7: Neri 2010:236, 45–46, 161–162.

6. Neri 2010:196–197, 236–237.

7. See also chapters 10 and 21.

8. On the Narce Painter and the Tomb of the Roaring Lions, see chapter 21.

9. Neri 2010:107–108, 239, and 430–431.

10. L. M. Michetti in Michetti and van Kampen 2014:107–108 n. 217 with bibliography.

11. Concerning this production of amphoras and the innovative aspects of the production at Caere, see also L. M. Michetti in Michetti and van Kampen 2014:105–106.

12. In the typology of Neri: *oinochoai* Cb 4d–e: Neri 2010:64–66; *skyphoi* Bc: Neri 2010:152–155; jars Dc 2d–e: Neri 2010:112–113.

13. Types Neri 2, Cb and Cc 1–2: Neri 2010:241–242. The composition with the tomb-group at Monte Aguzzo confirms the progressive standardization of shapes: L. M. Michetti in Michetti and van Kampen 2014:110.

14. Traditionally this technique has been considered a derivation from the Phoenician Red Slip. See ten Kortenaar 2011:313–323.

15. 290 Fa1; 290 Fc (2 earlier?)-4: ten Kortenaar 2011:157–158.

16. Types ten Kortenaar 150 F 2–3: ten Kortenaar 2011:96–97 with bibliography on the white-on-red examples.

17. Neri group Ce: Neri 2010:105–106.

18. ten Kortenaar 2011:296–298.

19. Necropolis of Volusia tomb 4: Carbonara in Carbonara, Messineo, and Pellegrino 1996:46–47, with bibliography concerning also a *lebes* from tomb XIII of Picazzano (both tomb-groups have been dated to the Late Orientalizing period).

20. This evidence has been recently confirmed by the excavation of Veii Piazza d'Armi. See *Veio* II, 132–141.

21. See I. van Kampen in Michetti and van Kampen 2014:121–122 with bibliography and n. 383 regarding the possibility of exports from Veii to Caere during the second quarter of the seventh century BCE.

22. B. Marchesini in Ambrosini et al. 2009:68 and n. 27 with bibliography. See also chapter 23.

23. On the chronology Neri 2010:210 n. 20.

24. All references are to Rasmussen 1979.

25. Boitani 2001:113.

26. Marchetti 2004:17–18.

27. I. van Kampen in Michetti and van Kampen 2014:153.

28. De Santis 1997:114.

29. Generally see Marchetti 2004, updated by I. van Kampen in Michetti and van Kampen 2014:128–130.

30. These types have been described by I. van Kampen in Michetti and van Kampen 2014:123–124 n. 411, and 126–127 n. 449.

31. Some fragments found around furnaces have been connected to vases belonging to this chronology in the contemporary necropoleis: L. M. Michetti in Michetti and van Kampen 2014:115 nn. 324–325 with bibliography.

32. See chapter 15.

33. Colonna 2006.

34. L. M. Michetti in Michetti and van Kampen 2014:112 n. 271–272, with bibliography.

35. L. M. Michetti in Michetti and van Kampen 2014.

BIBLIOGRAPHY

Ambrosini, L., B. Belelli Marchesini, G. C. Colantoni, B. Giuliani, M. R. Lucidi, and M. Merlo. 2009. "Il contributo degli scavi di Piano di Comunità alla conoscenza dell'abitato di Veio: Materiali dal riempimento di un pozzo sul pianoro sommitale." In *Veio* I, 65–123.

Bartoloni, G., V. Acconcia, and S. ten Kortenaar. 2012. "Viticoltura e consumo del vino in Etruria: La cultura materiale tra la fine dell'età del Ferro e l'Orientalizzante Antico." In *Archeologia della vite e del vino in Toscana e nel Lazio: Dalle tecniche dell'indagine archeologica alle prospettive della biologia molecolare*, ed. A. Ciacci, P. Rendini, and A. Zifferero, 201–275. Florence.

Boitani, F. 2001. "La tomba principesca di Monte Michele." In *Veio, Cerveteri, Vulci*, 113–118.

Carbonara, A., G. Messineo, and A. Pellegrino. 1996. *La necropoli etrusca di Volusia*. Rome.

Colonna, G., 2006. "Un pittore veiente del ciclo dei Rosoni: Velthur Ancinies." In *Tarquinia e le civiltà del Mediterraneo. Atti del convegno internazionale, Milan 2004*, ed. M. Bonghi Jovino, 164–175. Milan.

De Santis, A. 1997. "Alcune considerazioni sul territorio veiente in età orientalizzante e arcaica." In *Necropoli arcaiche*, 101–143.

Marchetti, M. H. 2004. "La produzione del bucchero a Veio: Alcune considerazioni." In *Appunti sul bucchero. Atti delle giornate di studi*, ed. A. Naso, 17–27. Florence.

Michetti, L. M. 2009. "Produzioni artigianali tra Veio e il Lazio nell'età dei Tarquini." In *Atti del XVII Convegno Internazionale di Studi sulla Stoiria e l'Archeologia dell'Etruria (Orvieto 2009)*, ed. G. Della Fina, 133–158. *AnnFaina* 17.

Michetti, L. M., and I. van Kampen ed. 2014. *Il tumulo di Monte Aguzzo a Veio e la collezione Chigi: Ricostruzione del contesto dell'olpe Chigi e note sulla formazione della Collezione Archeologica della famiglia Chigi a Formello*. *MonAnt* 16. Rome.

Neri, S. 2010. *Il tornio e il pennello: Ceramica depurata di tradizione geometrica di epoca orientalizzante in Etruria meridionale*. Officina Etruscologia 2. Rome.

Rasmussen, T. 1979. *Bucchero Pottery from Southern Etruria*. Cambridge.

ten Kortenaar, S. 2011. *Il colore e la materia: Tra tradizione e innovazione nella produzione dell'impasto rosso nell'Italia mediotirrenica*. Officina Etruscologia 4. Rome.

———. 2012. "L'impasto rosso." In *Veio* II, 132–141.

CHAPTER 19

ARCHAIC, LATE ARCHAIC, AND CLASSICAL POTTERY

MARIA TERESA DI SARCINA AND FEDERICA PITZALIS

This chapter presents a brief overview of pottery production at Veii during the Archaic (575–480 BCE), Late Archaic (480–425 BCE), and Classical (425–396 BCE) periods. These periods correspond to one of the apogees in the history of Veii, and the exceptional fortune of this Etruscan town is reflected in its material culture, especially the pottery.

As in other Etruscan towns, during the Archaic period pottery production at Veii had distinctive characteristics and showed a standardization of the different types, along with a partial continuity with the earliest production.[1] The discovery of the production area at Piano di Comunità, where bucchero and fine-ware pottery were locally made, has confirmed the diffusion of local craftmaking among the different urban workshops.[2] Our knowledge of the Archaic and Late Archaic pottery at Veii has increased significantly thanks to recent excavations in the settlement. Since 1996 the sites of Campetti,[3] Macchiagrande,[4] Piano di Comunità,[5] and the small plateau of Piazza d'Armi[6] were included in the extensive Veii Project by the University of Rome (map 3).[7] In addition, review of the data collected during the British School at Rome surveys in the territory of the town has revealed important new evidence.[8] The results of the new discoveries can now be combined with the outcomes of past research.

The area excavated by the British School at Rome near the North-West Gate (map 4:F) remains one of the most important contexts for the study of the Archaic pottery at Veii.[9] At the same time, the semi-subterranean building of Casale Pian Roseto (map 1: no. 8), along via di Santa Cornelia, which functioned as a sacred place within the territory of ancient Veii, constitutes another important case study.[10] From the religious areas, the different votive deposits represent other important data sets: the deposit at the Caere Gate[11] (map 4:K); the deposit at the Formello Gate[12] (map 4); the so-called Stipe Lanciani (map 4:X), located between Piazza d'Armi (map 4:Y) and Comunità (map 4:W)[13]; and finally the sanctuary of Portonaccio (map 4:S).[14]

In contrast to the previous period, the necropoleis present a limited amount of evidence from this time, due to the austerity of the funerary laws at Veii and the different towns of Latium Vetus.[15] From the beginning of the sixth century BCE through the entire fifth century BCE, a reduction in the number of artifacts characterizes the majority of the tomb-groups, which were also later affected by systematic illegal looting.[16]

IMPORTED POTTERY

The imports at this time were extremely limited in number and occurred either in funerary contexts or in votive deposits. A Laconian *kylix* discovered in the sanctuary of Portonaccio stands out among the most prestigious objects. A hirsute Gorgoneion in the medallion and an internal frieze with galloping horses formed the decoration of this *kylix* attributed to the Boread Painter (570 BCE).[17] East Greek pottery, consisting of cups with linear decoration, is poorly attested at Veii, in contrast with other sites of southern Etruria such as Tarquinia and Graviscae. It occurs only in the sanctuaries of Portonaccio[18] and Campetti. Despite the limited amount of evidence, this class had a significant influence over other local products, such as bucchero or fine ware.

The Attic pottery at Veii is known mainly thanks to the discoveries in the urban sanctuaries, in the deposit of Casale Pian Roseto, and in a few Late Archaic tombs.[19] *Kylikes* with figural decoration represent the majority of the known examples, together with more rare vessels (especially closed shapes), such as the black-figure *dinos* from Portonaccio attributed to the Antimenes Group[20] and the red-figure head-vases from the sanctuary of Campetti North.[21] The most significant examples date to the fifth century BCE. Other Attic fragments have been identified: (a) at Piazza d'Armi;[22] (b) in the Stipe Lanciani;[23] (c) on the main plateau, especially in the area of the later Roman forum, where the fragment of an open-shape vase with an Etruscan inscription was recently found;[24] and (d) one or more *stamnoi* with the representation of Dionysos, in an area north of the forum.[25]

The Attic black-gloss pottery, dating to the late fifth century BCE, consisted of tableware (*kylikes*, small plates, and *skyphoi*) and is documented at Casale Pian Roseto, at Campetti–Formello Gate, and in the well of Macchiagrande (*map 4:M*), where a fragment with imprinted palmette has been dated to the late fifth or early fourth century BCE.[26]

LOCAL FINE-WARE POTTERY

At Veii, the local fine-ware pottery prevails in all Archaic contexts. A comparison with contemporary productions in impasto/coarse ware allows us to suggest that the fine wares were especially subject to experimentation and innovation. This fact confirms the cultural dynamism of the workshops of the Etruscan town during the last century of its autonomous history. Despite some analogies with other sites in Etruria and Latium Vetus (especially Tarquinia), as in the case of bucchero, the development at Veii of a local tradition finds its origins in the Late Orientalizing period and its outcomes in red-gloss and black-gloss products. Different types of bowls, and especially those with a large

and almond-shaped rim, occurred in different classes. This circumstance reveals the existence of local trends, which the artisans adopted with different solutions.

The bucchero (fig. 19.1: nos. 1–10)[27] is one of the more frequently attested pottery classes, despite the fact that during the Archaic period its production decreased in quality, with the shapes appearing to become standardized and the color turning toward gray.[28] The finds discovered in the excavation at the North-West Gate and in the votive deposit of Casale Pian Roseto represent the most important repertoires for our understanding of bucchero during the Archaic and Classical periods. The open shapes were more common, especially the multifunctional vases, such as the carinated bowls, the types with vertical rim and conical basin, and the ones with horizontal rim and deep spherical basins, which widely circulated. The first group corresponds to Rasmussen bowl types 1 and 2, including the simple bowls or the bowls with larger rims, which were extremely common at Casale Pian Roseto.[29] The chalices were the most common drinking vases. The carinated type with short circular foot (corresponding to type Rasmussen 4) was the most widespread variation of this form. These types represent a simplification of shapes as compared to the elegant Late Orientalizing chalices (Rasmussen types 2 and 3).

The open-shape vases in bucchero at Veii were marked with the earliest-attested inscribed signs and letters. This evidence occurs especially in sacred contexts, such as the sanctuaries of Portonaccio and Campetti–Caere Gate and the deposits of Casale Pian Roseto and Campetti–Formello Gate, where in particular the representation of *sigla* such as the five-pointed star, the cross, isolated letters, and abstract symbols is attested on the small plates and on the bowls with short basin.[30]

Among the closed shapes, pouring vases were very common (*oinochoai* and jugs), together with containers for various liquids (*stamnoi* and jars), which were occasionally used as ossuaries for cremations. Miniaturistic vases (chalices, *kyathoi*, and small cups) had a ritual function and occurred especially at Casale Pian Roseto (more than forty specimens).

We can often find the fine ware decorated with bands (fig. 19.1: nos. 11–14) in layers dating to the Ar-

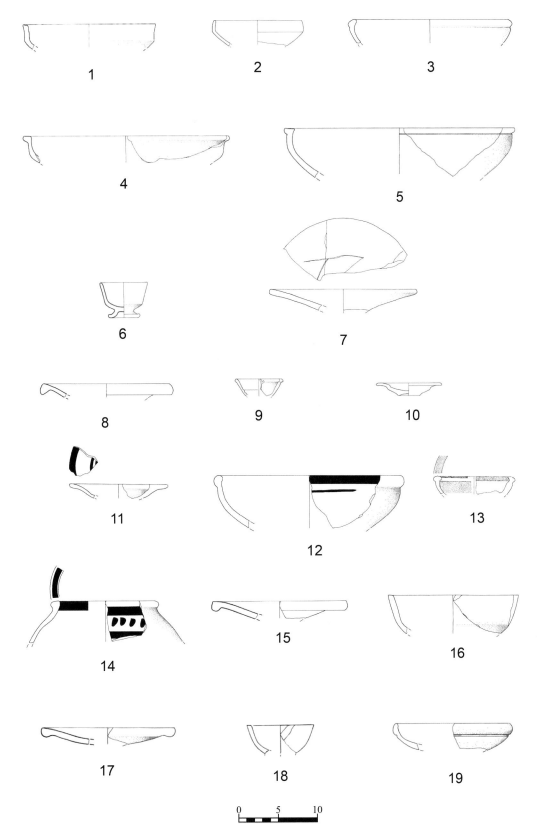

FIGURE 19.1. Local fine ware. 1–5. Bucchero bowls; 6. Bucchero small chalice; 7–8. Bucchero plates; 9. Bucchero miniature cup; 10. Bucchero miniature plate; 11. Fine cream-ware plate decorated with bands; 12–13. Fine cream-ware cup; 14. Fine cream-ware jar; 15. Black-gloss plate; 16. Black-gloss cup; 17. Red-gloss plate; 18–19. Red-gloss cups. (Copyright: M. T. Di Sarcina and F. Pitzalis)

chaic period at Veii, especially at Casale Pian Roseto and in the wells of Macchiagrande and Comunità. Therefore, it appears to have been one of the most representative pottery products during the Late Orientalizing and Archaic periods. Recent studies have demonstrated that during the two periods this type of pottery shared the same techniques and most of the typological repertoire.[31] The decoration consisted of redbrown, reddish orange, and purplish red bands. More complex decorative motifs characterize the *skyphoi*, the *oinochoai*, and the jars. In particular, the lines of dots and vertical indents or undulations reveal influences from colonial imitation of Ionic pottery and are seen to have occurred at Veii especially on the *skyphoi*.

In the layers of the end of the fifth and the first half of the fourth century BCE, black-gloss pottery fragments belong to open-shape vases, such as cups and small plates (fig. 19.1: nos. 15–16).[32] The techniques and the connection with bucchero pottery and fine ware with bands suggest a local production. The possible derivation from Attic black-gloss pottery, dating to the end of the fifth century BCE, reveals the existence of local workshops during the Late Archaic period. On the other hand, the red-gloss pottery occurs especially in Roman Republican contexts[33] and can be dated to the late fifth and early fourth century BCE (fig. 19.1: nos. 17–19).[34] The shapes attested at Casale Pian Roseto, at Comunità, and at Macchiagrande find comparanda in bucchero, cream-colored fine ware, and fine ware decorated with bands.

IMPASTO/COARSE-WARE POTTERY

Among the Archaic and Late Archaic pottery repertoires at Veii, impasto had a considerable importance, as reflected in its quantity, morphology, and function. The red impasto (*impasto rosso*) (fig. 19.2: no. 1) continued to have a significant presence in the Archaic deposits. During the entire sixth century BCE, this production consisted of late replicas of the typical forms of the Orientalizing repertoire. From the end of the sixth century BCE, the red impasto appears in forms mainly connected to the preservation and transportation of food commodities.[35]

Cream coarse ware (*impasto chiaro-sabbioso*) (fig.

19.2: nos. 2–3, 6–9) was also of importance. It consisted of semi-purified clay of a creamy color with an impasto full of inclusions, especially augite. From the end of the seventh century BCE, this mineral was used for pottery production in Archaic Etruria and Latium Vetus.[36] The cream coarse-ware production at Veii involved various cook wares and containers for the transportation or preservation of food or liquids. The types often displayed linear decoration painted in reddishbrown or red, and in most of the cases had an underlying white layer of pure clay. The most common open shapes were basins of conical or spherical form with surmounting handles. In later contexts, the types with enlarged rims or with beads occurred, both plain and with fingerprints. Different examples of incense burners (*thymiateria*) were identified in the various sacred areas. *Thymiateria* were also common in simple fine ware or with bands. Closed shapes included jars and jugs as well as the *situlae*.

The coarse ware is a common pottery not made of purified clay. Scholars have been giving different names to coarse ware, such as *impasto grezzo* ("rough impasto") and *impasto rosso-bruno* ("red-brown impasto"). In the tradition of studies on Veii, it is usually called simply "coarse ware." Coarse-ware pottery was used for both the preparation, cooking, and preservation of food and more generally.[37] The shapes are very simple, the fabric has numerous inclusions, and the surfaces are not polished and often bear traces of firing.

Coarse ware is documented in all the different parts of the settlement during the Orientalizing and especially the Archaic period at Veii,[38] and numerous examples also come from sacred contexts and burials.

The local repertoire was part of the larger *koinè* of the Tiber area. The ovoid and cylinder-ovoid jar was the most representative shape, and it seems to have been used during all the different phases of the preparation and conservation of food. It has been connected to the Latin *aula*, a container in which *puls* was prepared during the Archaic period. *Puls* was a soup made of different cereals, and it constituted the main meal in the central Tyrrhenian region in the period around the eighth through the sixth century BCE.[39]

Among the open shapes, bowls and basins are al-

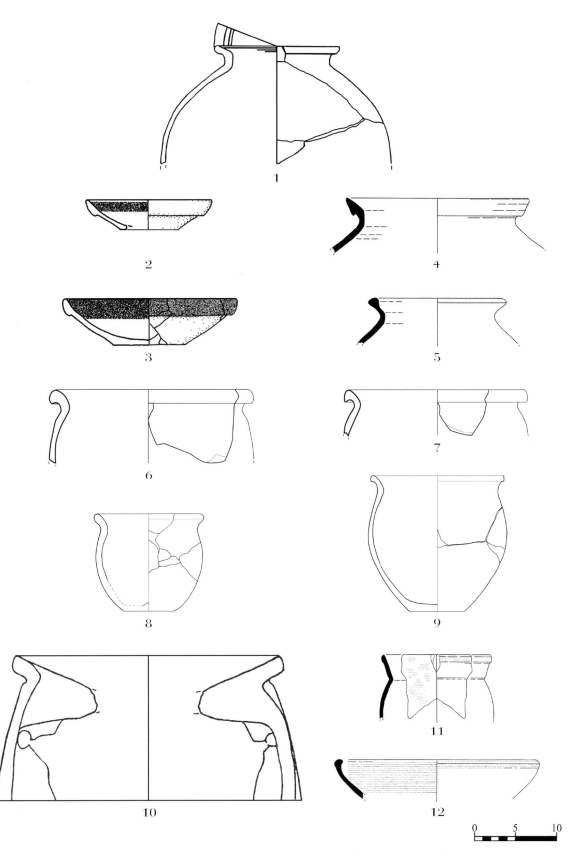

FIGURE 19.2. 1. Red impasto jar, Veii–Piazza d'Armi; 2–3. Coarse cream-ware, basin, Veii–Piazza d'Armi; 4. Jar, Veii-Campetti; 5. Pitcher, Veii-Campetti; 6–9. Coarse-ware jar, Veii–Piazza d'Armi; 10. Cooking-stand, Veii–Piazza d'Armi; 11. Internal-slip ware, jar, Veii-Campetti; 12. Internal-slip ware, basin, Veii-Campetti. (Copyright: M. T. Di Sarcina and F. Pitzalis)

most exclusively attested; they were used as well for cooking. Some cooking-stands were used specifically for food preparation, such as type Sheffer IIA (fig. 19.2: no. 10).[40] The shape, occurring mainly within the settlements, is characterized by an opening in the front and support indentations.[41]

Internal-slip ware (fig. 19.2: nos. 11–12) was a particular variant of coarse ware. A thin layer of fine clay reaching the rims was used to cover the internal surface of the vases and functioned probably to make it impermeable to water.[42] Vases in internal-slip ware are attested in both Etruria and Latium Vetus during the Late Archaic period and have been divided into standardized groups. A simple or an enlarged rim characterized the bowls. The majority of these vases were ovoid jars occurring in different varieties. From the late sixth century and especially in the fifth century BCE, the specimens with extended rim, more or less enlarged, were widespread in this region. The largest record of internal-slip ware vases comes from Casale Pian Roseto, from the wells at Macchiagrande and Comunità, and from the sanctuary at Caere Gate. The chronology of this production is still debated. Based on the evidence of the different contexts where internal-slip-ware finds are attested, this type dates between the Late Archaic period and the end of the fourth century BCE.[43]

In the Archaic period, transport amphoras do not appear in a significant number of contexts at Veii.[44] The bottom part of a Samian amphora (early sixth century BCE) and an Etruscan amphora of the Py 4 type[45] (end of the sixth to early fifth century BCE) were discovered in excavations in the well of Piano di Comunità. Other fragments were discovered at Piazza d'Armi during the British School surveys.[46]

In conclusion, it is evident that in the Archaic period a rich and distinctive pottery industry existed at Veii, a large-scale endeavor incorporating both innovative and traditional practices. Despite the circulation of high-quality imports, the prominent role played by local Veientine products in the pottery trade is an indicator of the apogee of the urban town of Veii.

NOTES

M. T. di Sarcina wrote the first parts of this chapter ("Imported Pottery" and "Local Fine Ware"); F. Pitzalis, the last part ("Impasto/Coarse Ware Pottery").

1. Cascino, Di Sarcina, and Rendeli 2012:354.
2. See chapter 23.
3. Fusco 2011, with bibliography.
4. D'Alessio and Di Sarcina 2014, with bibliography.
5. Ambrosini et al. 2009.
6. Acconcia 2012.
7. See the introduction to this volume.
8. See chapter 1.
9. *Formello*, 24–26. The author suggested an earlier chronology, beginning in the early sixth century BCE.
10. Torelli and Murray Threipland 1970; Torelli 2001; Di Sarcina 2012a.
11. Torelli and Pohl 1973. The published finds date between the sixth and the first centuries BCE.
12. On the 1937–1938 excavations: Vagnetti 1971. The frequentation of this area dates between the sixth and the first centuries BCE. A number of fragments come from later excavations: Comella and Stefani 1990:116–123.
13. See chapters 12 and 14.
14. See chapter 13.
15. See chapter 12.
16. An example in Drago 1997.
17. Michetti 2002:230, with bibliography.
18. Colonna 2001; Michetti 2002.
19. On the British School at Rome surveys: Cascino 2012a. For the most recent discoveries within the urban area: Ambrosini et al. 2009.
20. Baglione 2001:77–78. See also chapter 13.
21. Vagnetti 1971.
22. Bartoloni 2006.
23. D. Sarracino in Bartoloni and Benedettini 2011:708.
24. F. Fulminante and G. Cifani in D'Alessio 2001:18–20. See also chapter 15.
25. D'Alessio and Di Sarcina 2014.
26. D'Alessio and Di Sarcina 2014:112.
27. Vases in fig. 19.1 come from the sacred area of Caere Gate (nos. 1, 2, 5, 6, 10, 13) and Macchiagrande, trench Alpha and well (nos. 3, 4, 8, 11, 12, 14–19).
28. Cascino 2012b.
29. Torelli and Murray Threipland 1970:87 fig. 2, group A; 89 fig. 4, group D.
30. Concerning the pottery used as support for the markings see Sassatelli 1993; Maras 2009. See also chapter 15.
31. Bagnasco Gianni 1999.
32. D'Alessio and Di Sarcina 2014.

33. The bibliography on the presence of red-gloss pottery has been listed in De Lucia Brolli 2006:72 n. 19. See also Stanco 1994; Mantia 2002; and *Portonaccio* I, 237.

34. D'Alessio and Di Sarcina 2014.

35. ten Kortenaar 2011, 2012.

36. Merlo 2005, 2012; Di Sarcina 2012d.

37. Pitzalis 2009: n. 111; Di Sarcina 2012c.

38. Milletti and Pitzalis 2012.

39. Zifferero 2004.

40. Predan 2016:231–233.

41. Di Sarcina 2012c; Biancifiori 2012:156–157.

42. Di Sarcina 2012e.

43. Cascino and Di Sarcina 2008; Acconcia 2012:29–31, with bibliography. For a later chronology see Di Giuseppe 2008.

44. Di Sarcina 2012b.

45. Ambrosini et al. 2009:89–91.

46. Biancifiori 2012:162.

BIBLIOGRAPHY

Acconcia, V. 2012. "La sistemazione della strada secondaria e la struttura B." In *Veio* II, 25–32.

Acconcia, V., A. Di Napoli, G. Galante, M. H. Marchetti, M. Merlo, M. Milletti, V. Nizzo, V. Paolini, A. Piergrossi, F. Pitzalis, F. M. Rossi, F. Sciacca, S. ten Kortenaar, and I. van Kampen. 2009. "Veio–Piazza d'Armi. Analisi di due contesti abitativi alla luce della cultura materiale." In *Veio* I, 17–62.

Ambrosini, L., B. Belelli Marchesini, G. Colantoni, B. Giuliani, M. R. Lucidi, and M. Merlo. 2009. "Il contributo degli scavi di Piano di Comunità alla conoscenza dell'abitato di Veio: Materiali dal riempimento di un pozzo sul pianoro sommitale." In *Veio* I, 65–123.

Argento, A. 2006. "Le classi ceramiche: I periodi 1 e 2." In *La fattoria e la villa dell'Auditorium nel quartiere Flaminio di Roma*, ed. A. Carandini, 341–373. Rome.

Baglione, M. P. 2001. "Le statue ed altri oggetti votivi." In *Veio, Cerveteri, Vulci*, 69–78.

Bagnasco Gianni, G. 1999. "La ceramica depurata acroma e a bande." In *Tarquinia: Scavi sistematici nell'abitato (campagne 1982–1988): I materiali* I, ed. C. Chiaramonte Treré, 99–176. Rome.

Bartoloni, G. 2006. "Veio–Piazza d'Armi: Dallo scavo degli ispettori alle ricerche attuali." In *Archeologia in Etruria Meridionale. Atti delle Giornate di Studio in ricordo di Mario moretti, Civita Castellana, 2003*, ed. M. Pandolfini Angeletti, 33–48. Rome.

Bartoloni, G., and G. Benedettini. 2011. *Veio: Il deposito votivo di Comunità (scavi 1889–2005)*. Rome.

Biancifiori, E. 2012. "Instrumentum domesticum e anfore da trasporto." In *Veio* II, 154–162.

Cascino, R. 2012a. "La ceramica di importazione attica." In *Survey*, 105–108.

———. 2012b. "Il bucchero." In *Survey*, 141–162.

Cascino, R., and M. T. Di Sarcina. 2008. "L'*Internal Slip Ware* nella media Valle del Tevere." In *Mercator Placidissimus*, 559–585.

Cascino, R., M. T. Di Sarcina, and M. Rendeli. 2012. "Veii in the Orientalizing, Archaic, and Classical Periods." In *Survey*, 336–359.

Colonna, G. 2001. "Introduzione." In *Veio, Cerveteri, Vulci*, 3–4.

Comella, A., and G. Stefani. 1990. *Materiali votivi del Santuario di Campetti a Veio: Scavi 1947 e 1969*. Rome.

D'Alessio, M. T. 2001. "Macchiagrande–Vignacce." In *Veio, Cerveteri, Vulci*, 17–22.

D'Alessio, M. T., and M. T. Di Sarcina. 2014. "Lo scavo in località Macchiagrande a Veio: Un contesto di età tardo-arcaica e classica." *ScAnt* 20:105–125.

De Lucia Brolli, M. 2006. "Dalla tutela alla ricerca: Recenti rinvenimenti dall'area urbana di Falerii." In *Archeologia in Etruria Meridionale. Atti delle giornate di studio in ricordo di Mario Moretti, Civita Castellana, 2003*, ed. M. Pandolfini Angeletti, 65–90. Rome.

Di Giuseppe, H. 2008. "Produzione, circolazione e uso della ceramica lungo il Tevere in epoca repubblicana." In *Mercator Placidissimus*, 587–619.

Di Sarcina, M. T. 2012a. "L'edificio tardo-arcaico di Casale Pian Roseto." In *MAV*, 131–135.

———. 2012b. "Anfore da trasporto arcaiche." In *Survey*, 242–244.

———. 2012c. "La ceramica d'impasto da mensa e da dispensa di età orientalizzante ed arcaica." In *Survey*, 201–219.

———. 2012d. "La ceramica d'impasto chiaro-sabbioso." In *Survey*, 219–229.

———. 2012e. "L'*Internal Slip Ware*." In *Survey*, 229–235.

Drago, L. 1997. "Le tombe 419 e 426 del sepolcreto di Grotta Gramiccia a Veio: Contributo alla conoscenza di strutture tombali e ideologia funeraria a Veio tra il VI e il V secolo a.C." In *Etrusca et Italica. Scritti in ricordo di Massimo Pallottino*, 239–280. Pisa.

Fusco, U. 2011. "Il complesso archeologico di Campetti, area S-O." In *Culto degli Antenati*, 11.

Mantia, R. 2002. "Ceramica etrusca a vernice nera e a vernice rossa." In *Cerveteri: Importazioni e contesti nelle necropoli*, ed. G. Bagnasco Gianni, 461–466. Milan.

Maras, D. F. 2009. *Il dono votivo: Gli dei e il sacro nelle iscrizioni etrusche di culto*. Pisa.

Merlo, M. 2005. "Impasto chiaro sabbioso." In *Ardea: Il deposito votivo di Casarinaccio*, ed. F. Di Mario, 21–42. Rome.

———. 2012. "Impasto chiaro sabbioso." In *Veio* II, 153–154.

Michetti, L. 2002. "Considerazioni sui materiali." In *Portonaccio* I, 229–245.

Milletti, M., and F. Pitzalis. 2012. "Impasto rosso-bruno." In *Veio* II, 141–153.

Pitzalis, F. 2009. "Impasto rosso-bruno." In Acconcia et al. 2009:39.

Predan, C. 2016. "*Instrumentum* da fuoco, da dispensa e da mensa." In *Veio* III.2, 218–248.

Sassatelli, G. 1993. "Il bucchero e le ceramiche affini come supporto per iscrizioni e graffiti in area padana." In *Produzione artigianale ed esportazione nel mondo antico: Il bucchero etrusco. Atti del colloquio internazionale, Milano, 1990*, ed. M. Bonghi Jovino, 195–205. Milan.

Stanco, E. A. 1994. "Ceramica a vernice rossa di periodo repubblicano." In *Ceramica romana: Guida allo studio* I, ed. M. Balzano e A. Camilli, 91–104. Rome.

ten Kortenaar, S. 2011. *Il colore e la materia: Tra tradizione e in-novazione nella produzione dell'impasto rosso nell'Italia medio-tirrenica*. Officina Etruscologia 4. Rome.

———. 2012. "Impasto rosso." In *Veio* II, 132–141.

Torelli, M. 2001. "*Stata Mater in agro Veientano*: La 'riscoperta' di un santuario rurale veiente in loc. Casale Pian Roseto." *StEtr* 64:117–134.

Torelli, M., and L. Murray Threipland. 1970. "A Semisubterranean Building in the Casale Pian Roseto (Veii) Area." *PBSR* 38:62–121.

Torelli, M., and I. Pohl. 1973. "Veio—Scoperta di un piccolo santuario etrusco in località Campetti." *NSc* 1973:40–258.

Vagnetti, L. 1971. *Il deposito votivo di Campetti a Veio*. Florence.

Zifferero, A. 2004. "Ceramica pre-romana e sistemi alimentari: Elementi per una ricerca." In *Bridging the Tiber*, 255–268.

CHAPTER 20

METAL PRODUCTION

MATTEO MILLETTI AND LUCIANA DRAGO

BRONZE

Metallurgical activities at Veii during the Late Bronze Age cannot be compared to the output of the rich workshops of coastal Etruria, especially those in the area of the Tolfa Mountains. In fact, in terms of the amount of production as compared to surrounding Tyrrhenic regions, the absence of metal hoards is striking. At the same time, looking at its connections to other bronzeworking traditions, Veii did not reach high levels of typological variability. Only a small number of objects could have been manufactured in the city and its territory, and recovered artifacts have provided only a limited amount of evidence.[1] Nevertheless, the scarce data coming from the local bronze workshops indicate a similarity with the "Tolfa-Allumiere" group, which parallels other aspects of Veientine material culture, especially pottery production.[2] In addition, this very limited record could be explained as a matter of archaeological visibility, and perhaps new discoveries will at least partially fill the gap between Veii and the nearby regions.

The archaeological record of metal production during the Early Iron Age is more impressive overall. For the earlier phases, however, the number of metal objects, mainly discovered inside the contemporary tombs, is still limited, because of the isonomic Villanovan funerary ideology, which involved a strict reduction of funerary goods and ornaments in the burials. Around the end of the ninth and during the eighth century BCE, the increasing development of a local tradition is evident. At this time, the arrival at Veii of artifacts (or their imitations coming from central Europe, and later from Greece and the Levant) demonstrates the growing interactions with other traditions of metallurgy.[3]

During EIA 1, certain ornaments stand out, especially the fibulae, usually having a serpentine bow (made in two pieces), massive body, and deep ribbing (fig. 20.1: no. 1).[4] These fibulae are some of the earliest examples of a type that would later circulate widely.[5] Other fibulae have a series of metal disks around the bow (fig. 20.1: no. 3),[6] and have been considered to be local,[7] among a larger group that characterizes southern Etruria and Campania. Finally, a third type of fibula, with beads of amber and glass on the bow (fig. 20.1: no. 2),[8] may come from the area of Bologna.[9]

During the ninth century BCE, terracotta helmets were almost the only reference to weapons evident in the burials. An exception occurred in tomb OP5 in the necropolis of Quattro Fontanili (*map 3*), where an oval miniature shield was discovered (fig. 20.1: no. 4).[10] The presence of this shield probably indicates an attempt to imitate a funerary custom typical of the nearby area of Latium Vetus.[11] Razors were the most common gender markers (fig. 20.1: no. 5), and some particular types testify to the network of interactions between Veii and Bologna that began in the late ninth century BCE and continued into the following century.[12]

From the beginning of the eighth century BCE, the amount of evidence increases due to the growing complexity of the tomb-groups. A local toreutic tradition flourished and seems to have been inferior only to that of Tarquinia. Artisans coming from the north played a

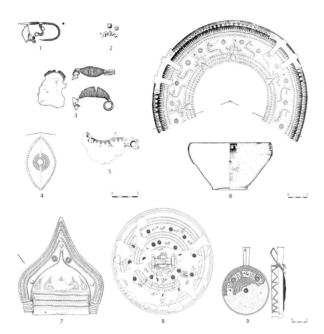

FIGURE 20.1. A selection of bronze objects from Veii.
1. Fibula with serpentine bow in two pieces; 2. Fibula with
beads of amber and glass on the bow; 3. Fibula with series of
metal disks around the bow; 4. Oval miniature shield, tomb
OP5 in Quattro Fontanili; 5. Razor; 6. Metal bowl covering
the ossuary of tomb 23 in Valle La Fata; 7. Crested helmet
from tomb AA1 in Quattro Fontanili; 8. Shield; 9. Pilgrim's
flask. (Copyright: M. Milletti)

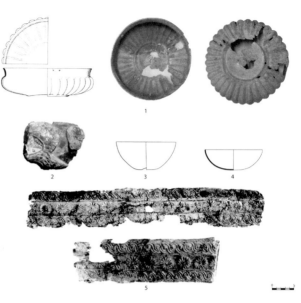

FIGURE 20.2. A selection of bronze objects from Veii.
1. Ribbed cups from tomb 871 in Casale del Fosso; 2. *Rhyton*
from Casale del Fosso; 3 and 4. Hemispherical cups; 5. Urn
from Monte Michele tomb 5. (Copyright: M. Milletti)

fundamental role in the development of a local tradition, producing masterpieces such as the incised metal
bowl covering the ossuary of tomb 23 in the necropolis of Valle La Fata (fig. 20.1: no. 6; *map 3*) and the
crested helmet deposited in the second half of the
eighth century in tomb AA1 at Quattro Fontanili (fig.
20.1: no. 7).[13] Objects made of sheet-bronze, such as
shields (fig. 20.1: no. 8) and "pilgrim's flasks" (fig. 20.1:
no. 9), with molded decorations representing horses
and ducks, have been considered local productions.
The pilgrim's flask is an Eastern shape that spread
widely in the Tyrrhenian region and functioned as a
container for precious liquids, such as, perhaps, a res-
inous wine of a high quality.[14] Contacts with Levantine
bronze workshops are evident in the tripod-stands[15]
and the tripod-bowls[16] dating to EIA IA. These forms,
just like the pilgrim's flasks, flourished especially in the
following periods.

As for bronze furnishings, we observe the presence
of trays in embossed foil with central basin and on

four wheels[17] that represent ritual carts and have been
connected to the Cypriot wheeled stands with four
sides that probably inspired the well-known Bisen-
zio wheeled incense burner.[18] Among the ornaments,
we should stress the presence of fibulae with enlarged
bows and bird-shaped elements. At the passage between local phases IIA and IIB and the end of the
Early Iron Age, Veii was probably a center of production of these fibulae.[19]

During the Orientalizing period, the number of
Levantine imports and especially ceremonial vessels
increased, as did the influence of the eastern Mediterranean metallurgies on the local productions. The lion
rhyton from Casale del Fosso (*fig. 11.1*; *map 3*) is one
of the earliest examples.[20] Dating to the second half
of the eighth century BCE, this *rhyton* (fig. 20.2: no. 2)
has been considered an Assyrian product,[21] and likewise the two ribbed cups discovered in tomb 871 of the
same necropolis, dating to the end of the eighth century BCE (fig. 20.2: no. 1).[22] The earliest imitations of
this shape at Veii followed these imports after a short
time, and the most common types were characterized
by a limited number of ribs.[23] The hemispherical cups
(fig. 20.2: nos. 3–4) also reveal a Near Eastern origin.
This shape was widely diffused as well in the western

Mediterranean. The ribbed and the hemispherical cups were replicated locally at Veii, in both metal and pottery, beginning in phase IIC.[24] The high ideological value of these cups is connected to wine consumption, which soon began to be a constant characteristic of aristocratic tomb-groups in Etruria. At the same time, they attest a strong network of economic and political interactions among the leading elites, who were fully acculturated to the Eastern models.

After the second quarter of the seventh century BCE, Veii played a fundamental role in the distribution of artifacts in embossed bronze foil with molded decoration, following an established tradition based on the earlier activities.[25] In most of the Etruscan cities local workshops existed and masters in bronze production followed their lords as *clientes*. Therefore, it is extremely difficult to distinguish specific local productions without analyzing in detail the decorative repertoires. We mention here some objects made of sheet-bronze from tomb 5 of the necropolis of Monte Michele (*map 4:B*)[26] and in particular the small urn, decorated on its sides by a series of palmettes and small stamped rosettes between two registers of guilloches with three interlaces (fig. 20.2: no. 5). The same decoration occurred on the plates lining the box of the chariot.[27] Similar considerations can be applied to the plates of the wooden barrel-shaped thrones,[28] on which the use of molded decorative reliefs is almost exclusive, and to the shields.[29]

The tradition of the high value of the bronze creations of Veii may be echoed by the legend of the great master Mamurius Veturius, who created the *ancilia* (ritual shields) of Numa. As different scholars have stressed,[30] his fascinating name implies an origin at Veii and especially a connection with Morrius or Mamorrius, king of Veii and descendent of Haleus, the mythical founder of Falerii.

From the beginning of the sixth century and throughout the entire fifth century BCE, the custom increasingly was to bury fewer grave goods (as in Latium Vetus),[31] which has affected our understanding of metalworking. The absence of data is only filled by the evidence in bronze from the settlement and the sanctuaries.[32] Concerning the bronzes, an evident reduction in the use of this alloy in several manufacturing categories—such as weapons—occurred together with an increase in iron production, which previously served as a precious metal in items decorated with inlay. Especially during the Archaic period, bronze continued to be used only for personal ornaments, due to its aesthetic value, and for vessels.[33] At this time, there occurs a large standardization of types, as in other areas of southern Etruria and Latium Vetus. Finally, the small bronze figurines of youths and maidens (*kouroi* and *korai*) found at Portonaccio (*map 4:S*) can be compared to similar specimens from votive deposits in Rome or in Latium Vetus.[34] These data suggest the birth of a regional artistic *koine*,[35] in which Veii participated until the Roman siege.

TIN, IRON, AND LEAD

The presence of metalworkers specialized in the use of tin is documented at Veii from the beginning of the ninth century BCE.[36] Small metal platelets were applied to the surfaces of ossuaries, their lids, and other vases in brown impasto. In EIA II, these metal platelets were applied to prestige objects having a connection with the military and/or religious status of the dead, such as bronze axes.[37]

The production of iron items is documented from the end of the ninth century BCE, but it was less widespread than bronze working. In the earliest phase, only distinctive ornaments for high-rank warriors and leaders were made, such as the rare serpentine bow fibulae with long or disc-shaped catch plates.[38] Around the end of the Early Iron Age and the beginning of the Early Orientalizing period, the use of iron became more frequent, with such objects appearing mainly in male burials. These finds consisted of small tripods,[39] vases and defensive weapons,[40] firedogs, knives, horse bits,[41] wheel rims and other parts of chariots, axes, spears, daggers, swords (and their sheaths), and also a few ornaments.[42] An exceptional object is the large iron club associated with the composite bilobated bronze shield found in the royal burial of the priest/warrior in tomb 1036 in the necropolis of Casale del Fosso (*map 3*), dated immediately after the mid-eighth century BCE.[43] At this time, iron was used also as an alternative alloy for a few leech-shaped and boat-shaped fibulae and for a few pendants.[44] In some cases, spindles and distaffs, often covered by amber,[45] were made of iron; these occurred in rich female tombs. Iron was also used for prestige objects in mixed materials, such as swords with bone or ivory hilts[46] and scepters[47] in princely male tombs.

During the Middle and Late Orientalizing periods, different types of fibulae—both dragon-type and enlarged bow—and other ornaments, such as bracelets,[48] were made of iron instead of bronze, as in the previous periods.

Among the few burials dating to either the sixth or the fifth century BCE, we can mention the Archaic cremation in tomb 2 at La Rotonda, where only one iron object was found, whose function is not certain (probably a rod which was bent on one end).[49] The few large iron nails found in tomb 426 in the necropolis of Grotta Gramiccia (*map 3*) date to the beginning of the fifth century BCE. These nails were probably related to the wheels and box of a chariot used to carry the dead woman during her funerary procession. Alternatively they may have functioned as part of a chest or of a funerary bed.[50]

For the period at the transition from the sixth to the fifth century BCE, the evidence of iron objects from the settlement[51] and from the sacred areas is very limited; there are nails for carpenters' work or for binding architectural elements.[52]

A small piece of lead foil found in the workshop area at Campetti (*map 4:G*) reveals that leadworking at Veii had already begun in the ninth century BCE.[53] In addition, the sixty small lead tubes found in tomb 5 of the necropolis of Monte Michele, which were considered at the time of their discovery "weights for a fishing net,"[54] date to the Early Orientalizing period. Three small lead foil pieces, forming a starburst on the knees of an infant body buried in the same princely tomb, are of uncertain date and function (perhaps ritual?).[55] Among the other small lead objects whose functions are not clearly understood, there were also some examples of egg-shaped "acorns"—believed to be sling bullets—found at the bottom of Villanovan trench tombs or near them.[56] During the Archaic period, lead was also used for carpenters' works and for the attachment of clay structural and decorative elements

on buildings, both sacred and civic.[57] A local workshop using lead is attested near the altars[58] of several sanctuaries. Here lead was probably used also to seal the joins of tufa blocks.[59]

GOLD, SILVER, AND ELECTRUM

Precious metals, such as silver, gold, and electrum, often in combination (and sometimes with bronze, amber, bone, or wood), came into use at Veii only between EIA II and the Orientalizing period. Precious metals occurred in the most prestigious tombs, especially female burials. The most common objects were wire earrings with amber rings;[60] spirals for hair braids (with plain ends or undulated edges);[61] beads[62] and other elements for necklaces;[63] bird-shaped pendants;[64] and different kinds of fibulae and clasps. In addition, thin gold plates, in the form of swastikas, worked in *repoussé* were decorated with geometric motifs, with little holes along the edges. These plates were sewed onto garments and formed part of the decoration of textiles and other parts of the adornment.[65]

During EIA II and the Early Orientalizing period, among the different types of fibulae, the following shapes were attested: (a) fibula with enlarged bow, covered with gold strips[66] or plates,[67] or entirely in gold, with an engraved chevron decoration,[68] and a short or slightly long catch; (b) leech-type fibula, with a thick bow entirely in gold[69] or an empty bow in gold and silver, decorated with wires applied on the surface,[70] with an elongated catch-plate; (c) fibula in two pieces, serpentine bow–shaped, covered with gold wires and ending with glass and amber beads (with a small gold plate disc on top), with a disc-shaped or elongated catch-plate;[71] (d) serpentine fibula in bronze, covered with silver wire, with an elongated catch-plate;[72] (e) fibula in bronze with a stick bow, covered with amber and bone discs, or only amber discs and a gold plate[73] (or with a single gold grain, or several amber discs with cavities in which small circular gold plates were inserted), with long catch-plate;[74] (f) dragon-type fibula, entirely in gold and silver, with long catch-plate;[75] and (g) fibula with enlarged bow in silver, with short or elongated catch-plate.[76]

Among the objects dating to the very end of the

FIGURE 20.3. Scepter in bronze, iron, amber, and gold, from Casale del Fosso tomb 1036. (Copyright: L. Drago)

FIGURE 20.4. Silver cup from Casale del Fosso tomb 804. (Copyright: L. Drago)

Early Iron Age and the beginning of the Early Orientalizing period, a small group of fibulae stands out. These fibulae were in gold, silver, and electrum or in bronze covered with silver with a very long catch-plate, an asymmetrical spring, and a serpentine bow partially forked and decorated with a small filigree band. They also were clad in gold wire and decorated with gold granulation.[77] These fibulae are among the earliest evidence of the local filigree technique and, along with some biconical beads, of the granulation technique, which were introduced at Veii during EIA II by Near Eastern artisans,[78] and later re-elaborated according to local taste.[79] The evidence of granulation is indeed limited to a group of high-ranking tombs and dates to the mid-eighth through the mid-seventh century BCE.

The use of gold, silver, and electrum highlighted the prestige of rising aristocratic individuals. Apart from the scepters of the priest-warriors of tombs 1036 and 871 at Casale del Fosso (fig. 20.3), and of one of the princes buried in tomb 5 of Monte Michele, it is important to mention the earlier hinged clasps found in other princely tombs and also in female tombs.[80]

Extant remains of rare metal vases are limited to two hemispherical cups made of silver discovered in the princely tombs 871 and 804 of the necropolis of Casale del Fosso;[81] the first one dates to 730–720 BCE and the second to the beginning of the seventh century BCE (figs. 11.3, 20.4–20.5). The later one has a more slender shape, between rounded and oval, with a hammered and inward-curved rim. Their shapes and mea-

FIGURE 20.5. Silver cup from Casale del Fosso tomb 871. (Copyright: L. Drago)

sures correspond perfectly to the blue glass cup found in the Bernardini Tomb in Praeneste, which dates to the second quarter of the seventh century BCE. These two cups at Veii were made for Etruscan clients by artisans of Near Eastern origins—probably Phoenicians, active in the West, who would have bought silver in mines located in Spain or Sardinia.[82]

Finally, evidence for jewelry belonging to wealthy women at Veii during the Archaic and Classical periods comes from several burials and includes: (a) a silver-mounted ring from tomb 4 of Pantano di Grano, of the sixth century BCE;[83] (b) a set of gold jewelry from the exceptional female cremation inside a heavy bucchero jar, found at Pantanaccio, dating to the third quarter of the sixth century BCE; (c) a ring made of a thin gold band, from the open-air cremation tomb

426 of Grotta Gramiccia, dating within the fifth century BCE;[84] (d) and a gold earring from tomb 9 and a silver earring from tomb 15 of the necropolis of Monte Michele, whose uncertain chronology varies between the sixth and the fifth century BCE.[85]

NOTES

Matteo Milletti wrote the first part of the chapter ("Bronze"), and Luciana Drago wrote the second and third parts ("Tin, Iron, and Lead" and "Gold, Silver, and Electrum").

1. Carancini and Peroni 1999; Lo Schiavo et al. 2013.
2. Berardinetti Insam 1990:15 n. 65; Barbaro 2010:71–72, 138–140.
3. Sciacca 2010a:5.
4. Bartoloni and Delpino 1979: n. 3, 49, pls. 9A3, 24a.
5. de Agostino and Gastaldi 1988: type 32A3, 50-41; Lo Schiavo 2010: type 322, 637–638.
6. For example Bartoloni and Delpino 1979: n. 4, 59, pl. 17.4; type 7, 86.
7. Babbi 2003:59–61 with bibliography.
8. Berardinetti Insam 1990:12, fig. 5 f.
9. Dore 2005: pl. 3.
10. Bartoloni et al. 1994:8, 1997:96.
11. De Santis 2011, with bibliography.
12. Bartoloni and Delpino 1979:97 n. 375; Bartoloni 1986: 47–52; Berardinetti Insam 1990:13–15 n. 56.
13. Iaia 2005:91, no. 41, 93, fig. 31, pl. XV.
14. See Marzoli 1989, 1998; Iaia 2010:33–35.
15. Colonna 1977; Iaia 2010:36–37.
16. Iaia 2007, with bibliography.
17. Naso 2006.
18. Torelli 1997; Iaia 2010:36–37.
19. Babbi and Piergrossi 2005:302–304.
20. See chapter 11.
21. Sciacca 2003, with bibliography.
22. Drago Troccoli 2006:101–102, fig. 13.4.
23. Sciacca 2005.
24. Mercuri 2004; Sciacca 2010b:46–53.
25. Strøm 1971.
26. Boitani 1983, 2001 with bibliography.
27. Strøm 2000:69.
28. Strøm 2000:67–73.
29. Geiger 1994: types 2a–c, 83–97.
30. Colonna 1991:97, with bibliography. See also chapter 7.
31. See chapter 9.
32. Bartoloni et al. 1994:38–40 with bibliography; Drago Troccoli 1997:268–278.

33. As in the case of different *oinochoai* from Portonaccio (Ambrosini 2009: nos. 595–596, 249–252).
34. Mazzocchi 1997: type III, 134–141. See also chapter 13.
35. Michetti 2002:242–243 with bibliography.
36. For the evidence from Grotta Gramiccia and Casale del Fosso see Drago Troccoli 2012a:758; from Valle La Fata, Bartoloni and Delpino 1979:76–78; from Quattro Fontanili, Toms 1986:84, 85, 87, 90, 92, 93; Guidi 1993:19, 27, 30, 31, 32, 34, 35, 43, 51.
37. Guidi 1993:41, 66, type 181, variety A, fig. 12/8; Berardinetti and Drago 1997:48; Boitani 2004:139–140 (Veii IIB).
38. Toms 1986:82, figs. 16, III 10; 20, III 11; Guidi 1993:50, type 103, variety E, fig. 6/7; type 109, fig. 23/6 (Veii IB–IIB).
39. Guidi 1993:37, 70, type 194, fig. 10/19; See also *QF* 1967: 154, 160, fig. 46, 13; *QF* 1972:222–223, fig. 19, 23: Quattro Fontanili, tombs FF 7–8 and CC 1–2 (Veii IIB).
40. The presence of the large iron *situla* of the Kurd type in tomb 871 at Casale del Fosso is exceptional. The rod that internally reinforced the folded edge of the circular shields was of bronze, and sometimes the handle was in iron.
41. Sometimes with bronze uprights, as in Boitani 2004:144, Quattro Fontanili tomb AA1.
42. Guidi 1993:29, 52, 54, 63, bracelets and rings type 116, variety D, E, F, and type 126, variety A, figs. 6/10, 23/11–13 (Veii IIA–IIC).
43. See chapter 6.
44. Palm 1952:64, pl. 18, 46; 66, pl. XX, 49; 70, pl. 26, 10 (Vaccareccia tombs VIII, X, XVII [Veii IIIA]).
45. Palm 1952:65, pl. 19, 60b (Vaccareccia tomb VIII); Boitani 2003:81, Monte Michele tomb 5 (Veii IIIA–B).
46. Guidi 1993:68, type 188, fig. 8/13, 10/18 (Veii IIB).
47. Drago 2012.
48. For example De Santis 1997:128, 133, 138, Pantano di Grano, tombs 1, 2, and 3.
49. Stefani 1953:95.
50. Drago Troccoli 1997:248–255, fig. 6.
51. Stefani 1953:104.
52. The evidence from Portonaccio is listed in Stefani 1953: 81–87; Martelli Antonioli and Martelli 2002:226–227; Michetti 2002:245; and from Campetti in Vagnetti 1971:154–155.
53. I thank F. Biagi for this information, provided via personal communication.
54. Cristofani 1969:13, 17–18 n. 5, fig. 1, tomb A (Veii IIIA).
55. Boitani 2001:113, and 2003, 81, "forse per trattenere un velo sul corpo" ("maybe to hold a veil on the body").
56. Drago Troccoli 1997:256 n. 41, 273 n. 93.
57. As in the case of the bronze figurine carrying an offering of a small pig (made of a high percentage of lead) discovered at Campetti (Santangelo 1952:46, pls. XV, XVI, 1), dating before the end of the fifth century BCE.
58. Martelli Antonioli and Martelli 2002:227.

59. Stefani 1953:43 (the paved area facing the altar to the north).

60. The example in gold from Quattro Fontanili tomb EE 7–8 B (*QF* 1967:131, fig. 26, 13–14).

61. Martelli 1983a:29–30, fig. 3, 4; 1983b:36. Buranelli et al. 1997:72, fig. 18; Drago 2013:31, 35, fig. 37, b; Boitani 2012:92.

62. Martelli 1983a:30, 1983b:37; Guidi 1993:25, 37, 67, 74, figs. 4/14, 4/15, 10/22, 25/29; Drago Troccoli 2005:92, 94, fig. 4, 7–8, 10; 2013:31, 32, figs. 29f, 37c; Boitani 2012:92, pl. II, 1.

63. Guidi 1993:67, 76, fig. 25/30; Drago 2013:31, 32, 35, figs. 29c, 37d.

64. Martelli 1983a:30, nos. 4–5; Martelli 1983b:36; 1983c:250–251; Guidi 1993:45, 60, 74, figs. 14/8, 17–18, types 150 and 232; Buranelli et al. 1997:72, fig. 17, Casale del Fosso tomb 1032 (Veii IIB, IIC, IIIA).

65. Drago Troccoli 2005:91.

66. Martelli 1983a:28; 1983b:75; 1983c:250 n. 3; Toms 1986: 78, 80, type I, 27, fig. 20B; Guidi 1993:42, 63, fig. 23/1, type 79 (Veii IIA–IIC).

67. Unpublished examples from Casale del Fosso (Veii IIB–IIC/IIIA).

68. Martelli 1983a:26, 32; Toms 1986:78–79, type I, 23, fig. 25 (Veii IIB).

69. Unpublished examples from Casale del Fosso (Veii IIB/IIC).

70. Quattro Fontanili, tomb LL 18 (*QF* 1963:254–255, fig. 117, u).

71. Martelli 1983a:28, 32, fig. 3, 1.

72. Martelli 1983a:26, 28; Guidi 1993:33, 50, fig. 8/3, type 107.

73. Martelli 1983a:28–29, fig. 3, 3; *QF* 1967:131–132, fig. 25, 16–17; *QF* 1970:190, 193, fig. 9, 22–23.

74. Martelli 1983a:28–30, fig. 3, 2; Drago Troccoli 2005: 91–92, fig. 4, 9, tombs 872 and 1000 at Casale del Fosso; Palm 1952: pl. XXXI, 1.

75. Palm 1952:63, pl. XVI, 30; Boitani 2001:115, 2003:82.

76. Boitani 2012:92.

77. Martelli 1983a:36, 1983c:268–269; Formigli 2003; Babbi and Niemeyer 2013; Niemeyer 2013a: figs. 1–2, 2013b:223–224, 226, figs. 1–2.

78. Martelli 1983b:36. See also Sciacca 2010:11.

79. Drago et al. forthcoming.

80. Martelli 1983b:40. See Palm 1952:61, 63, 72, pl. XI, 5, XVI, 29, XXXI, 6; Boitani 2001b:114–115, 2003:82–83.

81. Drago Troccoli 2005:97, 98, 102, 103, 105, 108, fig. 13, 2; Drago 2013:30–34, 40–41, figs. 31–36.

82. Benvenuti et al. 2015, forthcoming.

83. De Santis 1997:140–141, fig. 30.

84. Drago Troccoli 1997:248–255.

85. Mengarelli 1901:241–243.

BIBLIOGRAPHY

Ambrosini, L. 2009. *Il santuario di Veio a Portonaccio III: La cisterna arcaica con l'incluso deposito di età ellenistica*. Rome.

Babbi, A. 2003. "Le fibule della Raccolta comunale di Tarquinia: Alcune considerazioni tecnologiche." In *Fibulae: Dall'età del Bronzo all'alto Medioevo tecnica e tipologia*, ed. E. Formigli, 59–75. Florence.

Babbi, A., and B. Niemeyer. 2013. "Katalog: Metalli, Oro." In *La Tomba del Guerriero di Tarquinia: Identità elitaria, concentrazione del potere e networks dinamici nell'avanzato VIII sec. a.C. / Das Kriegergrab von Tarquinia: Eliteidentität, Machtkonzentration und dynamische Netzwerke im späten 8. Jh. v. Chr.*, ed. A. Babbi and U. Pletz, 233–245. Mainz.

Babbi, A., and A. Piergrossi. 2005. "Per una definizione della cronologia relativa ed assoluta del villanoviano veiente e tarquiniese (IC–IIB)." In Bartoloni and Delpino 2005: 293–318.

Barbaro, B. 2010. *Insediamenti, aree funerarie ed entità territoriali in Etruria meridionale nel Bronzo finale*. Florence.

Bartoloni, G. 1986. "Relazione interregionali nell'VIII secolo a.C.: Bologna–Etruria mineraria–Valle Tiberina." In *Studi e Documenti di Archeologia* 2:45–56.

———, ed. 1997. *Le necropoli arcaiche di Veio. Giornata di studio in memoria di Massimo Pallottino*. Rome.

Bartoloni, G., A. Berardinetti, L. Drago, and A. De Santis. 1994. "Veio tra IX e VI sec. a.C.: Primi risultati sull'analisi comparata delle necropoli veienti." *ArchCl* 46:1–46.

Bartoloni, G., and F. Delpino. 1979. *Veio I: Introduzione allo studio delle necropoli arcaiche di Veio: Il sepolcreto di Valle La Fata*. MonAnt 1. Rome.

———, eds. 2005. *Oriente e Occidente: Metodi e discipline a confronto. Riflessioni sulla cronologia dell'età del Ferro in Italia. Atti dell'incontro di studi, Roma, 2003*. Mediterranea 1. Pisa.

Bartoloni, G., et al. 1997. "Le necropoli villanoviane di Veio: Parallelismi e differenze." In *Necropoli arcaiche*, 89–100.

Benvenuti, M., D. Ferro, L. Drago, C. Bellafiore, and E. Scarsella. 2015. "Desde el Mar Tirreno a la Península Ibérica: El proyecto de investigación y los datos preliminares sobre el hierro, el cobre, el plomo y la plata." In *Minería y metalurgia en el Mediterráneo y su periferia oceánica. III Encuentros Internacionales del Mediterraneo*, 102–111. Mazarrón.

Benvenuti, M., M. Gnade, C. Bellafiore, and E. Scarsella. Forthcoming. "Oriente y Occidente: La circulación de metales en Etruria y el Tirreno central entre la Edad del Hierro y la Romanización: Resultados preliminares y perspectivas en el marco de una investigación interdisciplinar." In *Atti dell'VIII Congreso Internacional sobre Minería y Metalurgía Históricas en el Sudoeste europeo. Presente y futuro de los paisajes mineros del pasado: Estudios sobre minería, metalurgia y poblamiento, Granada, 11–15 giugno 2014*.

Berardinetti, A., and L. Drago. 1997. "La necropoli di Grotta Gramiccia." In *Necropoli arcaiche*, 39–61.

Berardinetti Insam, A. 1990. "La fase iniziale della necropoli villanoviana di Quattro Fontanili: Rapporti con le comunità limitrofe." *DialArch* 8:5–28.

Boitani, F. 1983. "Veio: La tomba 'principesca' della necropoli di Monte Michele." *StEtr* 51:536–556.

———. 2001. "La tomba principesca 5 di Monte Michele." In *Veio, Cerveteri, Vulci*, 113–188.

———. 2003. "Necropoli di Monte Michele, la tomba principesca." In *Formello*, 81–84.

———. 2004. "La tomba di guerriero AA1 dalla necropoli dei Quattro Fontanili a Veio." In *Scavo nello scavo: Gli Etruschi non visti. Ricerche e "riscoperte" nei depositi del Musei Archeologici dell'Etruria meridionale*, ed. A. M. Moretti Sgubini, 128–149. Rome.

———. 2012. "La tomba tardo-orientalizzante '6' di Veio-Monte Michele." In *MAV*, 91–96.

Buranelli, F., L. Drago, and L. Paolini. 1997. "La necropoli di Casale del Fosso." In *Necropoli arcaiche*, 63–83.

Carancini, G. L., and R. Peroni. 1999. *L'età del Bronzo in Italia: Per una cronologia della produzione metallurgica.* Quaderni di Protostoria 2. Perugia.

Colonna, G. 1977. "Un tripode fittile geometrico dal Foro Romano." *MÉFRA* 89:477–491.

———. 1991. "Gli scudi bilobati dell'Italia centrale e l'*ancile* dei Salii." *ArchCl* 43:55–122.

Cristofani, M. 1969. *Le tombe da Monte Michele nel Museo archeologico di Firenze.* Florence.

Cristofani, M., and M. Martelli. 1983. *L'oro degli Etruschi.* Novara.

de Agostino, B., and P. Gastaldi. 1988. *Pontecagnano 2: La necropoli del Picentino*, 1: *Le tombe della prima età del Ferro. AnnArchStorAnt* 5. Naples.

De Santis, A. 1997. "Alcune considerazioni sul territorio veiente in età orientalizzante ed arcaica." In *Necropoli arcaiche*, 101–143.

———, ed. 2011. *Politica e leader nel Lazio ai tempi di Enea.* Rome.

Dore, A. 2005. "Il Villanoviano I–III di Bologna: Problemi di cronologia assoluta e relativa." In Bartoloni and Delpino 2005:255–292.

Drago, L. 2012. "Veio nella prima età del Ferro: Struttura sociale e scambi." In *L'Etruria dal Paleolitico al Primo Ferro: Lo stato delle ricerche. Atti del X Convegno Preistoria e Protostoria in Etruria*, ed. Nuccia Negroni Catacchio, 757–766. Milan.

———. 2013. "Aspetti dell'Orientalizzante antico a Veio." In *Dall'Italia omaggio a Barbro Santillo Frizell*, ed. A. Capodiferro, 19–44. Rome.

Drago, L., D. Ferro, and B Marci. Forthcoming. *Fibule d'argento con arco decorato a filigrana dalla necropoli di Casale del Fosso a Veio.*

Drago Troccoli, L. 1997. "Le tombe 419 e 426 del sepolcreto di Grotta Gramiccia–Veio: Contributo alla conoscenza di strutture tombali e ideologia funeraria a Veio tra il VI e il V secolo a.C." In *Etrusca e Italica. Scritti in ricordo di Massimo Pallottino*, 239–280. Pisa.

———. 2005. "Una coppia di principi nella necropoli di Casale del Fosso a Veio." In *Dinamiche*, 87–124.

Formigli, A. ed. 2003. *Fibulae: Dall'età del bronzo all'alto medioevo tecnica e tipologia.* Rome.

Geiger, A. 1994. *Treibverzierte Bronzerundschilde der italischen Eisenzeit aus Italien und Griechenland. PBF* III.1. Stuttgart.

Guidi, A. 1993. *La necropoli veiente dei Quattro Fontanili nel quadro della prima età del Ferro italiana.* Florence.

Iaia, C. 2005. *Produzioni toreutiche della prima età del Ferro in Italia centro-settentrionale: Stili decorativi, circolazione, significato.* Pisa.

———. 2007. "Prima del 'simposio': Vasi in bronzo e contesto sociale dell'Etruria meridionale protostorica." *Revista d'Arqueologia de Ponent* 16–17:261–270.

———. 2010. "Fra Europa Centrale e Mediterraneo: Modelli di recipienti e di arredi in bronzo nell'Italia centrale della prima età del Ferro." *Bollettino di Archeologia On Line* 2010.1, F/F2/4:31–44.

Lo Schiavo, F. 2010. *Le fibule dell'Italia meridionale e della Sicilia dall'età del bronzo recente al VI secolo a.C. PBF* XIV.14. Stuttgart.

Lo Schiavo, F., P. Falchi, and M. Milletti. 2013. "Sardegna ed Etruria tirrenica: Identità in formazione. Ripostigli e scambi della fase di transizione fra la fine del Bronzo Finale e la prima età del Ferro." In Δόσις δ'ολίγη τε φίλη τε. *Studi in onore di Antonella Romualdi*, ed. S. Bruni and G. C. Cianferoni, 371–416. Florence.

Martelli, M. 1983a. "L'Età del Ferro." In *L'Oro degli Etruschi*, ed. M. Cristofani and M. Martelli, 26–34. Novara.

———. 1983b. "L'Orientalizzante." In *L'Oro degli Etruschi*, ed. M. Cristofani and M. Martelli, 35–51. Novara.

———. 1983c. "Schede critiche." In *L'Oro degli Etruschi*, ed. M. Cristofani and M. Martelli, 250–251, 268–269. Novara.

Martelli Antonioli, V., and L. Martelli. 2002. "Catalogo." In *Portonaccio* I, 161–227.

Marzoli, D. 1989. *Bronzefeldflaschen in Italien. PBF* II.4. Munich.

———. 1998. "Bronzene Feldflaschen aus hervorragenden Gräbern der italischen Eisenzeit." In *Archäologische Untersuchungen zu den Beziehungen zwischen Altitalien und der Zone nordwärts der Alpen während der frühen Eisenzeit Alteuropas*, 69–82. Bonn.

Mazzocchi, A. "Bronzetti votivi a figura umana di età arcaica di Roma e del Lazio." *QArchEtr* 26:129–185.

Mengarelli, R. 1901. "Veio (territorio di Formello): Nuove indagini nell'area della necropoli veientana." *NSc* 1901:238–246.

Mercuri, L. 2004. *Eubéens en Calabre à l'époque archaïque: Formes de contacts et d'implantation.* Rome.

Michetti, L. M. 2002. "Considerazioni sui materiali." In *Porto-naccio* I, 229–245.

Naso, A. 2006. "Un carrello cultuale bronzeo da Veio." In *Gli Etruschi da Genova ad Ampurias. Atti del XXIV Convegno di Studi Etruschi e Italici*, 357–370. Pisa.

Niemeyer, B. 2013a. "Technologische Untersuchungen an den Funden: Gold und Silber." In Babbi and Peltz 2013:96–99.

———. 2013b. "Restauro antico e moderno dei reperti: Alt- und Neurestaurierung der Funde. Metall. Gold und Silber." In Babbi and Peltz 2013:213–220.

Palm, J. 1952. "Veiian Tomb Groups in the Museo Preistorico, Rome." *OpArch* 7:50–86.

Rizzo, M. A. 1983. "Veio: Tomba a incinerazione." In *L'Oro degli Etruschi*, ed. M. Cristofani and M. Martelli, 287–288. Novara.

Santangelo, M. 1952. "Veio, santuario 'di Apollo': Scavi fra il 1944 e il 1949." *BdA* 37:147–172.

Sciacca, F. 2003. "Nota sul rhyton a protome di leone da Veio: Confronti e produzione." *ArchCl* 54:301–319.

———. 2005. *Patere baccellate in bronzo: Oriente, Grecia, Italia in età Orientalizzante.* Rome.

———. 2010a. "Veio: La metallotecnica orientalizzante e i rapporti con l'oriente." *Bollettino di Archeologia On Line* 2010.1, F/F7/2:5–19.

———. 2010b. "Commerci fenici nel Tirreno orientale: uno sguardo dalle grandi necropoli." *Bollettino di Archeologia On Line* 2010.1, F/F2/5:45–61.

Stefani, E. 1953. "Veio. Tempio detto dell'Apollo: Esplorazione e sistemazione del santuario." *NotSc* 1953:29–112.

Strøm, I. 1971. *Problems concerning the Origin and Development of the Etruscan Orientalizing Style.* Odense.

———. 2000. "A Fragment of an Early Etruscan Bronze Throne in Olympia?" *ProcDanInstAth* 3:67–95.

Toms, J. 1986. "The Relative Chronology of the Villanovian C Cemetery of Quattro Fontanili at Veii." *AION* 8:41–97.

Torelli, M. 1997. *Il rango, il rito e l'immagine: Alle origini delle rappresentazione storica romana.* Milan.

CHAPTER 21

WALL PAINTING

FRANCESCA BOITANI

In the ancient world, painting was the most appreciated of all the arts.[1] With the use of line and color the painter achieved extraordinary verisimilitude in the images, creating the illusion of reality. Famous personages were willing to pay enormous sums of money to acquire painted panels. Almost nothing is left of monumental Greek painting: the sacred buildings and the palaces that we know were beautifully decorated have not survived above their foundations, and the majority of tombs did not have paintings on the walls. We can catch some reflection of Greek painting in contemporary ceramic decoration, but it is the painted tombs of the different peoples of ancient Italy that fill this great void with a rich and well-articulated assemblage of direct evidence. Veii, as we shall see, was at the forefront of artistic and technological developments in its early wall painting tradition.

WALL PAINTING AND FUNERARY IDEOLOGY

Monumental wall painting in Etruria represents the most relevant corpus of ancient paintings because of the number of examples surviving and because it covers a wide chronological range (seventh through second centuries BCE). Further, this body of material is highly significant in articulating through images the evolution of a distinct funerary ideology.[2]

Beginning around 700 BCE, during the Orientalizing period, rich aristocratic chamber tombs were decorated with extraordinary wall paintings highlighting the political and social status of their owners. But the ensemble of paintings in a tomb did not merely convey prestige, nor did it have value just as decoration. The paintings reflected a primordial system of images of death as a long journey to an "other" and faraway world, an afterlife beyond the ocean, to be reached by land or by sea. The dead was lying in his burial chamber, waiting to begin the great journey to the afterlife (the possibility of spending the afterlife within the tomb was not then acknowledged).

In the case of Archaic painted tombs and of most tombs dating to the fifth century BCE, a number of scenes of games were represented in realistic settings, and these were connected to funeral rituals in the world of the living. At the same time, paintings often represented a banquet—connected to the sphere of dance by Dionysus—presumably located in the afterlife, which was meant to be a place for eternal pleasure, such as the Isles of the Blessed, just as the earliest great Greek poets had described it. From the fourth century BCE onward, when tombs came to be seen as the ending point of the great journey and the place where the deceased was to dwell permanently, the otherworldly banquet was depicted as taking place in the dark landscape of Hades, staffed by threatening demons who were the ushers of souls, such as Charun and Vanth. The participants are identified by inscriptions that give, as a lasting reminder to the relevant gentilicial group, their names along with the offices they had held across generations.[3]

Tarquinia played the most prominent role in funerary painting among all the Etruscan centers, producing a continuous and extensive body of material dating

from the end of the seventh through the second century BCE, but it is in the necropoleis of Veii that we find
the earliest wall paintings. These date between 700 and
670 BCE, which was when the earliest chamber tombs
gradually replaced the large trench tombs with burial
recesses typical of the Late Villanovan period. These
Veientine wall paintings are about twenty-five years
older than the earliest ones discovered in Caere, which
unfortunately are not in a good state of preservation.[4]

THE EARLIEST TOMBS

Two tombs provide the earliest evidence of wall painting at Veii: the Tomb of the Roaring Lions,[5] discovered
in 2006 north of the large protohistoric necropolis of
Grotta Gramiccia and close to the important road leading to Nepi, and the Tomb of the Ducks, discovered
in 1958 in the necropolis of Riserva del Bagno, near
the road that led toward Caere.[6] The painted decorations, the richness of the grave goods (even though
partially looted), which all date to the Early Orientalizing period, and their locations within a small group
of noble burials separated from other burial sites indicate that they belonged to influential people of a high
status.

In both these tombs, entirely carved into the bedrock, the skillfully colored paintings not only embellish the walls but also highlight some of the meaningful architectural features of the tomb. The colors,
derived from natural pigments, are those canonical in
the oldest mural paintings—red, black, and yellow.
In the Tomb of the Roaring Lions, colors were spread
over a light layer of mixed clay having the same color
as tufa, while in the Tomb of the Ducks a thin plas-
ter layer is attested. The figures are indicated by a pre-
paratory incised line, in places rather deep and often
showing repeated revisions. In the Tomb of the Roaring Lions they are drawn using a contour line, while in
the other tomb a silhouette rendering was produced
by an in-filling of color. According to Pliny the Elder
(*Nat. Hist.* 35.15), those were the two techniques originally used in painting, which was invented in Sicyon
or Corinth by tracing the outline of a human shadow.[7]

THE TOMB OF THE ROARING LIONS

The Tomb of the Roaring Lions, dating approximately
to 690 BCE, is earlier than the Tomb of the Ducks. The
quadrangular chamber was initially smaller (12.30 ×
11.50 feet) and only later was enlarged on the left-hand
side as one entered. The architectonic structure was
emphasized, with the flat ceiling, the vertical door
casings, and the external wall facing the long *dromos*,
painted red. A polychrome band runs around the internal walls, with a clear yellow stripe between two black
stripes, bordering the lower part of the wall, painted
in red, and marking the outline of the door. Thinner
stripes of the same colors border the perimeter of the
burial recess, on the back wall, close to the left corner.

Extraordinary decorative figures were represented
on the back wall and on the right wall. Eight waterfowl alternating in a double line, one above and one
below, are painted on the back wall. These waterfowl
appear to move from the burial recess to the entrance
and continue in a single line on the right wall. On the
lower part of the back wall, three lions move in a line
toward the burial recess; a fourth lion stands opposite
the first one (*plate 7*); all the lions have a threatening
appearance. The selection of the subjects depicted de-
pended on their symbolic value, which finds it origins
in early European protohistory. Death was perceived
as the journey of the deceased toward the afterlife, beyond the ocean: waterfowl (*plate 8*) acted as mediators
between earth and heaven and accompanied the deceased on this celestial journey, while the roaring lions
hint at the obstacles that must be overcome by the deceased individual during the journey.[8]

As for style, each waterfowl is unique in appearance, set apart by the various drawings on their bodies
and by different combinations of red and black colors.
These waterfowl are very different from the "herons"
that are monotonously repeated in contemporary sub-
Geometric pottery from Veii and Caere and from the
Faliscan and Capenate territories. Herons appeared
also, incised, on Orientalizing impasto and bucchero
products. Better analogies can be seen with the "ducks"
of the tomb named after them, which are more precisely outlined.

The lions are really exotic, with unusual "figure-8"

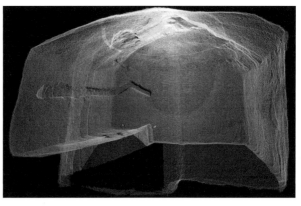

FIGURE 21.2. 3D scan of the Tomb of the Ducks. (Copyright: P. Brocato)

FIGURE 21.1. One of the lions from the Tomb of the Roaring Lions, back wall (detail). (Copyright: F. Boitani)

body structures, huge, wide-open mouths, full of teeth, and outstretched triangular tongues (fig. 21.1). Their clawed paws appear to attack; tails are raised and run parallel to their backs. The models inspiring the Etruscan painter can be identified in Late Geometric ceramics produced in Athens, especially among the artisans of the beginning of the seventh century BCE.[9] The lions can also be compared with those represented on vases made by an important potter from Veii, the Narce Painter, active in the first years of the seventh century BCE.[10] Many new vessels by the same hand have been recently recognized, such as a jar found among the tomb-groups of the same Tomb of the Roaring Lions. It is hard to agree with those scholars who suggest that the same artisan was involved both in the wall paintings and in the pottery decoration. Nevertheless, it may be admitted that at the dawn of the period of these great paintings the distinctions among different areas of expertise were not well defined, and reciprocal influences and cross-fertilization were probably common.

THE TOMB OF THE DUCKS

The Tomb of the Ducks dates between 680 and 670 BCE, a few years later than the Tomb of the Roaring Lions. It appears slightly different in terms of both architecture and painted decoration. The chamber is almost squared (fig. 21.2), small (about 11 × 10.2 feet), with a four-fold ceiling reminiscent of a tent, which would probably correspond to the real tent used during the funeral of the dead. The access corridor is shorter, but as in the Tomb of the Roaring Lions it has benches on the side near the entrance, which probably served as a space for burial ceremonies and rites. A large funerary bed made of tufa slabs in the shape of a sarcophagus was placed along the internal left wall, originally with a gabled lid, as suggested by the cuttings found in the same wall and in the adjacent back wall. This funerary bed was probably for a female burial and appears similar to examples found in Caere.

Each available surface of the tomb was fully colored, mainly in red and yellow. This yellow is from a higher-quality pigment than that used in the Tomb of the Roaring Lions. Those two colors were used alternatively for the ceiling slopes; the bottom parts of all walls are red, and the upper parts are yellow, while they were not painted in the older tomb. The same polychrome band decoration is here enriched, with two yellow and red stripes between black lines, which appeared also in the sixth-century BCE tombs of Tarquinia. Some scholars have argued that this decoration corresponds to a representation of the rainbow, an element connecting the cosmic spheres and, in this case, the chthonic dwelling where the dead was to be laid and the hereafter.[11] On the yellow back wall (*plate 9*), we can see five waterfowl moving toward the funerary bed, symbolically protecting the deceased during her journey.

They were painted in alternating schemes, in the outline and the full-color silhouette techniques. Their images, along with the uniform coating of the surfaces, produce an effect of symmetry and balance that is not found in the Tomb of the Roaring Lions.

THE CAMPANA TOMB

Another very interesting tomb with wall paintings at Veii is the Campana Tomb (*map 4:C; plate 10*), which seems to be a few generations later than the others.[12] The tomb is named after the well-known banker Giovanni Pietro Campana, who discovered it in 1842–1843. This is the most important Etruscan painted tomb of the Orientalizing period, even though today its paintings no longer show the rich and brilliant polychrome decoration that appears in the drawings made by Luigi Canina after its discovery (*plate 10*).

The tomb dates between 620 and 610 BCE and is located at the southern edge of the necropolis of Monte Michele (*map 3*), near the ancient road to Capena. In plan the tomb has two chambers on axis and two cells on the sides of the *dromos*, similar to the layout of contemporary aristocratic hypogea in Veii, which were not always covered with a tumulus, as also in this case. The burial was enriched by sculptural decoration, as suggested by the remains of two tufa lions at the sides of the entrance, and a wall with large polygonal stones reinforced the inner face of the entrance wall.[13] In the two cells are funerary "beds" with carved decoration.

The departure of the hero for hunting, perhaps alluding to the theme of the journey to the afterlife, appears in the paintings in two different registers—one above the other—on the back wall of the first chamber and at the sides of the door leading to the second chamber. In both the top registers the artist painted a person riding a horse toward the door. The man in the left painting is alone, while in the right register the man is followed by a dog, has a small panther crouched beside his shoulders as he sits on the horse's back, and is accompanied by both a groom holding the horse's reins and a bearer carrying a double-edged axe, the emblem of rank of the deceased prince. The two principal personages appear miniaturized, their dimensions reduced in comparison to the horses and the other figures.

These scenes are set in a landscape thriving with plants, flowers, and animals—even ferocious ones—and a sphinx: the scene is clearly alluding to the perilous journey to the Isles of the Blessed. In the rear chamber is a series of painted shields on two lines, emphasizing the high rank of the deceased. The complex and exuberant character of the Orientalizing style of the end of seventh century BCE is exemplified by the iconography and style of these paintings.

The great funerary paintings at Veii ended at this time. A few decades later, around the end of the sixth or the start of the fifth century, the rite of cremation again became widespread. In the new trench tombs, with steps descending to an open-air platform with niches for cremation, there was no longer space for wall paintings. The funerary austerity now linking Veii to other south Etruria cities and Latium Vetus (probably deriving from the Athenian funerary laws of Solon)[14] no longer permitted any ostentatious display of aristocratic status. Despite its glorious beginning, along with the rich tomb-groups, wall painting disappeared at Veii.

NOTES

1. Pliny, *Nat. Hist.* 35.1–43; Gentili 2012:343.

2. Pallottino 1952; Steingräber 1985; Pallottino 1989:11; Roncalli 2000:345; Minetti 2003.

3. Torelli 1997:122; Colonna 2014:27; Cerchiai 2014:37.

4. Naso 2005:19.

5. Boitani 2010:23.

6. Brocato 2012.

7. Colonna 1989:19.

8. Colonna 2014:27.

9. Boitani 2012:23; Martelli 2008:2.

10. See also chapters 10 and 18.

11. Roncalli 2014:53.

12. Rizzo 1989:109; Colonna 2014:30.

13. See chapter 22.

14. Colonna 1988:493; Drago Troccoli 1997:239.

BIBLIOGRAPHY

Boitani, F. 2012. "Veio, la Tomba dei Leoni Ruggenti: Dati pre-liminari." In *Archeologia nella Tuscia*, ed. P. A. Gianfrotta and A. M. Moretti, 23–47. *Daidalos* 10. Viterbo.

Brocato, P. 2012. *La Tomba delle Anatre di Veio*. Rossano.

Cerchiai, L. 2014. "Il dionisismo nell'immaginario funebre degli Etruschi." In *Il viaggio oltre la vita: Gli Etruschi e l'al-dilà tra capolavori e realtà virtuale* (exh. cat.), ed. G. Sassatelli and A. Russo Tagliente, 37–43. Bologna.

Colonna, G. 1988. "I Latini e gli altri popoli del Lazio." In *Italia Omnium Terrarum Alumna*, 492–493. Milan.

———. 1989. "Gli Etruschi e l'"invenzione' della pittura." In *Pittura etrusca al Museo di Villa Giulia nelle foto di Takashi Okamura* (exh. cat.), ed. M. A. Rizzo, 18–25. Rome.

———. 2014. "L'aldilà degli Etruschi: Caratteri generali." In *Il viaggio oltre la vita: Gli Etruschi e l'aldilà tra capolavori e realtà virtuale* (exh. cat.), ed. G. Sassatelli and A. Russo Ta-gliente, 27–35. Bologna.

Drago Troccoli, L. 1997. "Le tombe 419 e 426 del sepolcreto di Grotta Gramiccia a Veio." In *Etrusca et italica. Scritti in ri-cordo di Massimo Pallottino*, 1:239–280. Pisa.

Gentili, M. D. 2012. "Pittura e ceramografia." In *Introduzione all'Etruscologia*, ed. G. Bartoloni, 343–394. Milan.

Martelli, M. 2008. "Variazioni sul tema etrusco-geometrico." *Prospettiva* 132:2–30.

Minetti, A., ed. 2003. *Pittura etrusca: Problemi e prospettive. Atti del Convegno (Sarteano-Chiusi 2001)*. Siena.

Naso, A. 2005. *Pittura etrusca: Guida breve*. Rome.

Pallottino, M. 1952. *La peinture étrusque*. Geneva.

———. 1989. "La pittura etrusca." In *Pittura etrusca al Museo di Villa Giulia nelle foto di Takashi Okamura* (exh. cat.), ed. M. A. Rizzo, 11–18. Rome.

Rizzo, M. A. 1989. "Veio, la Tomba Campana." In *Pittura etrusca al Museo di Villa Giulia nelle foto di Takashi Okamura* (exh. cat.), ed. M. A. Rizzo, 109–111. Rome.

Roncalli, F. 2000. "La pittura." In *Gli Etruschi*, ed. M. Torelli, 345–363. Milan.

———. 2014. "L'aldilà: Dall'idea al paesaggio." In *Il viaggio oltre la vita: Gli Etruschi e l'aldilà tra capolavori e realtà vir-tuale* (exh. cat.), ed. G. Sassatelli and A. Russo Tagliente, 53–59. Bologna.

Steingräber, S. 1985. *Catalogo ragionato della pittura etrusca*. Milan.

Torelli, M. 1997. "*Limina Averni*: Realtà e rappresentazione nella pittura tarquiniese arcaica." In *Il rango, il rito e l'im-magine: Alle origini della rappresentazione storica romana*, ed. M. Torelli, 122–151. Milan.

CHAPTER 22

STONE SCULPTURE

IEFKE VAN KAMPEN

It is now generally acknowledged that Veii was the first Etruscan town to create wall paintings in a funerary context.[1] At the beginning of the seventh century BCE Veii also played a leading role in the early adoption of monumental sculpture, an artform in which Vulci later took the lead. Evidence for stone sculpture at Veii is not as well known as that of its later counterparts from Vulci. A. Hus, in his still-fundamental book on the subject,[2] listed only five pieces from Veii, all said to have come from the Campana Tomb (map 4:C).[3] Since then the number of pieces has increased slightly, but our understanding of them has changed substantially.

The sculptures known from Veii consist of the fragmentary statue of a figure seated on a throne from Veii-Picazzano (fig. 22.1; map 3);[4] a sphinx head in the Allard Pierson Museum in Amsterdam (fig. 22.2);[5] and a series of pieces from the Tomba Campana (fig. 22.3).[6] In 2008, some other parts of stone sculptures came to light during excavation of the Oliveto Grande tumulus (map 2: nos. 6–7), among which are a winged sphinx and some fragments belonging to felines, probably to be identified as the external decoration of the sepulcher.[7]

The Tomba Campana is a very problematic funerary context. Only in the 1980s[8] did it become clear that the tomb group, "discovered" in 1843 by Giovanni Pietro Campana, was actually a fake assemblage gathered by Campana himself. The finds are real, but they do not come from this tomb, at least not the great majority of them. Three funerary urns came from Luigi Arduini's excavations in Orte.[9] Two female sphinx heads in *nen-fro* are so similar to artifacts found in Vulci that they would have been attributed to Vulci "had they not been found in Veii" (fig. 22.3:B).

It is likely that these female sphinx heads did not in fact come from Veii, but this is not necessarily true for all the items of the tomb-group, and certainly not for the paintings. These paintings have been a point of reference for what has been called the "florid style" of the Orientalizing period, dated together with the tomb around 600 BCE.[10] As F. Delpino stated, in order to understand the original characteristics of the tomb, it would be very important to analyze the walls with remains of painting (if any).[11] The bodies of the felines still present on the side of the dromos of the tomb, heads now missing (fig. 22.3:C), and another sphinx head, probably of a male sphinx (fig. 22.3:A), might be genuine. The location of the tomb makes it quite difficult to reach, and it might have been easier to leave the very heavy pieces in their places. Moreover, the sphinx head in Amsterdam (fig. 22.2), from the art market but certainly coming from Veii, is similar in style, material, and features to the male sphinx head of the Campana Tomb. These sculptures date to the end of the seventh or the beginning of the sixth century BCE. They demonstrate the existence of sculpture workshops in the territory of Veii in this initial phase.

In a larger context, the flourishing of sculpture in the Faliscan area, culturally but not politically connected with Veii in this period, may also point in the same direction. The head of a statue from the Temple of Celle, at Falerii (fig. 22.4; map 5),[12] is very similar

FIGURE 22.1. Statue of a figure seated on a throne, from Veii-Picazzano. Museo dell'Agro Veientano, Formello, inv. 143684. (Copyright: I. Strøm)

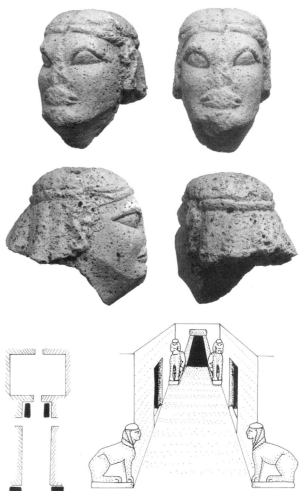

FIGURE 22.2. A. Sphinx head from Veii. Allard Pierson Museum, Amsterdam, inv. APM II.877. B. Reconstruction of the tomb with four different sphinxes. (Copyright: P. S. Lulof)

to the Campana head and the Amsterdam sphinx, and perhaps we may postulate the existence of a "Campana Tomb workshop."

One sculpture dates a century earlier than those listed above (fig. 22.1). Unfortunately, its origin is not precisely known. It was found during excavations carried out in 1982 by the Soprintendenza in the area of Veii-Picazzano, as documented by the single photographic film sequence preserved in the archives.[13] The sculpture is a fragment of a seated figure on a throne[14] and preserves a footstool composed of a horizontal element and two volutes supporting it. The edge of the robe has a curved line, indicating a kind of long, simple tunic,[15] probably made to appear more luxurious by other elements and colored by painting (or even combining other materials like bronze or cloth). The man (or the woman) might have been barefoot or might have been wearing sandals, which probably would have been painted.[16] The throne is freestanding and has a finely worked rear side.[17] The piece must be compared to the more complete seated figures from the Tomb of the Statues at Ceri, near Cerveteri. G. Colonna dated this tomb to the final phase of the Early Orientalizing period (690–670 BCE),[18] while F. Prayon suggested a date around the second quarter of the seventh century BCE.[19] The dimensions of the footstools in the two

tombs are very similar.[20] The footstool of Veii, apart from the fact that it is better preserved, seems to be a more refined version of those at Ceri.

It has been noted that, unlike the case of the throne, which probably had a local origin, the type of footstool is unusual in Etruria.[21] However, it has Near Eastern parallels, as it is similar to the Phoenician ivories found in Nimrud.[22] We can, however, exclude the possibility that the inspiration for creation of these three-dimensional footstools, found in both sculpture and a bronze-sheet version, originated from the imported ivories.

Within the framework of the Near Eastern imports in central Tyrrhenian Italy in the Early Orientalizing

FIGURE 22.3. Campana Tomb "assemblage." Museo dell'Agro Veientano, Formello. A. Inv. no. 12395: male head, Veientine production and probably coming from the tomb. B. Inv. nos. 12394/1 and 12394/2: two female heads, probably of Vulcentan production and forced into the context by Campana. C. Two feline bodies, private collection, probably pertaining to the tomb. (Copyright: I. van Kampen)

period (ca. 720–675 BCE) we can distinguish various components: (a) easily transportable objects such as amulets, scarabs, and glass pastes; (b) trade amphoras and other ceramics; and (c) metal works and luxury products, including bronze *paterae*.[23] These *paterae* were probably Syro-Phoenician and Assyrian products, as in the case of the *rhyton* shaped as a lion protome coming from Casale del Fosso.[24]

In this context, the presence at Veii of Oriental artists and craftsmen, from the end of the eighth century but especially from the beginning of the seventh century BCE, has been suggested in particular because of the diffusion of the granulation technique for goldworking.[25]

The presence of Oriental artists could justify the appearance of monumental sculpture, and in particular

FIGURE 22.4. Sphinx head from the temple of Celle (Falerii), Museo Archeologico dell'Agro Falisco, Civita Castellana, inv. no. 2498. (Copyright: I. van Kampen)

the scheme with the seated figure on a throne, as suggested by Colonna.[26] He suggests that among Etruscan cities, Caere was the first to actively invite such artists, much as Bologna did later on. According to M. Martelli, however,[27] we can refer only to a "Near Eastern patina" (i.e., "surface coating") for the production of luxury products, while the funerary ideology would have had Homeric roots. Taking the evidence for Veii into account, in particular tomb 5 at Monte Michele,[28] the existence of rites of Homeric inspiration is evident, but it is difficult to imagine the creation of monumental sculpture without a deeper meaning being assigned to it.[29]

For technical reasons we may also suggest the presence of Oriental craftsmen teaching new techniques, which make a sudden appearance in Etruria at this time. In Veii we find the earliest evidence for gold granulation,[30] which has been recognized as the first trace of Oriental craftsmen: the golden decorated bead of tomb LL 18 of Quattro Fontanili,[31] and a fibula decorated with filigree technique from tomb 446 at Grotta Gramiccia.[32]

The Picazzano sculpture can be compared with a funerary stele from Maraş,[33] of the Late Hittite period (1200–700 BCE), representing a couple holding grapes and a mirror. The footstool is really similar to our Ceri type. The Maraş stele belongs to a group of banquet scenes defined by the research of W. Orthmann.[34] The couple, sculptured in high relief, is represented in frontal view. However, we should imagine a small table in front of them (as shown by Orthmann's research), and thus we are dealing with a banquet scene. In this group of dining scenes we normally find one or two persons to be interpreted as humans and not as gods, seated at either side of a table, represented *en profile*. These scenes have been referred to as representing scenes connected with the cult for the dead.[35] In Ceri, the presence of two seated figures in the antechamber of the grave has been interpreted as representing the ancestors of the deceased, being venerated as in the atrium of a Roman house of high lineage.

If the identification of the north Syrian provenience of the prototype of the seated figure on a throne is correct, it confirms the diaspora of craftsmen coming from the small north Syrian states after the Assyrian conquest, in particular dating after 738–708 BCE.[36]

A real version of a bronze-sheet throne with curved back that has been identified as of Veientine production and dated around 650 BCE was offered in the sanctuary of Olympia.[37] Moreover, the most ancient "real" footstool of the Etruscan world comes from tomb 871 of Casale del Fosso at Veii, and has been attributed to the years around 720/710 BCE.[38] It is important to note that in the series of footstools now known, this is the earliest evidence. The territory of Veii has two other pieces at Trevignano Romano (*map 1: no. 33*), in the Tomba dei Flabelli (Tomb of the Fans). This tomb consisted of two chambers,[39] containing at least two inhumations and a cremation. The tomb-group, dating to the period between 675 and 600 BCE, was in use for more than one generation.[40] These examples suggest that indicating status by means of a footstool for a seated figure was a widespread convention in the area of Veii.

Based on the evidence presented, we can date to around 700 BCE the introduction of monumental sculpture in Veii.[41] The presence of Oriental artists in the city is known from the second half of the eighth century, and they remained in the town for at least the duration of the Early Orientalizing period, up to ca. 650 BCE. This date fits well with the presence of Syro-Hittite elements in the Bologna area in the second and third quarters of the seventh century BCE, if we consider that close contacts occurred between Veii and Bologna beginning in the Early Iron Age.[42]

In conclusion, we are now able to define the special role Veii played in the earliest phase of monumental sculpture in the Etruscan world and during its definite affirmation, after the end of the seventh through the beginning of the sixth century BCE. The strong cultural influence of the town is also indirectly proved by the flourishing of sculpture in the Faliscan area, culturally connected to Veii in this period, as is shown by what we have called the "Campana Tomb workshop."

NOTES

1. See chapter 21.

2. Hus 1961.

3. See chapter 21.

4. Museo dell'Agro Veientano, Formello, inv. 143684. Cf. van Kampen 2011.

5. Inv. APM 11.877 (head) and APM B 13.243/246 (four other fragments). Petrographic research has proved the pieces to belong to four different sculptures, probably four similar squatting sphinxes (see fig. 22.2:B).

6. Inv. nos. 12394/1–2 and 12395 respectively for the two female and male heads. Two feline bodies (see fig. 22.3:C), belonging to a private collection, are now on long-term loan to the Museo dell'Agro Veientano, inv. nos. MAV 1773 and 1774.

7. Boitani and Cerasuolo 2015. It is possible to suggest a date at the end of the seventh or the beginning of the sixth century, in particular considering the folded, stylized legs of one of the felines, similar to those of the Campana Tomb. Even if we do not know whether the pieces from Oliveto Grande belong to another grave inside the tumulus itself (not found as yet), or to the very rich sepulcher brought to light outside the tumulus perimeter, these data tally well with the chronology for the various depositions at Oliveto Grande, all dated to the end of the seventh or the beginning of the sixth century BCE.

8. Delpino 1984–1985:191–201; 1985:65–83 and 137–139; 1991; see also 2012.

9. Consider, in this context, the private pact signed on April 6, 1842, between Agostino Chigi, Pietro Campana, and Luigi Arduini to carry on excavations in the territories of Formello, Campagnano, Scrofano (now Sacrofano), Magliano Pecorareccio (now Magliano Romano), and Cesano (now part of Rome)—all Chigi properties of that period—stating that a third part of the outcome would belong to the Chigi prince (van Kampen 2012b:181 no. 3).

10. Cf. Colonna 1989:21–24; pl. II (620–610 BCE for the paintings); Steingräber 2006:59–60; Naso 1990:491–493 (610–600 BCE). See also chapter 21.

11. Delpino 2012:102. For a recent analysis of Veientine painting see C. Falcucci in Brocato 2012:175–186. Furthermore, the work-in-progress CO.B.RA Project, which began in July 2015, has involved ENEA and Around Culture, together with the Soprintendenza Archeologia, Belle Arti e Paesaggio and the Regione Lazio, and focuses on a series of case studies of Etruscan tomb painting, among which is the Tomba Campana.

12. Inv. no. 2498, Museo Archeologico dell'Agro Falisco, Civita Castellana.

13. We may possibly assume that the area of provenience was not very far from the Tomba dei Pilastri, the subject of the investigation of that day.

14. Ström 1997; van Kampen 2003, 2011, and 2012a.

15. Bonfante 2003; Prayon 1975b:171.

16. The space left empty next to its feet is larger at the right, perhaps indicating the statue was slightly turned toward the onlooker.

17. A lower part, left unfinished and ca. 9 cm in height, probably represents the part set into the ground.

18. Colonna and von Hase 1986.

19. Prayon 1975a:52.

20. Height of 22 and 16 cm for the Caeretan statues and 15.5 cm for the piece from Veii. It is not easy to compare their width because of the different shapes of the thrones, worked like a single block in Ceri (56 cm), and with a singular inclusion of the footstool inside the throne in Veii (49 cm).

21. Type S Sonderform in Steingräber's typology, now type Ceri (Jurgeit 2000).

22. Steingräber 1979:116, 176.

23. For the relationship between Veii and the Orient, see chapter 11. Recently, F. Sciacca has "added" a piece of Syrian importation in Veii to our list for this period, interpreting the truncated conical element in ivory of Monte Michele tomb 5 as such, on the basis of the iconography of the walking sphinx with head *en face* (Sciacca 2013:246).

24. See chapters 11 and 20.

25. Prayon 1998.

26. Colonna and von Hase 1986.

27. Martelli 1991:1069–1072 and cf. 1983a:31–32.

28. 680–670 BCE.

29. More than a century later, we find in Veii–Piazza d'Armi the sculpture group of a standing figure with his (or her) dog, to be interpreted as the ancestor of the house, dated in the second quarter of the sixth century (see chapter 1). In northern Etruria around 580 BCE we still find the iconography of the seated figure to represent the heroized ancestor in the so-called Second Palace of Murlo. For this and all other evidence on ancestor cult in Veii see *Culto degli Antenati*.

30. See chapter 20.

31. Dated in the third quarter of the eighth century (Martelli 1983b).

32. 750–730 BCE.

33. Akurgal 1961: pl. 104; Prayon 1977; Özgüç and Temizsoy 2002:358, no. 160.

34. Orthmann 1971:373–380.

35. Orthmann 1971:377 n. 39.

36. Van Loon 1974:24.

37. Fr. Ol. IV.1007 (Strøm 2000); cf. Steingräber 1979: 23–24, type Ia.

38. Phase between the Late Villanovan period (Veii IIC) and the Orientalizing period (Veii IIIA). Drago 2005:94 with bibliography. For chronology see Babbi and Piergrossi 2005.

39. The tomb preserves traces of red painting as in other Veientine contexts and has been excavated between 1966 and 1968.

40. The footstools have been dated around 640 but might actually be from the first deposition, as the pieces from Casale del Fosso and Trevignano are quite similar. Cf. Colonna and von Hase 1986:58, nos. 4–5 (ca. 640 BCE) and Caruso and Pisu 2002:32–34.

41. As already suggested by F. Jurgeit (2000:223) on the evidence of the footstool from Casale del Fosso.

42. Bartoloni and Delpino 1979:97; Drago 1981. See also chapter 20.

BIBLIOGRAPHY

Akurgal, E. 1961. *Die Kunst der Hethiter*. Munich.

Babbi, A., and A. Piergrossi. 2005. "Per una definizione della cronologia relativa e assoluta del Villanoviano veiente e tarquiniese." In *Oriente e Occidente: Metodi e discipline a confronto. Riflessioni sulla cronologia dell'età del Ferro in Italia. Atti dell'incontro di studi, Roma, 2003*, ed. G. Bartoloni and F. Delpino, 293–318. Mediterranea 1. Pisa.

Bartoloni, G., and F. Delpino. 1979. *Veio I: Introduzione allo studio delle necropoli arcaiche di Veio: Il sepolcreto di Valle La Fata. MonAnt* 1. Rome.

Boitani, F., and O. Cerasuolo. 2015. "Novità del tardo orientalizzante veiente dalla necropoli di Oliveto Grande." In *Novità*, 133–141.

Bonamici, M. 1974. *I buccheri con figurazioni graffite*. Florence.

Bonfante, L. 2003. *Etruscan Dress*. Rev. ed. Baltimore.

Brocato, P. 2012. *La tomba delle Anatre di Veio*. Rossano.

Caruso, I., and C. Pisu. 2002. *Trevignano Romano: Museo civico e area archeologica*. Trevignano Romano.

Colonna, G. 1989. "Gli Etruschi e l'"invenzione' della pittura." In *Pittura etrusca al Museo di Villa Giulia* (exh. cat.), ed. M.-A. Rizzo, 19–25. Rome.

Colonna, G., and F.-W. von Hase. 1986. "Alle origini della statuaria etrusca: La tomba delle statue presso Ceri." *StEtr* 52: 13–59.

Delpino, F. 1984–1985. "Sulla scoperta della Tomba Campana di Veio: In falso dell'archeologia romantica?" *RendPontAcc* 57:191–201.

———. 1985. *Cronache veientane: Storia delle ricerche archeologiche a Veio dal XIV secolo alla metà del XIX secolo*. Rome.

———. 1991. "I rilievi archeologici di Veio della collezione Lanciani: Appunti su Francesco e Ludovico Caracciolo." *BdA* 68–69:161–176.

———. 2012. "La Tomba Campana e la sua 'scoperta.'" In *MAV*, 97–102.

Drago, L. 1981. "Rapporti Veio-Bologna nell'VIII secolo." *ArchCl* 33:55–77.

Drago Troccoli, L. 2005. "Una coppia di principi nella necropoli di Casale del Fosso a Veio." In *Dinamiche*, 88–124.

Hus, A. 1961. *Recherches sur la statuaire en pierre étrusque archaïque*. BÉFAR 19. Paris.

Jurgeit, F. 2000. "Die Füssbänke vom Typ Ceri." In *Das Orient und Etrurien: Zum Phänomen des "Orientalisierens" im westlichen Mittelmeerraum (10.–6. Jh. v.Chr.). Atti del Colloquio Tübingen 1997*, ed. F. Prayon and W. Röllig, 219–226. Pisa.

Lulof, P.–S., and H. Kars. 1994. "Early Etruscan Stone Sculpture: Reconstruction and Petrography of Sphinxes from Veii." *BABESCH* 69:49–61.

Martelli, M. 1983a. "L'età del Ferro." In *L'Oro degli Etruschi*, ed. M. Cristofani and M. Martelli, 26–34. Novara.

———. 1983b. "L'Orientalizzante." In *L'Oro degli Etruschi*, ed. M. Cristofani and M. Martelli, 35–51. Novara.

———. 1991. "I Fenici e la questione orientalizzante in Italia." In *Atti del II Congresso Internazionale di Studi Fenici e Punici a Roma 1987*, ed. E. Acquaro, 3.1049–1072. Rome.

Naso, A. 1990. "All'origine della pittura etrusca: Decorazione parietale e architettura funeraria in Etruria meridionale nel VII sec. a.C." *JRGZM* 3:439–493, pls. 40:1–2 and II:2.

Orthmann, W. 1971. *Untersuchungen zur späthetitischen Kunst*. Saarbrücker Beiträge zur Altertumskunde 8. Bonn.

Özgüç, T., and İ. Temizsoy, eds. 2002. *Die Hethiter und ihr Reich: Das Volk der 1000 Götter* (exh. cat.). Bonn.

Prayon, F. 1975a. *Frühetruskische Grab- und Hausarchitektur*. MdI suppl. 22. Heidelberg.

———. 1975b. "Zur Datierung der drei frühetruskischen Sitzstatuetten aus Cerveteri." *RM* 82:165–179, pls. 41–50.

———. 1977. "L'Oriente e la statuaria etrusca arcaica." *Colloqui del Sodalizio* 5:165–172, pls. XXXVIII–XXXIX.

———. 1998. "Phöniker und Etrusker: Zur Goldlaminierung in der frühetruskischen Kunst." In *Archäologische Studien in Kontaktzonen der antiken Welt*, ed. R. Rolle, K. Schmidt, and R.-F. Docter, 329–341. Göttingen.

Sciacca, F. 2013. "Le prime sfingi in Etruria: Iconografie e contesti." In *Il bestiario fantastico di età orientalizzante nella penisola italiana*, ed. M.-C. Biella, E. Giovanelli, and L.-G. Perego, 239–285. Aristonothos 1. Trento.

Steingräber, S. 1979. *Etruskische Möbel*. Rome.

———. 2006. *Affreschi etruschi: Dal periodo geometrico all'ellenismo*. Verona.

Strøm, I. 1997. "Conclusioni." In *Necropoli arcaiche*, 245–247.

———. 2000. "A Fragment of an Early Etruscan Bronze Throne in Olympia?" *ProcDanInstAth* 3:67–95.

van Kampen, I. 2003. "Necropoli di Picazzano, scultura sporadica." In *Formello*, 80–81, pl. IVc.

———. 2011. "La scultura di Veio-Picazzano come testimonianza di artigiani orientali." In *Culto degli Antenati*, 5–6.

———. 2012a. "La statua di un principe da Veio-Picazzano." In *MAV*, 81–83, pls. 6:3.

———. 2012b. "Appendice. Lettera di G. Baronci a G.-A. Colini." In *MAV*, 181–182.

van Loon, M.-N. 1974. *Oude lering, nieuwe nering: Het uitzwermen der Noord-Syrische ambachtslieden in de late 8e eeuw v.C.* Amsterdam.

CHAPTER 23

KILNS AND EVIDENCE OF CERAMIC PRODUCTION

BARBARA BELELLI MARCHESINI

Veii has provided plentiful evidence (surface finds, kilns, and related structures) of long-lasting production activities, which were certainly performed inside the urban plateau. Ceramic wasters ploughed up in the cemeteries north of Veii probably highlight the presence of more workshops located immediately outside the town, although in the southern cemetery of Macchia della Comunità misshapen pottery was occasionally deposited in the tombs.[1]

EARLY EVIDENCE FROM CAMPETTI

Household industry during the Early Iron Age is well documented at Campetti by a sequence of several structures located next to the edge of the plateau, south of the North-West Gate (*map 4:F*).[2] These structures were found within a narrow trial trench and certainly belong to a much wider productive area that dates back to the earliest phase of the settlement (Veii IA). The area was definitively abandoned in the first half of the eighth century BCE, when it was overlapped by the defensive *agger*.[3]

The industrial zone features two main periods of exploitation. In the first, the productive area occupied a narrow strip of land, no more than 5 meters wide, which was fenced by palisades and reinforced by an embankment of earth and tufa stones on the opposite side. Due to the seasonal rhythm of the production work, the multiple structures required in the different steps of pottery production were dismantled, abandoned, and buried after use and the floor levels continuously renewed. The final result is a stratigraphical

sequence 70 centimeters thick, which includes at least ten kilns of different shapes and working activities.[4] The simplest type of kiln consists of an oval pit, which is provided with an opening for the fuel on the long side and perhaps covered by clay; the pottery was fired on the floor and placed directly on the fuel. Horizontal draft-kilns, which are widespread in Italy from the Late Bronze Age, are documented at Campetti, where there are two types of elongated ditches with an opening on a short side and provided with a flat or slightly inclined bottom; in this type of kiln the firing chamber is in the rear side and protected by a daub covering, and sometimes shaped as a distinct cavity.

Only one of the kilns is circular in shape. It was provided with a long corridor and may be identified as an up-draft kiln; in this type of kiln the furnace would have been superimposed over the firing chamber and a clay grill placed in between to support the pottery. Up-draft kilns attest substantial technological progress and allowed the firing to reach higher temperatures. It has been suggested that this type of kiln arrived in southern Italy during the Late Bronze Age together with the Mycenaeans and is documented in northern and central Italy during the Early Iron Age,[5] although its widespread diffusion dates from the Early Orientalizing period.

In the following period the productive area of Campetti underwent a substantial transformation with the construction of a large oval hut and a huge cavity. There were three adjacent rectangular ditches, partially brought to light in the excavation area (fig. 23.1).[6] The dividing walls were made with soil and modular clay

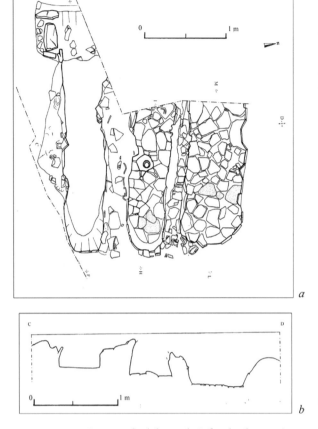

a

b

FIGURE 23.1. Rectangular kilns and pit for the decantation of the clay, Campetti. (Copyright: F. Boitani, after Boitani, Neri, and Biagi 2007–2008: fig. 7a)

slabs that have been interpreted as stocks of raw material; the bottom of the ditches and the top of the walls were carefully coated with ceramic shards. One of the ditches was slightly larger and used for the decantation of the clay; the other two (3.15 meters long) seem to be horizontal-draft kilns, although we lack specific parallels. The walls of these kilns were plastered with baked clay, and their covering was also made of clay provided with vent holes and supported by a vertical pole; the mouth for the fuel was lined with stones and vaulted.

THE LADY OF THE FURNACES

The abandonment of the productive and domestic structures at the end of the ninth century BCE was marked by the inhumation of a woman between forty and fifty years old, who was buried inside a rectangular ditch at the rear side of the hut (*see fig. 5.5*).[7] This female tomb, which is exceptional for its location inside the settlement, seems to be strictly connected to the crafts area itself. Whether the lady was a slave or a mistress is difficult to tell; nevertheless, the specific role of women in the control of household production during the Archaic period, highlighted by epigraphic evidence,[8] must be taken into account. To explain the inclusion of this formal burial on the urban plateau and not in the surrounding cemeteries, scholars suggest that the lady was perhaps a foreigner or was regarded as having magic powers because of her specific activity.

The archaeological evidence provided by the site of Campetti suggests that pottery production at Veii had already reached a high level of specialization during the Early Iron Age, even if it is not now possible to state whether the work was carried out in this period by different families or by expert members of the community at a larger scale. The discovery of bronze tools (small chisels and punches) in the filling of the kilns and a later furnace (dating to the second half of the eighth century BCE) suggests that metallurgic activities were also performed at the same site.[9]

EVIDENCE FROM COMUNITÀ

From the Orientalizing period onward, the entire southern district of Comunità (*maps 3, 4:W*) holds the function of a *kerameikos*, or potters' quarter, of the Etruscan town. The concentration of productive activities in this district is probably due to the presence of Pliocene claybeds, located southwest of the urban plateau and next to the Valle La Fata Gate (*map 4*).[10] The South Etruria Survey of the British School at Rome identified several concentrations of overfired and wasted pottery[11] that show the distribution of pre-Roman workshops along the main road crossing the town from north to south.[12] Surface evidence also includes the remains of a kiln dump or a proper kiln structure, with overfired pottery, fused clay, and fragments of kiln supports, ploughed out at the northern limit of Comunità. These data imply a long-lasting workshop that was in use up to the third century BCE and produced terracotta sculpture as well as pottery.[13]

The artisanal specialization of the southern district of the town is also highlighted by the appearance of misshaped pottery and pierced vases in the grave inventory of some tombs in the nearby cemetery of Macchia della Comunità.[14]

The excavations carried out by Sapienza University since 1997 on top and around the summit hill of Comunità have provided further information about the spatial organization and arrangement of this urban district in the pre-Roman period, bringing to light several structures and infrastructures related to the *kerameikos*. In addition to the evidence of production, both the surveys and the excavations have collected several architectural terracotta fragments dating from the second half of the sixth century BCE, which highlight the presence of a main sanctuary at Comunità. According to different scholars, the terracottas may belong to the temple of Juno Regina, which is said by Livy to be on the *arx* (citadel) of Veii (5.21.1–4; 10).[15] This temple probably stood on the summit hill and was replaced in the Republican period by a monumental complex (now dubbed Edificio Lanciani). The archaeological evidence suggests that from the Late Archaic period onward large-scale productive activities were performed at Comunità under strict control of public authority.

The close relation between sacred and productive spheres is evident in the fill of a water pit found in lower layers of the Edificio Lanciani, which included, in association with Late Archaic architectural terracottas, a large amount of fine wares, a few ceramic wasters, and several fragments of kiln tools.[16] The pottery from the pit belongs to the repertoire of fine-ware production at Veii throughout the sixth and fifth centuries BCE.[17] Archaeometric analysis of fine purified-clay ware and bucchero samples from this cistern have provided preliminary information about particular technical features of local wares and the composition of raw material.[18] The strata beneath the Edificio Lanciani have also provided evidence of ditches for the decantation of clay, dumps of overfired bucchero pottery, and storerooms.[19]

The most meaningful evidence is a potters' quarter, recently excavated on the southeastern slope of the summit hill (figs. 23.2–23.3).[20] The quarter includes different workshops arranged along the slopes of the

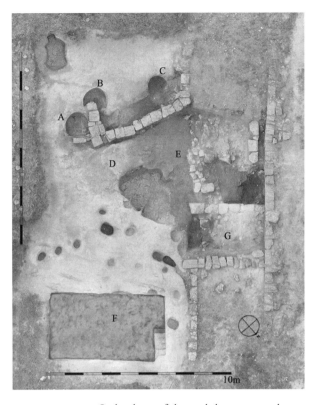

FIGURE 23.2. Orthophoto of the workshop area on the southeastern slope of the summit hill, Comunità. In evidence: the kilns (a, b, c); the burnt floors (d); the embankment of charcoal, bucchero shards, and refractory tools (e); the water tank (f); and the road trench (g). (Archive, Sapienza University of Rome. Copyright: B. Belelli Marchesini)

hill and along a road that departs from the main road of the town and stretches over more than one hundred meters, up to the limit of the fortification walls. This road was bounded by retaining walls of different periods and may have functioned also for water drainage. In the Late Archaic period the trench was filled in and the slope of the hill endowed with a terracing system.

The workshop dates from the end of the seventh century BCE onward and is characterized by the progressive exploitation of the sloping bedrock and by the seasonal renewal of the industrial structures. It includes circular up-draft kilns of small dimensions (diam. 130 centimeters), which fit into type I/a of the Cuomo di Caprio typology.[21] The kilns are cut into the bedrock and plastered with clay or provided with a revetment of soil and tufa chunks; traces of a central pillar indicate that there was a grill to support the pottery load.

The potsherds from the filling of the three excavated examples suggest that they were probably used for the firing of bucchero and other fine wares.

In addition to the kilns, the workshop includes a thick stratification of burnt circular floors (maybe fireplaces) that are connected with the surrounding enormous embankment of crushed bucchero pottery (mainly *oinochoai* and bowls, some misfired) and refractory kiln tools.[22]

The kiln tools from Comunità include modular tapering bricks,[23] rectangular in section and similar to the above-mentioned clay elements from Campetti. In Etruria few parallels are available (e.g., at Pyrgi and Tarquinia) and bricks are usually found in quadrangular kilns, such as the late Etruscan ones of Chiusi.[24] Plano-convex bricks of similar proportions were used at Mothya to cover the mouth of the channel for the fuel and to support the grill, according to Near Eastern models,[25] or they were used as fire-bars in a radial pattern to connect the central pillar to the walls,[26] recalling Romano-British pottery kilns.[27] At Comunità the bricks are always associated with slightly concave bowls with rough outer surfaces (spacers?) and refractory cover-tiles, which were perhaps used for crawlspaces.[28]

The workshop was surrounded by ditches of different size and shape, most provided with a stepped bottom and functioning for the decantation of clay. Water was collected in a nearby rectangular open-air cistern (3 × 6 meters), accessible through a staircase. Several hydraulic infrastructures have been also brought to light along the eastern slope of Comunità, suggesting that water management was strictly connected with the productive function of the hill. The most significant is a water tank (4 × 12 meters) flanked by a *cuniculus* and featuring a stepped bottom.[29]

WORKSHOPS AND SANCTUARIES

The district of Comunità has so far provided evidence of large-scale and long-lasting production of tableware. The location in this area of more specialized workshops, suggested by the monumental and particular bucchero shapes and the signature *velthur ancinies* on high-quality Etrusco-Corinthian pottery[30] from the sanctuary of Portonaccio, is highly hypothetical.

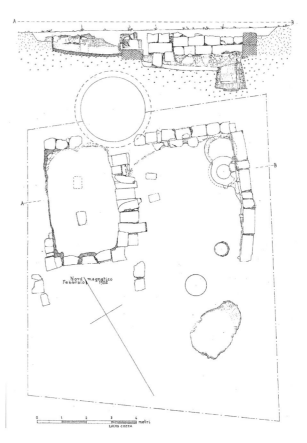

FIGURE 23.3. Plan of the workshop at Macchiagrande, drawn by Lucos Cozza. (After Colonna 2015b: fig. 29. Copyright: G. Colonna)

The kiln discovered at Macchiagrande (*map 4:M*) by M. Santangelo in 1952, near a Late Archaic temple,[31] and the mould of an antefix from the sanctuary next to the Caere Gate[32] prove on the other hand that productive activities took place next to the sanctuaries in order to supply architectural terracottas and to satisfy the needs of attendants to the several sacred areas located in the northern district of Veii. The workshop uncovered at Macchiagrande (fig. 23.3) included a horizontal-draft kiln, a water pit, and a ditch for the decantation of the clay, and its purpose was the production of architectural terracottas. In the period immediately after the Roman conquest, production activities took place in the northern district of the town. At this time, the connection between workshops and sanctuaries is well documented at Campetti next to the foundation of a Late Archaic temple, by infrastructure related to the cycle of production, and by significant finds, including misshapen pottery, the mould of a satyr's head antefix (third–second century BCE), and votive statues.[33]

From the available information, it is possible to state that in the Etruscan period ceramic production was undertaken within the urban plateau of Veii, as shown by surface finds from the northern cemeteries, and maybe in its surroundings as well. The site of Campetti has provided evidence of several EIA kilns located along the northern edge of the plateau, documenting the passage from household industry to workshops and reflecting the early improvement of firing techniques. From the seventh century onward, the southern district of Comunità was extensively exploited as the potters' quarter of the Etruscan town. We must not overlook, however, the presence of highly specialized workshops next to the several sanctuaries of the town, for the production of both architectural terracottas and votive gifts.

NOTES

1. Cascino (2017) provides an overall discussion of the topographical distribution of surface finds providing direct evidence of production activities.

2. Boitani, Neri, and Biagi 2007–2008:833–834, fig. 1; 2009:23, figs. 1–2. See also chapter 5.

3. See also chapter 16.

4. Boitani, Neri, and Biagi 2009:25–29, figs. 4–6, pl. II:B–C. See chapter 5.

5. di Gennaro and Iaia 2004:112.

6. Boitani, Neri, and Biagi 2007–2008:841–846, figs. 7–10; 2009:24, pl. IIa.

7. Boitani, Neri, and Biagi 2007–2008:839–841, fig. 6. See also chapter 5.

8. Colonna 1993.

9. Boitani, Biagi, and Neri 2017:141, fig. 3.1.

10. Peña 1987:293, area 8.

11. Cascino and di Sarcina 2005:289, fig. 5; Cascino 2008, 2017.

12. Belelli Marchesini and Cascino 2012: fig. 2.2.1.

13. Peña 1987:284–304, site 16, map 4; *Survey*, 70–71.

14. Cascino 2017:95.

15. See chapters 12 and 14.

16. Ambrosini et al. 2009.

17. Ambrosini and Belelli Marchesini 2009. See also chapter 19.

18. Ambrosini et al. 2009b.

19. Belelli Marchesini 2015:23, fig. 1.2.1.2.

20. Belelli Marchesini 2013; 2015:26–27, fig. 1.2.1.5–6; 2017: 111–116, pl. VII, figs. 2–3.

21. Cuomo di Caprio 2007:524, fig. 169.

22. See also chapter 18.

23. Belelli Marchesini in Ambrosini et al. 2009a:112–113, fig. 39; Belelli Marchesini 2017:117–119, figs. 6, 10a–h.

24. Pucci and Mascione 1993:380, pl. VIa.

25. Falsone 1981:69.

26. Cuomo di Caprio 1977.

27. Corder 1957.

28. Belelli Marchesini in Ambrosini et al. 2009a:113–114, figs. 39–40.

29. Belelli Marchesini 2015:24, fig. 1.2.1.3.

30. Colonna 2006.

31. Colonna 2015a:116, fig. 2.5.6; 2015b:86–91, figs. 25–31.

32. Di Sarcina 2017:134–135, fig. 5.

33. Jaia and Cella 2015:37–38; Cascino 2017:93.

BIBLIOGRAPHY

Ambrosini, L., A. Argentieri, B. Belelli Marchesini, A. C. Felici, A. Generosi, C. Giampaolo, S. Lo Mastro, B. Paci, M. Piacentini, V. Rossi Albertini, and M. Vendittelli. 2009b. "Studio archeometrico su ceramiche rinvenute nello scavo di Piano di Comunità a Veio." In *Atti della X Giornata di Archeometria della ceramica. Le classi ceramiche: situazione degli studi (Roma, 5–6 aprile 2006)*, ed. S. Gualtieri, B. Fabbri, and G. Bandini, 83–98. Bari.

Ambrosini, L., and B. Belelli Marchesini. 2009a. "Ceramiche a Veio tra V e III sec. a.C.: I materiali da un pozzo di Piano della Comunità." In *Suburbium II: Il Suburbio di Roma dalla fine dell'età monarchica alla nascita del sistema delle ville (V–II sec. a.C.). Atti delle giornate di studio sul suburbio romano tenute a Roma il 16 ottobre e 3 novembre 2004, 17 e 18 febbraio 2005*, ed. V. Jolivet, C. Pavolini, M. A. Tomei, and R. Volpe, 261–287. Rome.

Ambrosini, L., B. Belelli Marchesini, G. Colantoni, B. Giuliani, M. R. Lucidi, M. Merlo, and A. Celant. 2009a. "Il contributo degli scavi di Piano di Comunità alla conoscenza dell'abitato di Veio: Materiali dal riempimento di un pozzo sul pianoro sommitale." In *Veio* I, 64–123.

Bartoloni, G., V. Acconcia, B. Belelli Marchesini, F. Biagi, O. Cerasuolo, S. Neri, F. Pitzalis, L. Pulcinelli, and D. Sarracino. 2013. "Progetto Veio: novità dalle ultime campagne di scavo." *ScAnt* 19:131–154.

Belelli Marchesini, B. 2013. "Piano di Comunità: Indagini sul versante sud-orientale del pianoro sommitale: Il quartiere artigianale." In Bartoloni et al. 2013:142–144.

———. 2015. "2.1. Comunità. La funzione del distretto: Strutture e infrastrutture produttive." In *Novità*, 21–27.

———. 2017. "Evidenze di attività produttive nel distretto meridionale di Veio: Indagini in corso." In *Artigiani*, 111–126.

Belelli Marchesini, B., and R. Cascino. 2012. "Veio: Comunità." In *Atlante dei siti di produzione ceramica (Toscana, Lazio, Campania e Sicilia) con le tabelle dei principali relitti del Mediterraneo occidentale con carichi dall'Italia centro meridionale IV sec. a.C.–I sec. d.C.*, ed. G. Olcese, 215–217. Rome.

Boitani F., F. Biagi, and S. Neri. 2017. "Veio, la più antica area produttiva." In *Artigiani*, 139–142.

Boitani F., S. Neri, and F. Biagi. 2007–2008. "La donna delle fornaci di Veio-Campetti." In *Sepolti tra i vivi*, 833–868.

———. 2009. "Novità dall'impianto produttivo della prima età del ferro di Veio-Campetti." In *I mestieri del fuoco: Officine e impianti artigianali nell'Italia preromana*, 23–42. Officina Etruscologia 1. Rome.

Cascino, R. 2008. "Attività produttive ceramiche a Veio." *MÉFRA* 120:5–19.

———. 2017. "Il pianoro di Veio: Il quadro topografico della produzione." In *Artigiani*, 93–110.

Cascino, R., and M. T. di Sarcina. 2005. "L'abitato di Veio tra età orientalizzante e conquista romana: Interpretazione in base ai dati delle ricognizioni Ward-Perkins." In *Communities and Settlements from the Neolithic to the Early Medieval Period. Proceedings of the Sixth Conference of Italiana Archaeology (Groningen 2003)*, ed. P. A. J. Attema, A. J. Njiboer, and A. Zifferero, 287–291. Oxford.

Colonna, G. 1993. "Ceramisti e donne padrone di bottega nell'Etruria arcaica." In *Indogermanica et Italica. Festschrift für Helmut Rix zum 65. Geburtstag*, ed. G. Meiser, 61–68. Innsbruck.

———. 2006. "Un pittore veiente del ciclo dei Rosoni." In *Tar-quinia e le civiltà del Mediterraneo. Atti del Convegno Internazionale (Milano 2004)*, ed. M. Bonghi Jovino, 163–186. QuadAEI 77. Milan.

———. 2015a. "Novità sugli scavi Santangelo a Veio." In *Novità*, 111–117.

———. 2015b. "Gli scavi Santangelo nell'area urbana di Veio (1945–1952)." *ArchCl* 65:59–101.

Corder, P. 1957. "The Structure of Romano-British Pottery Kilns." *ArchJ* 114:13–27.

Cuomo di Caprio, N. 1977. "Una fornace a Mozia." *Sicilia Archeologica* 10:7–14.

———. 2007. *Ceramica in archeologia, 2: Antiche tecniche di lavorazione e moderni metodi di indagine*. Rome.

di Gennaro, F., and C. Iaia. 2004. "Evidenze relative alla produzione di ceramica a Fidene nella prima età del Ferro." In *Archaeological Methods and Approaches: Industry and Commerce in Ancient Italy* (BAR International Series 1262), ed. C. De Sena and H. Dessales, 109–119.

Di Sarcina, M. T. 2017. "Indicatori di produzione di terrecotte architettoniche nel santuario di Porta Caere a Veio." In *Artigiani*, 129–138.

Falsone, G. 1981. *Struttura e origine orientale dei forni da vasaio di Mozia*. Palermo.

Jaia, A. M., and E. Cella 2015. "Paesaggi urbani a Veio. Saggi di scavo della Sezione Topografia Antica della Sapienza." In *Novità*, 34–40.

Peña, J. T. 1987. *Roman-Period Ceramic Production in Etruria Tiberina: A Geographical and Compositional Study*. Michigan.

Pucci, G., and C. Mascione. 1993. "Un'officina ceramica tardo etrusca a Chiusi." In *La civiltà di Chiusi e del suo territorio. Atti del XVII Convegno di Studi etruschi ed Italici (Chianciano Terme, 28 maggio–1 giugno 1989)*, 375–383. Florence.

CHAPTER 24

ARCHITECTURAL TERRACOTTAS

NANCY A. WINTER AND CLAUDIA CARLUCCI

FROM THE LATE ORIENTALIZING PERIOD TO 510 BCE

Veii deservedly ranks as one of the leading Etruscan centers for the production of decorated terracotta statuary and roofs, as witnessed both by archaeological evidence and by ancient sources. Pliny (*Nat. Hist.* 35.157) mentions that King Tarquinius Priscus (616–578 BCE) summoned Vulca of Veii to Rome to make a terracotta statue of Jupiter that was dedicated on the Capitoline Hill, and that he also made a famous terracotta statue of Hercules.[1] Plutarch (*Poplicola* 13) recounts that King Tarquinius Superbus (534–509 BCE) commissioned from Veii, for the apex of the Temple of Jupiter Optimus Maximus on the Capitoline Hill, a terracotta quadriga, which magically expanded in the kiln as it was being fired.

The earliest evidence thus far of a decorated terracotta roof at Veii dates to 620 BCE and consists of special ridge-tile cover-joints excavated at Piazza d'Armi (*map 4:Y*), which carry a pair of "horn" acroteria that were attached to the roof apex.[2] While unprepossessing, these acroteria demonstrate that Veii was aware of contemporary roof decoration, as seen in nearby Rome and in northern Etruria (Poggio Civitate).

WHITE-ON-RED PAINTED DECORATION, 600–580 BCE

From the period 600–580 BCE, L-shaped raking simas, flat revetment plaques, and circular antefixes painted in the white-on-red technique have been excavated at Piazza d'Armi and Comunità (*map 4:W*).[3] The white-on-red technique was popular during the period, and earlier, for painted pottery at Caere and for painted terracotta decorative roof elements at Acquarossa, and again demonstrates that Veii follows contemporary Etruscan artistic fashions also in its roof decoration.

"FIRST-PHASE" ROOFS WITH MILITARY SCENES, 580–560 BCE

Around 580 BCE a new style of terracotta roof using figural scenes in relief, styled by Della Seta as the "First Phase," appears in Veii. Several of these roofs depict military scenes as their primary decoration. Veii may be the inventor of this new decorative system, which later spreads throughout southern Etruria. The roof of the *oikos* at Piazza d'Armi[4] of 580 BCE is characteristic of the new system: along the eaves of the building (fig. 24.1:A) revetment plaques protecting the wooden rafter ends are decorated with a chariot procession in relief and paint,[5] antefixes at the lower end of the row of cover tiles are capped at the ends with a female head, and eaves tiles (the bottom-most flat pan tiles on the slopes) have painted floral designs on the underside, visible as they projected from the walls of the building. Decoration of the pediment at the short end of the building (fig. 24.1:B), perhaps added ca. 560 BCE, included a raking sima above revetment plaques depicting a warrior's departure scene. The raking sima is similar to an example from Caere while the warrior's departure scene resembles one from Crustumerium.[6]

The roof of a "tower-house" on Piazza d'Armi[7] (for

A

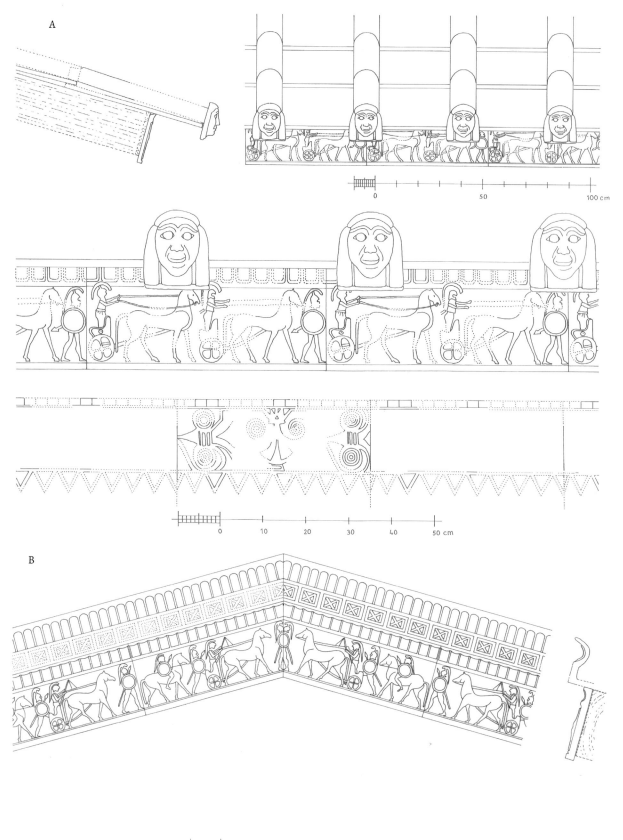

B

FIGURE 24.1. A. Reconstruction drawing of the *oikos* roof eaves at Veii, Piazza d'Armi, 580 BCE; B. Reconstruction drawing of the *oikos* pediment at Veii, Piazza d'Armi, 560 BCE; C. Reconstruction drawing of the roof eaves of the temple at Le Stimmate, Velletri, 530 BCE. (Drawing: Renate Sponer Za. Copyright: N. Winter)

the "tower-house," *see fig. 1.8*) included revetment plaques with a warrior's departure scene and a procession of felines; disc acroteria, one with a Gorgoneion; and an antefix with feline head.[8] This roof closely resembles ones of similar date found in Rome, Vulci, Rusellae, and Poggio Civitate.

Another group includes a cutout acroterion, a statue of a draped figure and dog, a lateral sima with feline-head waterspout, circular antefixes, revetment plaques with an armed rider, and tiles.[9]

ETRUSCO-IONIAN STYLE, 540–510 BCE

Refugee artisans from Asia Minor, fleeing the incursion of the Persian king Cyrus the Great, settled at several places in Etruria around 550–540 BCE, and their presence in local workshops can be detected in some of the roofs of Veii because of the new elements that appear in the terracotta roofs: relief meanders, often surrounding star-flowers and birds, floral patterns (painted and in relief), and scenes of chariot races. All of these new elements were features on terracotta roofs, dating before 550 BCE, excavated at the sites of Phokaia, Larisa am Hermos, and Sardis in modern-day Turkey.

The roof of the *sacellum* of Menerva in the Portonaccio sanctuary[10] (*map 4:S*), datable around 540–530 BCE, includes painted floral bands on both raking sima and revetment plaques, crowned by a relief meander, each with close comparisons in Asia Minor.[11]

Around 530 BCE a new decorative system appeared at Veii, Rome, and Velletri (fig. 24.1:C),[12] using shared molds; some elements are characteristic of earlier roofs in Asia Minor, while others are purely Etruscan. Traditional Etruscan elements are revetment plaques with figural scenes of armed riders, chariot processions to left and to right, a banquet scene, and a seated assembly, as well as a lateral sima with feline-head waterspouts flanked by antefixes with a female head. New East Greek elements are the relief meander on revetment plaques above the figured scene, and the new depiction of chariot races.[13] One L-shaped raking sima from Piazza d'Armi also carries a chariot race.[14] A group of Hercle and Menerva statues flanked by vo-

lutes sat at the apex of the pediment[15] and sphinxes at the corners of the roof.[16]

A possible replacement roof for the *sacellum* of Menerva in the Portonaccio sanctuary, dated 520–510 BCE,[17] has revetment plaques with floral decoration in relief, antefixes with female head, and eaves tiles with painted floral designs on the underside.[18]

VEII'S ROLE DURING THE "FIRST PHASE"

The role of the Veii workshops for terracotta roofs of the so-called First Phase is difficult to assess because they either copied so closely and so quickly other contemporary styles, or were so closely and so quickly copied themselves by others. The presence of East Greek terracotta roof makers at Veii already around 540 BCE, before any such presence can be noted in Rome, however, suggests that Veii was the key player in the invention of the Veii-Rome-Velletri decorative system, which may have required one workshop in Veii and another in Rome, using molds made from the same set of prototypes, as it was one of the most decorative and most popular styles of terracotta roofs during the period 530–520 BCE, producing some twenty terracotta roofs for temples throughout Latium as well as in Veii itself.

ARCHITECTURAL TERRACOTTAS AT VEII FROM THE LATE SIXTH CENTURY BCE TO THE ROMAN CONQUEST

From the second half of the sixth century BCE, architectural terracotta decoration at Veii characterized many public buildings and especially the urban temples. Temples soon became the preferred space for this type of art, which in ancient times was considered the most appropriate to portray different deities. Cult statues and pedimental groups with figures in high relief presented mythical narratives connected to individual deities.[19] During the Late Archaic period, the archaeological record of terracotta sculptures in ancient Etruria and Latium is extremely rich, but unfortunately very fragmentary. Identification of the existence of "schools" or recognition of the "hand" of an artist has rarely been possible, in contrast to studies of Greek marble sculptures.

Nevertheless, the providential discoveries at Veii in the sanctuary of Portonaccio brought to light one of the largest complexes of terracotta decoration ever found.[20] Exceptional terracotta statues were found together with numerous remains of the roof decoration of the temple, and a large number of votive statues, some of exceptional artistic value. All of these masterpieces can be attributed to different masters with distinctive personalities, although none of their names survive in the ancient sources, with a significant exception. In fact, all these artists probably were trained at the school of the master Vulca, whose name is the only one mentioned among the literary sources.[21]

The later cycle of acroteria created by the "Master of the Apollo"[22] appears to have been of even greater importance and testifies to the richness of the school of Vulca. In fact, this school probably functioned as a major attraction for extraterritorial commissions, since its masters were called several times to work in Rome during the sixth century BCE.[23] The statues represented Olympian deities and were placed on the *columen* (ridge beam) of the roof, forming different groups, which narrated different episodes of Greek myths.

This sequence suggests a sort of three-dimensional movie.[24] The strong physicality expressed in these sculptures is especially visible in the rendering of sculpted bodies, particularly in the folds of the garments, which seem to follow the movements of each figure. This physicality was also accentuated by a dynamic power the sculptor managed to express. This power appears especially in the episode of the fight between Aplu and Hercle, who had stolen the deer sacred to Artumes. The god is portrayed in the act of pouncing on the hero (*plate 11*). The first scholars who studied this group described Aplu as "a walking god"[25] (*plate 12*). This group testifies to the excellent narrative capabilities of the anonymous artist who made it. In fact, Hercle and his prey appear closely merged, in contrast to the more common depiction, which usually occurs in two different scenes.

Apart from the acroteria on the ridge, four statues representing fantastic animals decorated the slopes of the roof, such as a sphinx with lion body and a Siren with a female bust and full-figure body in the form of a bird. All the statues were placed on large terracotta bases.[26] Both pediments of the temple were also decorated.[27] One of the monumental statues probably occupied the apex. An open-work decoration was placed at its sides, covering the monumental raking simas. The simas functioned as background for a lively military scene: on the front pediment, small rampant acroteria portrayed horse riders battling barbarians; on the back pediment, a fight between panthers was depicted. Two mirror-image groups with horses and riders, connected by perforated volutes to two lower ram protomes, decorated the corners at the base of the gable on the façade (*plate 13*). The rear façade was decorated with projecting palmette acroteria.[28]

Along the sides of the temple, the decorative program of Portonaccio focused on a series of impressive antefixes alternating along the eaves of the roof. The large dimensions of the antefixes reflected the monumental scale of the acroteria, creating a unique visual match. Four subjects were here represented: (a) the Gorgoneion (*plate 14*, top), (b) two types of Achelöos (the half-man, half-bull monster), (c) a Silen, and (d) a maenad (*plate 14*, bottom).

All of these roof elements belong to one of the best-preserved decorative systems for a single temple ever discovered. This is also one of the earliest examples of the new decorative system, known as the "Second Phase." It excels in its unifying concept of far-reaching scope, apparent in all its components, from the sculptures to newly conceived nonfigural revetments. The project and its realization date to the end of the sixth century BCE.

Products of this workshop have been identified at Veii in urban sanctuaries, such as at Caere Gate, probably dedicated to Menerva, Vei, and Hercle,[29] all located near the city wall in the large area of Campetti. The evidence from a contemporary small temple on the hill of Pizzo Piede at Narce revealed the presence of an extraterritorial workshop of Veii.[30]

A group of fragmentary terracottas from the area of

FIGURE 24.2. Antefix with head of Satyr from
Portonaccio, 475–470 BCE. (Copyright: C. Carlucci)

FIGURE 24.3. First tile, connected to the *columen*,
on the left slope, from Portonaccio, 475–470 BCE.
(Copyright: C. Carlucci)

Comunità suggests the existence here of a cult place, probably connected to Uni/Juno Regina, with different phases from the last quarter of the sixth to the beginning of the fifth century BCE.[31]

During the years 475–470 BCE an important renovation of the decorative revetments is documented, testament to the appearance of a new system, another original creation of a workshop of the city (figs. 24.2–24.3). The great popularity of this workshop was not limited to the territory of Veii, but reached Caere, the Ager Faliscus, and Latium Vetus.[32] The presence of this new system in three major sanctuaries at Veii (Menerva at Portonaccio, Vei at Campetti North, and Menerva at Campetti-Caere Gate) demonstrates the effort by the town to renovate its sacred spaces during the second quarter of the fifth century BCE. In the sanctuary of Campetti North, two new types of full-figure antefixes are also attested: (a) a single maenad playing the crotala (castanets) (*plate 15*), and (b) a satyr and maenad. The presence of these new types suggests an increase in the iconographic repertoire at Veii, which was inaugurated earlier by the antefixes with a full-figure Siren.

Finally, another series of antefixes with full-figure nymphs carrying a *stamnos* comes from a newly discov-

FIGURE 24.4. Cut-out frame from Portonaccio,
late fifth century BCE. (Copyright: C. Carlucci)

ered sacred area, previously unknown, in the locality of Macchiagrande (*plate 16*).[33]

The rich repertoire of full-figure antefix types created for the new decorative systems proves the uninterrupted predilection for sculpture by the terracotta school of Veii. This school, thanks to the vibrant culture of Veii, was able to create high-quality master-pieces with constant innovation in the iconography.

Finally, it is important to note that the excavations at the sanctuary of Portonaccio revealed elements of a new decorative system, which dates to the end of the fifth century BCE, just a few years before the Roman conquest of the Etruscan town in 396 BCE (fig. 24.4). This system represents one of the last testimonies to the exceptional building vitality of the free town.

NOTES

Nancy A. Winter wrote the first part of the chapter ("From the Late Orientalizing Period to 510 BCE"), and Claudia Carlucci wrote the second part ("Architectural Terracottas at Veii from the Late Sixth Century BCE to the Roman Conquest").

1. See also chapters 12 and 13.

2. D. Sarracino, "Elementi di decorazione architettonica," in *Veio* III. Cf. Winter 2009:22, 1.E.1, fig. 1.4 right, Ill. 1.6.3 (Rome), and 100, 2.E.1, Ill. 2.7.1 (Poggio Civitate), with earlier bibliography.

3. Belelli Marchesini 2011a. Cf. Wikander 1981–1988 (Acquarossa).

4. Winter 2009:224–228, roof 4-1, Ill. roof 4-1, with earlier bibliography.

5. Fragments from the same mold have been found at Portonaccio, Macchiagrande, and Campetti: Belelli Marchesini and ten Kortenaar 2011:108, fig. 1, pl. V.a–b. The Macchiagrande fragment (pl. V.b), said to be a variant of the procession to left, instead appears to belong to the procession to right, with the foreleg of the left horse, wheel of the right chariot, and tail of the right chariot horse. Variants of these revetment plaques with departing warrior scenes have been excavated at Piazza d'Armi: Winter 2009:255–257, 4.D.2.b, 4.D.2.d, 4.D.2.e, figs. 4.9–10, Ill. 4.6.3–4, with earlier bibliography; D. Sarracino, "Elementi di decorazione architettonica," in *Veio* II:164–165, pl. XLII.

6. Raking sima from Caere: Winter 2009:240, 4.A.1.a, with earlier bibliography. Revetment plaques from Crustumerium: Belelli Marchesini and ten Kortenaar 2011:108, fig. 3.a–c, with earlier bibliography.

7. See chapter 1.

8. Bartoloni et al. 2011:132–135, figs. 14–17, pl. VII.a, with earlier bibliography; Belelli Marchesini and van Kortenaar 2011:110–111; Bartoloni et al. 2013:142–143. A similar "tower-house" (Building β) in the Portonaccio sanctuary also had revetment plaques with warrior's departure scene and feline processions: Belelli Marchesini and van Kortenaar 2011:110, and Belelli Marchesini 2011b:281, with earlier bibliography. For

the feline processions, cf. examples from Rome: Winter 2009: 175–178, 3.D.1.a, figs. 3.9–11, Ill. 3.4.1, and 178–180, 3.D.2.a, fig. 3.13, Ill. 3.5.1, with earlier bibliography. For the disc acroterion, cf. the relief Gorgoneion on *columen* plaques from Poggio Civitate (Murlo) and Vulci: Winter 2009:192–193, 3.D.9.a, fig. 3.24, with earlier bibliography. For the feline-head antefix, cf. the *antepagmenta* from Poggio Civitate (Murlo): Winter 2009:193–194, 3.D.10, figs. 3.26–28, with earlier bibliography. A revetment plaque with a similar departure scene comes from Crustumerium: Belelli Marchesini and van Kortenaar 2011:111, fig. 3.d, with earlier bibliography.

9. Bartoloni et al. 2011:136–142, figs. 18–19, 25.a–b, pl. VI; 2012:87–120, figs. 16–45; 2013:143–144, figs. 8–9. See also chapter 11.

10. See chapter 13.

11. Winter 2009:495, roof 7-1, Ill. roof 7-1, with earlier bibliography; Belelli Marchesini 2011b:282–283. Relief meander on a lateral sima at Sardis: cf. Åkerström 1966: figs. 23, 23a. Floral band: cf. a raking sima from Sardis: Åkerström 1966: pl. 50.3 (upside down). The dates of the decorated roofs at Sardis have recently been raised by stratigraphical excavations to fall between 585 and 560–550 BCE: Ratté 1994.

12. Winter 2009: ch. 5, with earlier bibliography; Lulof forthcoming. Historical considerations as well as stylistic comparisons with Pontic vases, metalwork, and sculpture provide the date: Colonna 1984:405; Fortunati 1989:63. At least five roofs at Veii (Piazza d'Armi, Portonaccio, Comunità, Campetti, and the crossing of *cardo* and *decumanus*: Belelli Marchesini 2011b:283–285), four or five at Rome (Sant'Omobono, Capitoline Hill, Palatine Hill [Casa di Livia and Casa dei Grifi], area of the Regia in the Roman Forum, and possibly near the Comitium: Winter 2011a), and one at Velletri (Carlucci 2011b) have been documented. Petrographic analyses and neutron activation tests have shown that the roofs in Veii were made with local clay and inclusions, while the roofs in Rome and Velletri were made with clay and inclusions linked to Rome, in all three places mixed to the same formula: Winter 2011b, with earlier bibliography.

An isolated fragment has also been found at Praeneste: Gatti 2011:246, fig. 5. New excavations at Gabii may also have produced fragments of a roof of this type: Lulof forthcoming.

13. For earlier examples of chariot races on architectural terracottas at Sardis in Asia Minor, see Åkerström 1966:70–71, nos. 4–6, fig. 22, pls. 39–41; Winter 1993:238. For the dating of the decorated roofs at Sardis between 585 and 560–550 BCE, see Ratté 1994.

14. Winter 2009:328–330, 5.A.1.a, fig. 5.1, Ill. 5.1.1, with earlier bibliography. At Velletri there was an S-shaped sima with relief tongues above a torus with painted scale pattern: Carlucci 2011b:224–225, fig. 7. A similar S-shaped sima from Sant'Omobono in Rome, originally attributed to the first-phase temple roof (Winter 2012:62–63, fig. 4.1), should probably

now be assigned to the second-phase temple roof, based on the new information from Velletri. No similar S-shaped raking simas have been documented thus far at Veii.

15. Winter 2009:377–381, 5.E.1.a (Hercle and Menerva) and 383–384, 5.E.2 (volute acroteria), with earlier bibliography.

16. Belelli Marchesini 2011b:284–285, pl. XII.b. Cf. Winter 2009:384–386, 5.E.3 (Sant'Omobono in Rome and Velletri), with earlier bibliography.

17. See chapter 13.

18. Winter 2009:495–497, roof 7-2, with earlier bibliography.

19. Pliny, *Nat. Hist.* 35.157–158; Pallottino 1979a:1004; Colonna 2008:54–55.

20. See chapter 13. For the history of the excavation and details of the discoveries, see Stefani 1953; Colonna 1985:99–109, 2001:37–38; and Baglione 1987.

21. Colonna 2008:54. See also chapter 13.

22. Colonna 2008:59–63.

23. Pliny the Elder described the statues, which decorated the temple of Jupiter on the Capitoline Hill. In addition, according to his description, the cult statue was still visible inside the *cella* before the destruction of the temple in 83 BCE. A statue of Hercules was also preserved in the Forum Boarium until the Imperial period. These two statues have been attributed to Vulca, while the famous *quadriga* (four-horsed chariot) on the ridge of the temple of Jupiter was a masterpiece by an unknown artist: Pallottino 1979a:1003–1005; Colonna 2008:54–56.

24. For three-dimensional statues in southern Etruria during the Late Archaic period, see Pallottino 1979c:1067–1069.

25. Pallottino 1979a:1007.

26. For the statues, see Carlucci 2001:57–59; 2008:201–202; 2011:123–124. For the bases, see Michetti 2011; Maras 2011.

27. Carlucci 2005, 2011.

28. Carlucci 2011:116–121.

29. Torelli and Pohl 1973 and Carlucci 2012; Vagnetti 1971 and Carosi 2002; Fusco 2011, 2013–2014, and 2015.

30. Baglione and De Lucia Brolli 2004; Carlucci 2013: 136–140.

31. Belelli Marchesini 2001.

32. Carlucci 2005, 2013.

33. Carlucci 2006:11, 1.VIII, fig. 1.2; Colonna 2014, 2015.

BIBLIOGRAPHY

Åkerström, Å. 1966. *Die architektonischen Terrakotten Kleinasiens.* Lund.

Baglione, M. P., and M. A. De Lucia Brolli. 2004. "Il santuario urbano di Pizzo Piede a Narce." In *Scavo nello scavo: Gli Etruschi non visti* (exh. cat.), ed. A. M. Moretti Sgubini, 89–102. Rome.

Bartoloni, G., V. Acconcia, B. Belelli Marchesini, F. Biagi, O. Cerasuolo, S. Neri, F. Pitzalis, L. Pulcinelli, and D. Sar-racino. 2013. "Progetto Veio: Novità dalle ultime campagne di scavo." *ScAnt* 19:133–156.

Bartoloni, G., V. Acconcia, E. Biancifiori, C. Mottolese, D. Sar-racino, and V. Basilissi. 2012. "Veio, Piazza d'Armi: La fossa del cane." *ArchCl* 63:55–126.

Bartoloni, G., V. Acconcia, F. Boitani, F. Biagi, S. Neri, and U. Fusco. 2013–2014. "Le ricerche dell'Università degli Studi di Roma 'La Sapienza' a Veio." *RendPontAc* 86:1–82.

Bartoloni, G., V. Acconcia, A. Piergrossi, S. ten Kortenaar, and I. van Kampen. 2011. "Veio, Piazza d'Armi: Riconsiderazioni e novità." In *Tetti di terracotta*, 116–174.

Belelli Marchesini, B. 2001. "Comunità." In *Veio, Cerveteri, Vulci*, 23–28.

———. 2011a. "Veio: Un frontoncino da Piano di Comunità." In *Tetti di terracotta*, 175–186.

———. 2011b. "Il tetto di Caprifico a confronto: Veio." In *Tetti di terracotta*, 278–288.

Belelli Marchesini, B., and S. ten Kortenaar. 2011. "Veio: Considerazioni sulle lastre di rivestimento con fregi figurati." In *Tetti di terracotta*, 107–115.

Carlucci, C. 2001. "Portonaccio. Il tempio: Le statue acroteriali e le loro sottobasi." In *Veio, Cerveteri, Vulci*, 57–59, 62–64.

———. 2005. "Gli apparati decorativi tardo-arcaici del tempio di Portonaccio a Veio." *StEtr* 70:33–46.

———. 2008. "Il sistema decorativo del tempio del Portonaccio nella fase dei 'Grandi acroteri': La coroplastica." In *Etruschi: Antiche metropoli del Lazio* (exh. cat.), ed. M. Torelli and A. M. Moretti Sgubini, 115–127. Rome.

———. 2011a. "Roma: Novità dal Colle Palatino." In *Tetti di terracotta*, 202–215.

———. 2011b. "Il sistema decorativo del tempio delle Stimmate di Velletri tra Veio Portonaccio e Roma-Palatino." In *Tetti di terracotta*, 220–236.

———. 2011c. "Il repertorio figurativo del ciclo acroteriale del tempio dell'Apollo a Veio-Portonaccio." In *Deliciae Fictiles* IV, 115–127.

———. 2012. "Il maestro dell'Apollo di Veio-Portonaccio: Una nuova acquisizione." In *MAV*, 109–113.

———. 2013. "Linee di sviluppo della coroplastica falisca tra le età tardo arcaica e classica." In *Tra Roma e l'Etruria: Cultura, identità e territorio dei Falisci*, ed. G. Cifani, 135–172. Rome.

Carosi, S. 2002. "Nuovi dati sul santuario di Campetti a Veio." *ArchCl* 53:355–377.

Colonna, G. 1984. "I templi del Lazio fino al V secolo compreso." *Archeologia Laziale* 6:396–411.

———, ed. 1985. *Santuari d'Etruria*. Milan.

———. 1987. "Il maestro dell'Ercole e della Minerva: Nuova luce sull'attività dell'officina veiente." *Lectiones Boëtianes* 6:7–41. *OpRom* 16.1.

———. 2001. "Portonaccio." In *Veio, Cerveteri, Vulci*, 37–44.

———. 2008. "L'officina veiente: Vulca e gli altri maestri di statuaria arcaica in terracotta." In *Etruschi: Le antiche metro-*

poli del Lazio (exh. cat.), ed. M. Torelli and A. M. Moretti Sgubini, 52–63. Rome.

———. 2014. "Gli scavi Santangelo nell'area urbana di Veio (1945–1952)." *ArchCl* 45:59–102.

———. 2015. "Novità sugli scavi Santangelo a Veio." In *Novità*, 111–117.

Deliciae Fictiles IV = *Deliciae Fictiles* IV: *Architectural Terracottas in Ancient Italy: Images of Gods, Monsters, and Heroes. Proceedings of the International Conference held in Rome (Museo Nazionale Etrusco di Villa Giulia, Royal Netherlands Institute) and Syracuse (Museo Archeologico Regionale "Paolo Orsi") October 21–25, 2009*, ed. P. S. Lulof and C. Rescigno (Oxford, 2011)

Fortunati, F. R. 1989. "Il tempio delle Stimmate." In *Museo Civico di Velletri*, 57–87. Rome.

Fusco, U. 2011. "Il culto di Ercole presso il complesso archeologico di Campetti, Area S-O, a Veio: Testimonianze dall'età etrusca a quella romana." *ArchCl* 52:379–412.

———. 2013–2014. "Aspetti cultuali e archeologici del sito di Campetti, area sud-ovest, dall'età arcaica a quella imperiale." *RendPontAcc* 2013–2014:309–345.

Gatti, S. 2011. "Praeneste. Le terrecotte architettoniche di 'Prima Fase': Problemi e contesti." In *Tetti di terracotta*, 237–250.

Lulof, P. S. Forthcoming. "Temples a l'age de Tarquin le Superbe: Espaces artisaneaux et réseaux des centres religieux dans Italie archaïque central." In *Espaces artisanaux, lieux de culte dans l'Antiquité (Actes de Journée d'Études de la Société française d'Archéologie Classique–INHA, Paris, 15 Marz 2014)*, ed. O. De Cazanove. Paris.

Maras, D. F. 2011. "Gli dei sul tetto: Le basi acroteriali del tempio di Veio-Portonaccio. Messa in opera e funzione." In *Deliciae Fictiles* IV, 107–114.

Michetti, L. M. 2011. "Gli dei sul tetto: Le basi acroteriali del tempio di Veio-Portonaccio. Struttura e apparato decorativo." In *Deliciae Fictiles* IV, 96–106.

Pallottino, M. 1979a. "La scuola di Vulca." In *Saggi di antichità* III, 1003–1024. Rome.

———. 1979b. "Un grande nudo maschile della officina plastica veiente." In *Saggi di antichità* III, 1025–1036. Rome.

———. 1979c. "Il grande acroterio femminile di Veio." In *Saggi di antichità* III, 1037–1092. Rome.

Ratté, C. 1994. "Archaic Architectural Terracottas from Sector Byzfort at Sardis." *Hesperia* 63:361–390.

Stefani, E. 1953. "Veio. Tempio detto dell'Apollo. Esplorazione e sistemazione del santuario." *NSc* 1953:29–112.

Torelli, M., and I. Pohl. 1973. "Veio. Scoperta di un piccolo santuario in località Campetti." *NSc* 1973:40–258

Vagnetti, L. 1971. *Il deposito votivo di Campetti a Veio*. Florence.

Wikander, C. 1981–1988. *Acquarossa* I: *The Painted Architectural Terracottas*. Stockholm.

Winter, N. A. 1993. *Greek Architectural Terracottas from the Prehistoric to the End of the Archaic Period*. Oxford Monographs on Classical Archaeology. Oxford.

———. 2009. *Symbols of Wealth and Power: Architectural Terracotta Decoration in Etruria and Central Italy, 640–510 BC.* MAAR Suppl. 9. Ann Arbor.

———. 2011a. "Roma. Testimonianze di tetti dei sistemi decorativi Veio-Roma-Velletri e Roma-Caprifico." In *Tetti di terracotta*, 216–219.

———. 2011b. "Analisi petrografiche di campioni da tetti dei sistemi decorativi Veio-Roma-Velletri e Roma-Caprifico." In *Tetti di terracotta*, 289–291.

———. 2012. "Monumentalization of the Etruscan Round Moulding in Sixth-Century BCE Central Italy." In *Monumentality in Etruscan and Early Roman Architecture: Ideology and Innovation*, ed. Michael L. Thomas and Gretchen E. Meyers, 61–81. Austin.

PART IV

LEGACY OF THE CITY

Our narrative ends in 396 BCE with the siege of Veii, led by the consul M. Furius Camillus—whose historical existence is authoritatively discussed in this final part of the volume. The Roman conquest is indeed not the end of the history of Veii. The identity of the town survives in the refoundation of its center in 12 BCE by Augustus. The Municipium Augustum Veiens did not reach the same level of importance as the city of Etruscan times and was limited in both space and time, and it rapidly disappeared during the medieval period.

CHAPTER 25

FURIUS CAMILLUS AND VEII

CHRISTOPHER SMITH

The history of Rome and Veii has at its heart a moment of destruction, an ending. Everything leads up to the fall of Veii, and arguably everything in the narrative was constructed around that ending.[1] In our conventional dating, in 396 BCE, after a siege lasting ten years, Rome finally gained the upper hand over Veii, and the Roman hero of the day was M. Furius Camillus.

The siege is well known from Livy's account, but few of those details are reliable. The length of the siege is suspiciously equivalent to the siege at Troy. The conflict began after a haughty answer to a Roman delegation and was stoked by the Veientine choice of an unnamed king as a ruler, which Livy suggests was as unpopular with other Etruscan cities as it was with Rome. However, the war itself was also unpopular with the Roman people, with the result that Livy's narrative oscillates between Roman reluctance, Veientine success, and Roman response. Veii is supported by Capena and the Faliscans (who perhaps had a relationship to Veii similar to that of the Latins with Rome).[2]

Many omens attended this event that marked Rome's first great victory over a major foreign city. Written prophecies and omens foretold doom. A soothsayer and the Delphic oracle both urged the draining of Lake Albano, and there is indeed a still-functional tunnel that serves to regulate the level of that lake. The tunnel is nearly 2.5 kilometers in length, approximately 1.5 meters high, and just over a meter wide on average. Although it is usually dated to the sixth century, it appears in the history of Veii perhaps because the siege at Veii was itself broken by a tunnel.[3] The Roman sappers even overheard a soothsayer proclaiming that whoever sacrificed a particular victim would gain the victory, and they broke through to steal the animal and take it to Camillus.

The capitulation of Veii, when it came, was total. The Romans proposed to remove the goddess Juno from her temple—and so they did when allegedly she herself, with a nod, assented. The territory of Veii would be distributed to the Roman people.

Camillus had vowed a tithe of the spoils to Apollo, but most of the plunder was taken by the Roman soldiers. A dispute arose as to how to honor the vow; the senate and Camillus expected the people to pay, and Roman women gave up their ornaments. In the end a golden bowl was sent to Delphi, but Camillus was unpopular as a result of this episode. His next deed, however, was one of great nobility. The Romans were conducting a war against the Faliscans, and a schoolmaster led out the children of Falerii to offer them as hostages to conclude the war. Camillus rejected this unacceptable betrayal and ordered the schoolmaster to lead the boys back to Falerii. The Faliscans, overcome with gratitude, came to terms. Facing prosecution, and rejected by his own city, Camillus went into exile, praying to the gods that if he were innocent, the Romans would wish they had him back.

Yet the Camillus story, as we see it, was not just about Veii, but bound up with the near-contemporary moment, just six years later, when Rome suffered its own catastrophe and was captured by the Gauls. Rome was disgraced and desperate, but a way was found to bring Camillus back from exile in Ardea. The citadel of Rome, the only part of the city the Gauls had not taken, was preserved by the geese that sounded the alarm. The Gauls, suffering from illness, decided to demand a ransom, and famously weighed down the scales. When the Romans complained, their leader responded *vae victis*, "Woe to the conquered!" Just in time Camillus arrived, scattered the ransom, and began the fight anew. The tide turned, the Gauls fled, and Camillus went on—and on. He became involved in settling disputes between the patricians and plebeians and in establishing the *concordia ordinum* afresh.[4] He died in 365 BCE at the age of more than eighty years, and had been fighting almost to the last.

Camillus was celebrated for as long as Rome had an empire; he was the *fatalis dux*, the fateful leader.[5] In this account, the fall of Veii is inserted into a larger narrative, dominated by one extraordinary man, one of victory, personal tragedy, national catastrophe, and the recovery of leader and state, all the while with the gods at hand. Inevitably such a dramatic and thrilling tale raises questions. Camillus himself is relatively colorless, a virtuous Roman machine.[6] How much can we actually believe? Did Camillus even exist? And what, in the end, can we say about the Roman sack of Veii?

MOTIVATIONS

The Romans had a clear sense that Veii had been an enemy from the very beginning. The list of Roman triumphs, an official list of Roman victories inscribed in stone compiled at the time of Augustus, may very well have recorded, in a missing line, Romulus's victory over the Veiians, which is reported in several of the sources; it does preserve that of Rome's fourth king, Ancus Marcius. Valerius Publicola triumphed over the Veiians in the very first year of the Republic, 509 BCE.[7] Conflict between the two states was persistent. On one occasion, on February 13, 477 BCE, the Fabian clan, which had undertaken the war against Veii by itself to free other Romans to fight elsewhere, was slaughtered, with only one survivor.[8]

Our sources do not spell out the reasons, but we may presume that the issue was control of the Tiber River and the valuable resources along its banks. It is important to note, however, that the motivation

for the final reckoning is set out in Livy. The Veiians were internally at odds, precisely at the time when a twenty-year truce with Rome was coming to an end. The Romans held back, but in the end received a rude response. War was declared. Tired of fractious annual elections, the Veiians chose a king, one who disrupted solemn religious festivals with the other Etruscan city-states. The Etruscans, we are told, hated kings on principle, and this one for good reason, and they turned their backs on Veii. Alone, Veii was vulnerable. Rome prepared for a siege.

The king is never named, but the Veientine family most usually associated with kingship is that of the Tolumnii.[9] Lars Tolumnius was killed in battle by Aulus Cornelius Cossus in 437 BCE, an event that led to a rather complex debate at the time (into which Augustus entered) over Cossus's status.

It is interesting that we see so clearly the perspective of the other Etruscan city-states, and it is not unreasonable to assume that the defeat of Veii might have left a mark on Etruscan historiography, alas now lost to us. However, what follows, a siege of ten years, is transparently modeled on the siege of Troy in Homeric epic; all the more so, because the chronology is off. The twenty-year truce is brought to an end too soon, and we know that the Romans inserted years to try to manage some discrepancies later on in their history.[10] Already we can see that the Veientine story was open to manipulation.

THE HISTORIOGRAPHICAL STRUCTURE OF THE ACCOUNT OF CAMILLUS[11]

All the surviving sources for Camillus date from the Late Republic and the Imperial period. That is, they were written several centuries after the event. Reading them with care reveals three key points:

1. The older layer of the tradition associated Camillus with the Roman siege of Veii, the city's capture, and his later military exploits.
2. A more recent layer of the tradition added the drama of Camillus's own life—his prosecution,

exile, return, and intervention to liberate Rome from the Gauls.

3. The most recent layer was added before the time of Livy, who began writing probably in the 30s BCE.

We can see that the character Camillus acquired many characteristics that were similar to those of great Romans of the historical period. He utters a prayer similar to that of Aemilius Paullus after the victory at Pydna in 168 BCE;[12] the episode of his trial and exile is similar to the experience of the Scipiones after the defeat of Hannibal;[13] his dictatorship has parallels with that of Sulla;[14] and so on. This transference of details is a common enough feature of Roman writing on the city's early history, where imagination had to fill the gap left by the paucity of surviving information.[15]

The difficulty is to establish what genuine elements may have been passed down. We cannot assume that the older tradition must be historical, because at least one of the elements, the inordinate length of Camillus's career, has been questioned. There have been many suggestions that in fact what we see is almost entirely fictional.

THE CONSTRUCTION OF A GREAT MAN—THE CAREER OF CAMILLUS

For the Romans, the example of the *maiores*, the ancestors, was always before their eyes. Funeral processions carried the busts of the ancestors to family tombs. Family trees were inscribed in the atria of the great houses. Perusing the lists of the magistrates, citizens could see the repeated names of families such as the Claudii and the Fabii. The monuments of the city recalled the victories of the past. Poetry and drama celebrated victory and defeat.[16]

Camillus's story was a major exemplum for the Romans of the virtues of the past and was regularly cited. Cicero for instance repeatedly refers to Camillus, perhaps most significantly when he himself returns from exile. Pompey may have referred to Julius Caesar as leading a second Gallic invasion, while the senate celebrated the victorious Caesar with reference

to Camillus. For Augustus too, the example of Camillus was attractive and alluring.

A speech at the end of book 5 of Livy has Camillus addressing the Roman people. They look at their destroyed city and consider whether it would not be better to abandon it and start again at Veii. Camillus's moving speech to dissuade them led him to be thought of as a second founder after Romulus. It is one of the great set-piece speeches in Livy—and entirely fictional. However, it can be assumed that other historians also placed a speech at this juncture, and although the theme of a threatened move of the capital was not uncommon in the Late Republic, this is an original and powerful statement of the connection between Rome as a place and Rome as the seat of Roman gods and traditions. Augustus's focus on Rome (as opposed to Mark Antony's alleged plan to move the capital city to Alexandria), his emphasis on the civic merits of virtue, piety, and justice, and the fact that both celebrated a triple triumph are ways in which Augustus—or at least the writers around him—used the Camillus paradigm.[17]

So we can see why poets and historians from the second century BCE onward would have wanted to develop the Camillus story as an example of civic virtue and military renown. Bringing Camillus into the story of the sack by the Gauls clearly made sense; the action could be concentrated on the great hero. The end result is a satisfying narrative in which Camillus's fortunes and Rome's are interwoven. But where did the figure of Camillus originally come from, and how does the analysis of this critical figure in the story of Veii affect our understanding of that city?

THE MYTHOLOGY OF CAMILLUS—DUMÉZIL

One answer has been to see in Camillus not a historical personage at all but rather a figure of myth who was brought into the story and became more human. The greatest modern exponent of the idea that Roman history can be understood as the transformation of mythical archetypes was Georges Dumézil.

Dumézil noticed that Camillus was closely connected with the deity Mater Matuta, the Roman god-dess of the dawn. Every one of Camillus's battles was won at dawn. His vow to Apollo is an indicator of a connection with the god of the sun. Camillus was therefore a solar entity, who was at some point (Du-mézil hesitantly suggests the fourth century[18]) turned into a historical one. The hints and clues that make up the bulk of the argument are remnants of a very distant set of identifications, a mythology lost almost without trace.[19]

CAMILLUS AS A ROMAN MYTH

An alternative approach was offered by Christer Bruun. Bruun noticed the appearance of an individual called Marce Camitlnas[20] on a famous fourth-century wall painting at Vulci, in the François Tomb.[21] The figure appears to be taking part in an event that would have made sense as a quasi-legendary one from around 500 BCE; other participants, Macstrna (a name sometimes associated with Servius Tullius), the Vipinas brothers, and Cneve Tarchunies Rumach (presumably a Tarqui-nius) all recall events in Rome's regal period.

The name Camitlnas/Camillus may have been a conflation with the role of the *camillus*, a young boy who served the priests in rituals. So what we would then have is a name associated with piety, associated with a more-or-less generic figure from ancient his-tory, who was merged into a historical personage. As Bruun notes, one member of the Furian clan whom Livy rather overlooks was L. Furius L. f. Sp. N. Me-dullinus, who appears in the lists of magistrates twice as consul and seven times as military tribune with con-sular power. Perhaps Camillus took over some of the activities of the real Furius, who was then oddly rele-gated to a rather negative position.[22]

Uwe Walter focused on the appearance of the Camillus story in Ennius, whose great epic poem of Rome, written in the earlier second century BCE, was enormously influential. It is likely but not provable that Ennius gave Camillus a role; Livy might have been echoing Ennius when he wrote the speech in which Camillus persuaded the Romans not to aban-don their city.[23] Walter also points to three poten-tial early records: the three gold dishes inscribed with

Camillus's name that were in the temple of Capitoline Jupiter until the fire of 83.[24]

We know therefore that the tradition on Camillus is complex and has many layers. We know also that there were several moments at which it made sense and was appropriate to develop the story, because the example of Camillus was significant as a forerunner of a con-temporary individual or could be harnessed as a posi-tive parallel.

What we do not know for sure is whether anyone called Camillus actually led the Romans in the fourth century BCE. However, the skeptical accounts are not without difficulty. Dumézil's reconstruction of early Roman history on the basis of a lost mythology is tenu-ous, and Bruun has to rely heavily on the evidence of the François Tomb, which strictly speaking only shows that not long after the sack of Veii, someone inserted a homonymous individual into a story about conflict between Rome and the Etruscans.

Another way of looking at this would be that the Romans mythologized their actual past. It is not im-possible that in the showdown between Veii and Rome, a Camillus played a part. That part was elabo-rated over time, and perhaps deep structures of Roman thought—the metaphorical language that arose from a profound belief in the sustaining support of the gods for the pious and the victorious, coupled with familial histories and historiographical practices of concentrat-ing success on a few figures to assist the narrative—all built the imposing example of the life of Camillus from a tiny core. Yet Camillus is intimately connected with the Veientine story; without Veii he does not pos-sess the critical elements that define his passage from triumph to disgrace to restitution.

VEII WITHOUT CAMILLUS

On the other hand, if we ask what difference this makes to our understanding of the history of Veii, the outcome may be rather different. Suppose Camillus had never existed, how far would we need to rewrite our history?

The answer is . . . surprisingly little. Most of the Camillus story is so patently fabricated that it has never had a significant role in modern Etruscan studies. A ten-year siege, the omens and portents, the tunnel, all this can be abandoned without undue concern. Three elements remain of critical historical interest, although none of them relates to Camillus: the motivation for the competition between the two states; the nature of Veientine politics; and the fate of Veii.

On the first, there seems every reason to believe that the Tiber was an important and tense frontier zone. Rome's encroachment is mentioned variously in the sources. The importance of the Roman foundation of Ostia at the mouth of the Tiber, probably also in the fourth century, and Roman use of tufa taken from the north bank of the Tiber—but only from the fourth century BCE onward—are two indices. The colonies of Sutri and Nepi, founded by the Romans shortly after the defeat of Veii, are proof that Rome began to move into the Faliscan area, which it could only have done after Veii had lost its influence over that territory. Even without reference to any individual, Roman ambitions are clear.[25]

Was Veii beset by particular internal political difficulties? Archaeology cannot tell us, but we have other references to the instability of the Etruscan city-states and can fathom something of their political structures.[26] It is not unthinkable. As for Veii's relationship with the other Etruscan towns, that too may have been compromised by Veii's relationship with the Faliscans. Nothing rests on the reliability of Livy's account here, but it is an interesting speculation that whilst the Romans were exaggerating the role of Camillus, the Etruscans too would have needed some story to tell; and perhaps they made Veii's fall the consequence of her own choices. Whether this influenced the François Tomb is hard to say.

Lastly, what of the *evocatio* of the goddess Juno from Veii? The large votive deposit at Piano di Comunità is now thought to represent the Veientine temple of Juno, but it does not end in 390 BCE. Juno may have nodded to the Romans, but Veii continued, yet with a much stronger Roman presence. Altars at Macchiagrande with dedications in Latin to, among others, Jupiter, Libertas, Minerva, and Victoria tell the story of the Roman conquest.[27]

In fact the account of the siege is at odds with the archaeological evidence that may show some disrup-tion at Veii but equally shows a good deal of continuity (just as the account of the sack of Rome six years later is massively exaggerated). The story of Veii and Camillus was part of a narrative of success and failure that was exemplary in various ways—of Roman prowess, and of the dangers of hubris, of the Roman capacity to come back from disaster, and of their need always to remember the gods. Just as, at the outset of the Roman story, Alba Longa was a sort of mirror to Rome, so Veii and ultimately Carthage would offer powerful alternate versions of their own identity, which Rome would have to face on a military and a more symbolic and ideological level.

CONCLUSIONS

In the end, however, we do not need to decide whether Camillus was a real person or a historicized myth in order to be able to say something about the history of Veii in the early fourth century BCE. The competition for resources between Rome and Veii was real enough. The approximate date of the Roman conquest is given by the sequence of Rome's subsequent interventions in the nearby territory. Even if Roman dominance was less overwhelming at first than the sources claim, there is no doubt that the Romans overcame resistance. Probably by the early second century BCE, Camillus was already the hero of the day for the Romans, and he remained so ever after.

NOTES

1. The key surviving narrative sources are Livy books 5–6 (with Ogilvie 1965 and Oakley 1997–2005); Dionysios of Halikarnassos books 13–14; Plutarch, *Life of Camillus*.

2. On Veii and the Faliscans see Cifani 2013; Biella and Tabolli 2017.

3. D'Ambrosio et al. 2010.

4. Momigliano 1942.

5. Bruun 2000:41 n. 3; *fatalis dux*: Livy 5.19.

6. Cornell 1995:317.

7. Degrassi 1937:534–535.

8. Richardson 2012.

9. Livy 4.17–20. See also chapter 15.

10. On the chronological complexities see Ogilvie 1965: 629–630; Cornell 1995:399–402.

11. Gaertner 2008 gives full reference to the history of this debate, and informs this summary.

12. Livy 5.21.15; cf. Valerius Maximus 5.10.2.

13. Livy 5.32.8 and Plutarch, Life of *Camillus* 12; cf. Livy 38.60.9.

14. Gaertner 2008:32; Täubler 1912.

15. Wiseman 1979.

16. There is a huge literature on this subject; see for entry points Flower 1996; Walter 2004; Wiseman 1998; Coudry and Späth 2001; van der Blom 2010.

17. Gaertner 2008; Burck 1991; Badian 1993; Miles 1995.

18. Dumézil 1980.

19. In general see Graf 1993.

20. See also chapter 15.

21. Moretti Sgubini 2004.

22. Bruun 2000; Oakley (1997–2005: IV.506) responds: "I should not wish to take scepticism so far."

23. Walter 2004:382–407; Skutsch 1980:314–316; but cf. Gaertner 2008:41.

24. Livy 6.4.3, with Oakley *ad loc.*

25. Bispham 2000; Cifani 2003, 2013; Harris 1971.

26. Wills Becker 2013.

27. Macchia Grande: *CIL* I² 2628–2632, Torelli 1999:25–29; Piano della Comunità: Bartoloni and Benedettini 2011.

BIBLIOGRAPHY

Badian, E. 1993. "Livy and Augustus." In *Livius: Aspekte seines Werkes*, ed. W. Schuller, 9–38. Xenia 31. Konstanz.

Bartoloni, G., and M. G. Benedettini. 2011. *Veio: Il deposito votivo di Comunità (scavi 1889–2005)*. Rome.

Biella, M. C., and J Tabolli, eds. 2017. *I falisci attraverso lo specchio. Atti della Giornata di Studi per festeggiare Maria Anna De Lucia Brolli, MAVNA (Mazzano Romano), 31 ottobre 2015*. Officina Etruscologia 13. Rome.

Bispham, E. 2000. "'Mimic': A Case Study in Early Roman Colonization." In *State Identities in the First Millennium B.C.*, ed. E. Herring and K. Lomas, 157–186. Accordia Specialist Studies on Italy 8. London.

Bruun, C. 2000. "'What every man in the street used to know': M. Furius Camillus, Italic Legends, and Roman Historiography." In *The Roman Middle Republic: Politics, Religion, and Historiography, c. 400–133 B.C.*, ed. Christer Bruun, 41–68. Rome.

Burck, E. 1991. "Livius und Augustus." *ICS* 16:269–281.

Cifani, G. 2003. *Storia di una frontiera: Dinamiche territoriali e gruppi etnici nella media Valle Tiberina dalla prima età del Ferro alla conquista romana*. Rome.

———, ed. 2013. *Tra Roma e l'Etruria: Cultura, identità e territorio dei Falisci*. Rome.

Cornell, T. J. 1995. *The Beginnings of Rome: Italy and Rome from the Bronze Age to the Punic Wars (c. 1000–264 BC)*. London.

Coudry, M., and T. Späth, eds. 2001. *L'invention des grands hommes de la Rome antique = Die Konstruktion der grossen Männer Altroms. Actes du colloque du Collegium Beatus Rhenanus, Augst, 16–18 septembre 1999*. Paris.

D'Ambrosio, E., B. Giaccio, L. Lombardi, F. Marra, M. F. Rolfo, and A. Sposato. 2010. "L'attività recente del centro eruttivo di Albano tra scienza e mito: Un'analisi critica del rapporto tra il vulcano laziale e la storia dell'area albana." In *Lazio e Sabina 6. Atti del Convegno. Roma 4–6 marzo 2009*, ed. G. Ghini, 211–222. Rome.

Degrassi, A. 1937. *Inscriptiones Italiae* 13.1: *Fasti Consulares et Triumphales*. Rome.

Dumézil, G. 1980. *Camillus: A Study of Indo-European Religion as Roman History*. Berkeley.

Flower, H. 1996. *Ancestor Masks and Aristocratic Power in Roman Culture*. Oxford.

Gaertner, J. F. 2008. "Livy's Camillus and the Political Discourse of the Late Republic." *JRS* 98:27–52.

Graf, F., ed. 1993. *Mythos in mythenloser Gesellschaft: Das Paradigma Roms*. Stuttgart.

Harris, W. V. 1971. *Rome in Etruria and Umbria*. Oxford.

Miles, G. B. 1995. *Livy: Reconstructing Early Rome*. Ithaca.

Momigliano, A. 1942. "Camillus and Concord." *CQ* 36:111–120.

Moretti Sgubini, A. M., ed. 2004. *Eroi etruschi e miti greci: Gli affreschi della Tomba François tornano a Vulci*. Rome.

Oakley, S. P. 1997–2005. *A Commentary on Livy Books VI–X*. Oxford.

Ogilvie, R. M. 1965. *A Commentary on Livy Books I–V*. Oxford.

Richardson, J. 2012. *The Fabii and the Gauls: Studies in Historical Thought and Historiography in Republican Rome*. Stuttgart.

Skutsch, O. 1980. *The Annals of Quintus Ennius*. Oxford.

Täubler, E. 1912. "Camillus und Sulla." *Klio* 12:21–233.

Torelli, M. 1999. *Tota Italia: Essays in the Cultural Formation of Roman Italy*. Oxford.

van der Blom, H. 2010. *Cicero's Role Models: The Political Strategy of a Newcomer*. Oxford.

Walter, U. 2004. *Memoria und res publica: Zur Geschichtskultur im republikanischen Rom*. Frankfurt.

Wills Becker, H. 2013. "Political Systems and Law." In *The Etruscan World*, ed. J. MacIntosh Turfa, 351–372. London.

Wiseman, T. P. 1979. *Clio's Cosmetics: Three Studies in Greco-Roman Literature*. Leicester.

———. 1998. *Roman Drama and Roman History*. Exeter.

CONCLUSIONS

JACOPO TABOLLI AND ORLANDO CERASUOLO

The importance of the Etruscan town of Veii has been detailed throughout the different chapters of this book. The unpublished data presented here (together with information appearing for the first time in English) allow the reader to gain a new understanding of the development of Veii and its territory throughout the centuries as well as its interactions with nearby ancient settlements and territories in central Tyrrhenian Italy. This development appears to have been gradual and was certainly not uniform and consistent throughout time.

The fundamental outline of precise "phases" and "periods" in the history of Veii is provided by the rich archaeological record available for this town. We must keep in mind, however, that any such periodization is a modern construct, and in antiquity the transitions between the different phases would have been more fluid. Our impulse to define specific periods in the history of Veii risks obscuring the factors of continuity. Consequently, a few general tendencies that appear in the different chapters of this volume are summarized here.

As a premise it is important to stress that the city of Veii is the protagonist of an important demographic, urban, and cultural development, which allowed this town to become over the centuries one of the leading cities in ancient central Italy. From an economic point of view, this development was based on a consistent exploitation of the different resources of the territory and on a continuous interaction with the nearby communities, thanks to its convenient geographical location. The development of a strong economic system occurred alongside the gradual structuring of the society

and the creation of political institutions that in turn drove this process.

In particular, during the history of Etruscan Veii, we can trace three moments that possibly were the principal phases of development, each constituting a sort of "apogee" period: (1) the eighth century BCE, (2) the end of the seventh century BCE, and (3) the end of the sixth century BCE.

THE FIRST APOGEE: VEII IN THE EIGHTH CENTURY BCE

Veii in the eighth century BCE was already a city with at least one hundred years of history. During this century, all the most urgent questions connected to the everyday life of this large and centered community appear to have been resolved, including the necessity for political and social organization, sustenance, defense, public infrastructure, and religious spaces.

At the end of this long process of adjustment, the city seems to have been enjoying an extremely vibrant life. Large gentilicial groups, partially in competition against each other, ruled the different areas of the settlement, holding control over specific economic districts. The distribution of the evidence throughout the plateau and the presence of separate necropoleis testify to the complex political articulation, which has been fully recognized in excavation in only a few cases, such as at Piazza d'Armi. At least three levels of social rank are visible in the necropoleis: warrior leaders and their spouses, soldiers and associated females, and common people. Unfortunately we have very little data on the lower classes and the community of craftsmen, which would have formed a large portion of the social body of Veii.

During the eighth century BCE the connection of Veii to its territory still relies on its links with those ancestral pre-urban communities that took part in its formation. The economic basis of Veii is the exploitation of the natural resources of its territory, especially agriculture and sheep-farming. The extremely different geomorphological areas in its territory provided a variety of economic opportunities for Veii as well as important trade routes: the seashore, with the salt-pans, or Salinae; the Tiber Valley, with the lower hills and the other small rivers; the Sabatini volcanic "mountains" with Lake Bracciano; and, indirectly, the more impervious Faliscan territory.

Continuous interactions with the surrounding Etruscan, Latin, Faliscan, Capenate, and Sabine communities are especially evident in the eighth century BCE. These relations were based on complex, often not equality based, exchanges of goods, in which Veii appears to have played a central role. At this time, the first conflicts against Rome probably took place.

As different authors of our chapters have stressed, the earliest international interactions with Greece and the Near East played a particularly important role in the society of Veii during the eighth century BCE. These connections not only affected the economic sphere (transforming processes of industrial production) but also resulted in important assimilations within the local culture. The Veii of the *principes* and of the primitive kings is now one part of a Mediterranean mosaic whose components appear to have been deeply connected and interdependent, even before the beginning of the Orientalizing period.

THE SECOND APOGEE: VEII AT THE END OF THE SEVENTH CENTURY BCE

Veii at the end of the seventh century BCE was a highly developed city, in which kings held the power in the society. According to the epigraphic evidence, at this time the aristocratic families began to adopt gentilicial (family-based) names, in order to stress the genealogical and power links within the clans and social groups connected to the different leaders. This cultural legitimation of political supremacy is a fundamental aspect of the period. Among the aristocrats, Oriental goods and styles spread, recalling heroic and especially Homeric traditions. Monumental tumuli and chamber tombs with wall paintings were built, together with public buildings functioning as cult spaces and royal residences and decorated by rich terracottas.

These transformations corresponded to a new organizational phase in town planning, involving a higher density of structures, large infrastructure for water collection (such as monumental tanks), and buildings characterized by stone walls made of tufa squared blocks and roofs with terracotta tiles. Foreign artisans and masters were now entirely part of the social body of Veii and labored in this renovation of the town along with the non-elites of the city. Massive serial production of pottery is attested, such as the Etrusco-Corinthian pottery produced at Comunità, together with votives, as the evidence from Portonaccio shows. This sanctuary and its "oracle" played a fundamental role in strengthening wide-ranging political interactions. At the same time the structuring of the territory of Veii created a complex system of sites along its borders.

THE THIRD APOGEE: VEII AT THE END OF THE SIXTH CENTURY BCE

Veii at the end of the sixth century BCE was a city surrounded by strong town walls, with new streets and an internal organization based on regular blocks. Kings and magistrates regulated its complex society and its powerful economy. A marked change in the dynamics of social representation is observable. Economic energies were now expended in the public sphere, especially in the sanctuaries, while a drastic reduction in previously typical aristocratic funerary excess is attested. As many of our authors have observed, this phenomenon was not limited to Veii but corresponded to a social transformation that took place in different areas of the Mediterranean around this time, and it manifests in Rome in the funerary laws reflected in the Twelve Tables, dating around 450 BCE.

The society of Veii in this period was highly educated and imbued with elements of Greek culture while maintaining a strong originality. Contemporary pottery and terracotta art, such as that produced in the workshop of the Master of Apollo, demonstrated this high cultural level. It is important once again to emphasize that it was the most famous Veientine master, Vulca, who was called by the last Roman king to realize part of the decoration of the temple of Jupiter.

THE EVENTS OF 396 BCE

From this perspective, the long-standing relationship between Veii and Rome—a city only four hours distant on foot—described in the ancient sources leads the two cities to their final clash during the fifth century BCE. This is the most consequential moment in the history of Veii.

While the victory of Rome constitutes the end of our story, it must be noted that the siege was not the "last chance" for Veii to overcome Rome. As C. Smith mentions in his chapter, after the disastrous attack of the Gauls on Rome (ca. 390 BCE), the Romans discussed the possibility of abandoning the ruined site of their own town and starting again at Veii (Livy 5.51). Even if the famous speech of Camillus against this option is a later invention inserted in the literary source, the episode itself reveals once again the lasting link between the two parallel stories of Rome and Veii, at the very end of an Etruscan *époque*. Until the final conquest, even the Romans themselves were probably saying (paraphrasing G. Dennis's words) that "of all the cities of Etruria, none takes so prominent a place in history as Veii." Nevertheless, Veii was not lucky enough to be chosen, and its glorious past did not revive.

A FIRST GLIMPSE OF ROMAN VEII

What did happen at Veii following the siege of 396 BCE? The four centuries between the Roman conquest and the foundation in 12 BCE of the Augustan *municipium* (Municipium Augustum Veiens) witnessed the radical transformation of Veii from an Etruscan to a fully Roman small town. This metamorphosis has become more and more evident in the most recent excavations and a rereading of past surveys.[1]

FIGURE 26.1. Columns from the Forum of the Municipium Augustum Veiens now incorporated into the Palazzo Wedekind in the Piazza Colonna in Rome. (Copyright: J. Tabolli)

According to Livy (5.21–22), after the conquest Veii was partially depopulated, because many Veiians were massacred or sold in Rome as slaves. Given the silence of the ancient sources, apart from the above-mentioned mythical/historical narration of the role of Veii during the Gauls' attack on Rome, the city itself appears to have been left lifeless in the mid-fourth century BCE.

It was only around 338 BCE that the first Romans settled in the area of the town, either revitalizing most of the cults and productive areas at Macchiagrande, Campetti, and Comunità or establishing large rural villas (in the locations with the most dramatic views). The future of the city was uncertain, however. In fact, even attempts to revitalize the center, and especially the area of Macchiagrande, in Augustan times by veterans, and later in the third century CE, were unsuccessful.[2] The foundation of the *municipium* followed the well-defined political ideology of Augustus, which aimed at revitalizing all sites with political and religious value for the history of Rome. Physical embodiments of this ideological propaganda—the famous columns of the Roman forum at Macchiagrande—are visible now at the Palazzo Wedekind in Rome (fig. 26.1), near the Palazzo Chigi, the seat of the current Italian government, once again "at the center of the power."

Indeed most of the areas of the Etruscan city had been abandoned and become rural. The desolate and bucolic picture of Veii depicted in the first century BCE by Propertius seems to be accurate. At that time, only the central part of the plateau (around the forum at Macchiagrande) was occupied by a settlement, with some public buildings that were briefly in use but almost disappear after the mid-Imperial period.

THE LEGACY

As this volume demonstrates, the archaeological excavations conducted in the past decades have revealed a new face of the Etruscan town of Veii and its territory.

This result has been possible only thanks to the real teamwork and synergy among the universities, the Soprintendenze and the museums. In closing this book we may hope that the Veii Project will continue to be an amazing archaeological opportunity for the Etruscan town of Veii, in the urgent need to disseminate what has been discovered and to engage the public in this fascinating story.

NOTES

1. *Survey*, 359–376.
2. P. Liverani, *Municipium Augustum Veiens: Veio in età imperiale attraverso gli scavi Giorgi (1811–1813)* (Rome, 1987).

APPENDIX

A CHRONOLOGY OF VEII

This chronological list presents an overview of the life of the Etruscan site of Veii, with the mythical, historical, and cultural elements mentioned by the different authors in this volume. It provides a short list of the most significant events after the fall of the city in 396 BCE, from Roman and medieval times as well as the major excavations between 1641 (year of the rediscovery of the city) and 2016.

In the first line of each, the dates (according to the traditional chronology) are accompanied by the corresponding cultural phases that characterize all of Etruria: Early Iron Age, Orientalizing, and so forth, followed in relevant instances by the phase names of the periodization of Veii itself (Veii IA, Veii IB, etc.).

SEVENTEENTH-FOURTEENTH CENTURIES BCE / MIDDLE BRONZE AGE (MBA)

First settlements in the future territory of Veii—Pottery with Apennine decoration

THIRTEENTH CENTURY BCE / RECENT BRONZE AGE (RBA)

Earliest settlement at Isola Farnese, adjacent to the plateau of Veii

TWELFTH-TENTH CENTURIES BCE / FINAL BRONZE AGE (FBA)

Halesos, legendary ancestor of King Morrius and founder of Falerii—Tiberinus Silvius, legendary king of Alba Longa (ca. 922–914 BCE), after whom the Tiber River was named—Remains of huts at Isola Farnese—Bronze Age settlements of Falerii and Narce—Cinerary urns at Pozzuolo (FBA 1–2), Casale del Fosso (FBA 3B), and perhaps Quattro Fontanili

LATE TENTH CENTURY BCE / EARLY IRON AGE 1 (EIA 1)

Agrippa, legendary king of Alba Longa (ca. 914–873 BCE)—Foundation of proto-urban Veii and contemporary depopulation of the territory—Earthen ramparts constructed at Campetti—Urn fields (cremations) around Veii, apparently not displaying status differentiation

EARLY NINTH CENTURY BCE / EARLY IRON AGE 1 (EIA 1)/ VEII IA

Romulus Silvius, legendary king of Alba Longa (ca. 873–854 BCE)—Beginning of the so-called Villanovan I period—Burial of the founder at Piazza d'Armi at the center of a *heroon*

MID-NINTH CENTURY BCE / EARLY IRON AGE 1 (EIA 1) / VEII IB

Aventinus, legendary king of Alba Longa (ca. 854–817 BCE)—Pottery kilns at Campetti

LATE NINTH CENTURY BCE / EARLY IRON AGE 1 (EIA 1) / VEII IC

King Propertius, founder, together with the Capenates, of the sanctuary of Lucus Feroniae—Procas, legendary king of Alba Longa (ca. 817–794 BCE)—Kilns at Campetti no longer in use and a female burial lies on top of them—Scepters found in

Veientine tombs—Earliest evidence of inhumations in simple trenches

EARLY EIGHTH CENTURY BCE / EARLY IRON AGE 2 (EIA 2) / VEII IIA

King Vel Vibe in Veii—King-like figures rule the city and control long-range trade—Amulius, king of Alba Longa (ca. 794–752 BCE)—Beginning of the so-called Villanovan II period—Falerii, Narce, and Capena are founded by Italic groups under the political control of Veii—Imported Greek *skyphoi* or local imitations are relatively common status symbols; the fast wheel is introduced in pottery production—Almost complete abandonment of cremation well-tombs with move to inhumation in trenches, differentiation in tomb typology and articulation—Foundation of the Greek colonies of Pithekoussai in 770–760 BCE and Cumae in 740–730 BCE

MID-EIGHTH CENTURY BCE / EARLY IRON AGE 2 (EIA 2) / VEII IIB

Romulus (ca. 753–716 BCE), the traditional foundation of Rome (753 BCE), and the first conflicts between Rome and Veii—Burial of a young man at Piazza d'Armi, close to the founder—Tombs of leaders appear in Valle La Fata tomb 23 and Quattro Fontanili tombs AA1 and Z15A—At least three social ranks are visible in the necropoleis: warrior leaders and their spouses; soldiers and relevant females; lower people—The production of red impasto begins

LATE EIGHTH CENTURY BCE / EARLY IRON AGE 2 (EIA 2) / VEII IIC

Dionysios of Halikarnassos (2.54.3) names Veii at this time "the most powerful city of the Tyrrhenians . . . as big as Athens"—Complex articulation of the society—Renovation of the defensive system at Campetti—Clustering of tombs (family groups) and numerous rich burials, some belonging to *principes*, with weapons for men and jewelry and textile tools for women—Assyrian beaker found at Casale del Fosso

CA. 720–675 BCE / EARLY ORIENTALIZING PERIOD / VEII IIIA

King Morrius in Veii—King Numa Pompilius in Rome (ca. 715–674 BCE)—Earliest evidence of Veientine epigraphy—Italo-geometric pottery (i.e. Narce Painter, ca. 700–660 BCE),

together with brown impasto—Reoccupation of the territory via the foundation of small settlements—Casale del Fosso tombs 1036, 871, and 872—Near Eastern silver cups in tombs 804 and 871—Earliest chamber tombs: Casale del Fosso tombs 1089 and 1090—Earliest wall paintings: Tomb of the Roaring Lions (ca. 690 BCE) and Tomb of the Ducks (ca. 680–670 BCE)—Funerary statue at Picazzano

CA. 675–630 BCE / MIDDLE ORIENTALIZING PERIOD / VEII IIIB

King Tullus Hostilius in Rome (ca. 673–641 BCE)—The Corinthian Demaratus, later father of Roman king Lucius Tarquinius Priscus, settles in Tarquinia—Orthogonal town planning at Piazza d'Armi—Early cult activities at the sanctuary of Portonaccio—Veientine craftsmen begin to produce bucchero pottery—Crane Painter—Earliest Corinthian pottery is imported (Chigi Vase, 640 BCE)—Monumental tumuli spread all around the city (Monte Aguzzo)—Monte Michele tomb 5, with luxury goods—A system of settlements defends the border of the territory, together with several control points along internal roads and waterways

CA. 630–575 BCE / LATE ORIENTALIZING PERIOD / VEII IIIB

Kings Ancus Marcius (ca. 640–616 BCE) and Lucius Tarquinius Priscus (ca. 616–579 BCE). Ancus Marcius conquers the salt-pans at the mouth of Tiber and Silva Maesia, then founds Ostia—Veii at its apogee, dense occupation of the territory, but also losing political control of the Ager Faliscus and Capenates—Building of the *oikos* at Piazza d'Armi and the rest of an aristocratic palace (statue of a man with his dog); white-on-red terracottas (600–580 BCE)—Cisterns in tufa blocks at Piazza d'Armi—A cult precinct at Campetti South-West—Oracular cult of Menerva at Portonaccio—Pottery kilns at Comunità; Etrusco-Corinthian pottery made at Veii (Castellani Master, ca. 630–620 BCE)—Rich depositions at Oliveto Grande (ca. 630 BCE), Vaccareccia (ca. 630–620 BCE), and Campana Tomb (ca. 620–610 BCE)

CA. 575–540 BCE / EARLY ARCHAIC PERIOD / VEII IV

King Servius Tullius (ca. 578–535 BCE) wages war against Veii—Aulus and Caelius Vibenna at Rome—Massive defensive town wall made of tufa blocks—*Hestiatorion* at Portonaccio, where Aulus Vibenna makes offering—Rich architectural terracottas (so-called First Phase, 580–560 BCE) of Near Eastern style—In chambers tombs fewer grave goods due to austerity of the funerary laws and return to cremation

CA. 540–480 BCE / MID-ARCHAIC PERIOD

King Lucius Tarquinius Superbus in Rome (ca. 535–509 BCE)—The Veientine craftsman Vulca is invited to Rome to create the statue of Juppiter Capitolinus—New roads and blocks of buildings—Investments in sanctuaries and public buildings (such as palaces, squares, and water tanks)—Terracottas in Etrusco-Ionian style (550–510 BCE)—The polyadic temple of Uni/Juno Regina (Livy 5.21.1–4 and 10), probably in the area of Comunità—Second phase at Portonaccio with sacellum and altar, together with an *oikos* (statues of *kouroi*, Turms, Hercle, and Menerva)—Intensification of countryside occupation

LATE SIXTH CENTURY

Temple at Portonaccio with acroteria made by a refined school of coroplastic art (Master of Apollo)—Attic pottery (Antimenes Painter, Nikoxenos Painter) and other imports at Portonaccio—Sanctuary of Vei-Demeter at Campetti North (since ca. 530 BCE)—So-called Second Phase in terracotta decoration

CA. 509 BCE

Republican Rome wins against Lucius Tarquinius Superbus, exiled in Veii, at battle near the Silva Arsia

EARLY FIFTH CENTURY BCE

Abandonment of Piazza d'Armi and contraction of building activity—Stipe Lanciani and votive deposits at Caere Gate—Restorations and transformations at Portonaccio, with new terracottas—Statues of Hercle and Aeneas in the sanctuary of Campetti South-West

CA. 496–480 BCE?

Late Archaic period—Fourth phase at Portonaccio: burial of the Aplu group and a new altar to Menerva

CA. 477 BCE

Battle of the Cremera, fought for Rome by the Fabii (February 13)—Veientine troops reach the walls of Rome—Evidence of battles and renovation of the defensive system at Campetti Bastion

CA. 473 BCE

Veii takes control of Fidenae

CA. 450–449 BCE

Rome adopts the first written laws, the Twelve Tables, with rules to limit funerary luxury

UNTIL 437 BCE

Lars Tolumnius king of Veii (Livy 4.18–22)

AFTER 425 BCE–LATE FIFTH CENTURY BCE

Beginning of the Classical period—Tomb of the Pillars, the only chamber tomb known at Veii so far for this period—Vestibule tombs, with niches for cremations

CA. 405 BCE

Beginning of a period of truce with Rome

CA. 396 BCE

After a siege lasting ten years Veii is conquered by the Roman M. Furius Camillus—Evidence of destruction and battle at the site of Campetti Bastion

CA. 390 BCE

The Gauls attack Rome (July 18)

BEFORE 386 BCE

Sutri and Nepi, north of Veii, come into the hands of Rome, marking the collapse of the territory of Veii—Earliest archaeological evidence of the *castrum* of Ostia, dating to the fourth century BCE, demonstrating the final control by Rome of the mouth of the Tiber

FOURTH–SECOND CENTURY BCE

Most of the area of the ancient Etruscan town is occupied by Roman rural farms—Few sanctuaries survive the siege

46 BCE

Caesar assigns to his veterans parts of the land of Veii and creates a colony

41–40 BCE

During the war of Perugia parts of the battle take place on the plateau of Veii

12 BCE

Augustus founds the Municipium Augustum Veiens in the central area of the plateau (Macchiagrande and Campetti)

256 CE

Last Roman inscription on the plateau of Veii, dedicated to the Roman emperor Costantius Clorus (discovered in 1774)—The area of the city is entirely abandoned

780 CE

Pope Adrian I (772–795) founds the Domusculta Capracorum (via di Santa Cornelia)

NINTH–ELEVENTH CENTURIES CE

Medieval fortified settlement of Piazza d'Armi

1641 CE

Luca Holstenius and Famiano Nardini identify for the first time the location of the ancient city of Veii

1812–1817 CE

Excavations in the Roman forum of the Municipium Augustum Veiens reveal columns (located today in Piazza Colonna in Rome)

CA. 1820–1830 CE

Antonio Nibby and William Gell extensively survey the area of Veii

1832 CE

William Gell publishes the first archaeological map of Veii

1838–1839 CE

Excavations funded by the Princess Maria Cristina—Discovery of the necropoleis of Quattro Fontanili (1838) and Picazzano (1839)

1841–1843 CE

Luigi Canina surveys the area of Veii and excavates in different locations

1843 CE

Giovanni Pietro Campana discovers the Campana Tomb

1882 CE

Prince Mauro Chigi excavates the tumulus of Monte Aguzzo and discovers the Chigi Vase

1889 CE

Rodolfo Lanciani discovers the Roman villa and the Stipe Lanciani at Piano di Comunità, probably in the area of the Temple of Uni/Juno Regina—Excavations in the necropoleis of Vacca-reccia and Picazzano

with Massimo Pallottino to direct excavations at Quattro Fon-tanili (1961–1974)

1913–1916 CE

Excavations by Ettore Gabrici and Natale Malavolta in the ne-cropoleis of Grotta Gramiccia and Quattro Fontanili, in which more than one thousand tombs were discovered

1916 CE

Giulio Quirino Giglioli discovers the statue of Aplu and the other acroteria in the sanctuary of Portonaccio

1920 CE

Beginning of the exhibition of material from Veii in the Na-tional Etruscan Museum, housed in the Villa Giulia in Rome

1922 CE

Enrico Stefani excavates the *oikos* temple at Piazza d'Armi

1939–1940 CE

Excavations by Massimo Pallottino at Portonaccio

1944–1952 CE

Excavations by Maria Santangelo at Portonaccio and in other areas of the ancient town

1946–1974 CE

J. B. Ward-Perkins is the director of the British School at Rome and promotes the South Etruria Survey—Ward-Perkins teams

1980 CE

Discovery of tomb 5 in the necropolis of Monte Michele (the necropolis had been already explore in 1900–1901 by Fausto Benedetti)

1996–2015 CE

The Veii Project of the Sapienza University of Rome directed by Giovanni Colonna and later by Gilda Bartoloni and Maria Teresa d'Alessio—Excavations at Piazza d'Armi (Gilda Barto-loni), Comunità (Giovanni Colonna and Gilda Bartoloni), Campetti (Gilda Bartoloni, Andrea Carandini, Maria Fenelli, and Marcello Guaitoli), Portonaccio (Giovanni Colonna), and Macchiagrande (Andrea Carandini)

2003 CE

Gilda Bartoloni discovers the tomb of the founder of Veii at Piazza d'Armi

2008 CE

Francesca Boitani discovers the Tomb of the Roaring Lions in the necropolis of Grotta Gramiccia

2014 CE

Alessandro Guidi excavates the FBA necropolis of Pozzuolo

2016 CE

The Museum of the Ager Veientanus in Formello is reopened to the public with a new collection

INDEX